Benjamin Banneker and Us

Benjamin Banneker and Us

Eleven Generations of
an American Family

Rachel Jamison Webster

with Edith Lee Harris, Robert Lett,
Gwen Marable, and Edwin Lee

Henry Holt and Company
New York

Henry Holt and Company
Publishers since 1866
120 Broadway
New York, New York 10271
www.henryholt.com

Henry Holt® and 🅷® are registered trademarks of
Macmillan Publishing Group, LLC.

Library of Congress Cataloging-in-Publication Data is available.

ISBN: 9781250827302

Our books may be purchased in bulk for promotional, educational, or business use. Please
contact your local bookseller or the Macmillan Corporate and Premium Sales Department at
(800) 221-7945, extension 5442, or by e-mail at MacmillanSpecialMarkets@macmillan.com.

First Edition 2023

Designed by Kelly S. Too

Printed in the United States of America

1 3 5 7 9 10 8 6 4 2

Contrary to what you may have heard or learned, the past is not done, and it is not over. It's still in process, which is another way of saying that when it's critiqued, analyzed, it yields new information about itself. The past is already changing as it is being reexamined, as it is being listened to for deeper resonances. Actually it can be more liberating than any imagined future if you are willing to identify its evasions, its distortions, its lies, and are willing to unleash its secrets.

—Toni Morrison

We are in the middle of an immense metamorphosis here, a metamorphosis which will, it is devoutly to be hoped, rob us of our myths and give us our history.

—James Baldwin

CONTENTS

AUTHOR'S NOTE

I wrote this book to explore a more honest version of my own ancestry, and a more honest version of American history. I have always been interested in the past and in the stories of my elders. But the idea of ancestry became more real to me in the last decade, as consumer DNA testing connected my family to genealogies and historical records that were previously unknown to us. As I write this, Ancestry.com has more than fifteen million members in its database, and 23andMe has more than twelve million members, and each of these members connects to thousands more ancestors and living relatives through those sites.

The collective, crowdsourced quality of this information demands a more collaborative approach to history. Knowing the names and birth dates of our ancestors also *personalizes* history and reveals that our ancestors were real, resilient, and imperfect, as we are. Learning about them and their lives can expose hidden injustices and ongoing denials. It can help us untangle what is the myth and what is the truth in our personal and collective stories. In my family, for instance, we lost track of our African American ancestry, in a denial that was mirrored in our wider nation's denial of African presence and genius in its origin stories.

The ancestors I write about here include a dairymaid from England, a kidnapped and enslaved man from Senegambia, a multiracial family who sued their Ohio county in 1840 for their children's right to a public education, and, most prominently, Benjamin Banneker. Banneker was a free person of color living in the Revolutionary era. He published the first almanacs by a Black man in the new United States, he helped to survey Washington, D.C., and he corresponded with Thomas Jefferson, calling out Jefferson on his hypocrisy as an enslaver who wrote about freedom.

As I learned about these ancestors, I knew that I wanted to write about them. But I did not know how to write about my Black ancestors ethically, as a white person. In creative nonfiction, aesthetic decisions are also ethical decisions, and to understand our ethical relationship with a work of writing, we must first examine our position of power and relationship to the story being told. Even though I was writing about my own forebears, I knew that I had to acknowledge the fact that my branch of the family "passed" as white several generations ago, losing track of these figures and failing our responsibility to our Black brethren. I decided that it was impossible for me to tell a story of Black genius and resistance without questioning my own position as a white woman and studying the origins and ramifications of whiteness itself.

Luckily, as I was in the throes of this internal debate, my Black cousins got in touch with me, and we began the collaborative sharing that became this book. My cousins' kinship, generosity, and intelligence made this writing possible and allowed the book to find its proper form as a conversation between the present and the past, between our ancestors and ourselves. Our conversations represent a new integration in our family. They also embody a truth about ancestry. Ancestry is always a collective inheritance and not an individual one, and discovering our ancestry is as much about cultivating healthy relationships in the present as it is about unearthing the names of ancestors from the past.

In writing about these figures, I adhered to all the facts available to me. I read more than one hundred books and articles; I did research in the Maryland Archives, where our ancestors' earliest records are located; and my cousins and I were given exclusive access to the archives at the Benjamin Banneker Historical Park and Museum. We also studied Banneker's almanacs and manuscript journal, which are in the Special

Collections of the Maryland Center for History and Culture. My cousins shared the oral histories that had been passed down through many generations of the Banneker-Lett family, and I was able to read the first oral histories that were recorded about Banneker's ancestry in the early nineteenth century. Finally, my cousins passed along their research to me—photographs, articles, wills, census records, and land deeds—that they had collected over the last forty years. These recorded histories provide the parameters for the book's historical chapters.

But after researching the details and contexts of our ancestors' lives, I allowed myself to imagine their thoughts and feelings, because I wanted them to live on the page as more than just names and dates. We need our imaginations to "feel with" one another, to heal our hierarchical relationships, and to experience both the specificity and the commonality of our humanity. This work of grounded imagination becomes most important, even necessary, when we are writing about people of color, women, and other marginalized members of society, because they are largely absent from historical documents. Most Black Americans were only recorded *as people* beginning in the 1870 census. And even those who were fortunate enough to be noted in the historical record—like Benjamin Banneker—were not given the same respect as white figures. I had only one of Banneker's journals to quote from, for example, because his other writings were lost when his cabin was set on fire on the day of his funeral. These all too common acts of violence are another reason why we have far less documentation to access when we write about ancestors of color. And yet, as our family's meticulous research reveals, these stories can still be discovered.

This biography of Benjamin Banneker and his lineage is more than just a family story. It is also a grappling with our nation's racialized history and racialized present. It was written for my ancestors, living relatives, and fellow Americans in an attempt at narrative reparation. As our country becomes more and more multiethnic, and as we continue to develop more complex notions of history and selfhood, I hope that these ancestors' stories will help us to celebrate Black brilliance and female resistance, and will replace some of our falsehoods with our truths. I hope they will help us imagine a more humane and inclusive future for our children and grandchildren, and for their children and grandchildren.

—Rachel Jamison Webster,
Evanston, Illinois, 2022

Benjamin Banneker and Us

CHAPTER 1

Letter to the Future

Ellicott's Mills, Maryland, 1791

BENJAMIN BANNEKER TIPPED back his chair and rubbed his eyes. It had been a four-candle night. When his final candlestick guttered out, he set his quill in the inkpot. He stood up, but his feet had fallen asleep in the long hours of sitting, so he hobbled a bit on them, rocking from his toes to his heels.

Benjamin stepped onto the porch and looked out over his land. The world was awakening, coming on in birdsong and rooster calls, in sunlight burning off the mist over the orchard. He had spent many nights lying in those fields, looking up through a telescope, jotting down notes. He had tracked the stars and planets as they passed the meridian, and had made the equations necessary to predict the precise times of an eclipse, as well as equinoxes and solstices, sunrises and sunsets. He had drawn out the phases of the moon and had projected all the major astronomical events for the coming year. His almanac for 1792 was finally complete.

Benjamin took a quick walk around the orchard, clearing his mind. He twisted the stiffness out of his back and stretched his arms up toward the sun. He knew that being in relationship with the sun and the stars had always been a matter of survival. His people in Africa had followed the stars in their sky maps, and now he had the mathematical skills to track celestial events on paper, in an almanac that would be of practical use. The almanac would help farmers plan the best time to plant their crops, and fishermen to safely cast out into the tides.

Benjamin checked his beehives and plucked some chives from the garden. Then he walked to the chicken coop and pulled two warm eggs from a nest. He stood at his kitchen hearth, stirring the eggs and chives into a skillet, preparing his breakfast while preparing his thoughts. He knew what he had to do next.

* * *

BENJAMIN CLEANED THE nib of his quill and smoothed out a fresh piece of paper. As he addressed the letter to *Thomas Jefferson, Secretary of State*, he felt his hand tremble and clench a bit. His practiced, elegant penmanship was boring down on the page. He began cordially, acknowledging the fact that Jefferson had probably never received a letter from a Black man:

> Sir,
>
> I am fully sensible of the greatness of that freedom which I take with you on the present occasion, a liberty which Seemed to me Scarcely allowable, when I reflected on that distinguished, and dignifyed station in which you Stand; and the almost general prejudice and prepossession which is so prevalent in the world against those of my complexion.

Benjamin reminded Jefferson that he was a free man, endowed with the same liberties as Jefferson himself. Then he contrasted his own situation with that of most African Americans, who were still enslaved.

By the third page of the letter, Benjamin was directly addressing the founders' hypocrisy. He reminded Jefferson of the Revolution and began quoting his most famous written work—the Declaration of Independence—back to him, writing:

> This, Sir, was a time in which you clearly saw into the injustice of a State of Slavery, and that you publickly held forth this true and invaluable doctrine, which is worthy to be recorded and

remembered in all Succeeding ages. "We hold these truths to
be self-evident, that all men are created equal, and that they are
endowed with certain inalienable rights, that among these are life,
liberty and the pursuit of happiness."

. . . but Sir, how pitiable it is to reflect, that although you were so
fully convinced of the benevolence of the Father of mankind, and
of his equal and impartial distribution of those rights and privileges
which he had conferred upon them, that you should at the same
time counteract his mercies, in detaining by fraud and violence
so numerous a part of my brethren under groaning captivity and
cruel oppression, that you should at the Same time be found guilty
of that most criminal act, which you profoundly detested in others,
with respect to yourselves.

Benjamin Banneker sat back in his chair. He was surprised by his
own clarity, by the way the words had flowed out on a rhythm of truth.
He concluded the letter to Jefferson by admitting that he had not set
out to write such a long message, but his "sympathy and affection" for
his enslaved brethren had caused the letter's "enlargement."

Benjamin put the almanac and letter into an envelope, addressed it
to Thomas Jefferson, and walked the three miles to the Ellicott & Co.
Store so it could be posted. As he left the package and walked back over
the stone bridge, along the wooded paths beside the Patapsco River, he
took long, deep breaths of the fresh air. He felt expansive, almost elated.
He felt that one of the central purposes of his life had been completed.

CHAPTER 2

Denial in the Bloodline

Asheville, North Carolina, October 2016

To CONSIDER YOURSELF part of a family, or a nation, is to live inside a story of what that means. We didn't know it yet, but ours was shifting, exposing fault lines and omissions that had been in it all along, revealing itself to be just that—a story. In need of revision.

My extended family was gathered in Asheville, North Carolina, for my cousin Laurel's wedding. It was the night before the reception, and we were out on my aunt Janice's deck, eating chili, drinking beer and lemonade. The weather was mild, and we were enjoying one of the last evenings of the year when we could wear short-sleeved shirts and sundresses. It was the last month that I would believe in a shared national narrative, the last week that I would assume I lived in ordinary times.

My 102-year-old grandmother sat in the best chair in the living room, with my cousin on the floor beside her, holding her hand. My grandmother had always said that she would live to be 100, and somehow, she'd made it—through her own stubborn determination and the devotion of her daughter who cared for her at home. My grandmother's great-grandchild, Haley, had also brought her children to the celebration, and as Haley bounced nine-month-old Teagan on her lap, I observed five generations of women together.

I was watching them through the window, so I don't know what they were talking about, but it probably wasn't the conversation we were having out on the deck. Earlier that day, the *Access Hollywood* tape had leaked that showed Donald Trump bragging about sexually assaulting women. We were debating whether he would be forced to drop out of the race by other Republicans, who tended to denounce such behavior patriarchally, as protective fathers and husbands. Tension had been rising all election season. It seemed that the entire country was balanced on a fault line between Republicans and Democrats, blue states and red states, one way of understanding America and another.

"I think we are just going to have two countries," my nine-year-old daughter had declared. "I think we'll have the red states and the blue states, and we'll decide that we don't want to be the same country anymore."

I told her that the nation had experienced similar rifts before. The years and months leading up to the Civil War, and the war itself, must have felt like this. The years leading up to the Revolution must have felt like this too. Even the years following the Revolution were tumultuous, as many citizens wondered if it had been right to break with England. We tend to talk about history as if it was easier back then to be courageous, and as if American success had been preordained. But it was always a long shot, and our success—that is, any functional national unity—has always been a patchwork job. The United States was the most ideological governmental experiment in history, but huge swaths of the country were excluded from its legalized liberties because they were African American, Native American, non-white, or female. Now, as we found ourselves at another turning point in history, the question seemed to be whether we would finally confront our nation's foundational hypocrisies or stay in denial about these historical and ongoing inequities. We were at a narrative divide, with the people of the country occupying at least two drastically different stories of what America *means*.

Even my own field of creative writing was being roiled and split around issues of cultural appropriation, literary ethics, and representation. I began my career creating workshops for teens, all of whom were students of color, through the Urban League of Portland, Oregon, and the City of Chicago. After a decade of learning from these students and working to decolonize education, I began teaching at the highly privileged Northwestern University, where I diversified reading lists and implemented social justice training as part of the creative writing curriculum. I had been waiting my entire adult life for the kinds of conversations that were taking place, but I was disturbed by the vitriolic blaming that seemed to be driving the discourse. Shame creates shutdown rather than openness to transformation, and as an educator, I had to believe in transformation. The conversations of our time had become so polarizing that I had begun to worry that my wisest, most sensitive students—of any ethnicity or background—would become too afraid of backlash to even take the risk of writing.

My creative writing students and I had spent the fall quarter asking the question of who gets to tell which stories. Some of the most vocal students said that we should only write about characters who look like ourselves, who occupy the same basic socioeconomic and racial categories as we do. Some said that we should always ask permission of who we tell a story about, and that we should be prepared to drop our project if the answer from a marginalized group is "no." One student—a young Black woman and Black Lives Matter activist—pointed out that we were having this conversation as if the playing field was level, and it is not. She argued that the issue is not about storytelling as much as it is about power and access. Many said that we were obligated both to write our own stories and to widen the field of literature for writers of color or any writers who had been marginalized in the past.

I was moved by their emotional intelligence, and I agreed with their insistence that systems of power needed to diversify. I also agreed that representation is important, that no one can imagine the stories of a group better than a member of that group itself. We talked about the fact that freedom of speech and expression have never been applied equally in our culture, and oftentimes those who call for freedom are calling for their own immunity, or even the right to engage in harmful speech.

But I still wanted the students to consider what would be lost to us—as writers and as humans—if we really decided that it was impossible to imagine what it is like to be a person from a different background. Narrowing our subject matter that dramatically would collapse the work of learning in writing, the expansive discovery that happens when we research and imagine something beyond our personal experience. It would also shut down our relationship to unknowing, which is probably the most fruitful relationship a creative writer can have. Creative writers do not write simply to advance an argument, after all, but to discover what they do not yet know, and the best writers and the best writing change right on the page. We were living in an age of opinion, but most literature is not an argument for what *should be*, as much as it is a depiction of the tangled, poignant mix of *what is*.

We were trying to make space for one another's truths in that classroom, and it was frightening. It felt almost impossible to talk about these issues without saying something problematic. Afterward, one of my students from Singapore wrote, "My voice was shaking, my hands were sweating, but this was important. I thought, this must be what *citizenship* feels like."

Ironically, the students who were most militantly against cultural appropriation were white, progressive, newly sensitized to the Black Lives Matter movement, and to issues of equality as they related to elite education and the elite worlds of publication—worlds that they were set to inherit. These were the students most likely to insist that we should write only about ourselves or characters in our own demographics. As young adults, they had not yet exhausted their interest in themselves, and they did not trust any impulse to tell stories that lay outside of their experience. We all lived within the machine of capitalism, after all, and within capitalism, encounters with other cultures usually lead to absorption and exploitation.

Many of my ethnically diverse students had more complicated responses that reflected their own complex identities, and sometimes stemmed from a feeling of responsibility to their communities. "As an Asian American woman, I can feel pigeonholed that I just have to write about being Asian, but I grew up at boarding schools in the U.S. and have had a 'white,' privileged education," one said. "Can I write about that?"

"As a mixed-race person," one young man said, "I would think that I would feel invited to write about myself and my ancestry right now. But I feel more afraid and shut down than ever. My grandfather crossed the border illegally and spent his life as a migrant worker in the fields, but I have never worked in the fields, so how can I write about him? Am I allowed, and do I have the imagination necessary, to write about my own grandfather?"

One student said that maybe the future of writing would be more collaborative, and we agreed that our notions of authorship needed to evolve, to catch up to the collective change-making happening through activism and social media. We discussed ways that stories could adhere less to the myth of the individual, seeing that individualism is itself a product of the dominant culture that most of us wanted to challenge. After all, every individual is a result of families, communities, societies, both personal and structural connections.

"How can we undertake *ethical* collaborations in our writing?" I'd prodded them. "And in addition to literal forms of collaboration, how can we think about collaboration more broadly? Who is to say that if J.D. sat alone in his room for two years, writing about his grandfather working in the fields, that he was not also engaging in some form of collaboration with his ancestor, some co-creation between the self and other that happens in the space of the imagination?"

The students just stared at me then. I was getting a little too woo-woo for them. They distrusted any cloudy thinking in an age when truth itself was under attack. Although they were all creative writing majors, ostensibly apprenticing in the arts of the imagination, our politicized time had attuned them more to activism than to other forms of art-making.

"There is a mystery to the imagination," I'd continued. "We can feel intimately connected to others' stories. We can feel like we almost *remember* things that we have not actually lived."

* * *

I WAS OUT on my aunt's deck, telling my cousin Nathan about these conversations in my classes. He was squarely in the camp of "writers should only write about their own demographics" and said that we all need to read more books by people of color. Then he said, "But these questions become more interesting when you take into account most Americans' mixtures of ancestry, including our own non-white ancestry."

"What do you mean?" I asked.

"Didn't Melissa tell you? She was researching the Webster genealogy this summer and found out that we are related to Benjamin Banneker, the colonial African American clockmaker and almanac writer. You know, the guy who helped to survey Washington, D.C.?"

I went blank. I was embarrassed to admit that I didn't know. Any of it.

*　*　*

LATER THAT WEEKEND, I found a moment to talk to our cousin Melissa alone, and she confirmed what Nathan had told me. One of our great-aunts and a cousin had looked into our Webster genealogy over the years in an attempt to determine if we were related to Noah Webster, who had compiled the first U.S. dictionary, or Daniel Webster, who was a congressman in the nineteenth century. But we were descended from neither of them.

"Because all of that had already been done," Melissa said, "I decided to look back through Grandpa's mother's line, where Grandpa's sisters had not seemed interested in researching. In the census records, all of these people had an *M.* next to their names."

For "mulatto," she realized. This line went back through our grand-father's mother and her father, through the generations to Jemima, Benjamin Banneker's sister, and their parents, Mary and Robert, before ending with Molly Welsh and Bana'ka—the British woman and Afri-can man who were our first American ancestors.

After the wedding, I asked my parents if they knew about this, and they confirmed that, yes, they had heard this story but had forgotten to tell me. For Christmas the year before, my brother and I had bought them DNA tests through Ancestry.com. I asked my brother to email me the results of our dad's DNA test, and there it was. On my dad's genealogical map, England, Ireland, and France were filled with bright colors, denoting most of his origins, and the other countries that were filled in were Senegal and Guinea.

Somewhere along the way, my family had swallowed a silence that I hadn't known we'd had.

*　*　*

I GREW UP in rural Ohio, as a flag-waving, American girl. We had a large extended family, and we all got together for reunions every summer. We ate salted tomatoes and buttered sweet corn from my grandparents' garden, and afterward, my grandmother made strawberry shortcake. She'd cut out biscuits on the floured kitchen counter with a jelly jar, and when they were still warm from the oven, she'd cover them with strawberries we had picked from the garden, sliced and mashed with sugar. Then she'd top it all with a dollop of Cool Whip.

On Independence Day, my dad would put his record of John Philip Sousa marches on the turntable and give the kids miniature American flags, and we would all march around the yard to the swelling crescendos of that patriotic music. I had a small red drum that I played in time to the march, and I smiled as I led the parade. I was proud to be my parents' daughter, proud to be my grandparents' granddaughter, proud to be what they told me we were: Americans.

I had marched with them all in the Bicentennial Parade of 1976 when I was just eighteen months old. My grandmother, mother, and aunts had sewn us all colonial outfits—long dresses, aprons, and muffet bonnets for the girls, knee-length breeches and buttoned greatcoats for the boys. Later, I learned there was a Revolutionary War rifle in the family, that our ancestors had been present for the founding of the country. That history existed as just a footnote, though. We did not think of America as finished, but as a living concept that we loved and took shelter in. We lived with an earnest sense of what America had been, an assumption of what America would go on being, and a hope for what it still could become.

I was a sentimental child, nostalgic for the moment I was in even while I was living it, as if I knew that my childhood already belonged to the past. It was, after all, something out of the annals of America, and an echo of my father's own childhood. There was the broad front porch with dark green wicker furniture, where we sat drinking iced tea and playing cards late into the summer evenings. There was my grandfather's strawberry patch raked with shining straw. Pints of strawberries and bundles of sweet corn that we sold from the side of the road, set out in balsa wood baskets on a painted yellow table. My grandmother's flower beds, filled with black-eyed Susans, peonies, snapdragons, and rosebushes that she had raised from sprigs—the red rose taken from her mother's garden and the pink rose taken from my grandfather's mother's garden. That was how we planted our flower beds then. Relatives would bring over cuttings from their plants, so you'd have gardens filled with nodding blossoms that reminded you of your family, your ancestors.

My father was a mailman, like his father before him, and we were able to afford this good life in a small town in Northeastern Ohio where our family had lived since it was declared the Western Reserve and allotted to the Revolutionary War veterans. My grandparents had never taken for granted the fact that they'd been able to buy their own home and a couple of acres of land where my grandfather grew our vegetables, and they counted this place, and our family, as our greatest privileges.

Every morning, my dad raised the flag in front of our house, and every evening at dusk he carried it inside again, rolling it around the flagpole with the golden eagle on the end. He wore an embroidered eagle on his Postal Service uniform too, a connection to the founding of the country and the Pony Express—those patriots who rode fast on their horses to bring newspapers and letters to every corner of the country, to make sure that every citizen had access to information, regardless of their location or economic class. My dad, like his father before him, read the newspaper every morning and discussed it with us in the evenings, arguing and explaining politics as we watched the evening news. And on summer evenings, he came home, changed out of his uniform, and took us out on Lake Erie in our little boat—a fourteen-foot bow-rider that he had bought used from one of his Post Office friends. He had fitted the boat with a polished teak flagpole, and we raised another American flag out on the water.

The flag meant something different then. Or maybe we just hadn't grappled with what the flag really meant, what it was covering up along with what it was declaring. We knew enough to be grateful for our peaceful American life. But we did not know enough to question whom that peace had excluded.

* * *

AFTER I LEARNED about my family's African ancestry, I racked my mind to come up with stories about race in my family. I didn't have many, which is itself a story about race. I had been born into the group of people who thought they didn't have to think about race—people who did not realize that our category of whiteness was a historical invention that had been weaponized to remove people of color from the guiding myth of America, and from its ongoing safeties and privileges. Sometimes willful and sometimes accidental, our ignorance was our privilege, and it was apparent in the fact that we did not think of ourselves as a race at all but quite simply as "Americans."

My small Ohio town was so homogenous that I went to school with only one Black student in twelve years of public education. When I was in third grade, another Black family moved to town, but they left weeks later when their tires were slashed and a cross was set on fire in their front yard. *Am I remembering that right?* I wonder now. *Was it really a cross, or a pile of tires, or something else that the neighbors set on fire as a way of terrifying them and driving them away?* I do remember that the family left town very quickly, and I felt disgust and shame about what had happened to them. That was when I began to question the nostalgia of small-town America and distrust the way it preserved its self-proclaimed innocence by excluding those people and ideas it considered "other."

Around that time, I came upon a pile of broken beer bottles in the woods, scattered around a burnt pile of books, their pages obliterated into gray, crenellated fans of parchment, ruined past all legibility. I was already a big reader, always trying to get my hands on more books, and I was sickened by those ruined pages and that willful celebration of ignorance. I felt a sudden nausea, an awareness that someone who could burn a book could do an even worse thing. I remember it now in a strange blurring of time, as if that charred heap was reminding me of something from both the past and the future.

I must have been nine or ten then, wearing a bonnet and a long skirt. I had been out in the woods all afternoon, gathering berries and leaves for my soups and "cures." I used to pretend I lived in the past all the time then, wearing *Little House on the Prairie* clothing and stirring up stews of bark, pine needles, and pollen in old pots that I kept in the cupboards of my playhouse. I sometimes found arrowheads poking up through the sandy soil of our backyard. And I knew where the secret rooms were located, under a hidden trapdoor in my grandmother's bedroom, and under the Unionville Tavern. These hidden cellars had once been used to hide people as part of the Underground Railroad. The past was under us all along in that town that time had forgotten. All I had to do was squint my eyes a bit, and I could almost see it.

* * *

BEFORE I LEFT for college in Chicago, all of my travel had been to visit family. My grandparents spent their winters in a retirement community in central Florida—a gathering of mobile and manufactured homes around an inland lake where people who had been teachers and mailmen, dry cleaners and butchers, lived out their golden years. We always spent our spring break with them at that park. In the year I was seventeen, I remember telling my grandparents that I was training to become a lifeguard. I was a slight five-foot-four-inch female, and I was proud of the tows I'd learned that allowed me to rescue people twice my weight. The roughest rescue I had done in training was with a huge linebacker of a man. He thrashed around just like a real drowning person would, while I did barrel rolls across the pool, towing his resistant body twenty-five yards to the wall.

I was recalling this tow and explaining the steps of CPR to my grandfather, when he said in his teasing voice, "Let me ask you something. What if it was a Black man who was drowning? Would you give him CPR?"

"Grandpa! Of course I would!" I answered. "That's a ridiculous question."

"Why would he say such a thing?" my dad said afterward, embarrassed by his father. It occurs to me that things haven't improved in the twenty years since we found that comment so offensive. In fact, they have gotten worse.

I can guess why my grandfather teased me that way. I had just published my first letter to the editor of our local Ohio newspaper. My letter was a defense of "the rioters" who took to the streets after the police beating of Rodney King. I had argued that the plunder of their neighborhood had historical roots and was based on an anger that stemmed from slavery and our country's ongoing economic injustice and mistreatment of them. I was upset by the way the news channels looped King's beating over and over, repeating the violence against him. That event—which we all indelicately referred to as "The Rodney King Riots"—had introduced me to the idea of racial justice, although I did not know to call it that then. My grandparents had clipped the letter from the paper and put it up on their fridge, proud that their granddaughter had been published. But I do not know if they agreed with its sentiments.

My grandfather's racist question—Would you help a Black man? Would you *kiss* a Black man?—was shaped by the socially constructed idea that Black men are dangerous, and by the old patriarchal insinuation that white women needed to be protected. It drew on the oldest, most divisive stereotypes in America. It also referred to several generations of his ancestry, although he didn't know that.

* * *

When I left home for college in Chicago, it was not as much for the school but for my desire to live in a city. I wanted to live around artists and diverse groups of people and get away from small-town judgments. I loved Chicago, and when I left two years later to transfer to a college in Portland, Oregon, I missed Chicago's urban energy and sought it out again. For my senior honors project, I wrote a thesis exploring the writings of Adrienne Rich and Audre Lorde and created a writing workshop with the Urban League of Portland. I worked alongside the poet Derwin Boyd, and we taught teens who had been kicked out of public school. All of them were students of color, and many were living without homes, or trying to extricate themselves from gangs. I learned the importance of consistently showing up to gain their trust and hear their truths.

I loved this work so much that after graduation, I moved back to Chicago and assisted First Lady of Chicago Maggie Daley to help build her after-school arts program for city teens called Gallery 37. I worked as Maggie's writer and public relations person and helped expand the program to include literary arts and reach thousands of Chicago Public School students. Creative writing allowed these students to appreciate their experiences, articulate their inner lives, celebrate their heritage, and imagine new futures for themselves. It also allowed them to release some of the trauma they had experienced—by voicing it in stories and poems, getting it out of their bodies and onto the page. Many of the students were writing through poverty, incarceration of loved ones, and gun violence. And all of them were writing about families, neighborhoods, food, music, living, and inherited cultures. For several years, I was their teacher, but the students were teaching me just as much—about resilience, joy, and the deep and necessary wellsprings of creativity.

"What *are* you?" a student would invariably ask me on the first day of class. It was always the first thing they needed to know.

"Well, I am a mix of Irish, English, French, Native American, and Hungarian," I would say, citing all the strands of ancestry I knew of at the time. I had tan skin and knew that my background could be hard to place, and I was painfully aware of my privilege when I entered those classrooms. But the term "white" had always felt off to me. I had not yet studied the legal construction of race in this country, so my response was not founded on legal history but on an emotional awareness of all the societal gaps that existed between me and my students. I wanted to meet them in a way that did not alienate us from one another. I also wanted to invite them to consider their own complex strands of ancestry—and inheritances that had nothing to do with money and everything to do with family, community, and culture.

My answer to them was incomplete, I know now, but I was not wrong to answer them in terms of ancestry rather than race. Race is not a biological reality as much as it is a weaponized fiction. While varying skin tones and differing cultures are, indeed, realities, there is no biological marker for race. We share 99.9 percent of our DNA with all other humans, regardless of ethnicity. And we can have more genetically in common with someone of different ethnicity and skin tone than someone who resembles us closely. In the years since the first decoding of the human genome in 2003, we have ample evidence that race is not a biological fact as much as it is "a technology of power" used to per-petuate dominance and exclusion. The establishment of race, and the idea of a dominant white race against which other races are measured, has always been a politically and economically motivated lie.

But our entire society was structured on this lie, and our lives are still shaped by it. Racism is a collective brainwashing and legalized caste system that influences law enforcement, property ownership, education, voting rights, media depiction, and every other aspect of citizenship. In those years when I was teaching at the Urban League and in Chicago Public Schools, I could see that structural racism had influenced almost every aspect of my students' lives.

I remember so many students from that time, but one in particu-lar comes to mind. Cordero was a slender, fourteen-year-old boy, with long, thick eyelashes. One day, my co-teacher, Keturah Shaw-Poulos, and I put a bunch of photographs out on a table and asked the students to pick one to write about. Cordero chose a black-and-white photo of a small white church, its clapboards peeling, its churchyard guarded by a huge live oak tree dripping with Spanish moss. It was a scene from the old South, timeless and still. Cordero sat and looked at the picture for a long time, not writing in his notebook, just gazing at the scene with his sweet face, his eyebrows furrowed.

"I never seen a place like this, but I feel like I know it," he said, as if he wanted me to explain how that could be possible. Some of our stu-dents had never left their neighborhoods on the South and West Sides of Chicago. A few expressed intense anxiety just boarding a bus to go downtown to give a reading at the end of the school year. One wrote that her dream was to go to a place far enough from the city and its light pollution that she would finally see stars in the night sky.

"I know what you mean," I told Cordero. "Sometimes places just feel familiar. Write into the feeling. Imagine yourself there, in the past, or in a story."

"Can I keep this?" he asked, holding up the picture.

I told him he could, and his openness in that moment served as a quiet affirmation for me—that writing can be healing, that Cordero *did* remember that church on some cellular level because what we remem-ber strangely exceeds our individual lifetimes. Cordero's ancestors may have built a church like that with their own hands, then stood within its shelter to worship, sing, hug, pray—and find the joy and strength for their survival.

My other memory of Cordero is much more difficult to bear. One day, he was very jumpy. He'd sit down for a minute and then get up and begin pacing the room. Then he'd try another seat at another table, stay there a minute, and walk around the room again.

"Cordero, please just choose a seat and *stay put*," I said.

That's when my co-teacher, Keturah, leaned over to me and whispered that Cordero's cousin had been shot and killed that week, and he seemed to be afraid to sit anywhere near a window or doorway. He was afraid they were coming to shoot him next.

I felt like the clueless, authoritarian white adult in the room. I also felt a helpless rage about the way these kids had been abandoned by our society. Then, as now, a Chicago Public School student was shot and killed roughly every week and it was hardly granted a mention in the news. We were in a Chicago Public High School on the West Side of the city. Every morning, our students had to pass through two policemen at each entrance, along with metal detectors, sometimes being frisked as they entered their place of learning. We taught in a room that looked like a cage, with metal bars across the windows and a heavy padlock keeping us out until it was time to lead our writing workshops. An ROTC training center had been established inside the school so that students could be recruited right from their classrooms to go to the Gulf Wars. We heard the recruits marching and chanting in the hallways while we wrote our poems. But there was no funding for a school nurse or a counselor. There was no trauma therapy for Cordero or for the hundreds of other children who were losing their classmates, siblings, and cousins to the ongoing epidemic of gun violence.

These stories are all connected, I realize now. The ancestors who worshipped under that live oak tree until they had the lumber to build their church, who sang and offered their questions and praises up to God, were intimately connected to Cordero—the boy with the long-lashed eyes who came to school even though he was terrified, who tried to find a safe place to sit and write his poems. The police roaming the halls and the ROTC officers marching outside were not so different from the patrollers and overseers of the old South. And I was a repeating character too—the well-meaning white lady who did not know the half of what the people around me were really going through.

* * *

WHEN I BEGAN researching our Banneker ancestors, I learned that they had arrived on this continent in the very years that race was being constructed as a political tool. Our English ancestor Molly was sentenced to indenture in the Colony (then called the *Company*) of Maryland in 1683. She survived her indenture and became a free tobacco planter in the colony. Then, around 1690, she was said to purchase two male slaves from Africa. She married and had children with one of them—a Wolof man from Senegambia named Bana'ka. Molly and Bana'ka's oldest daughter, Mary, became known as a healer and herbalist in the area, and Mary's African husband, Robert, was enslaved as a boy and young man, before he earned his own freedom. Mary and Robert had five children. One was Benjamin Banneker, and another was our ancestor, Jemima.

Benjamin Banneker was born in 1731. He attended a Quaker school for a few years and continued to study natural sciences, higher mathematics, history, and music on his own. Benjamin achieved fame as a young man when he constructed a working clock out of wood— one of the first mechanical clocks in the region. Later in his life, Banneker was hired by George Washington and Thomas Jefferson to help survey Washington, D.C. Afterward, Banneker began compiling and publishing almanacs, becoming a symbol of Black intelligence for abolitionists. He went on to publish best-selling almanacs in Maryland, Pennsylvania, and Delaware from 1792 to 1797.

Benjamin's sister Jemima—our ancestor—married Samuel Delaney Lett, a mixed-race man of indigenous and European ancestry who had been raised by a free Black man and identified as Black, and they had nine children. After the American Revolution, the Banneker-Lett family was stripped of their right to vote and driven from their land, so they migrated to the new Northwest Territory of Ohio. They and a few other free families of color came to collectively own one thousand acres in southern Ohio that they called the Lett Homestead. Then, in the 1840s, the Letts sued their township for the right to a public education for their children.

According to the oral history that Mr. Turner Simpson Jr. recorded about Meigs County, Ohio, the "octoroon" Aquilla Lett settled in the county, paid his taxes, and insisted on sending his children to school, which was a radical act in the early days of the new country:

> There lived in the southeastern corner of Meigs township a colored man (a Quadroon) named Aquilla Lett. This man owned a good farm, and, paying a good round tax, naturally enough conceived the idea of educating his children. With this idea in view, he sent his daughter, Margaret, then twelve years of age, and his two younger children, Henry and Susan, to the district school.
>
> The news soon spread like wildfire that there were "niggers in the school," and the directors (Jacob Wharton, David McCarty, and Burr Reed) ordered the teacher, Miss Louisa Harmon, to put the "niggers" in a corner by themselves until a meeting could be had. The teacher attempted to comply, but Margaret refused to be separated from the other scholars, on the plea that she "was not a nigger."
>
> The next day the directors came and ordered the teacher to separate the scholars. The teacher then refused on the ground that Mr. Lett's children were attentive and orderly, and she would not disgrace them by any such unenviable distinction. She also refused to point them out.
>
> Mr. McCarty, after some parleying, addressed Margaret with, "Say, my gal, ain't you one of them?"
>
> Margaret inquired: "One of what?"
>
> "Why, Africans."
>
> The rejoinder was: "No sir, I am as white as you are."

This story illustrates the family's activism and commitment to education. It also illustrates the impossibility of living as a whole person in a racist society. Margaret's whiteness was not complete, as much as it was a denial that would allow her to get an education. By this time in

America, becoming white was the primary way to gain admission into safety, privilege, learning, and livelihood. Miss Harmon, the teacher who had tried to protect the Lett children by refusing to identify them, was fired after that day and replaced with someone who would refuse the children their education.

But Aquilla Lett Jr. still insisted on sending his children to school. After they were beaten, harassed, and tormented by the neighboring white folks, he sued the county and won the funding to erect a new schoolhouse for "colored children" on the Lett homestead. White townspeople burnt that schoolhouse down three times, trying to further terrorize the families, but the Lett Settlement persisted, successfully educating several generations of Black and brown students at their school.

By this time, my ancestor Peter, Aquilla Jr.'s brother, had moved to Crawford County, Pennsylvania. His daughter, Susan, would later move with her husband and siblings to Lake County, in Northeastern Ohio, where my family still lives. In the census of 1850, Susan was listed as "mulatto," and she gave her parents' birthplaces correctly as Ohio and Pennsylvania. But in order to be legally married in Mentor, Ohio—the very town where my father would spend forty years delivering mail—couples had to find a sponsor to swear that they were entirely white. Although he knew of the family's African ancestry, Susan's brother-in-law attested to the family's 100 percent whiteness, and by the final census of her life, Susan was listed as white and her parents' birthplace was listed as Germany. Just through these census and marriage records, in other words, we can see how Susan's story made a narrative arc away from the family's complex ancestry and into the fiction of whiteness. Susan was the great-grandmother of my own grandfather, a person I saw almost every day during my childhood, and one of the closest, most adored people of my life. But he never told me about Susan.

*   *   *

My cousin Nathan called me a week after we got home from the wedding. "I just found a children's book about Benjamin Banneker, Molly

Welsh, and Bana'ka, and I ordered it for all the kids in the family for Christmas," he said.

"Thanks!" I responded. "This is such an important story for them to know."

"I agree," Nathan said. "I called my mom, because I thought she'd be as excited as I was about it. But the weird thing was, she said, 'You'd better check with their parents before you send it, to make sure it's okay with them that their kids know this story.'"

"Your mom said that?" I asked. My aunt had worked in city government, as a Democrat. "She seems like the least likely person in our family to say that."

"I guess we are all a product of our generations," Nathan answered. "And you know, Grandma and Grandpa did not have the most progressive views on race. We didn't have to grow up with that."

"True," I agreed. "What did my brother say?"

"He thought it was cool, but he said, 'Wow, I bet Rachel is *really* excited.'"

"I am!"

"I know you are," Nathan said. "But if you write about this, whatever you do, you have to write about the fact that our branch of the family *hid* this history. That cowardice is as important to the story as the courage of Mary, Robert, Benjamin, and Jemima Banneker."

"I know," I said. I looked out the window. Our letter carrier, Will, was walking up my front steps, his back a little stooped. I waved and he waved back.

"Whatever you do, don't act like this makes you Black."

CHAPTER 3

The Milkmaid

England, 1680

There is nothing that is less in our power, and less our own than our birth. And therefore of all pretenses a man takes hold of to value and prefer himself to others, that of his birth appears the most groundless; and the truth is, a man does seldom insist on it, but for want of another merit.

—Banneker's Almanac of 1794

I RETURNED FROM my cousin's wedding and began researching this branch of the family. I was especially interested in the women of the line, but working-class women and women of color remain largely undocumented, and when they are listed on ships' manifests and land records, they usually merge into a big blur of Marys whose last names disappear into that of their husband's or "master's." In the case of our Marys—Molly (Mary) Welsh and Mary Banneker—the only reason we know their names at all is that Benjamin Banneker achieved so much in his lifetime that people recorded his ancestry.

Most of what we know about Benjamin Banneker begins with a biography written in 1836, thirty years after his death, by Martha Ellicott Tyson. Tyson was the daughter of Banneker's best friend, George Ellicott, and she grew up knowing the "sable astronomer," as he was then called. In the years after Benjamin's death, Tyson interviewed his sisters, nieces, and nephews, as well as other townspeople, in order to construct an accurate record of Banneker's remarkable life. Excerpts of Tyson's *Sketch of the Life of Benjamin Banneker, Afric-American Astronomer* were read before the Maryland Historical Society in 1854, and this provided the narrative basis for all of his later biographies.

"The ancestry of Benjamin Banneker, the Afric-American astronomer, can only be traced as far as his grandparents," Tyson's biography begins. It goes on to describe his British grandmother, Molly, as "a person of exceedingly fair complexion" who was an "involuntary emigrant to America." According to her great-grandchildren, Molly was a servant in England when she was "accused of stealing a bucket of milk, which a cow had kicked over." For this offense, Molly was sentenced to indentured servitude in Maryland, only "escaping a heavier penalty because she could read."

* * *

WHEN I IMAGINE Molly, I picture her as a thirteen-year-old girl, fair and slight like my niece Gwyneth, and wryly observant like her too. Molly wakes with the rooster, drinks a dipper of water, then wets her fingers and swipes the sleep from her eyes. She pulls a skirt over the linen shift she's slept in and ties a coif over her hair. After scattering some feed for the chickens, she grabs a heel of bread and a boiled egg from the larder and sets off down the lane, half running, half stumbling. She knows her chances of finding work will be best if she arrives early.

Her mother had died the month before, and the loss was fresh enough that Molly still woke to it bitter and unbelieving. Her mother had been widowed when Molly was very young and had turned to spinning and sewing to support them. She was literate and owned her own Bible, and as much as folks came to buy her bodices and petticoats, they also came to see the Holy Book set out on the oiled kitchen table. The neighbors gave her mother a shilling here and there to help them decipher their work contracts, marriage certificates, and letters. That is how Molly herself had learned to read and write, by sitting with her mother and listening to her soft voice reading passages from the Bible.

Through the long weeks of her mother's illness, Molly had sat beside her on the bed, reading her the verses she loved, telling silly stories, trying to make her laugh. When her mother's hands went cold and turned a stony blue, Molly rubbed them between her own to bring the warmth back. She washed the soiled bedsheets and smelled the foul discharge that came from her bowels. She saw the fear in her mother's eyes, her very gaze apologizing to Molly for falling ill. But the whole time she cared for her, Molly thought that surely her mother—her bright and witty mother—surely, *she* would recover. Molly refused to imagine that she could lose the one person who loved her in the world. But it had happened to her, as it had to many others. Her mother's lips had drained of color, her hands had unclenched, and she had gone very still. Molly put her hand on her mother's chest and waited, but her heart did not beat again.

Afterward, Molly took the linen that was left on the loom—fine linen meant to be sold to one of their wealthier customers—and stitched her mother into a shroud. Every stitch was rending her own heart, but she made them even and straight enough so that her mother would approve. When mourners and gossips stopped by, she went to the door and smiled and nodded. Yes, her mother was a very fine woman, and yes, thank you, she would manage.

A few days after the funeral, Molly took inventory of her remaining food. Some neighbors had dropped off porridge and a side of bacon, but that was already gone. She had a few eggs from the hens, carrots, turnips, and a small basket of potatoes in the larder, but only one cup of flour left, and no access to any shillings.

So Molly felt old, much older than she'd been just a month ago, as she walked the eight miles to the Collins farm.* It was a farm somewhere between a yeoman's and a nobleman's. The Collinses worked alongside their laborers, unlike the gentry, but kept more livestock than they had need of themselves. They hired lads to tend the crops, and girls to milk the cows and process the milk into curds, butter, and cheese. Then they sold the products to regional markets. Theirs was one of the company farms that was changing English agriculture, shifting it from subsistence

---

* Collins is an invented name. We have not located the farm in England where Molly was employed, but she told her family that she worked as a dairymaid.

family farms to larger holdings that hired gig workers and specialized in a single product—a scaling-up process that was setting the stage for large colonial plantations. Molly knew that there wasn't much stability in work like this, that farmers like Collins kept their workers just through seasonal contracts and didn't always pay full wages. But she was not a good enough seamstress to continue her mother's profession, and a girl could not just read and write for a living.

Molly made it to the farm just as the sun was rising above the tree line and the workday was beginning. She saw the broad pastures and wondered what that would feel like—to own so much land that you couldn't even see the edge of it. The little yard attached to her cottage was tiny and had been grazed down to bare earth so her hem was always heavy with mud. The Collins farm was bustling, almost a town unto itself, with chickens waddling around and boys going out to plow, and outbuildings filled with various workers. She looked into a long cow barn, where several girls sat on stools, milking. She stepped in, the grassy smell of cattle sharp in her nose and her eyes adjusting to the sudden dimness.

Molly asked the young women where she could find the master.

"The man himself?" one girl scowled.

"He'd be round about in the stables," another said.

Molly found him there, a portly man in tall boots polished to a shine. He was giving orders to a boy who was forking hay. She stood silently until the man noticed her, and then, in a soft voice, told him she had come to present herself as a willing worker.

"Pipe up!" "Master" Collins laughed, making some joke about how he'd see how willing she was. Molly pretended not to get his meaning, although she knew as well as anyone that to become a milkmaid was to set yourself up for certain slurs. Everyone knew the jokes about dairymaids who called to the plowmen to sow their seeds. To be a milkmaid was to be solidly of the working class and considered a lusty sort of slut. Rumor had it that "masters" liked to hire good-looking girls for the job.

Collins, predictably, asked after Molly's people, and when she said her mother's name, he looked her over, considering. The girl was spindly and short, but his wife had known her mother, and he figured he could do his part to keep one more wench out of the workhouse. He walked Molly back to the milking cabin, red-faced, and told each of the other girls to give Molly one of their cows. The girls nodded obediently, but when he left, their demeanor changed. One walked over to Molly and squeezed her upper arm. "Like a limp turnip," she said, pinching her.

"It'll mean reduced wages for all a' us," another said, under her breath.

"Ye can have this cow I'm milking now," one girl offered, kicking over her stool. This startled the animal, who kicked and shuffled. The girl leaned back and began to eat an apple, chewing loudly as Molly struggled to calm the cow.

As the day wore on, the girls explained that they each had a dozen cows to milk and that they also saw to the curding, butter churning, and cheese-making. They were paid once a fortnight. A *fortnight*? Molly thought anxiously. That would mean two weeks before she could buy food or give anything to the landlord. She'd have to make do on grubbed garden roots, and maybe a dipper of milk. *Were they allowed to drink the milk?* she wondered.

Molly returned, morning after morning, and proved to be a steady worker, small as she was. She rationed her food, eating one meager meal at dawn and waiting until hunger gnawed at her stomach. Then she'd slowly chew one of the wild onions that she'd found growing by a streambed on the way to the farm. They made her stink, she knew, but they also cut her hunger. At the end of each workday, the other girls walked off without her, arm in arm, but Molly didn't care, because it allowed her to stay a little later. She'd duck down for one more pull on the teat, letting the milk stream directly into her tin cup, which she kept tied to her apron. She willed that one long drink of milk to keep her stomach quiet until morning.

While they worked, the girls gossiped about the people they knew. The stable groom and the shopkeeper's daughter who had married in a rush, and didn't they guess it, she had a round loaf rising under her apron not a month later. The Millers' son who had gone to the plantations with an indenture and now owned his own farm. And Becky's cousin who had been sent to Barbados and was either dead or rich because they hadn't heard from him in years. Molly asked how a person got one of those indentures, and the other girls laughed at her ignorance. Molly hated being uninformed and always blushed a ruddy pink when she didn't already know a thing.

"Ye don't want one," one girl said. "The bonds is mostly for the lads, or women who get renned with child, or kencrackers—thiefs, you know, who are stupid enough to get themselves caught."

Molly tried to understand, but her mind was too muddled from grief and hunger to think clearly. She seemed to be waiting for something, but she didn't know what. It was a feeling like a low and smoggy sky.

*　*　*

"Master" Collins looked in on the dairymaids more often than usual and seemed to take a special interest in Molly. He leaned over her while she milked, telling her how best to do it. Soon he was catching Molly when she came outside to use the privy, trying to back her against a wall so he could reach up her skirts and rub himself against her. She allowed it a few times—what could she do? Then she grew shaky and nervous from trying to avoid him. She always asked one of the girls to go to the "necessary" with her, but they usually refused, thinking her too tenderfooted. The girls would be docked pay, or worse, out of a job, if they didn't milk their part. And all of them had to help feed their families.

Molly ventured past the barns and stables alone, toward the outhouse. She set her shoulders straight and walked quickly, but sure enough, there was Mr. Collins again, striding toward her. *Did he never work?* Molly wondered. She greeted him, but instead of answering, he scooped her off her feet and ran with her, toward the woods that bordered the fields. Molly wanted to scream, but her throat was strangely dry, and what came out was no more than a pathetic croak. She dug her nails into his arms, twisted up her body, and spit directly in his eye. Collins dropped her, and she ran back to the barn and her milking stool.

Molly milked the rest of the morning in a haze of distraction. She had gotten away, but at what cost? Now Collins would be looking for a way to get rid of her or to extract even more of a ladies' payment. She had one fortnight's worth of wages, enough to eat for a few days, meagerly, and not nearly enough to pay the rent. Maybe she could convince the landlord to let her stay. But if Collins put out word that Molly was not a good worker, it would be impossible to find a job on any of the area farms.

At the end of the day, Molly busied herself with a little extra milking. "Master" Collins walked in with a flushed face. She didn't seem to be as willing as she'd promised, he said, and he reckoned she'd be starving if it weren't for her wages and the milk she was stealing.

Molly trembled. Usually she could summon up a witty deflection, but her mind had gone blank. She admitted that she'd been hungry and asked what she could do to make up for it. But when he reached for her, Molly jumped back. The cow started and kicked over the bucket where she'd been milking.

"That's larceny!" Collins called out, as she backed out of the stall. "A theft from the farm!"

Molly ran most of the way home.

Molly did not return to work the next morning. Or the next. The day after that, a warrant for her arrest was read aloud in the town square. She was charged with grand larceny—the theft of salable property belonging to her venerable "master."

*　*　*

MOLLY'S CHARGE OF grand larceny was the most common crime of the late seventeenth century. It was defined as theft of property worth at least a shilling—which would equal about eight dollars today—and was punishable by hanging. At that time, people were so impoverished in England that most of these thefts were of clothing items or food and were committed out of dire necessity. According to the editors of the book *Crime and Punishment in England*, more than two hundred crimes were subject to the death penalty, including "stealing property worth a shilling or more, setting fire to a heap of hay, breaking down the head of a fish pond so the fish may escape, defacing Westminster Bridge and cutting a hop-bind in a hop-plantation."

But while hundreds of English citizens were threatened each year with the gallows, only about a quarter of the people convicted of these crimes were actually hanged. Murderers were those most likely to die of the death penalty. In the case of theft, sometimes magistrates or juries devalued the goods that were stolen and convicted the accused of petty larceny instead of grand larceny. And sometimes individuals appealed to the church courts and were given the "benefit of clergy." If a criminal could prove that he or she could read the Bible and was a devout member of the Church of England, they could be granted a pardon through this benefit.

Most likely, Molly would have stood trial before the county magistrate, in the magistrate's own home, without supporting witnesses or a jury. Molly's "master" would have come himself to accuse her of the crime. I imagine that Molly trembled with a mixture of fear, anger, and inarticulate shame as Collins towered over her. He had assumed the bruised manner of a man who had tried to help a young girl, only to be rewarded with insolence. He told the magistrate that he didn't even have need of another dairymaid but took Molly in on account of what had happened to her mother.

The magistrate listened with a dour face. He and Collins were old friends, and the magistrate knew that Collins liked to give young ladies a leg up in life. He asked Molly to state her defense.

"The cow was frenzied," Molly said. "It kicked over the bucket. Not me."

"Did you know you can hang for this offense?" the magistrate asked.

"I know now, your Honor," Molly replied, lifting her chin.

The magistrate gave her a mildly punishing look. If there was anything he found unbecoming, it was a rustic woman too haughty for her station.

Then Molly asked if she could "call for the Book."

The magistrate nodded, surprised. He knew that commoners sometimes memorized Bible verses, but not many of them could actually read. They had already sworn upon the Bible before the hearing. Now he opened it at random to the Psalms and told Molly to read the verses beneath his finger. Molly bent toward the book, squinted a little, and read the passage in her flat, clear voice.

> For a day in thy courts is better than a thousand.
> I had rather be a doorkeeper in the house of my God,

than to dwell in the tents of wickedness . . .
O LORD of hosts, blessed is the man that trusteth in thee.

Molly smiled to herself at the random passage. It was as if her mother were somewhere close, reminding her to have faith. And the magistrate had to admit that Molly could read, as well as his own daughters who had been taught by a private tutor. He considered the matter. Then he sentenced Molly to seven years of indentured servitude in the American plantations.

Molly's knees dipped, her stomach sloshed, and she felt strangely outside her body, as if she were watching herself from up in the rafters. She was relieved not to be headed to the gallows, but she could hardly believe that she would be exiled from England, sent across the ocean, just for "spilling a bucket of milk." She thanked the magistrate for his pardon and curtsied to him, bristling at the servility of the act even as she did it.

The magistrate called for the constable, who looped a rope over Molly's wrists and led her to the county jail.

* * *

THIS IS JUST one of many stories I imagine for Molly. I see her as spirited and strong-willed and, at the same time, defenseless and poor. She was likely dependent on any part-time work she could find and was most likely orphaned. During her parents' lifetimes, the economy of England had changed drastically. Lands that had once been publicly owned had been parceled out to wealthy individual landowners in a shift that left people jobless and homeless. England became overrun with vagrants and gig laborers who migrated to the larger cities looking for work, and to rural areas that specialized in specific agricultural products. The authors of *Crime and Punishment in England* explain that those migrating included "dispossessed cottagers and copyholders, unemployed rural laborers, orphans and unmarried mothers . . . forced by economic and social pressures. Many of these immigrants were young and single; youth crime was a constant worry to the authorities." Stripped of their own homes and farms, these migrants were dependent on meager pay and fluctuating jobs. They found themselves in large, unstable communities of people without long-term ties whose judgments determined their standing in the eyes of the law. Like all capitalist centers, these communities were marked by competition, scarcity, and shifting opportunities.

But for the first time, young women like Molly were able to find paying work outside the home, and this shift made women's labor, and women themselves, a subject of increasing debate among clergymen and lawmakers. Females were seen as subservient humans and were generally only as safe or respected as the men in their family. Spilling a bucket of milk that belonged to the company farm was robbing from a central societal institution. For someone like Molly without the protection of money or a father, it was cause enough for the death penalty. Or with the rare skill of literacy, it was cause enough for exile to the colonies.

This process of exporting criminals in indenture had been begun by King James I in 1615, when he authorized the transportation of convicts who could "yeild a profitable service to the Common wealth in parts abroad where it is found fitt to imploie them." Those convicted were forced into indenture, but many more impoverished and ambitious young people volunteered for their indentures, signing up with the recruiters who roamed the cities. Indentured servants— known then as bonded servants, "King's Passengers," or "Seven Year's Passengers"—were contracted to work for a term of years without pay, in exchange for their passage to the colonies. The ship's captain sold their contracts when they got into port and that money helped to pay the ship's expenses. Sometimes servants got to draw up the terms of their contracts before leaving England. Other times, servants were fitted in among the cargo, almost like a tax. It was the other products—tea, dry goods, and wool—that determined where the ship was headed, and not the human cargo.

Molly would have waited months before merchants found a place for her on a ship. At that time, British servants were being sent primarily to the Chesapeake in North America—a region including the colonies of Maryland and Virginia—and to the West Indies in the Caribbean. Maybe Molly campaigned for an indenture to Maryland, or maybe she was simply lucky. The Chesapeake had fewer mosquitoes and tropical diseases than the Caribbean, and British people were more likely to survive their indentures there than in the West Indies.

In the seventeenth century, two hundred thousand people left England for Maryland and Virginia, and 60 percent of them were indentured servants like Molly. These migrants were part of a solution of removal that allowed England to pull out of its recession and stop the starvation of its people. By the end of the century, England's population had thinned—in part through plague, starvation, and death in the overcrowded cities, and in part through this mass exporting of young people. This immigration allowed England to reach new stability and prosperity. It allowed the colonies to establish large-scale plantations. And ultimately, it initiated a new model of capitalism that was dependent on expendable laborers.

CHAPTER 4

Reverse Migration

Meigs Township, Ohio, and Baltimore, Maryland, 2017

THE SUMMER AFTER learning about Molly and the Banneker family, I took my daughter Adele and niece Gwyneth on a road trip to explore this history. They were fifth graders at the time, which is when the Common Core curriculum in the public schools covers colonial and revolutionary U.S. history. I wanted to teach them histories that were different from the white, male, military accounts that I had been taught in school. So I decided to do the Great Migration in reverse, beginning in Ohio—the state that had once represented the free North to our ancestors.

Benjamin Banneker's nephew and our ancestor, Aquilla Lett, moved his family to Ohio in the 1820s, after they and other free people of color were stripped of their voting rights and their farms in Maryland. The Lett brothers traveled with a few other free families of color into what was then known as the new Northwest Territory. They worked on others' land at first, and eventually joined together to purchase more than one thousand acres in Meigs Township, Muskingham County, Ohio. They named that cooperative the Lett Settlement and together established a self-sustaining community. They built their own homes and a church, baked their own bricks, cut their own lumber and shingles, grew their own food, and did their own blacksmithing and sewing.

I drove us back and forth through the county, looking for the historical marker that I'd seen online, hoping to see the old church or schoolhouse, but we couldn't find any trace of the Lett Settlement. We stopped at two gas stations, and a Subway, where we bought chips and made conversation with the locals, who were all white farmers and workingmen. No one had ever heard of the Lett Settlement.

Then I used data on my phone and headed toward the little pin where Google had located the Lett Settlement historical marker. We drove down a long gravel road, beside undulating fields, with thick woods off in the distance. We could see a green metal gate up ahead that I hoped was a turnoff into a farm with the sign. But it turned out to be an African safari park called "The Wilds."

The girls and I got out of the car, hot and thirsty. A female ranger walked up and explained that the place had been established as a wildlife conservatory and nature theme park in 1984. She told me that I could pay $25 each for the kids to go ziplining through the woods, or $100 to ride in a jeep and see the wildlife. We would see American bison and a number of African animals roaming free, including wild dogs, zebras, giraffes, and rhinos. "It's a lot like being on an African safari!" she assured me cheerily.

I felt a sudden nausea. Our ancestors had been kidnapped from Africa, had found a way to survive in America, and eventually buy this land, in the early nineteenth century. But they were forced off the land in the early twentieth century when lawyers purporting to represent them, but really representing coal interests, convinced them to sell it to the Southern Ohio Coal Company, who began strip-mining the fields. Then, in the beginning of the twenty-first century, the mine was closed and the land was converted into an African safari park? It seemed we had stumbled into a particularly American example of historical erasure—a half-told story that moved from resilience to exploitation to the domestication of wildness, and that all ended in a gift shop.

The gift shop was filled with stuffed African animals, and it made me think of the souvenirs of Disney World—a place I had loved as a child. I had absorbed a Disney-like version of American history too, I realized, filled with tales of orphans, explorers, and upward mobility. I thought about Americans' penchant for happy endings, about how desperately optimistic our stories have been, in order to hide the denials behind them. Americans have had an insistence on our historical

REVERSE MIGRATION · 35

innocence that manifests in an absurd prolonging of childhood. If we are only children, the logic goes, then of course we must be innocent.

I asked the rangers if they knew about a commemorative marker for the Lett Settlement. They said that it was around somewhere, in a storage shed. But apparently, a worker kept accidentally running it over with his truck.

My daughter begged to stay and go ziplining, but I was a single mother on a tight budget, and the place just cost too much. It was 90 degrees outside, and only getting hotter. I bought the girls ice-cream sandwiches at the snack bar and asked them to stand with me on the hill and imagine what our ancestors would have seen when they looked out at that land two hundred years ago.

"They had to clear these fields by hand," I said. "This place would have represented hope to them, this land over the Ohio River, finally in the 'free' North." The girls nodded, tiredly, and I wondered how much they understood, how much any of us understood.

We took a photo with the fields and woods in the background and got back into the car.

* * *

WE CONTINUED DRIVING south, and two days later, we arrived at the Maryland Historical Society, now called the Maryland Center for History and Culture. Both Gwyneth and Adele were excited. They had pictured a whole room dedicated to Benjamin Banneker, telling his story, showcasing his almanacs, and connecting him to other notable Black people of Maryland like Frederick Douglass and Harriet Tubman. I had read them several children's books about Benjamin Banneker and his family. The girls knew that his grandmother Molly had come from England and that his grandfather Bana'ka had come from Senegambia. They had seen illustrations of Grandmother Molly teaching Benjamin to read, and other renderings of Benjamin designing and building a clock as a young man. They knew that Benjamin had helped to survey the city of Washington, D.C., and had written and published his own almanacs. I explained that the almanacs had been a sensation—not only because they were accurate and readable but because they had been compiled by a Black man. They were proof that African Americans were capable of intelligence and even genius, in a time when African people were being cruelly enslaved and not even seen as full humans.

The girls approached the security guard at the doorway and proudly told him we were related to Benjamin Banneker. They were both grinning widely and almost hopping up and down with excitement about it. The guard glanced down at them. He did not seem all that impressed but did tell us that we could see a copy of one of Banneker's almanacs there in the museum.

We went upstairs and looked around. But there was no room for Benjamin Banneker, or for the other free people of color of the Chesapeake. No exhibit dedicated to the horrors of slavery or to the Quaker abolitionists of Baltimore County. Instead, we walked through room after room hung with giant, gold-framed portraits of white men in colonial finery. One gallery was a little homier, with folk quilts on the wall and small, dusty clay dioramas depicting tobacco cultivation. Dozens of four-inch-high brown figurines stood bent-backed in a case, pushing plows, washing laundry, cooking over fires, and bundling leaves. They looked exhausted, as if their story were a worn-out, little thing.

Beside this room, we found a single glass case devoted to Benjamin Banneker, with one edition of his almanac on display. It was in the hallway, between the bathrooms and the microfiche library.

The girls were incensed. "He should have a room! Or at least a wall!" my daughter kept saying. I agreed but told them that we could still find out more about him. They stood at my side as I settled in to do some research. I gave them shifts turning the knob on the microfiche machine, and between their bickering about who was turning the knob too fast and who was turning it too slowly, we saw the pages of Banneker's journal. They were filled with expertly drawn arcs beside mathematical equations, little rhyming poems, descriptions of his dreams, math story problems, and columns of astronomical computations in which the cosmic and the earthly came into conversation. Benjamin Banneker had been studying nature and the cosmos all his life, and compiling almanacs was the culmination of his dream: to publish his astronomical findings and present his intellect to the world.

After that, we went to look for Benjamin Banneker's sister, Jemima, our ancestor, the one biographers had once called "unknown" or "unnamed." I opened a heavy file cabinet labeled "L–M" and saw a very old manila folder with LETT typed on the tab. I pulled it out and read from a yellowed, typed page. Jemima Banneker had married Samuel Delaney Lett in 1757, in Baltimore County, Maryland, and they were the parents of nine children, eight of whom survived into adulthood, including our ancestor Aquilla Lett, who had traveled to Ohio with his wife, children, and brothers. There they were.

"Look, they were *real!*" I told the girls.

But they were still in a drawer.

CHAPTER 5

At Sea

Atlantic Ocean, 1683

Hail! Thou multitudinous ocean! Whole waves chase one another down like the generations of men.

—Banneker's Almanac of 1792

WHILE I WAS in Maryland, I pored over the lists of early convict servants and Carson Gibb's *The New Early Settlers of Maryland* but did not find one woman listed as Molly or Mollie. But I knew that Molly was sometimes a nickname for Mary. These databases list more than a thousand Marys arriving in Maryland between 1670 and 1690 and 434 women named Mary who were transported to Maryland just between 1680 and 1684, when her great-grandchildren said she'd arrived. Maybe one of these women was our ancestor Molly, or maybe she was one of the many more servants and convicts who entered the colony as an undocumented immigrant. According to historian Kenneth Morgan, the servant trade was largely unregulated, and most of the names of indentured and convict servants are lost. If Molly was a petty convict, as the oral histories say, she may have been transported through an under-the-table deal between sheriff and captain. Historians estimate that between 1615 and 1699, English courts sent approximately twenty-three hundred convicts to the American colonies, mostly in a haphazard manner that involved merchants negotiating the passages directly with English courts and jails.

Molly may have been one of a few convicts packed onto a ship bearing woolens, crock ware, shoes, and other exports from England, or she may have been on a ship filled primarily with other servants. In that case, she would have traveled with 150 to 200 other people, mostly between the ages of fifteen and twenty-two. All of them would have been fed stingy rations of dried biscuit, salted meat, dehydrated peas, and cheese. And their passage to Maryland would have taken anywhere from 50 to 140 days, with tiring stops in northern English ports and setbacks from storms that battered the hull in terrifying, mountainous waves.

* * *

I IMAGINE THAT Molly hated the ship—the way the decks sloshed and slid, the unsettling absence of land, and water in all directions, steep and swelling, at best a gray-green rippling that never ceased slipping from its colors. The trip was a nauseous dream of dawn and then dusk, and only when she had passed through her fear and anger, like taking off a dirty linen shift, did she feel it. A shimmering glint—of hope? curiosity?— that leapt up through the waves of her mind and flashed its insistence on her right to be here. Even if *here* was just a creaking wooden schooner in the middle of the ocean. The horizon, like a ring of smoke all around, was sometimes obscured so completely in fog that she felt not only outside of place, but outside of time. It hardly helped to count the days. But she did. She knew she had to keep her wits about her.

On the ship, the crew didn't treat Molly and the other women like hardened criminals, but like upstarts, waifs, and sexual conquests. As they would be in the colonies, women were outnumbered by men by at least three to one. The men flirted with them and harassed them, and at times the women reciprocated. Lying with a sweaty deckhand was sometimes better than being crowded down in the hold of the boat, among sacks of grain, barrels of whiskey, and crates of chickens—a corner that had a ripe, fermented smell that Molly thought she would never clear from her nose. She set up there with her bedroll and chamber pot and tried to look away when the others got sick. Worse than a farm smell, by far, was the smell of human sickness, that stench of sour stomachs and slop buckets.

I picture Molly crammed in beside several other convict women. Martha, who had "pled the belly" and found that her illicit pregnancy saved her from the gallows. She'd had to leave the baby behind just after giving birth, not even able to nurse the child. Ruth, a tall tough one who had grown up in a London workhouse and was a professional thief, and not a once-caught like Molly. And Betty, who had run a Southwark brothel with her husband, though her husband had not been convicted. All of them but Molly were hoping to get to the plantations, serve their time, and then marry. They had heard that there were so many men in the Americas that just to arrive there as a woman was to be taken up as a rich man's wife. Betty had that husband back at home, but she said it would all be worth it if she could marry a landowner. No one would ever know, and maybe her first husband could come over and work for them as a servant. Ruth said things like, "Look at these arms, who wouldn't want this for a wife?" It was true, she had the strapping look of someone who would survive. And while that hearty stubbornness had made them distrusted back in England, they had heard that on the plantations such pluck held the winning hand. The women had a bawdy sense of humor and a last-ditch feeling of freedom. "I reckon life'll be what we make it now," Ruth said.

Molly had once had an unblemished sense of herself, back when she was a girl and her mother was still alive. And as much as she missed her mother, she missed the life her mother had wanted for her—with her own home, clean aprons, and a tidy garden. But being marked as a convict and this *other* kind of woman left her open to abuse, but it also granted her a strange new feeling of freedom, because she no longer had to behave like she had been taught to behave. Sure, she had been exiled from England and would be owned by a "master" for at least seven full years. But what happened now would be between her and God. She vowed that now the life she made would be *her* life.

The boys were singing loudly again, volleying verses and making up limericks to pass the time. They were a rough-and-tumble bunch who had been recruited into indenture because they were starving, struggling, or convinced by tales of wealth and plenty. Most of them had grown up laboring in workhouses, scrapping in the alleys of London, or climbing the chimneys as sweeps. And now, way out there on the ocean, there was not enough for them to do, and too much time to worry the mind. So, the boys made up races, climbing the masts as the clips clattered below them. They mended the sails with hemp thread and wooden needles. They whittled awkward animals from fishbone, then laughed at their creations before throwing them into the sea. But none of it could quiet the sloshing feeling of waiting or quell the aching restlessness in their arms and legs. So they sang—sea shanties and ballads that were about sex and women, crimes and adultery, and always about leaving home. Some of the boys had been sold into servitude by their parents. Many had witnessed their parents' deaths by starvation, illness, and even execution, and now they improvised on their own unlikely luck:

> *Oh they calls me Hanging Johnny*
> *Away, boys, away*
> *They says I hangs for money*
> *So hang, boys, hang*
> *At first I hanged my daddy*
> *And then I hanged my mammy*
> *Away, boys, away*
> *Oh yes, I hanged my mother my sister and my brother*
> *I hanged my sister Sally*
> *I hanged the whole damned family*
> *Away, boys, away*
> *I'd hang the mate and skipper*
> *I'd hang them by the flippers.*
> *I'd hang to make things jolly*
> *I'd hang Jill, Jane, and Polly*
> *Away, boys, away.*

The songs were a mix of humor, violence, lust, and survivor guilt. They were characterized by the orphaned opportunism that would become central to the culture of the "New World." The songs knew that the boys would never see their families or homeland again. Despite the recruiters' promotional fliers and all the grand talk about the colonies, the boys must have known that not all of them would survive the ship's passage or their indentures. And what they suspected was probably even better than the truth, as only half to two-thirds of indentured servants lived to see the end of their contracts. Most of those who *did* survive would be dead before the age of forty.

The Lutheran pastor Gottlieb Mittelberger wrote about the misfortunes of indentured servants in his book *Journey to Pennsylvania*, published in 1756. His first-person account starkly contrasted with the popular tracts of the time that promised abundant land and prosperity, alongside glowing tales of adventure. Mittelberger told a much bleaker story that began with the ship's passage. "During the voyage there is on board these ships terrible misery, stench, fumes, horror, vomiting, many kinds of seasickness, fever, dysentery, headache, heat, constipation, boils, scurvy, cancer, mouth-rot, and the like," he wrote, "all of which come from old and sharply salted food and meat, also from very bad and foul water, so that many die miserably." He described terrifying storms that raged for two to three consecutive nights, and a horrific rate of infant mortality. On his own passage, thirty-two children had died of fevers and illness, and all were unceremoniously thrown into the sea.

According to statistics, Molly would have seen several of her shipmates pass away on the voyage. Maybe the women in Molly's berth grew sick with fevers and gradually recovered, and then Ruth went into an early labor, shocking her shipmates who hadn't even known she was with child. Although Molly and Martha did all they could to help her, Ruth died along with a tiny baby boy, a child fully formed but so small and transparent that they could see through his skin. Afterward, the captain and crew rolled Ruth and her stillborn baby into a blanket and hoisted them off the ship's deck. A clergyman held a tattered Bible, read the Twenty-third Psalm, a few people bowed their heads in prayer, and that was it. A chill settled in Molly's bones that would not leave. From then on, people kept dying, and the passengers found themselves breathing in a rancid death-smell alongside the fumes of nausea and dysentery, mouth-rot and urine.

* * *

By the time the ship finally docked, Molly had lost count of the days. She was so hungry that her vision had gone spotty. Hunger made her feel sharp and mean. She was sick of the other girls—their whining and bravado, all those tiresome tips about how to trap a man. For the last month, there had been lice and maggots everywhere, crawling from the bags of flour they rested upon, teeming over their legs. Mold had spread a gray-green fuzz over the dried peas, hardtack, and cheese, and although she had scraped it away with her fingernail, its musty taste had settled in her stomach. Taste of the past, Molly decided, and as hungry as she was, she could not imagine ever eating her fill ever again. The muscles in her arms and legs had gone slack, and her smock stank and hung loose on her body.

Molly had thought that when they got to Maryland they would all run off the dock barefoot and sink their toes into mud, breathing in the smell of the trees. She was surprised by how much she had missed the feeling of solid, unmoving land. But even after they docked in the harbor, the captain refused to let the servants off the ship. He and the sailors kept them locked on board for another week, overfeeding them, trying to fatten them up. The ship hands gave the boys rough haircuts and passed around wooden combs to scrape the lice from their skulls. They brought barrels of water onto the deck for them to bathe, all of them sharing the water until it was floating with lice and oily gray. They powdered and greased their bodies to hide their sores and fleabites. Molly found the rocking in the harbor even worse than the rocking out at sea, with the netted fish, mud, and livestock forming a miasma in the air.

While the ship was docked, the captain and his crew were onshore, meeting in taverns and advertising the ship's arrival in order to make some sales. Announcements were pasted around town that positioned the servants almost like any other products. "Just imported from Bristol . . . Fifteen Convicts, men, women and lads . . . who are to be sold on board the said Ship, on this Day . . . ," they read. Some of the advertisements made merry with the servants' circumstances, offering the sale of "Sixty-eight of His Majesty's Seven Years Passengers, who had too much Ingenuity to be suffer'd to live in England."

And so the ingenious Molly was led off the ship with a rope around her neck. The first mate spun her around and talked a big game about her, saying that she could sew, cook, and pick tobacco. Molly found the rope and the auction barbaric, even ridiculous. Here in the colonies, where the old ranks didn't matter as much, where any poor commoner could rise to the level of landowner or even burgess, they had to make their servants look to be of a different breed, no better than cattle. And yet, she had been used harshly back in England and would be used harshly here. It was not all that surprising.

Because Molly was able to read, she would have been less likely to be swindled in the terms of her indenture. Once her contract was notarized, Molly would have been passed from the deckhand to the overseer. There were very few wagons in the colonies, even then, so she and the other servants would have been led over the wooded paths they called "the rolling roads," because planters would roll their casks of tobacco along them. The servants probably would have trekked for several days, through woods and beside marshes, before arriving at the plantation they'd now call their home.

CHAPTER 6

The Park and Museum

Oella, Maryland, 2017

ON OUR SECOND day in Maryland, I drove the girls to the Benjamin Banneker Historical Park and Museum in the tiny town of Oella, which is in the Patapsco Valley State Park just east of Ellicott City. The park exists on the actual land that the Banneker family farmed from the 1730s through the 1800s. It includes 142 acres of meadow and woods, a creek that branches off from the Patapsco River, a kitchen garden, one hundred pear trees of Benjamin's favorite variety, and a one-room log cabin that replicates the cabin where Benjamin once lived.

While the girls ran and played outside, I had a conversation with one of the park's docents, Dorothy.* We had spoken on the phone weeks earlier, and she knew that I was in town doing research on the Bannekers.† We had also told her that we were distant descendants of Benjamin's sister, Jemima, a fact that the girls were very proud to share and repeat, but that I was suddenly feeling self-conscious about, given the state of our whiteness.

"Oh yes," Dorothy said, "lots of people over the years have claimed to be related to Benjamin Banneker. I don't know how much of it is true."

---

* Not her real name.
† The family name evolved from Bana'ka, to Beneca, to Bannaky, to Banneker.

I understood her impulse to protect Benjamin's story from inter-lopers. His story was a public monument to Black genius, not a private acquisition. Dorothy told me about the architectural dig that they had conducted on the site of the Banneker property in 1985, excavating the site of the cabin that was burnt down during his funeral. Then she walked me through the museum exhibit, explaining how they had reproduced the cup and plate that Benjamin would have used based on shards of pottery found at the dig. She also showed me a working wooden clock modeled on the clock that Banneker had carved as a young man. She had been telling Benjamin Banneker's story for years to school groups and museum visitors, and although it was a story that all of us needed to hear, I felt that Black people, including Dorothy, had much more claim to it than I did.

Dorothy and I continued to chat as I took notes on the exhibit. I was inspired by Benjamin's passion for learning and his determination to share his naturalistic observations with the world. But while Benjamin delighted most in being a thinker and astronomer, he also knew his success could be used for larger purposes of justice. This mission to help his enslaved "brethren" was why he sent his first almanac manuscript to Thomas Jefferson and penned that enclosure letter. It also explains why Benjamin described his race as "of the deepest dye" in that letter, footnoting the phrase by explaining that his father was a slave from Africa. Because of this insistence, many biographers have wanted to deny that Banneker had any European ancestry, and some have questioned Molly's role in this lineage, despite her presence in the oral histories as Benjamin's grandmother.

The longer I talked with Dorothy, the more I felt that she was also questioning my presence in the story. I think she only began to trust me when she referred to the "accidental" fire that consumed Benjamin's cabin during his funeral.

"Right, an *accident*," I blurted out. "The neighbors—white supremacists—burned it down!"

"I always thought so too." She smiled. And I was reminded of how guarded Black people have to be around white people, how much racism is still unacknowledged in the dominant culture's outlook. As we found more common ground, Dorothy began to share some skepticism about the story that she had spent years retelling to visitors, educators, and schoolchildren.

"I just don't know," she said. "Some of it doesn't quite line up. How did Molly buy two slaves as a woman *alone*? How did she have enough money to do that?"

"I've wondered about that too," I said. "I wonder if she had the help of some Quakers or abolitionists living nearby."

"Who knows? But I do think that people make way too much of Molly," Dorothy said. "Almost every book tells the story like it was Molly who made Benjamin a genius, because it was Molly who taught him to read."

"Good point," I agreed. "It's like the story is still attributing too much of Benjamin Banneker's success to her, almost as if it still needs a white protagonist to be told," I said.

"Exactly! Why does no one talk about his father, Robert? Now, that man had to be smart. He somehow got himself out of slavery, and he farmed so well that he bought two tracts of land—more than one hundred acres. And he had the foresight to put the land in his name *and* his son's, to secure freedom for at least another generation. I think Robert must have been the really smart one."

"He had to be brilliant," I agreed. "And you're right, we don't hear enough about him." Dorothy and I had compared notes. We had both read a dozen books about Benjamin Banneker, as well as a contentious recent paper by a genealogist who conjectured that Benjamin's grandmother Molly was actually the family's *owner*.

And Dorothy was getting at something that had already bothered me about the framing of the Banneker story. Although his biographies were all progressive for their times, and certainly abolitionist in nature, they always had a tone of exceptionalism about them that alienated them from their full social impact. This was partly because the Bannekers lived a very different reality than most people of color, who remained enslaved. But it was also because each telling had been influenced by the teller's position and time in society. When white people told Banneker's story, for instance, they tended to qualify their praise, as if he were brilliant not *because* he was African American, but because he was *different* from most African Americans.

And Benjamin Banneker's grandfather, Bana'ka, was always described not as a kidnapped and enslaved African but as a Wolof prince, as if to suggest that Benjamin was a genius because his African ancestry was lettered and exceptional. Meanwhile, his mother, Mary, is rarely mentioned. And his father, Robert, who converted to Christianity and was so devout and hardworking that he was able to secure his own freedom and purchase one hundred acres of land for the family, is generally mentioned less in the biographies than either Molly or Bana'ka. I suspected that was because Robert's and Mary's stories were about their own self-actualization as Black people, and not about a "white savior" who freed them.

As our conversation continued, I wondered if I *could* tell this story without beginning with Molly. But I didn't think I could. The oral histories, recorded biographies, family trees, and, now, DNA breakdowns, all suggest that Molly was a real person and our actual ancestor. There are many things that DNA cannot tell us, of course, especially this far back. But even so, we have little reason to distrust the story that was passed down through the generations of the Banneker-Lett family.

It is also true that, like Benjamin, Molly seems to stretch the bounds of what people can imagine. In her biography of Banneker, Martha Tyson wrote that Molly took a special interest in Benjamin's learning, cultivating his desire to read. But Benjamin himself never publicly mentioned his grandmother Molly, and in the 1800s, his early biographers hoped to prove that Banneker had no English ancestry. These writers were disappointed to be corrected on this count by Martha Tyson, who knew the family personally. When these biographers found that Banneker was not "strictly of African parentage," they deemed his story less useful for the cause of abolition because they feared that his intellect would be attributed to his English bloodline. This is why when Molly is acknowledged in his early biographies, she is almost always mentioned as having low or average intelligence. This too is part of the story, I realized—America's racist and sexist structures that have made honest nuances of ancestry and intelligence almost impossible to express.

But I was feeling that Molly's presence in the story was the only way that I could justify my own telling of it, my own *presence* in it—not only because she was my actual ancestor but because she was a white woman like me and writing about her was a way of addressing my own demographic and "staying in my lane."

Benjamin Banneker's first biographers were also white women, so it didn't surprise me that they too began with his grandmother Molly—this woman who was more than a wife and mother, more than an invisible participant in an unjust culture, someone who did something courageous and completely out of step with her time, something technically illegal but overwhelmingly right. She had children with the man she loved. She saw him as a man and not as property. She lived in a time that seems distant now but was actually much like ours—a time of change and political upheaval, a time when economic systems were in transition and laborers were unprotected. A time when Black people were being forcibly incarcerated, and divisions between working people were being exploited and inflamed. Molly dared to conduct herself with independence, and her actions suggest that she dared to hope for a positive future for her children. Maybe Molly has to be here in Banneker's story for us as white people more than for Black people, I thought, as a way of asking ourselves if we too could act with independence and courage, if we too could do something against the law and outside the norm, but quite simply *right*.

"I agree that Robert must have been a genius like his son Benjamin," I said to Dorothy. "But I'm tired of all the histories being about men. Molly survived her trial and her indenture. She raised four girls to honor the African traditions of her husband. Her daughter Mary became known as a local healer and herbalist. I think the women of this family must have been really smart and strong too."

Dorothy smiled at me. Nothing I said had surprised her. But she was understandably over the "white savior" chapter of the Banneker story. And I was reminded again that history—even well-researched history—is subjective and alive. It is always being seen through the lens of the present.

CHAPTER 7

The Company of Maryland

Baltimore County, 1680s

Needles first made in London, by a Negro, from Spain, in the reign of Queen Mary; but he dying without teaching the art, it was left till 1566, when it was taught by Elias Grogose, a German.

—Historical facts featured in Banneker's Almanac of 1792

THE SMELLS WERE different in Maryland, the trees and the climate. The woods were thick with maples, oaks, walnut and chestnut trees, and teeming with deer and wolves, badgers and hawks—more wildlife than Molly had ever seen back in England. The air, too, was less laden with rain. Clearer. People's stories felt like that too, lighter, unburdened. In Maryland, you didn't have to carry the past with you but could start anew—could invent, embellish, or deny what you wanted.

I imagine that Molly half liked Maryland, despite its roughness, despite the circumstances. Living on that scrubby, untilled plantation felt like going back in time, back to before the Romans, the servants would joke. "The New World feels a whole lot like the Old World," they'd say, laughing and shaking their heads, unsuckling their feet from the mud. Sure, they'd reminisce about the cobbled streets of England, the taverns with steep roofs and polished tables, but they didn't miss the dead-end struggle of living there. In Maryland, if they survived, they could one day farm their own land instead of toiling their whole lives for a "master." Such a thing had become impossible back in England.

* * *

No RESEARCHERS—INCLUDING myself—have found an indenture contract for Molly. But a court record discovered in 2021 involving her daughter Mary tells us that Molly was "a white woman servant of John Newman." I discovered that a settler named John Newman bought three tracts of land in Maryland in the decade that Molly arrived in the colony. He purchased two hundred acres called Bedworth in June 1681; fifty acres he called Newman's Addition in June 1681; and one hundred more acres he called Newingham in October 1683. Molly's great-grandchildren remembered her as arriving in Maryland in 1683, and this date now seems to be remarkably accurate, suggesting that Molly was part of the large indentured labor force brought in to work on Newman's tobacco plantations.

Molly would have labored with at least twenty other indentured servants who would have come from all over England, Scotland, and Ireland, along with a few African people who had been brought up from the West Indies. The Dutch, Portuguese, and English firms that were trafficking in kidnapped Africans were not yet importing them directly into North America, so the African people whom Molly would have met during her first decade in Maryland most likely would have come from Brazil or Saint Domingue (what we now call Haiti), having been born or enslaved there before arriving in the Chesapeake. These people would have brought a mix of traditions with them from their African nations, from the colonial influence of Catholicism, and from the vibrancy of the Caribbean, and they would have slept and worked alongside the European servants. Power was structured around gender then and was not yet organized around race, so the servants would have lodged in one bunkhouse for the women and one for the men, regardless of their skin tone or nationality.

Staple agriculture was dependent on a large, cheap labor force, and tobacco was a finicky crop that needed to be closely tended at every stage. Male and female servants worked side by side, and each was responsible for tending roughly ten thousand tobacco plants—hoeing, raking, plowing, planting, transplanting, weeding, cutting, and curing the leaves. Molly's hands would have blistered and split from the work.

She would have felt aching jabs in her ribs and back from bending to pull the fat, sticky worms from the plants. She developed cuts and calluses from chopping the coarse leaves and tying them up with twine. Her cheeks turned red, her skin toughened, and her shoulders grew broad. But there was an anonymity to the work that she did not mind, a freedom in being one of many laboring in the fields, rather than being singled out and starving in a company town. As hard as the labor was, Molly was alive—not hung up on the gallows or buried in the potter's field, not a drunkard's daughter or a beaten housewife. None of those things had anything to do with her now.

She and her fellow servants were scrappy and brash—the kind of people considered "undesirables" by the upper classes. They had next to nothing and had lost all of that nothing to come to this humid place of pin oaks and arum, skunk cabbage and mountain laurel. They had the humor, grit, self-interest, and ingenuity of survivors. They also had the kinds of friendships forged through long hours of working and living in close quarters. They made tinctures from barks and pollens, nursed one another when they were sick, and tried not to fall ill themselves. They slept side by side in the bunkhouses, on straw pallets under thin woolen blankets. They knew who cried in their sleep, who snored, who snuck out to lie with another, who was crawling with lice. Every one of them had known sharp pangs of hunger back in England and still had a constant, hollow worry in the gut that there was not enough to go around. That had been their only experience, and that was what their "masters"—who had more than anyone really needed—would have them believe.

Lord Baltimore had initially established Maryland as a Catholic colony, a refuge for those who followed the Roman way. Then, in 1649, the colony passed the Maryland Toleration Act, making it the first American colony to protect religious freedom and to welcome diversity. But for all of its ideological claims, the colony was, above all, a business investment. Catholic investors wanted to spread the word about their superior working conditions to attract more cheap labor, and Lord Baltimore himself published several pamphlets advertising opportunities for workers in the colony. A former servant, George Alsop, also touted the benefits of indenture in his 1666 book, *A Character of the Province of Maryland*, writing that those indentured in Maryland had "the least cause to complain, either for strictness of Servitude, want of provisions, or need of Apparel." But the truth was that servitude was grueling, and only half to two-thirds of the servants survived the hunger, working conditions, and illnesses that awaited them in the Chesapeake.

A letter home to England from Elizabeth "Betty" Sprigs, who was, like Molly, indentured on the Patapsco River, conveys the strain of this life. "What we unfortunate English People suffer here is beyond the probability of you in England to Conceive," Betty wrote to her parents. "Let it suffice that I one of the unhappy Number, am toiling almost Day and Night, and very often in the Horses drudgery . . . tied up and whipp'd to that Degree that you'd not serve an Animal, scarce any thing but Indian Corn and Salt to eat." Betty described herself as "almost naked no shoes nor stockings to wear, and the comfort after slaving during Masters pleasure, what rest we can get is to rap ourselves up In a Blanket and ly upon the Ground, this is the deplorable Condition your poor Betty endures." She then ended the letter begging her parents to send her some clothing on any of the ships bound to "Baltimore Town."

We do not know if Betty ever got her clothing, or if she was forced to go on sleeping on the ground. Indentured servants were seen as expendable laborers, and they often lived in deplorable conditions, with "masters" withholding food and extending their terms of work at the littlest provocation. Servants were legally required to work six days a week in the tobacco fields and forbidden to leave their plantations without a written pass. If a servant tried to escape, "masters" could inflict strict punishments on him or her.

Perhaps Molly's "master," John Newman, was more benevolent than that of Betty Sprigs. Or maybe Molly had special skills that helped her to survive. I imagine Molly as someone good at "having a crack," and getting people laughing, and I think she must have been the type to pitch in to help, doing the mending in the evenings, sewing a torn seam, or adding a patch to a fellow's breeches. Maybe she penned letters for fellow servants like Betty. She showed them how to make walnut ink and fashion a quill from a turkey feather to sign their names, and taught them how to recognize a few essential words so that they could avoid signing unfair contracts that would extend their bondage.

Most laborers at this time were illiterate, and many fell prey to this exploitation, laboring without pay for years longer than necessary, and sometimes their whole lives, because they were unable to read their own contracts.

We do not know the details of Molly's indenture, but we can assume that it held specific vulnerabilities for her as a woman. Servant women were legally forbidden to marry or become pregnant before their indenture was through, because the pregnancy would interrupt their owed labor and cost their "master" part of his investment. Sociologist Jacqueline Battalora explains that these laws made female indentured servants "particularly vulnerable to sexual exploitation and to the extended exploitation of their labor." When women became pregnant during their indentures, "masters" extended the women's contracts and held their children in servitude as a way of increasing their own wealth. A few servants sued their "masters" for denying them and their children their freedom, but to do so they had to summon extraordinary emotional and financial resources. The courts always favored the upper class, the legal process was slow, and servants were usually sent back to their "masters" after the trial, where they faced retribution in the form of physical, psychological, and sexual abuse. These laws policing female servants like Molly were setting the groundwork for a new type of capitalism that would increasingly legislate female reproduction.

Molly and the other servants would have been well aware of themselves as men and women, as gendered and sexual people. They also would have thought of themselves as British or Irish, Ashanti, Ibo, Portuguese, or French. But the servants would not have thought of themselves as white or Black, because those designations were just beginning to be written into law as a way to divide the working class. In the seventeenth century, 120,000 indentured and convict servants had been imported from England into Virginia and Maryland to work on the tobacco plantations. There were hundreds of indentured Africans in the colonies at this time, and they lived alongside these Europeans and had the same rights. When their indenture was up, servants were given their freedom, permitted to vote, marry, own land, and run for office— regardless of their skin color or country of origin.

Historians T. H. Breen and Stephen Innes have studied the high number of free Africans in early colonial Virginia, noting the ways that they used the courts, ran for office, owned land, and intermarried with other free people of both African and European descent. They estimated that on the Eastern shore of Virginia, 30 percent of the Black population were free by 1668. By reading the wills and court records of these free Black people, they deduced that these families fully expected to retain their freedom, and likely thought that chattel slavery was a moral and economic aberration that would be outlawed in the coming decades. These free people of color were leaving land, livestock, and belongings to their children in their wills, picturing prosperous futures for them. They were not foreseeing the increasingly racist society that would transpire.

In Molly's time, European and African servants still ate and danced together, labored in searing heat and stiffening cold, cared for one another when they fell ill, prayed, and slept together. Studies of the criminal courts of Philadelphia up to the late eighteenth century reveal that Europeans and Africans of the lower classes accepted, trusted, and cooperated with one another. The closeness of their relationships can be seen in the escapes that British and African servants often plotted together. The most famous of these escapes took place in 1640, when two British men and one African man fled their Virginia plantation for the more tolerant colony of Maryland. In a chilling prelude to the way that race would be weaponized in the coming decades, a Virginia court prescribed different punishments for the men. All three men received thirty lashes, and the British servants were sentenced to four years of extra servitude. But the African servant, John Punch, who had never been enslaved before, was sentenced to a lifetime of slavery in punishment for attempting the same escape.

Over the next decades, the racial categories that influenced John Punch's sentence would become more and more legally defined. Beginning in the 1660s, the colonies passed legislation that broke with long-standing English law and declared that the freedom of children born in the colonies would depend on the status of the *mother* rather than the *father*. Inheritance in English society had never been conceived of in this way. This rewriting of inheritance to "follow the condition of the mother" would go on to intimately shape Americans' experience of race by constructing racial hierarchies through women's bodies and offspring. This switch made enslavement appear to be a "natural" status and ultimately led to the legalized rape of enslaved African women by European men.

The colonial courts followed these changes with additional laws that named a new social category of "whiteness." In 1676, Bacon's Rebellion united European laborers and laborers of color as they demanded that Virginia's ruling elite grant them greater compensation for their work. British forces stamped out the uprising, and lawmakers retaliated with laws that would divide the interests of the working class. These new laws linked the rights of citizenship to whiteness, separating British and other European servants from those of African and Native American descent and stripping people of color of their previous rights.

The first of these laws naming whiteness was passed in Maryland in 1681 and made it illegal for a "white" woman to marry an enslaved African American man, saying that the women would be enslaved for the duration of their husbands' lives, and their children would be enslaved until their twenties. This law effectively reserved white women as the biological property of white men. This restriction on marriage was a significant setback to men of color and a rich source of privilege for these newly named white men, who would have the household help and long-term security provided by wives and offspring.

Additional laws that named whiteness followed, forbidding any African or Native American man to vote, to hold public office, to gather in public places, to own weapons, to have servants, to own property, or to testify against a white person—all the basic rights of citizenship that African and Native Americans had previously enjoyed. Poor white people were then put in charge of policing the removal of these rights, becoming the overseers and patrollers of the very people they had recently lived and labored alongside.

By inventing this new category of whiteness, lawmakers achieved several things for themselves—the wealthy, ruling class. First, they increased their control over white women and their reproductive rights, making white women victims of the white patriarchy as well as its beneficiaries.

Second, they created a mythical connection that linked poor

laborers like Molly to wealthy landowners. The category suggested that the laborers were related to the upper class in an "us versus them" narrative that used racism to hide the fact that these white laborers were still being economically exploited. This designation then led to real economic advantages over time, as whiteness became the prerequisite for privileges like voting, political representation, and landownership.

Finally, and most horrifically, these laws set the stage for the trade that would go on to import more than four hundred thousand kidnapped African people to North America. The slave trade was underwritten by American and English investors, who grew more comfortable with these business ventures when they were buttressed by laws that codified notions of white supremacy and Black inferiority. Historian Kathleen M. Brown explains that although Europeans had been engaged in condescending descriptions of Africans since the 1530s, the "single-minded emphasis of blackness and inferiority did not begin until the late seventeenth century, after the English were solidly committed to the slave trade." Subsequent generations would then accept racial hierarchies as natural, without question, because those who *knew* that this hierarchy was not natural had been disenfranchised from citizenship and stripped of the ability to argue for their rights or change the laws.

While these colonial laws were ideological, in other words, they served a clear economic function of dividing the laboring class from one another and increasing wealth for large plantation owners. In this way, a cruel capitalist system was hidden behind a racial mythology that poor white people would come to vehemently defend.

* * *

BUT WHEN MOLLY was indentured, these racial designations were still new and had not yet taken over the culture. Despite her fatigue as a laborer, Molly must have found it exciting to be around people from all over the world, who brought their music and stories, cures, recipes, prayers, and dances with them. The servants were allowed one hour of recreation each evening and were free on Sunday afternoons. I picture them together—one man from Ireland playing reels on his closely guarded fiddle, others teaching one another dances from home, still others doing some mending and darning while having a chat.

In those years, the servants were mostly from England and Ireland, but I imagine that after a few years, a few African people arrived on the plantation, including an elegant young woman I'll call Adaora. Adaora was a good foot taller than Molly, but they both were deemed "head-strong," which meant that they did not pretend to know less than they did. The two became friends. They liked to walk off into the woods on Sunday afternoons to look for roots, walnuts, and morels together. Adaora was always devising ways to make something out of nothing—weaving reed baskets and straw hats, and sewing scraps of cast-off fabric into exuberant quilts.

When the other servants complained and went on and on about the grand house they'd build someday and all the food they'd eat when they got their own land, Molly saw anger simmering under her friend's silence. Adaora would give the braggart a withering glance and speed up at her task—roughly scrubbing the potatoes, or quickly stitching a hem. She was the only one among them who was enslaved rather than indentured, and even worse than the long hours, the meager food, and threadbare clothing was the knowledge that they would all move on and she would remain there, aching and aging, doing the same unpaid drudgery in the same pale place. In these moments, Molly always tried to catch Adaora's eye to let her friend know that she saw her. But what good did that do?

CHAPTER 8

The Untangling

Arlington, Virginia, and Evanston, Illinois, February 2020

AFTER OUR TRIP to Maryland, I continued to do research about these ancestors and the contexts in which they lived. Then in 2018, I wrote an Op-Ed that was published in the *Pacific Standard* and titled "White Lies and Fiction." The essay examined my family's construction of whiteness and the denial of African ancestry in our origin story, and attested that this denial was mirrored in our nation's official origin stories. I wrote about the Banneker-Lett ancestors, who were just a few of the people of color who had built and protected our country—not only through their labor but through their talents and expertise.

Then two years passed. I went silent. I continued to read and educate myself about the legal construction of race, and I searched out anything I could find about the Banneker and Lett families. I sensed that what these ancestors had experienced when the nation was just beginning could illuminate our own tumultuous moment, when it seemed like our democracy was on the brink of dissolution. But I did not know how to work with these ancestral stories ethically, as a white person, as someone who respected Black culture and knew that it was not my own. I got very self-conscious whenever I talked about these stories with my Black friends. I was even shy about mentioning them to my immediate family.

"There is something particularly obnoxious about a white person claiming Black ancestry right now, especially a famous Black ancestor," my brother pointed out.

"I know," I said. "Maybe, at this moment in history, it is not unlike what our ancestors did before us, when they claimed entry into a society that they wanted to be a part of." Were my interests in sharing this story now the same thing that our ancestors had done then, when they passed over into whiteness? Was I trying to gain access to power—to a community or identity—that I could not access otherwise? That was a question that had to be asked.

All I know is that a huge wave of self-doubt rose up in me, a doubt so complete that it tipped me into self-loathing.

"That silencing is also your ancestors," my friend Erika Allen said. We were at our friend Geeta's long dinner table, and Erika had heard me share the story of the Banneker-Lett family and then wonder aloud if it would be ethical for me to write about them. It wasn't that these ancestors seemed "other" to me. In fact, I had felt a deep inner recognition when I learned about them, as if they finally explained my orientation in the world. And it was almost like I could feel them with us that night, as I sat surrounded by friends who had stumbled into a conversation about our ancestors.

"Look closely at your doubt, your fear," Erika went on. "Get to know it. That is your ancestors' break in communication with the family when they passed as white. That is *their* doubt and fear." Erika is a Black woman and Iyanifa by training and ordination, a diviner who is working with ancestral guides to do her work in the present time. She cofounded the Urban Growers Collective, which plants organic farms in unused urban spaces in Chicago, and employs Black youth to farm, harvest, and provide fruit and vegetables to schools and food-insecure communities. Her organization is providing the South and West Sides of Chicago with healthy produce and helping to return Black people to their rightful ancestral connection to the land. Her own ancestors farmed, as did mine and most African Americans and Native Americans in earlier centuries. This continent was cultivated by their labor, their expertise, and their relational understandings of nature. But most Native Americans were driven from their land by government settlement, treaty trickery, and land theft in the eighteenth and nineteenth centuries. And most African Americans fled their land for urban crowdedness after Restoration, when the "40 acres and a mule" promise of landownership was rescinded and the era of Jim Crow unleashed lynchings and terror across the South.

"We say 'The Great Migration' like it was this wonderful, exciting thing," Erika explained, "but it was also people of color being run off their land by white people, forced off the land of their ancestors into crowded Northern cities."

My ancestors, I knew now, were part of that story, and my research into their lives was introducing me to new understandings and relationships. For this, I was thankful. It wasn't that I couldn't imagine their mixed-race families and communities. I had sought out similar communities in my own life. My hesitation came from the fact that I knew that white narratives—not to mention white people—were known for disregarding and generalizing the joy, wisdom, and specificity of people of color's experiences. We white people are not very good at knowing what we do not know, at getting out of the way and acknowledging that there are many ways to tell a story.

* * *

A WEEK AFTER Geeta's dinner party, I logged on to Facebook and saw a message from someone named Edie Lee Harris. "I saw your Op-Ed and I would love to talk about our family," she wrote. The Op-Ed had been published two years earlier at this point, so I was excited, and a little surprised.

I scanned her Facebook page. I learned that Edie was an attorney who was very involved in Democratic politics. She had grown up in Springfield, Illinois, and now lived in the D.C. area. Like me, she traced herself back to Aquilla Lett, and before that to Jemima and Samuel, Mary and Robert, Molly and Bana'ka.

She messaged me. "I periodically do a Google search of family names to see what comes up. And when I saw your article, I was like, 'Who is this woman writing about my family?' Then I realized you're one of ours!"

One of ours. It was such a kind thing to say, and I felt my face flush with gratitude. Edie wrote that she had done more than thirty years of research into the Banneker-Lett family line, and now she was busier than ever, compiling sources and sharing documents, photographs, and historical records through Ancestry.com.

Edie and I decided we would talk on the evening of February 5, 2020. News outlets had just begun reporting on a strange new virus overseas, but I didn't understand why they were giving it airtime because there was so much political turmoil going on at home. That week, Donald Trump had been acquitted in his impeachment by the Republican Senate. The night before, he had given the State of the Union address in which he falsified his successes and justified what I saw as dangerous erosions of our democracy. He was using the same divide-and-conquer techniques that I had been studying in history, the same weaponizing of race to make working-class people think that they were aligned with his wealth just because of their whiteness.

Edie and I began there. We had already scanned each other's Facebook profiles and knew that we were both Democrats. I rarely posted, and when I did, it was usually about something writing related. Edie posted several times a day, and almost always about politics or ancestry research.

"I'm a news junkie," Edie began. "I have the news on pretty much all the time, and I could not even watch his full speech. I watched for about ten minutes," she said, "and I heard four or five lies within that time."

"I listened on NPR," I said, "and what I heard was all fear, talk of stopping so-called 'aliens' at the border, and illegal immigrants that have gone on crime sprees. It was a whole lot of 'othering.'"

We went on to discuss the crowded field of Democrats vying for the presidential nomination and then turned to voting rights. The day before, an app had malfunctioned to make the results of the Iowa caucus two days late, and distrusted.

"What does it say about our democracy when a privately designed app has the information that reporters and government agencies can't even access?" I said. "What kind of shape is our democracy even *in*?"

"I hear you, but that is too scary to even think about," Edie said.

"I know. I tend to be an optimist," I replied, "but right now, I do not feel optimistic about the state of our country."

"I am afraid we have entered a dark time," Edie agreed.

Then she told me that, for her, political interest began in the family. "My father was a doctor," Edie said. "He was the only Black physician in Springfield, Illinois. He would get home around five, and my mom would have dinner all ready. He'd put on the news, and one of the rules in our family was that we did not talk during the news. My father would say, 'This is the one thing I ask! Just let me watch my news!'" She laughed.

"It was the same at my house," I said. "My dad would come home, change out of his uniform, and we would all watch the news while we ate dinner. I realize now that it was like a constant, running civics lesson. We had an awareness of being part of the nation, part of a shared reality that I don't think people in our country really have anymore."

"Our parents taught us that it was our *duty* to be informed," Edie said. "It was our duty not to be ignorant. My dad had served in World War II and had volunteered for the service. He'd worked as a surgeon in the army, so he was patriotic. But he'd always say, 'Don't be a flag waver. Don't trust those people who are advertising their patriotism. They have an agenda, and sometimes when they're waving flags, it means they want to take your rights away.'"

I felt a little embarrassed when I thought of my family's flag, of how little we had understood.

"You said something in your essay about how you and your family thought of yourselves as Americans but didn't realize you were also African American," Edie continued. "You know, that's all my people want too. To be seen as Americans. I think people assume that Black people always want to be talking about racial issues. But that's not true. Black people would be happy to never have to say anything else about race. It's just as uncomfortable for me to be talking about it as it is for you to be receiving it. But if we don't say anything, people will think that the way things are is acceptable, and they aren't."

"They really aren't," I agreed. We continued talking politics, then I asked Edie if she would tell me about her genealogical research.

"I began researching because my mother was adopted, and she wanted to learn more about her birth family," Edie began. "But it was long before anything like Ancestry.com or 23andMe existed. You had to look through all the census records, marriage certificates, and death certificates on your own, in person. Then I found a little group that was also doing research on the Banneker-Lett family. We were a little motley crew researching the Ohio Letts—a white woman from Idaho, a Black man named Robert Lett from Pasadena, a white man named Darren Rockhold from Peoria, Illinois, and me.

"And it turns out that the white man was not from Peoria, but was from Pekin, Illinois. Do you know anything about Pekin?"

"No." I felt a stiffening in my chest.

"It was known as being a sundown town."

"I was afraid you were going to say that."

"Yep. It was an all-white town. When I was growing up, it was always like, 'Don't go into Pekin. Don't stay after dark in Pekin. Bad things will happen if you go there.' Whenever we'd play them in basketball or something, there would be these big fights along racial lines. Stuff like that. Anyway, Darren from Pekin, his line goes all the way back to Zachariah Lett. He and I got really close, and he'd always say to me, 'I don't understand how I am connected, but I feel that I am.'

"Now, Zachariah was the bastard, 'mulatto' son of Mary Lett. Did you read that? She was tried and convicted of 'bastardy' for having a child out of wedlock. And as her punishment, Zachariah and his sisters were sold into indenture."

"How awful," I said. I had been in a committed partnership, but unmarried, when I had my own daughter, and the thought of losing her took my breath away. I realized I had covered my heart with my hand.

"Anyway, this white man said, 'My family has done all this gene-alogy work, but when they get to Zachariah, they always say that he was a German immigrant who arrived in New York in the 1720s. But there was no record of a Zachariah Lett who did that. But there was our Zachariah Lett living at the exact time as his ancestor, in Maryland. We have the conviction of his mother Mary, and then later, we have a will in his name."

"My relatives did almost the same thing," I said. "We had cousins and aunts who researched our genealogy and were very proud that we were Daughters and Sons of the American Revolution. But it wasn't until 2016, when my cousin Melissa started doing research, that she noticed that one strand of our grandfather's heritage from the Lett family had never been examined. Others must have stopped their genealogy research when they got to the people who had an *M* next to their names in the census."

"Oh yes, that happened. Even among those doing research online, there was always this big separation between the Black Letts and the white Letts." Edie continued, "But Robert kept saying, 'I just think Zachariah is one of ours. I just think he's one of ours.'"

One of ours. There it was again. The feeling.

"It was a feeling as much as anything," Edie said.

"I know what you mean," I said, my eyes filling. I was so glad that Edie had found me.

"We were lucky," Edie said, "because we actually had the original birth certificate for my mother, where it gave the name of her birth parents. I started looking into them and that led me to the Letts and then eventually to the Bannekers.

"When Mom was a teenager, she started writing letters to her biological mother, who was in Youngstown, Ohio, by that time," Edie went on. "And her adopted father drove her up so she could meet her birth mother. She told me that the only thing that she remembered about her mother's house was that there were books everywhere, on every surface in every room, books lined up along the floor, even in the kitchen. And I was like, 'And that is different from our house *how*?'"

We laughed. I swung my laptop around to show Edie my office, which had piles of books lined up along the floor. "When you run out of bookshelves," I said, "the floor becomes a shelf!"

"It is kind of fitting that Molly saved her own life by being able to read," Edie said. "The idea that books are sacred runs in our family. My brother Edwin and I always had our noses in books, and our mom would routinely burn dinner because she was so wrapped up in her book, she wouldn't hear the kitchen timer."

"I would have loved your mother!" I said, laughing. I told Edie about my aunts, how we can tune out everything if we are reading a book. "In a milder sense, I feel like reading saved my life too," I said. "It is what allowed me to get scholarships and an education, and live the life I wanted."

"You know, because my mother was adopted, she didn't know that she had this ancestry," Edie continued. "But she was fiercely devoted to our learning. She taught us all the constellations, and sometimes, she would wake me and Edwin and our other brother up in the middle of the night to show us the stars, or to see a comet. Believe me, there was nobody else on our street at night, lying in the grass, looking up to see a comet!" She laughed.

We continued trading stories, but after about an hour, I had to cut the conversation short. I was walking to the Block Museum of Art, to attend a talk by the textile artist Sonya Clark. Edie and I were both a little giddy, feeling the happiness of having connected with kin who really felt kindred.

"Meeting you is such a gift," I said. "Ever since I learned these stories, I have been wanting to research and write about these ancestors, but I didn't want to do it alone. And I know that Benjamin Banneker is very important to Black culture."

"I'm excited too," Edie said. "To think that I have done almost forty years of research, and here you are, a writer! And this is an absolutely epic story. And the thing is, this family story is so big, you *can't* get the whole thing by yourself. It's just too big for that.

"And you're right. This is an important story to Black culture," Edie said. "But our family has always been of mixed ancestry, since before the Revolution. That is what makes this such an American story. These ancestors could have only met and married in this country. Their stories would only be possible in *this* country."

"That's true," I said. "It has also helped me to be learning about their lives now, and to remember that they lived through much darker times than these. They lived through cycles like this one, when it was probably going to get worse before it got better."

"Oh, yes, they sure did," Edie said. "And now it's time to go back to the well. We have a deep history there, of surviving and thriving."

"That was beautiful!"

"Well, you can quote me!" Edie said. "That was my mother speaking through me. Next time we talk, I will tell you more about my mother. She was just amazing."

* * *

I SLIPPED INTO the back of the auditorium to hear Sonya Clark's talk. I felt buoyant and porous, my face flushed and my energy open, like Edie and I had been connecting to something much larger than ourselves.

Sonya Clark began by saying, "This talk is dedicated to my late parents, who are ancestors now." Then she began showing slides of her artwork, which she always created with some form of group participation. In one exhibit, she and community members painstakingly unraveled Confederate flags, leaving them on exhibit as twisted, hairlike heaps of dyed thread.

The piece that moved me most was one that Clark made for the art museum at the University of Virginia, a campus modeled on Thomas Jefferson's plantation, Monticello. It is called *Black Hair Flag*, and is a Confederate flag overlaid with an American flag made of hair—with black cornrows for the stripes and braided knots for stars. The piece has a haunting, visceral quality to it, as if the hair has been growing out of the symbol, insisting on bodily presence. To see the *Black Hair Flag* is to *feel* the enslaved African people who made the country's prosperity and independence possible. It is to be reminded that the country itself was made from their presence, their work, their bodies.

In the Q and A afterward, someone asked Sonya Clark about the use of human hair in her work. "If I pluck a hair," she answered, "it is holding all of my ancestry. Every Black woman has a story about her hair. Hair is a place where we get divided, but it is also a place where we connect. And this becomes really complicated when I sell artwork. If I am selling a piece of art that has my hair in it, I am also selling a piece of artwork that has my DNA in it. So, in some sense, I am also selling my ancestors."

Then Clark talked about her next work, an installation in New Bethlehem, Pennsylvania, which had been a stop on the Underground Railroad. For this project, she collaborated with inmates at the local prison—most of whom were Black men—to scatter heirloom seeds on sheets of fabric, which were then painted with a cyanotype solution. As the sheets sat in the sun, the photos developed, and the scattered seeds became constellations of stars on the deep blue fabric. The stars would be draped across the museum's ceiling, and visitors would navigate the exhibit with the help of just a little flashlight. Sonya Clark said that she did not want to create something too beautiful, or to suggest that she was replicating the experience of escaping from slavery—braving hounds and patrollers, guns and whips, to walk through marshes and woods in the middle of the night. Instead, she wanted to create a meditative space to reflect on the journeys that these brave refugees took, guided by their courage, faith, and collaborations—and by the light of the stars.

As I was picturing those stars, I was thinking about Edie as a little girl, lying on her front yard in Springfield, Illinois, looking up at the constellations. And I was thinking of Benjamin Banneker, lying out in his fields, looking up at the stars, tracking the zodiac and phases of the moon. *Yes*, I thought. *There is a connection between the stars and the seeds that goes way, way back.*

CHAPTER 9

Stolen

Senegambia and the Atlantic Ocean, 1690

How pitiable it is to reflect, that although you were so fully convinced of the benevolence of the Father of mankind . . . that you should at the same time counteract his mercies in detaining by fraud and violence so numerous a part of my brethren under groaning captivity and cruel oppression.

—Benjamin Banneker to Thomas Jefferson,
a letter reprinted in his Almanac of 1793

BANA'KA'S ANCESTORS WOULD have traveled across the desert for salt by way of the stars. As a boy, walking beside his grandfather with his staff, he would have learned their stories and memorized the Wolof constellations—stars as story shapes and navigation tools, stars as ancestors and illumined guides. After all, Bana'ka knew who he was and where he was in Western Africa because of the grandfather who walked beside him, and the ancestors above them, who participated in the family as spirits. When Bana'ka came of age, he was given a carved spear with a bone tip, and a shield made of copper disks lashed together with cured hide. He wore that shield over his caftan, which was embroidered with silk thread. Once he heard a traveling griot reciting from Al-Bakri, *The Book of Routes and Realms*, and he half wished that he could apprentice with this man, become a griot who went from village to village, sharing Wolof stories, maps, and lineages in the form of songs and poems. But as one of the ruling merchant class, he knew he could not enter the caste of griots—artisans who spent their lives in service to the family's and culture's stories.

According to the family histories, Bana'ka was born around 1670 in Senegambia as part of the Wolof people. Martha Tyson wrote, "The first that is known of the name of Banneker is that it was borne by an African prince. He was the son of the king of his country" who was "captured and brought to America as a slave." Today, we in the family can see in our DNA breakdowns that we do have at least one ancestor from Senegambia.

By the time Bana'ka reached adolescence, he would have outgrown his mother's and siblings' hut and would have slept in a structure that was built as part of his coming-of-age ritual—round, with walls made of mud-millet adobe, and a conical thatched roof. In his home, Bana'ka slept under a quilt his mother and aunts had sewn for him. The quilt was made of brightly dyed fabric painted in the design of the quincunx—a four-pointed star that symbolized the four directions of the earth, with the wisdom of Allah branching out from the fifth element of the center. Around the quincunx, his aunts had embroidered sacred words. Words in Islamic Wolof culture were not just used to list belongings and record sales and deeds, but were sound-shapes imbued with spiritual power, charged with the history and vibration of their tones. Words were written on parchment, worn in amulets, and used in incantations to pray, to thank Allah, to enact healing, and to confer protection. The verses on Bana'ka's quilt expressed his family's hopes for him, preserved the lineage of his name and people, and made prayers for his protection.

But they could not protect him. In Bana'ka's time of the late seventeenth century, Western Africa was being ravaged by the slave trade. Dutch and Portuguese traders were forming alliances with African nations, who would then battle their neighbors and sell the prisoners of war to the traders. When the Portuguese, the Dutch, and the English began exporting human beings, they exploited existing divisions between peoples and employed Africans to capture other Africans.

As one of the Wolof ruling class, Bana'ka would have known about slavery, because his family would have held slaves themselves. But slavery in Africa existed in a different form than it did in the American colonies. There were both voluntary and involuntary kinds of slavery in Africa, with most enslaved people retaining human rights like the right to marry, earn an independent income, and hold property. Slaves were often adopted into families to assume and safeguard a lineage. While European culture was perpetuated through the linked institutions of church, courts, and trade, African societies were organized along these lines of kinship. Kinship and family formed the very center of meaning in African cultures, and kinship was defined expansively. It included the unborn; living family members like children, parents, and grandparents, uncles, aunts, and cousins; and all the ancestors who were still remembered by the living. These departed were thought of as "the living dead" and were seen as vital participants in the community.

In one possible story of Bana'ka's capture, Mandingo bandits raided the village early one morning, when the men were away on a trading journey. The warriors burst into Bana'ka's hut, pulled off his blanket, and began beating him. One man held Bana'ka down and another locked shackles around his ankles. Bana'ka tried to scream for help, but he had been gagged with a leather strap. They put a burlap hood over his head, and dragged him from the compound. Bana'ka heard wailing and commotion, girls screaming and throwing hot water at the raiders, and men and boys fighting. He recognized the voices of the other captives when they cried out, as he did, in pain, anger, and fear.

After the chaos and bloodshed of the raid, the captors put the kidnapped people in chains and led them miles away from home, on foot, through swamps, woods, and fields. Bana'ka tried to memorize the directions they were pulling him. He tried to remember what his grandfather had taught him, to follow the stars and to recognize the smells of trees and directions of the rivers, so when he escaped, he could make his way home again. But he was so hungry, his head was throbbing from the blows, and his right eye was caked with blood and swollen shut. He and the other captives were given only a bit of gruel and water in the evenings, as if their captors knew just how little food was required to keep them alive. The kidnapped people watched with cramping, rumbling stomachs as their captors cooked meat over the fire and fed themselves before throwing oily bones and fat to their dogs, not offering any at all to the captives. When one of the Wolof boys collapsed on the path in thirst, hunger, and exhaustion, the captors left him to die alongside the road. Bana'ka had known the boy since they were infants. They were cousins. When he was forced to walk on and leave his cousin behind, something in Bana'ka died too, leaving a hard, scarred anger in its place.

Bana'ka's wrists and ankles blistered and split from the shackles, and his mouth became parched with a choking thirst. He didn't think he could lift his feet to take another step, and yet he did, again and again, prodded forward by the men's whips and his own staggering insistence to survive them. He tried to call on everything his grandfather and father had taught him, but within days, he had to admit that he did not know where he was. The climate had changed, had become more coastal, and the smells were no longer familiar.

He had been kidnapped with four other young people from his village, but now only three remained. At fifteen, he was the oldest, and as the son of the chief, he felt guilt and responsibility for all of them, as well as a prickly sense of entitlement, disbelief that this could be happening to *him*. At the end of the journey, they were all thrown together in one dank and stinking cell, the only comfort being that they could at least speak of home and discuss their plans for rescue or escape. Escape seemed unlikely because they were all shackled together by the ankles and armed slavers stood guard outside. But they still believed in rescue. They still hoped that their fathers would return to free them. But what if the men did not yet know about the raid? Had the women survived it to find them?

Fadia was the one girl who'd been kidnapped. She'd always had a matter-of-fact way about her, but now her directness had flattened into despair. "They are going to put us on one of the *tumbeiros*," Fadia said, "and sail us off the edge of the water." They had heard of the ships called *tumbeiros*, floating tombs, because it seemed that everyone who went on them died.

"No, it is a ruse. Only for money," her younger brother, Saiko, argued. "Our fathers will come and buy us back."

"Ñoom lañu dem ci lekk ñun. They are going to devour us," Fadia said vacantly. Her shoulders slumped and she shivered uncontrollably. Her body had already been so violated, it didn't even feel like her own anymore. The only relief was that she'd been put in a cell with Saiko, who had always been adored and coddled by Fadia and their mother. He was the plump one, the funny one. But even his hope was waning.

By the end of the third day, Saiko too had begun to cry and curse, while Fadia sat beside him in stunned silence. Bana'ka insisted that they would not go to all the trouble to capture them and march them across the country if they only meant to kill them. Pau agreed and said wearily, "They mean to get years of work out of us." Saiko raised his arm weakly. He hardly needed to say what he was thinking. Once he had been hearty, but now he was almost as skinny as Bana'ka. How could they work, when their captors were starving them?

The captives were furious and humiliated that they had been taken from their own village. Their parents had warned them to look out for kidnappers when they were herding their goats, playing in the woods, or walking to meet their mothers in the far fields. But they had not known that they could be taken from their very own cots. The bandits had raided the village early in the morning, just after the women had left to plant the blue millet. They must have heard the soft singing of the women as they walked down the lane, Bana'ka realized. They must have heard the songs of their mothers and taken that as their cue to kidnap the children.

Some had fought back. Their friend Kebba had grabbed his father's spear and drove it through an invader's throat. *How had he done it?* the boys wondered now, proud and a little envious of him. The man had fallen, but his comrade had shot and killed Kebba with his musket. Pau too had fought, just enough to give his sisters time to run and hide in the bush. His sisters knew how to hide. And he hoped—no, he knew, he told himself that he *knew*—that the girls had made it to safety.

Had the Mandingo taken over the village or just plundered it for its wealth—primarily its salable people? The boys simmered with rage at these men, dishonorable cowards who did not have the courage to fight with their equals but took boys and girls from their beds. They also blamed themselves for not sleeping with their spears beside them, for not protecting their village and resisting the invaders, who were twice their age and number, and armed with European muskets.

Bana'ka could not stop thinking about his mother. If she was still alive, she would have known that he had been kidnapped and sold to the slavers. Was she glad that he was alive, or would she have rather seen him die a brave warrior death like Kebba? Then she could have buried him, and kept him with the land, as a guardian spirit to his family. Instead, he had been wrenched from the natural order of things. Now his mother could not see his face in the sand crane's, could not speak to him in a cool wind that tickled her shoulder. Or would she? All of his things—his embroidered robes and headwraps, his amulets and shield, his blanket, his knives, his gold utensils and copper pots—all of that had been stripped from him. But nothing was as terrible as being stripped from his family and destiny, wrenched from his kingdom and nation.

The captives fell into a thick silence. They had been free in their village, and being enslaved was not something they could even imagine. Pau told them that they had to try to stay together, that whatever they did, staying together was the most important thing. Pau was ever practical, ever strategizing. He told them to look around when they were led onto the ship and try to hide in another group.

"They will try to separate us," Pau said. "When you see one of us, step forward, but do not make it obvious that you want to be together. Make your faces blank. Do not let them know we are family."

* * *

AFTER HOLDING THE kidnapped people for three weeks, the captors sold them to the Portuguese slavers who were filling a ship to cross the Atlantic. Those colorless men were already known to Bana'ka. His uncles and father had traded with them, but now they would not listen to his claims of who he was. Bana'ka used every Portuguese word he knew. But none of those pale men would look him in the eye or acknowledge him when they saw him in the coffle with other kidnapped people, dozens of men and women who were Wolof, Ibo, Ashanti, and Fanti, all shocked, depressed, and terrified, starving and bent with pain. Armed with muskets and swords, the Portuguese sailors put the captives on small boats and rowed them out to a huge ship that would take them across the Atlantic Ocean, on what we call the Middle Passage.

This launch onto water represented another death to the captives because it meant that now they were beyond rescue. To those from Western Africa, water was sacred, but the ocean was terrifying. In their cosmologies, the sea represented unknown, never-ending change. It was a source of supernatural power, but it was not an element fit for humans to live on. Many Africans thought that the pale people who sailed out onto its wide waters were not quite human at all, but emissaries from a shifty and alien world. To become rootless, landless, was to lose the earth, the mother who had birthed them and who would take them back into her body to return them, as sure as she did the shoots from the seeds. It was to be set adrift from the tides of time that had always allowed them to come back onto the family land as ancestors, returning again as descendants.

When the four were led onto the ship that would take them to the Americas, they made their faces blank and acted as if they had no knowledge of one another. By some luck and maneuvering, Bana'ka found himself in the same group as Pau. Then Bana'ka looked up to see Saiko running across the deck, his chains clattering, trying to join his sister Fadia. But it was too late. The Portuguese sailor held a whip. As Saiko cowered to cover his head, the whip sliced open his broad, smooth cheekbone, cutting the face his mother had declared beautiful, which the other boys had teased him about, calling him "Rafet," mama's boy.

Saiko cried out, and Fadia looked back and caught her brother's eye as blood ran down his cheek and neck. They had whipped Saiko merely for trying to stay with his kin, making an example of him as they would of many others. The brother and sister were led to separate sides of the ship, for no reason other than to break their spirits, and all of the captives were taken down into the hold.

They were stacked three on top of one another, chained by the ankles into bunks with no cushions and bases made of lattice-boards. In this way they were flattened and forced to lie under the urine and diarrhea, nausea and tears, of one another. Nothing in their lives had prepared them for the horrors of that ship. Any stories they had heard about the thieves who roamed the villages and took boys and girls to the traders seemed like child's fables in comparison to what this was.

Perhaps, before he was taken belowdecks, Bana'ka shouted loudly in Portuguese to one of the sailors, and then made sure the man also heard him speaking in Wolof, Ashanti, and Mandinka. He wanted to differentiate himself as someone who could communicate with the captives and translate the captain's orders. His plan may have won him a top bunk, or a little more time in the upper air. I can imagine that, in this way, Bana'ka came to translate the reprehensible slavers to the captives, and the terrified captives to the slavers. He listened to the Portuguese crew and reported on their plans to the kidnapped. He told his fellow inmates they would not be burned in the way some of them feared, but that they would be used to fuel some larger fire. He told them they would reach land, they would see the sky again, in just a few more days, weeks, months. He told them that wherever they were headed, it had to be better than the stench, dying, and darkness of the *tumbeiro*.

I imagine that between speaking to his fellow captives and speaking to the sailors, Bana'ka learned to split his spirit. Laid out on his bunk, flattened and chained in that floating, crowd-choked coffin, he would slip back into his mind and close himself away, behind his eyes. He would send part of his spirit back over the roiling waters, over the steep wave-faces veined with salt, pulling through foam whiter than the fur of goats.

And in the fifth day of sailing, when there was no land to be seen to those up on deck, that half of Bana'ka that was a spirit felt himself leave the raging waters and touch down. He felt land under his own feet again, and it was his family's land. He began running then, free of the ropes and the hood, free of the irons that chafed and cut, back through the forest and along the little muddy river that rushed over rocks and trickled into a stream. He balanced on those rocks and bent to wash his blistered hands in the waters. He stood at the edge of the clearing that marked his village. He saw his feet on the red earth, his toes stretching out free and certain, one orange baobab leaf under his right heel. He stood watching them. His family. For the rest of his life, he would walk himself back like that, in a ritual of vision, his eyes shivering under his lids, his legs taking to the terrible waters until he touched down again. On Wolof land.

That is how he saw it all behind his eyes. He saw when his mother was raped by one of the warriors who waited for the women to return from the planting. He saw the way she swallowed her disgust and stiffened her face, looking into the middle distance whenever she had to lie with that man who later claimed her as a wife. He saw his older sister dance her womanhood dance and then marry the man she had wanted. He saw his cousin grow hard and harder, participating in the coup, closing his memory of him, snapping it shut like a box inlaid with ivory. He saw men tending to the fire, boys inspecting their mothers' copper pots, mothers scolding them, chasing them with laughter, just like his own mother had done. He saw the women tying bright scarves in their hair, dancing through the seasons of celebration, even after all that loss, moving powerfully with their hips and hands, their slender wrists chiming with bracelets. He saw them sitting, eating together on ordinary evenings, and laughing. He stood at the edge of the world, and he watched them. His family.

Maybe, to them, Bana'ka was a flash in the forest, a painful memory that made the eyes sting, a little darkening green that sometimes his mother caught in the corner of her vision. His youngest sister in her fever would see him most clearly. During that time, Bana'ka was there with her, sitting vigil, every day. He was not yet an ancestor contracted to the earth, but neither was he an object. He was not back with his family in Africa, but neither was he absent.

* * *

IT IS NOT possible to accurately imagine the horrors of the Middle Passage. And there are very few firsthand accounts from African people who were kidnapped and forced onto those ships. One of our only first-person memoirs of the experience comes from Olaudah Equino, from Nigeria's Igbo people. Equino was kidnapped as a child and bought and sold repeatedly before he was purchased by an officer in the Royal Navy, who permitted him to learn to read and earn his own freedom. In 1789, Equino published his memoir, *The Interesting Narrative of the Life of Olaudah Equino*. The book became a bestseller that was released all over Europe and reprinted in the United States in 1792, the same year that Benjamin Banneker published his first almanac. Both Equino's memoir and Banneker's almanac were read aloud in the English Parliament and influenced laws that repressed the slave trade, including the British Slave Trade Act of 1807, which abolished it in England.

Equino depicted the vibrant Igbo culture of his home before his kidnapping and described his wrenching separation from his sister, who was taken during the same raid on his family's compound. He noted the many times his "masters" changed his name to suit themselves, where once he was called Jacob, and another time Michael, and another time Gustavus Vassa. He summarized the cruelties of the slave ship and told of sailors having their way with kidnapped girls of no more than ten years old. He described "the stench of the hold" where people were chained together as "intolerably loathsome" and "absolutely pestilential." After writing about fellow enslaved people who were half hanged, and then burned on the ship, he declared, "Thus by repeated cruelties are the wretched first urged to despair, and then murdered."

Most of our information about the slave ships and the Middle Passage comes not from the kidnapped people themselves, but from historians like Stephanie Smallwood who have studied the ships' logbooks and analyzed the notes that were taken about the passages. These notes were not made to protect the captives on board but to secure the ship's profits. Investors, then as now, did market studies to determine how to get the best returns on their investments. They studied how far the captives could be deprived without dying and determined that they could lie weeks in the hold, chained to the bunks or to one another. The captives were given one meal a day—no fish or meat—but a gruel of water and grains and a few dried peas. A similar cost-benefit analysis taught the enslavers to allow the captives up onto the deck once a week to breathe the sea air and have saltwater poured over them in a brusque, rushed kind of bath. The captain and crew unchained the men and women in small groups and let them walk the decks, while the people gulped at the wind, trying to scour the stench of illness and excrement from their noses and mouths.

* * *

I IMAGINE BANA'KA up on deck like this, gasping to breathe in as much fresh air as possible, as he rubbed his slender arms with salt water. Maybe he watched, as a man named Mannu pushed the bucket of water back up into the sailor's face and won himself just enough time to leap overboard. Bana'ka saw the confused skirmish and then Mannu, flailing in air, his naked body falling into the freezing waves. He saw Mannu's face as a momentary terror was overtaken by his will. It was the resolve of a man putting on a ritual calm, and then he was under the waters, and gone.

The crew chained everyone up after that, whipping and cursing them for the loss. It wasn't a loss of a man to them, but of property. Afterward, the slavers only let the captives out one by one, because they were afraid of them jumping overboard or gathering together in groups to overtake the crew. Back in his bunk in the hold, Bana'ka could not stop thinking about the man with iron on his ankles who was probably still sinking. How long would his body fall like that?

Bana'ka thought about how he had walked his own spirit back over the waters, and he told the others on the bunks around him that they would have to sing a way back for Mannu. Some grumbled, many said nothing, but some tried, whispering with their dry, swollen throats songs that they thought would help Mannu's spirit return to his village and family. They tried to say the names of his people, all the names braiding together into a rope he could pull himself home on. But they were so thirsty, and there were only so many names they could chant, maybe not enough to weave Mannu back to his family. So Bana'ka guessed at them, filling them in, knowing Mannu's nation and tribe. He knew that the larger a family becomes, the more names it will contain, that each syllable can break open into a rhythm that is something like a bloodbeat, and in that pulse the true name may slip through. Some whispered their own names, and the names of their mothers and grandmothers, those sacred lineages fraying behind them. There were twelve different languages there in the boat, from several nations and tribes, but they tried.

Other captives pounded their heels on the boards of the boat to beat out some of their anger, and to echo the memory of the drums. The splintered wood of the bunks was nothing like the roll and rumble of the goatskin. But the rhythm helped them remember the djembe, the tamu, the dundun. It helped them to call up their dancing, their heartbeats. It reminded them that their bodies and blood were still alive, despite being held in more filth than they would have imposed on their enemies' goats.

After Mannu, three more people went the same way, by jumping overboard, one by squeezing himself out of a porthole. The ship lost more to sickness and despair. They died with no one to hold them. No one to wipe their brow with cool water or remember them when they were younger—the smile they'd flash their mother when they wanted a treat, the tender way they held their sisters' hands, the little pranks they played on their brothers. Bana'ka wanted to die too, but something would not let him. And he realized that he was learning something new about time, about how excruciating suffering can somehow be survived.

Alliances formed, and something beyond friendship. Bana'ka and Pau had been friends and sometimes rivals back in their village, but during that passage, they became brothers. They could not have imagined it then, but they would survive. And bloodlines would branch out from them, wider than the nets that the slavers had used to catch them, wider than the foaming veins on the towering waves, wider than the roots of the banyan trees they had played beneath as children.

*　*　*

OR MAYBE IT was not that way at all. Maybe Bana'ka stayed silent and groaning through the journey and said nothing to his fellow captives. Maybe he devised a way to sit at the side of the captain. Maybe he simply tried to continue breathing, shallowly, through the stench. We do not know. All we know is that he survived. It is enough that he survived.

Statistically, a third of those confined to the slave ships died at sea and many more were close to death by the time they arrived in the colonies. Another third of those who survived the passage would die during what was called their "seasonings," in their first years on the plantations.

But when Bana'ka's ship sailed into port in the West Indies, the captain and crew would have assumed a carnival air, swathing the ship in the giddy atmosphere of a marketplace. Advertisements were posted around town and run in the papers, announcing the ship's arrival and the auction of its "human cargo" to be held the following week. Those listed as "very ordinary cargo" were people who were old or blind, sick or emaciated. Those described as "bursten" were covered with sores. But most of the African captives were advertised in the braggadocio of market-speak. They were called "strong" and "lusty" and were described not really as people but as tools to labor and create wealth for others.

The captain and crew kept the captives locked on board the ship, and spent more than a week preparing them for sale—bathing them, scraping them of lice, shaving their bodies and heads, and oiling their skin to hide their chafing, sores, and bug bites. Then, on the day of the sale, they invited buyers on deck and served them brandy, wine, and pastries, so that the landowners would be loose and addled as they bid on the "cargo." As well-dressed buyers milled about with drinks in hand, the captives were stripped naked for inspection. Buyers noted the size of their breasts and genitals and joked about their anatomy.

Fadia watched as Saiko was ordered to walk across the deck and lift a huge sack of flour while the white women looked him up and down. Somehow, amid her disgust and despair, Fadia felt a thread of relief because now she knew that her brother *had* survived the passage. Saiko bravely lifted his eyes to see the strangely costumed people who were bidding on him and tried to catch the eye of one who looked the least cruel. Some captives were loudly chanting prayers and lamentations in their home languages to call in spiritual protection. Some were rolling their eyes and acting deranged in order to avoid the sale. Most were ill from the journey, swaying on their feet, and terribly quiet. The guns, whips, and relentless violence of the enslavers had shown them that outward resistance would be futile or deadly, and had forced them to dissociate from their bodies.

Fadia and Saiko were sold to separate bidders. Afterward, they ran to each other on the deck. They embraced, their shoulders shaking. Fadia touched Saiko's wound from the whip, which was now an infected gash across his cheek. Then she put her thumb to her brother's forehead, between his eyes, as if to say *Watch for me. We will find each other again.*

They did not see Bana'ka or Pau, and each assumed that the two had not survived the journey. But Bana'ka was down in the hold, ill with a fever, and Pau had been given leave to tend to him. The crew had decided that these two would remain on the ship and go with them up to the next port. The captain wanted to check out what was supposed to be an exciting new market for the slave trade: the Chesapeake.

CHAPTER 10

The White Horse

Pasadena, California, and Evanston, Illinois, May 2020

EDIE TOLD ME that before I did anything else, I had to get in touch with Robert Lett, our cousin who lived in Pasadena. Robert and I first met over email. In his initial message, he wrote out a long list of the ancestors and living cousins who had done genealogical research and preserved the stories of the Banneker-Lett family. I told him I was grateful to be included, and we began talking on the phone every week, often chatting for two or three hours at a time.

Meanwhile, the entire world had shifted due to a global pandemic. Like most people, I had been quarantined at home due to COVID-19. I taught classes on Zoom from my home office, while supervising my daughter's middle school education, which was transpiring on an iPad in the living room. As the weather warmed, I held classes from my front porch, and I took walks—even just around the block between meetings—to get away from the screen and remember that I was a human in a body, on the earth.

Talking on the phone for hours at a time was similarly disembodying, so I was walking around barefoot that day when I first spoke to Robert. I was trying to reconnect to the ground, pulling up dandelions in my backyard. I'd watch their starred seeds shake out in little clouds and wonder if I was doing more harm than good.

Robert had just turned seventy but seemed much younger. He was a coach and high school guidance counselor, a musician and an athlete—and above all, a born educator who spoke with intention and sincerity. He exuded a kindness that could almost mask his sharp intelligence. And he felt very familiar to me.

"Really, I'm more of a healer type," Robert said that day. "I like to connect people and then kind of get out of the way." I related to that. The healing aspects of writing interested me at least as much as the products, and I could usually tell when I had come upon a subject or conversation in which something deep and confused needed to be brought up into language.

"And as remarkable as our history is," Robert said, "it is much like the history of many other families. It's just that our history can be documented. We have the oral histories, and we can connect those with written documentation, and that is very unusual for African American people.

"I was part of a coalition of African American families a few years back," he continued. "The Woodson family was there, and the descendants of Simon Northrup—you know, from *Twelve Years a Slave?*—the Hemings family, and the Quander family. You don't know who the Quanders were."

"No, I don't."

"Because I didn't even know who they were! The Quander family was on Washington's plantation. And there were descendants of those who were enslaved on former president Zachary Taylor's plantation there too. We were all together in Washington, doing a press conference about the caste system in this country, on behalf of the lowest caste in India."

"Oh," I said. "We don't talk about racism being a caste system in this country, but that is exactly what it is."

"Yes," Robert said. "And what I learned from being on that panel is that every family has its own remarkable story. The difference is that our story happened to be the oldest."

We talked about Molly's and Bana'ka's arrival dates in the late 1600s, and then went on to talk about the treatment of Banneker's story by his biographers.

"I have noticed," Robert said, "that African American scholars treat Banneker's accomplishments more warmly than Euro-American scholars. They seem to have more empathy for what Benjamin Banneker experienced."

I got up and sat at the picnic table to make sure I could hear him clearly, could pick up on even what he did not say. Although Robert was already generously sharing the family's oral histories with me, I anticipated his skepticism of me as a white writer. I knew that he was educating me not only about our ancestral stories but also about the ongoing story of American racism.

"You have white scholars writing about Banneker's 'self-taught' quality like it was a pitiable thing," Robert continued, "which is very different from the way it is treated with the white 'Founding Fathers'—as a way of exalting them and confirming their self-discipline."

"Yes," I agreed. "The Founding Fathers are called Renaissance men, while Benjamin Banneker is not given that respect, although he clearly was one too."

"Banneker is depicted as a poor tobacco farmer," Robert said. "But he and his father owned one hundred acres—which was a lot of land for anyone, of any race, to own at that time. And by the time Benjamin was an adult, the Banneker family had diversified their crops and were growing far more than tobacco.

"You need lots of labor for a tobacco farm to be productive," Robert went on. "It was basically a 1-to-1 ratio. You needed one enslaved person to farm about one acre of tobacco, full-time, working all the time. That's why tobacco plantations were so large. And then tobacco took seven to eight steps to produce. It was a very labor-intensive crop. I know this firsthand because my grandfather and uncles in Northern Kentucky grew tobacco. As a child, I'd go with them, and we'd set the tobacco plants by hand with a team of horses. You would take three fingers and stick them in the dirt and then set the plant in."

I had been deadheading the pansies in a pot on the picnic table, as my grandmother had taught me to do—pinching off those flower heads that were dried and dead. I could picture Robert as a little boy, out on the farm with his uncles, and I remembered walking through my own grandfather's fields, picking plump ears of sweet corn, tomatoes ripe and heavy in the hand.

Robert and I then turned back to Benjamin Banneker and the way his story had been written in the past, as opposed to the way we would tell it now. We were especially interested in a biography by Silvio Bedini published in 1972 and reissued in 1999, which was the most thoroughly researched biography of Benjamin Banneker to date.

"So many scenes come to mind that could have been written," Robert mused. "Bedini was amazing at documentation, but sometimes that book turns back on itself and becomes a kind of documentation loop. And because he was writing as a white man, there are some things that he just couldn't imagine about the African American experience."

"Yes, of course," I said. I wanted Robert to know that I heard him, that I also did not believe that a white person could fully comprehend the experience of being Black. "Like what?"

"Well, imagine this scene, from the point of view of Bana'ka. You are these Black African guys, on a slave ship, packed below deck like pancakes, laid out on lattice boards. Someone above you defecates and it drips down onto you. Every once in a while, you're taken on deck and someone splashes some seawater over you to clean you off. It's two months of this. Then finally you arrive. You're taken on deck and splashed with seawater again and this time you're scrubbed and oiled and cleaned. You're in a new land, in the bright sun, and you're walked out to auction, where your body is prodded and pulled, and before you know it, you're chained to the back of somebody's wagon. And as you blink in the sun to see what this is all about, you squint to see who's driving, and it's a little white lady!

"What are you thinking!" Robert laughed. "What now? Is some alien going to jump out at me?

"And then she starts driving you back into the woods," Robert continued. "She's taking you into some remote landscape where no one else lives. Imagine what's running through your mind at that point. So they go back into the woods and get to her land, and where did they sleep?" Robert asked.

"They must have slept in her cabin, right?" But as I said it, it sounded naive, like I had accepted a childish fairy tale about Molly and Bana'ka's marriage without even realizing it. "Or maybe in her barn?"

"I don't know. Maybe Molly built them their own place to sleep. But apparently in rapid fashion, Bana'ka and the other man clear the land and plant the crops, and give her a working farm, and then she frees them. But Molly and Bana'ka have taken a liking to each other, so they marry. But they all would have had to go into town together to sell their tobacco crops, and I imagine that Bana'ka would have ridden in the back of the wagon with the tobacco. They wouldn't have wanted to upset the locals by putting their relationship on display. You have to remember that they were living in a rural wilderness area, surrounded by indentured servants. And for indentured servants, it was all about survival.

"But here is something I've noticed from my African American perspective," Robert went on. "Twenty years ago, our white cousins began to get in touch with me, wanting to know more about their Native American ancestry. Now, in the whole family line, we have only two documented instances of our ancestors marrying Native Americans. But these family members would say, 'What about Aquilla? Wasn't he Native American? Didn't he live on Native land?' And I'd say, 'Yes, he did live on Native land, but he was African American.' I would have to say to these relatives, 'I don't think you have Native American ancestry. I think it's *African* blood.' After I let them know this, some of them would humbly fade back into the shadows. But some remained connected."

"We thought we were part Native American in my family too," I admitted. "That was the story we were told to explain our 'tan' skin. Not everyone has it, but it runs like a thread through the generations— from my grandfather, to my dad, to me, to my daughter. It sounds like there was a tendency among white-passing people to romanticize Native American ancestry and deny their African American ancestry."

"Yes, it seems so," Robert agreed. "Another thing that is kind of interesting is that I've been contacted by more white descendants looking for their ancestors than Black descendants. It may be that the Black descendants already know this ancestry. Still, in all these years I have never had anyone contact me from Peter Lett's line, until you. I'd wonder, 'Who are the people descended from Peter who are interested in these stories? When are they going to get in touch?'"

I smiled. I felt a tension easing in my chest, a relief that I was connected.

"What did you say Peter did when he was in Western Pennsylvania?" Robert asked.

"Well, according to the census, he was a laborer," I answered.

"You know the family oral history about Peter, don't you?" Robert asked.

"No," I said. "We did not even know about Peter until a couple of years ago." But weeks earlier, I had had a dream about him. In it, he was leaning against a brick wall, wearing a blue workshirt rolled up, his forearms sunbrowned and smoothly muscled. He was tall and had squinty eyes and a rakish confidence—he had a style like some of the other men in my family. He reminded me of my cousin Joshua, and I loved him in the dream, the way I love my cousin, with a deep recognition that is also a fascination for what in him will always remain unavailable to me. A staunch activist conviction, a solitary confidence paired with a male goodness that has always made me want to be beside him. "Leave me out of this story," Peter said in the dream. "Don't write about me."

"Well, the story goes that Peter came to the family on a large white horse," Robert began. "He said he was leaving the Lett Homestead because he had to go up North to do some work. He rode off on that horse and was never seen by the family again."

A white horse? Was that a metaphor for passing into whiteness? I wondered. *Or a real horse? Was Peter like he'd been in my dream—a handsome loner who kept his secrets?* I was amazed that Robert could introduce me to Peter 190 years after he rode away from home.

"I always wondered if Peter had some connection to John Brown," Robert continued. "John Brown had a tannery in Guys Mills, Pennsylvania, in Crawford County, and that was exactly where Peter moved after he left the Lett Settlement."

"John Brown, the famous abolitionist?" I asked.

"Yes, you know, John Brown was very interesting," Robert said. "His father taught at Oberlin. And our cousins Henry Cornelius Lett and Hannibal Lett went there during those years to get a teaching certificate. Henry, Hannibal, Peter, and John Brown would have been around the same age, so they probably met as young men."

"Do you think they were all involved with the Underground Railroad?" I asked.

"Well, we know that the Lett Settlement was part of the Underground Railroad," Robert said. "There are oral histories and articles written about the family's work to help fugitives from slavery. The fact is, you had ancestors who worked for abolition on both sides of the color line."

I smiled, noticing that Robert had called them my ancestors as well as his.

"Those who could pass 'the eyeball test' and work as white people did that," Robert said, "and those who were Black . . . well, it does not make sense to call them abolitionists, per se, because they were Black people, working for their own freedom and their people's freedom. But we can tell from where their children were born, in Ohio, then down in Maryland and Virginia, then back in Ohio again, that the family was moving whiskey or grain or people—they were moving *something*.

"At that time, in the 1830s through the 1850s," Robert went on, "there were many networks of free families of color helping people around West Virginia and southern Ohio, because, as our cousin Henry Burke used to say, 'Who could you trust to keep a secret more than your family?' A white abolitionist who was captured could always appeal to the courts. But a Black antislavery activist found harboring an escaped slave would be accused of stealing property and would be lynched. There was no due process for you, so you needed the protection of your extended family."

"That makes sense," I said. I felt whole worlds opening up, histories I had never been taught.

"I've always wondered if Peter left so he could work at John Brown's tannery," Robert said. "But this is not a mystery we are going to solve today!"

"How sad that must have been for Peter," I said, "to ride away from the family and never see them again."

"Well, he did stay in touch by letter," Robert said. "Peter was named in Aquilla's will, so we know that he stayed in touch with the family.

"And you know, I have no judgment of those who passed," Robert went on. "Just understanding. It wasn't easy to be Black in this country. And how you were seen determined everything—where you could live, what kind of job you could have, what kind of education you were allowed to get. So, I don't have judgment."

"That is generous of you," I said. I felt my lungs expanding. I still felt outside of these stories, and dependent on Robert's permission to know them.

"This is your story too, you know," he said.

"Thank you," I answered. I was looking at the trunk of the birch tree in my backyard. I knew I would remember this moment.

"Another thing that was true about our ancestors is that they loved and married people from other backgrounds," Robert said. "In almost every generation they did this. My feeling is that they always knew about their differences. They weren't hiding it from each other. I think they just decided to take the risk together."

CHAPTER 11

The Elders

Maryland, 1690–1700

If one hour were like another; if the passage of the sun did not show that the day is waning; if the change of season did not impress upon us the flight of the year, quantities of duration equal to days and years would glide on unobserved. If the parts of time were not variously colored, we should never discern their departure or succession, but should live thoughtless of the past, and careless of the future.

—Banneker's Almanac of 1792

MY COUSINS AND I may think of Molly and Bana'ka as the first American ancestors in the Banneker-Lett lineage, but they would not have thought of themselves as Americans because the country had not been established yet. They would not have thought of themselves as Black or white, either, because those categories were not yet the divisive political tools they would go on to become. Molly would have thought of herself as British; Bana'ka would have thought of himself as Wolof. If the stories of their origins are true, Molly would have expected to serve others, and Bana'ka would have expected to be served by others. Both were exiles, forced into Maryland against their wills, but maybe Molly would have thought of herself as a settler, a lucky one, after she survived her indenture. I do not imagine that Bana'ka ever recovered from the anger and grief of being kidnapped and wrenched from his kingdom and kin.

Family oral histories said that Molly worked through her indenture, and bought her own land. Then, around 1690, she purchased two enslaved men "from a ship anchored in the Bay." Biographers have always depicted Molly bringing the men back to her land to help her raise tobacco. But questions have remained, including how Molly would have been able to homestead alone, and how she, as an ex–indentured servant, would have had the funds to purchase two enslaved men.

During the first decades of settlement in Maryland, every indentured servant was given clothing, shoes, a mule, a gun, and a tract of land after their indenture was through. A Maryland act of 1640 listed these "freedom dues" as "one good Cloth suite of kersey or broad cloth, or a Shift of white linen, one new pair of stockins and Shoes two hoes one axe 3 barrells of Corne and for women Servants, a Years Provision of Corne, and a like proportions of Cloths & Land." But by 1663, indentured servitude had become more widespread, and "masters" were no longer legally required to offer such "freedom dues." Since legal rights and citizenship had been tied to landownership, voting planters feared that they would be outnumbered by former indentured servants who now owned land and were, after all, just illiterate commoners. By the time Molly finished her indenture, land grants were rare.

The British were settling the area rapidly, stealing it from the Susquehannock, Powhatan, Piscataway, Shawnee, and Lenape peoples through battles and treaties. Indigenous peoples thought of the land intimately, as the great mother and sustainer of their lives, and not as a privately owned commodity. They were sometimes unprepared for the British claim of the land as a source of capital, and even when they were prepared, they were often swindled through altered, indecipherable, or rescinded treaties and through European alliances with warring tribes. The colonial economy depended upon these two legally supported exploitations—cheap or free land made possible by the displacement and genocide of indigenous peoples, and a steady supply of inexpensive labor made possible by the indenture and enslavement of workers.

During Molly's first decade in Maryland, the Chesapeake economy had transitioned from a dependence on indentured servants from

Europe to a dependence on kidnapped and enslaved people from Africa. In 1660, the Royal African Company was established in London, and it began operating the triangular route that would become the hallmark of the slave trade. First, London ships were loaded with textiles and metalware to sell and barter on the West Coast of Africa in exchange for kidnapped people. These people were then taken on the Middle Passage across the Atlantic and sold in the West Indies and North America. Once emptied, the slave ship was loaded again with colonial products—sugar and rum from the West Indies or rice or tobacco from the American colonies—to be brought back to England for sale. This triangular route took well over a year to complete, but its multipoint exchange offered a high return for investors, who ignored the injustice of slavery for the sake of these tripled profits.

At first, the market of the Chesapeake was not big enough to attract such investors, but as English demand for tobacco grew and Chesapeake profits became more consistent, the Royal African Company began including the region on their routes, and slavery became much more common in Virginia and Maryland. In Maryland in the 1670s, European servants like Molly outnumbered African and Caribbean servants four to one. But by the early 1690s, when Bana'ka arrived, these numbers had flipped, with African people now outnumbering European servants four to one.

The details of Molly's indenture are unknown, but indentures like hers usually lasted at least seven years. Maybe Molly was able to rent some land afterward and homestead for a season or two before realizing that she would need to hire or purchase help if she wanted to survive. Maybe she did indeed purchase Bana'ka and Pau and bring them back to her little landholding near the Patapsco River.

Or maybe Molly met Bana'ka before her indenture was through. Molly, Bana'ka, and Pau may have been workers together on Newman's plantation, and Molly and Bana'ka could have developed their relationship as they labored and lived side by side. Molly would have worked alongside the men, tending to the tobacco plants, cutting down brush, dragging logs, weeding the garden, chopping wood, and grinding corn for the winter. While they worked together, they would have talked, Molly teaching Bana'ka English and learning his phrases of Wolof.

They would have tried out these words in their mouths, sometimes laughing and teasing each other as they did so.

Perhaps Molly saw a spark in Bana'ka, a quiet defiance, that she recognized in herself. She seemed small, but she had a wildness in her that liked to pull out plants at the root, that didn't mind snapping the neck of a chicken, that prized freedom and self-sufficiency above all else. And she liked the way that being with Bana'ka made the small-minded folks on the plantation uncomfortable and gave her a break from their prying. Being with him made her feel freer, even though they and their labor were officially "owned" by John Newman—her for a term of years, and Bana'ka, unbelievably, for life.

Bana'ka radiated so much intelligence and rarity that he was intimidating, and he liked it that way. Before Newman had them shaved—for spite—Bana'ka wore his braids long, sometimes piled up on his head like a crown, and strung with shells and feathers. He painted his body with symbols and fashioned bells for his wrists and ankles. This made him seem even taller, and he already stood several inches above the other servants. His face often had a faraway look on it, like he was seeing through this drab, hardscrabble place to his real home back in Africa, where the women wrapped their hair in colorful scarves, and the drummers played stories, and people moved to the rhythm of the dance more than to the rhythm of toil. Although he said very little, other indentured servants regarded Bana'ka as someone to be avoided or respected. Whatever it said on the white man's papers, he knew who he was, and his strength lay in his refusal to become anything like the men who had kidnapped him.

Bana'ka was said to be from Senegambia, on the Gold Coast of Africa. His family would have been part of the great Mali Empire, which had been trading in salt and gold for three hundred years by the time of his kidnapping, and which had science, learning, literature, and education rivaling any country in Europe. In 1777, the missionary Christian George Andreas Oldendorp interviewed enslaved people in the West Indies who remembered their homes and talked about the communities that traded along the Gold Coast. He noted that "the Negro merchants who do this trade can reason mathematically and read," and he praised African artisans who did elaborate metalwork in gold and silver. Then he went on to describe their Islamic religion, explaining that they called God Allah and worshipped him in temples, using a book during the service.

"They hold their morning and evening prayers very punctually," Oldendorp wrote. "They get up before the sunrise and observe a deep silence until they have washed themselves. As soon as the sun appears, the father of the house kneels down with his family on a mat and leads the prayer with his face toward the sun. The evening prayer is done similarly after having washed their faces, hands and feet."

When the oral histories say that Bana'ka "practiced his African religion," I envision him praying this way, washing and rising with the sun, sitting in silence, and then reciting Islamic verses. Some scholars even connect Benjamin Banneker's mathematical genius to his grandfather Bana'ka's Islamic thought—a system of study that included advanced astronomy and mathematics within a spiritual framework. Ron Eglash, an ethno-mathematician, studies the ways that mathematics and cultures intersect. He sees Banneker's descent from his grandfather's Wolof people and his father's Guinean people as playing a key role in Benjamin's understanding of sacred geometry and higher mathematics. Eglash writes that African and Islamic systems of numerology passed down through the family likely shaped Benjamin Banneker's complex mathematical thinking.

Family histories say that the strong, unnamed man that I've called Pau was a good worker, but that the tall, frail Bana'ka had distances in his eyes and was more inclined to hunt and meditate than to labor in the fields. According to their descendants and neighbors, Bana'ka was "a man of bright intelligence, fine temper, with a very agreeable presence, dignified manners and contemplative habits." The name *Banne*, one researcher has noted, was given by Wolof mothers to their sons. It was related to the word for "nectar," or honey, and denoted a person with a "sweet or serene" disposition. Other scholars have traced the name "Banakas" to royalty in the Walo region of Senegambia.

*   *   *

I IMAGINE AN early autumn morning, with a few gold leaves glinting in the trees. Bana'ka had gone down to the river to pray. He did this every morning—washed himself, made ablutions, and bowed low in prayer as the sun rose out of the tree line, and then did so again when it balanced highest in the sky. He sat in meditation with his eyes closed, absorbing the light, quaking with the energies around him, which were cosmic and earthly, and which he understood as Allah. There, beside that branch of the Patapsco, he listened to the water running over rocks, rumbling on like the chatter of ancestors. He opened the crown of his head to his God and his kin, and his body trembled like a reed on the riverbank. He bowed to the sun. He understood that the same sun shone down on his mother and sisters, and sensed that as he greeted it, his mother said goodbye to it, releasing it like a great glowing orb. The waters, too, were the same waters, the river moving fast and foaming over rocks until it met the ocean and swam backways like that, slapping against prows of ships to lap again on the sandy shores of Africa. There, the water would offer its pocked face to the rain or trickle into little creeks moving inland, back to his family's land. Bana'ka's meditations always took him on journeys like that.

He sat with a drum in his lap that he had made from a giant dried gourd, stretched across with deerskin. He liked to close his eyes and patter out a rhythm with his thumbs as if the drum were talking to the water. And it was as if he heard the water answering. Sometimes, he asked a thing outright to the air, or made a complaint, or had a conversation in which he heard the voices of his father and his father's father echoing in his mind.

Molly also rose early, but while Bana'ka went out to pray, she started a cooking fire and hung an iron pot of hominy over the hearth to warm. She scattered feed for the chickens and went into the woods to gather morels and walnuts, hitching up her skirts to do so, wiping her face with her apron. Her mind was almost entirely crammed with tasks. There was not much spaciousness in it, but busyness, industry, utter capability.

That morning, when she returned from her foraging and saw Bana'ka walking back from his dawn ministrations at the river, his whole body seemed to glow, as if he had caught the rising sun and it poured gold along his limbs. His face had filled out and matured since he'd arrived in the colony, but it was still dominated by his large, liquid dark eyes. His chest was bare, and his gris-gris bag—a little deerskin pouch he'd hung around his neck—was filled with, what? she wondered. Protective herbs and minerals. Sand for getting back to Africa, sage and black cohosh for protection, and the red feathers of cardinals for flight. Bana'ka walked toward the cabin, half muttering to himself, his hands making the shapes he used when he told her a story. His face brightened then, thinking of something unknown to her, and Molly filled with a feeling of good fortune. She was glad she hadn't settled for one of those Brits who'd badgered her. Their osnaburg waistcoats stank of boiled meat and their sour, unwashed bodies. And their strained proposals had been presented to her almost like business contracts, as if life was just a transaction and she wasn't her own woman.

Molly respected Bana'ka. She respected his refusal to become anything British or enslaveable or broken, despite the exile of the place and the unending work. He was as Wolof as the day he'd first arrived. Molly felt humble before the wonder of him. She'd done it, and she would do it again. She'd give up those other versions of power for him, for this, for something more powerful.

* * *

OF COURSE, WE cannot know the details of Molly and Bana'ka's relationship, but we can learn something about ourselves in the way we imagine it. If we see Molly and Bana'ka's love as radical, it is only because we are seeing it through the lens of America's long historical perversity. It is only because we are looking back through centuries of racist laws that pathologized unions between white women and men of color, while normalizing white male enslavers' sexual coercions of Black women. By outlawing mixed marriages undertaken in love and respect, and excusing sexual liaisons undertaken for power and profit, these laws programmed generations of people to treat mixed unions as perversions, rather than natural responses to human proximity, affinity, and desire.

When Molly partnered with Bana'ka and they had children, their choice was not nearly as unusual as it would go on to become. Newly freed British and European women of the lower classes were so inclined to marry and have children with Native American and African American men, in fact, that the very first law naming the category of whiteness did so as a way of reserving these women for British men.

But these laws were inconsistently and haphazardly enforced, and hundreds of women like Molly were prosecuted for breaking them. The database of *Free African Americans of Maryland and Delaware from the Colonial Period to 1810* records more than six hundred families that descended from a relationship between a British woman and an African man. These were just the unions that were recorded, so we can assume that many more were happening off the record. According to Paul Heinegg, who compiles this database, "Over two hundred and fifty British women were prosecuted in Maryland for the offense of bearing children with an African man. Some had a number of children, indicating long-standing relationships." When historians take into account how many colonial court records were lost to fire, floods, and neglect, they estimate that thousands of people were resulting from unions between British women and African men. In fact, the idea of female convict servants coupling with African men became a negative stereotype of the early eighteenth century. It was the subject of a racist rant by Virginia governor William Gooch, who declared that most "free-Negros and mulattos" were "Bastards of some of the worst of our imported Servants and Convicts."

In 1664, the first Maryland law against mixed marriages stated that a woman who married an enslaved "Negro" man would be sentenced to slavery herself, and her children would be enslaved until the age of 30. It read:

Forasmuch as diverse freeborn English women forgetful of their free condition and to the disgrace of our Nation do intermarry with Negro slaves by which also diverse suits may arise touching the [children] of such women and a great damage doth befall the

Masters of such Negroes for prevention whereof for deterring such freeborn women from such shameful matches,

Be it further enacted by the authority advice and consent aforesaid that whatsoever freeborn woman shall intermarry with any slave from and after the last day of this present Assembly shall serve the master of such slave during the life of her husband, and that the [children] of such freeborn women so married shall be slaves as their fathers were. And be it further enacted that all the [children] of English or other freeborn women that have already married Negroes shall serve the masters of their parents til they be thirty years of age and no longer.

This law was designed to protect the loss of profits of "great damage" to the "masters," but it hid this economic agenda in moral language, admonishing these women for their "disgrace to the nation" and "shameful matches." Shame was used against women as a tool of surveillance and was employed by both church and state to keep women in silenced, subservient positions. Someone who was pilloried or put in the stocks—common punishments for women then—was pinned with her hands and head in a yoke of wood set in the middle of the town square. Townspeople would yell at the accused, spit on her, whip her, or find other ways of punishing her. Similarly, the common sentence of "lashes" was a public whipping designed to publicize the fact that the accused person had broken a social contract. These shame-based techniques were especially used to punish women, homosexuals, and anyone who was seen to have committed a sexual abnormality. As colonial courts grew increasingly obsessed with policing citizens' sexuality, mixed marriage was prosecuted as one of these sexual crimes and was positioned as a threat to the very identity of the "Nation."

"White political elites specifically targeted white women who participated in sexual acts across racial boundaries as a way to enhance their patriarchal authority," explains historian Warren Eugene Milteer. "Punishing white women who challenged elite ideas about proper racial boundaries enhanced the power of white men over white women. It also enhanced the power of white men over men of color who were the partners of white women, and supported the idea that white men, alone, had the right to access the bodies of white women." Milteer notes that these laws requiring "mulatto" children to act as servants through their own prime reproductive years also made servitude an "inherited status for many free children of color."

Historian A. B. Wilkinson studies multiracial families like that of Molly and Bana'ka's and attests that examining this early Chesapeake legislation allows us to trace the establishment of racial hierarchies in all of colonial America. He writes that "magistrates in Virginia and Maryland consciously engineered legal systems to punish parents and children of blended families as a method of stemming the tide of inter-mixture." Again, this intermixture was a *tide*—a widespread, natural response to the proximity and affections of working people. The orig-inal construction of race on this continent happened as a way of stop-ping that affinity, dividing the working class, and increasing profits for owners.

This racial hierarchy was established through women's bodies. It began with prosecuting women for their free choice of reproduction, continued with the forced servitude of their offspring, and would go on to strip enslaved women of color of all freedoms regarding their children. Enslaved women would be forced to bear children even when they did not want to, to lie with the "master" or other men against their will, and to watch, powerless, as their children were sold away from them. For this reason, reproductive rights have a profound sig-nificance for women of color. Even today, Anna Malaika Tubbs writes, "When a Black woman is able to choose when she will bring children into the world of her own accord, it is a revolutionary act in the context of American history."

Because of this, Black families have long understood that their pre-served family histories are essential vessels of meaning. As historians Stephen Innes and T. H. Breen explain of early free families of color, "Within the Black communities themselves, the family was the central institution. It provided an opportunity to become fully human, to give and receive affection, to express intimate thoughts, to achieve a mea-sure of security in an otherwise frenetic environment, to consider a future that included children as well as grandchildren. It was, in fact, a vehicle for the transfer of culture from one generation to the next." When the dominant culture declares your union illegal and your offspring not fully human, then preserving the family becomes an essential act of resistance. It becomes a way of safeguarding both future and memory, and protecting what is dear.

In our case, the strongest evidence of Molly and Bana'ka's union exists in their children. According to oral histories, they integrated two different strands of culture and ancestry into four strong daughters who lived to adulthood. This family was both their greatest source of meaning and the key to their survival.

* * *

MOLLY AND BANA'KA could have been married, as our oral histories insist, even if there is no legal record of their marriage, and even if they both remained in servitude. Perhaps they convinced the overseer to give them their own cabin, out past the bunkhouses, the last in the row. They knew the other servants were watching them askance, wondering how their first child would turn out—with a father as tall and dark as Bana'ka, and Molly petite and sun-freckled. But if anyone could carry it through, it was Molly. She had delivered babies for her fellow servants on the plantation and had an unflappable way about it—staying awake with the laboring mother for days on end, reaching her small hands to cradle the head and shift the shoulders as the baby came. It never ceased to amaze her—the difficulty of birth, the blood and pain that wanted to wrench the mother in half, and then—like that—another life among them, pinched-faced and squalling.

But there was no one else like their firstborn, Mary. She was born in 1699, on the cusp of a new century. Even as a toddler, Mary was calm and observant like her father, resembling him in more than just appearance. Bana'ka always walked through the woods with a carved staff, and as soon as Mary could walk, she would grab a stick and accompany him, toddling to keep up, listening as he talked. She would stand tall and look off into the distance, as he did.

Molly had shown Bana'ka care and respect when he'd first arrived in the colony and had made it almost bearable to be there. But it was Mary, their daughter, who finally made him want to stay alive. Sometimes Bana'ka could see his mother and sister flickering in her features. Mary tied him back into the rounds of life again. And he realized he would have to somehow accept this place that had wronged him, because *she* was here, and she could not have been born in any other place.

CHAPTER 12

Juneteenth

Springfield, Illinois, and Evanston, Illinois, 2020

EDIE'S BROTHER EDWIN Lee and I decided to talk on the evening of Juneteenth. Before I dialed Edwin, I took a walk around my block. I could hear music, laughter from parties in open garages, kids shooting off fireworks in the alleys, dogs barking in response.

I live in a neighborhood in Evanston, Illinois, that had been one of the town's Black wards before gentrification and high taxes began driving people of color farther west, out of their ancestral homes. My neighborhood has unpaved alleys, interlinked one-way streets, and unassuming frame houses that once housed people who worked in "service" in the mansions beside the lake.

My house first belonged to Ms. Mabel Jackson, who came to Evanston with her family as part of the Great Migration in 1890. Mabel bought her home as a single Black woman in the first years of that decade. Although it is a small farmhouse, it has two fireplaces, a wraparound front porch, and tall front windows—Southern architectural features that Mabel must have insisted on. The house stayed in the Jackson family for ninety years before it was bought by a civil rights lawyer—another single Black woman—in the 1980s. A white couple bought the house early in the 1990s. Then it inexplicably sat on the market for six years before I bought it in 2011.

I didn't tell anyone that I was looking at a house that day, because they would have told me I was crazy. My partner Richard had been sick with the degenerative disease ALS for two years at that point, and we were living hand to mouth. We knew he had just months or weeks left to live. He had no Social Security or life insurance, and we had a three-year-old daughter whom I would have to raise on my modest nontenured salary. Anyone would have told me that it was not the time to make a big decision. But I knew that if I didn't take a risk, I would have to rent smaller and sadder places, or be forced to leave my job and move back in with my parents in Ohio. I wanted to find a way to continue living and teaching in Evanston, and I wanted my daughter to have a safe place to grow up. I loved the house when I had seen it online, and even though it was out of my budget, I knew that it had a small coach house in the back that I hoped I could rent to tenants and then use that money to help pay the mortgage.

After my realtor told the sellers about my situation and presented my offer, they accepted, although it was 25 percent less than their asking price. They even left me some of their furniture and dishes. We moved in three weeks before Richard died and a month before Adele turned four. In those first, precious weeks in the house, Adele learned to ride a bike on the front sidewalk, while I sat on the front porch tending to Richard. He sat in his wheelchair and watched her, sometimes with tears running down his face. "He's so glad he got to see where Adele is going to grow up," his hospice nurse said.

Since then, the house had been a protective shelter for us and a hub for the neighborhood kids. I had always felt that it was Ms. Mabel Jackson who had allowed us to live there, that Mabel understood what it was to be a caregiver, how tired I was, but also how determined to create a beautiful place to raise my daughter—the way Mabel herself had insisted on this same safe place to raise her children, her grandchildren, nieces, and nephews.

There were still a few Jacksons in the neighborhood, including Mr. Jackson, who lived on the next block and was set to turn one hundred that summer. Now that it was warm enough, his granddaughter brought him outside in the afternoons and sat him in the front yard on his walker. He always wore a straw hat, a blue button-up shirt, and pants with suspenders—an elder from another time. He would sit watching the children play on the wooden bridges and lookouts of

Penny Park. Mr. Jackson was a handsome mahogany-skinned man. But in his lifetime he had seen the children of the park, and the people of the neighborhood, become increasingly white.

That night, on Juneteenth, Penny Park was overrun with kids squealing and running around, and hipster parents in handmade cloth masks, standing around talking. A few blocks west, teenagers were shooting off fireworks and smoke bombs. The air was charred and mouthwatering with the smells of barbecue. Someone was playing electric bass in his garage. Someone else was drumming. *Someday soon*, I thought, *these kids will not remember that we haven't always celebrated Juneteenth.* The evening felt edgy and a little risky after all those months spent alone and indoors during COVID-19. It felt like a lively counterpoint to the scrubbed-up patriotism of Independence Day. It felt like a holiday we'd been needing.

⚜ ⚜ ⚜

I SAT DOWN on my front porch and punched in Edwin's number.

"Rachel!" Edwin answered.

"Edwin! How are you?"

"Great! It's a gorgeous evening out."

"It is!" I agreed. "I'm so happy to reach you!"

"Me too, Cuz!"

We began by talking about a group phone call we had had with several of our cousins the week before to discuss current events and the Black Lives Matter movement. One of our cousins had taken issue with our use of the terms "Black" and "white" in conversation, saying that they were historical constructions in the first place, and that we all needed to transcend these politicized labels.

"Of course, the one human family thing is the ideal," Edwin said. "But some of what this cousin was saying was just bullshit. You have ninety-nine percent of the people in this country not there yet, still seeing things in terms of Black and white. A whole generation is going to have to die before we get rid of that.

"But he is right that the African American story is a mixed-race story," Edwin continued. "According to Ancestry.com and 23andMe, we have one cousin that is fully African American. Only one cousin out of the twenty-four thousand people in our family tree has no European DNA."

It was a compelling statistic. And I was amazed that Edie had connected twenty-four thousand people in the family tree. Any acquisitional claiming of ancestors became absurd, I realized, when you considered how many thousands of others were equally connected to the same people.

"Most African Americans are aware that they have European DNA in their backgrounds, but white people are not as aware of this," Edwin added.

"I've noticed that too," I said. I knew that most white people did not see their shared ancestry with Black folks. And I had spent hours watching DNA-reveal videos online, a trend in which people would open their DNA results live on YouTube. I'd noticed that when white people saw that they had African ancestry, they didn't know what to say, or they got nervous, or they glossed over those statistics quickly. When Black people read their DNA results live, they tended to do so with much more ceremony and emotion. When they came to the European percentages in their DNA, they didn't look surprised, but they didn't look comfortable either. They often breathed deeply, or went momentarily silent as they took in the genetic mixing with whiteness that was likely the result of the rape of their female ancestors and the disregard of their white patriarchs.

"We always had a picture of Great-Grandfather hanging on the wall," Edwin said. "We were told who he was. We knew he was the enslaver of my great-grandmother, back in Hinds County, Mississippi. He had a child with her, in the same year he had another child by one of his other enslaved women. He also had a whole family by his white wife."

"Oh," I said. There it was. I loved Edwin's honesty already.

"The very first DNA test I took was the Y DNA test, only for the male Y sex chromosome," Edwin went on. "Then there is the mitochondrial DNA test, for the woman's X chromosome. That is what African Ancestry uses. That mitochondrial DNA tracing goes back thousands of years and tells people that they hail from countries that didn't even exist back then, so that is why I am not as interested in those tests.

"But according to both tests, I am seventy percent African and thirty percent European, and this is the usual breakdown for African American men," Edwin said. "Most African American males have thirty percent Y European DNA from European men. At the same time, only two percent of African American males have mitochondrial DNA from European women."

"Those are such telling breakdowns," I said, "because it proves that most of the mixing was coming from male enslavers having children with their enslaved women. It shows how terribly prevalent that was."

"Exactly. And it shows how rare it was for a white woman to be with a Black man," Edwin said.

With that, we started talking about Molly and Bana'ka. "There's no proof that they were married," Edwin said. "That's kind of a fairy tale, if you ask me." He laughed. "But they did do *something*. Evidently! They had four daughters.

"And about the indentured servitude part of this story," Edwin went on. "People like to call indentured servitude 'Irish slavery,' but it wasn't the same thing."

"I agree," I said. "I find the use of the word 'slavery' for that offensive." We had both seen recent posts on Facebook referring to people's indentured ancestors as "Irish slaves." The posts had proliferated during the racial awakening of the last months and had seemed to be a subconscious or conscious way for white people to avoid looking at anti-Black racism and replace it with a story of their own oppression.

"Indenture was definitely not the same as slavery," I went on. "Indentured servitude was really difficult, and it is true that only half to two-thirds of the servants survived their indentures, but if they survived, they would often be granted land, and clothing, and plows . . ."

". . . and sometimes even money to get their start!" Edwin added. "And a white person could move somewhere else, and no one would ever know they had been indentured. They got to be white then and become anything they wanted to be or could be. Whereas a person of color could not do this. From my research, it looks like the very first

Africans were indentured. It was only later that they created the slave trade and enslavement for life."

"Yes, that's what I've been learning too," I said. "And because slavery became associated with African ancestry, even free people of color were always in danger of being captured back into slavery."

"I think that's why our Banneker-Lett family had to keep moving across the country," Edwin said. "Things got bad in Maryland, and so they went up into Ohio. They worked so hard to establish the Lett Homestead and open the church and the school for their children, but then they started getting messed with and had to leave Ohio and move on up into Michigan. Did you notice that they began to leave Ohio right at the time of the Fugitive Slave Act?"

"I did," I said. "I've been reading about the Northwest Territory of Ohio. It was seen as such a hopeful place at first, because the charter laws said that any landowner could vote there, regardless of skin color. But then the legislatures took away that privilege, and as more and more white people moved into the state, citizens began hunting down people of color and anyone who was helping on the Underground Railroad."

"I think that's why the family moved up into Michigan," Edwin agreed. "William Lett was my great-great-grandfather who left Ohio and went to Michigan. Who was your ancestor again?"

"We are also descended from Aquilla and Christina Lett, like you, and then from their son, Peter," I said. "He was the brother closest in age to your ancestor, William."

"A lot of the Letts that passed as white seemed to come from Peter's family," Edwin said.

"True," I admitted. I felt embarrassed, but I was learning that the only way through that feeling was honesty.

"We did not even know about this ancestry until my cousin Melissa began doing research a few years ago," I added. "Other people had done genealogical research, but they had avoided looking into this line, probably because these family members all had an 'M' next to their names in the census."

"And Lett is not a typical surname of African Americans," Edwin said. "It sounds German. That's probably why when the white descendants did genealogy, they said, 'This can't be right that they're "mulattos,"'" so they made them German. They just decided, 'This can't be true!' Like the branch out in Oregon. They changed their name to DeLett and said they were French!" Edwin laughed.

I laughed with him. I really liked Edwin—his intelligence, his humor, his straightforward way of talking about it all.

"One of the problems with America is that many people can't go back past their grandparents, because people came here and erased their heritage or had it erased from them," Edwin continued. "Even white people think they're one hundred percent German or something, but really they're more of a mix. People don't really know what they are.

"But one thing that's surprised me is that all of the genealogical research that Edie's been doing through these years is now being confirmed by DNA testing," Edwin said. "That's kind of special."

"It really is," I agreed. "And it seems especially important to share these stories now, at this moment of rising awareness about Black history and Black lives."

"Yeah, but you have to be careful," Edwin said. "You and I are outsiders." I noted his kindness in calling himself an outsider, when we both knew I was the real outsider.

"We didn't grow up knowing about this heritage," Edwin continued. "Neither of us did, so you have to be very careful when telling these stories. Ours is a mixed family, but it is also an African American family that goes back to before the founding of the country. That is not common. There aren't hardly any African American families that can do this kind of documentary verification. There's plenty of white families that can do this if they try, but not many African American families. And this is a very important story to Black culture."

"I know," I said.

"My dad grew up in Mississippi, and I only have to go back in time to my great-grandparents, and three out of four of them were enslaved people," Edwin added. "Slavery is not as far back as people think. And the effects of slavery are still with us—psychologically, economically, emotionally, and socially."

While we'd talked, I had been hearing police sirens a few blocks farther west. The fireworks had continued, but now it sounded like something bad had happened. "I know," I said.

"But I do think the goal of this DNA testing, and ancestry research, and even all this storytelling is to find the commonness of our humanity," Edwin said. "When you realize you can be connected to any kind of person, well . . . that changes things."

CHAPTER 13

Mary

Oella, Maryland, 1700s

Until the reformation in our code of penal jurisprudence takes place, it will be in vain to attempt universal and perpetual peace in our country.

"A Plan for the Peace Office of the United States,"
Banneker's Almanac of 1793

ACCORDING TO MARTHA Tyson, Bana'ka "died early, leaving his wife with four young children. The family tradition tells us nothing further until Molly had a daughter grown to adulthood." This daughter, Mary, was described by those who knew her as "a woman of uncommon intelligence. She had a knowledge of the properties and uses of herbs, which was often of advantage to her neighbors. Her appearance was imposing, her complexion a pale copper color . . . and she had an ample growth of long black hair, which never became gray."

*　*　*

WHEN I IMAGINE Mary, I sense her grace and capability. She raises the wooden yoke to her shoulders to walk to the well for water. She packs a wagon with baskets of bread and bacon, apples, boiled eggs, greens, and hominy and heads to Ellicott's Mills to feed the workingmen their lunch. She chases down a chicken and quick-snaps its neck, then plucks its feathers right there at the edge of the woods. She watches the feathers take to the wind and knows what the weather's going to do.

The land was animate to Mary, a vast network of plants and creatures that she observed respectfully and in detail. She could see where plants liked to grow, and which plants they favored as their neighbors. She noticed when they were sodden at the root, or had a blight burrowing into the leaves, or when they were almost glowing with good health and healing. Each plant had a meaning and a purpose, a specific way of working. Sometimes the plant's appearance announced its healing properties. The red vesicles of the ruby mustard, for instance, would clean the blood and keep it running swiftly, while the sponge-like yellow of the yarrow would break a fever. Mary had learned the English cures and "physiks" from her mother, Molly, had learned some West African cures and medicines from her father, Bana'ka, and had gleaned additional plant medicines from her neighbors, and she added that knowledge to her own observations. This gave her a lifelong ability to gather healing leaves, roots, and barks from the woods, and to know which plants to have on hand in her garden. Later, Benjamin would include "receipts" and cures in his almanacs much like those he had learned at home from his mother, including recipes to treat whooping cough, asthma, and jaundice.

"Mary Banneky had a great interest in herbs," wrote Benjamin's biographer Silvio Bedini. "During her years on the farm she sought out woodland plants that had medicinal value and she collected information about herbs and remedies from her neighbors. She raised sassafras, ginseng, and snakeroot. She also sought out the bayberry bushes and carefully collected the berries, useful for making candles. She may have raised some flax and hemp and a little cotton, which she could spin and weave for cloth to be used in the home as well as for clothing."

Mary knew that for both bodies and land to thrive they had to be brought into balance. Burn back that bramble wanting to take over, cart buckets up from the river full of mud and waterweeds to feed the soil that was getting tired. The body was little different, so when Mary was doing a healing, first she tuned in to what was too wet or too dry, and then she let the body itself tell her what it needed. Sometimes the cure would come to her, stark and sudden, based on her years of study.

Then she'd make a tincture or a tea, infusing it as she worked with her prayers, in which she pictured the person working, walking, laughing, whole—the bleeding stemmed or the fever cooled, and balance restored to the body. Mary respected her mother's God and her father's Allah, but she saw divine intelligence most clearly in nature.

* * *

THESE STORIES ABOUT Mary all take place later in her life, after she had married Robert Banneker and had become the mother of Benjamin. We have never known what Mary's life was like before those years. But in 2021, Paul Heinegg, the researcher who compiles the database *Free African Americans of Colonial Maryland and Delaware*, stumbled upon an entry in the Maryland Provincial Court Records from May 1731 that provides a possible window into Mary's early life.

The trial opens with a "mulatto" woman, Mary Beneca, arguing for her children's right to freedom. She begins her testimony by saying that she, "your petitioner, was born of a white woman who was a servant of John Newman of this county." She then explains that she was indentured until the age of thirty-one, when she was "adjudged to be free by the Justices of Baltimore County," and while she was in servitude, she had several children "born of her body," including Sarah Lett, Zachariah Lett, and Deborah Lett. She attests that she has paid 7,000 pounds of tobacco for the children's keeping to a landowner named William Rogers, and tells the court that, even so, her children have been unjustly charged with indenture until they each reach the age of thirty-one years. Like Mary herself, the children had done nothing wrong to be charged with this indenture but had simply been born of the union with an African man.

Mary goes on to argue for her daughter Sarah's freedom. Her claims reach their highest pitch when she declares that the indenture ruling "is *erroneous*, and *repugnant*, and that the said Sarah by law is entitled to her freedom." Mary then "beseeches your Honors to order a citation against the said William Rogers to answer the promises, and to . . . adjudge your petitioner's children to be free when they attain the age of sixteen and twenty-one years." The note following the testimony records that William Rogers was summoned for a trial and that Mary Beneca did, in fact, win her case.

This extraordinary document tells us that Mary spent her first thirty-one years in indentured servitude. It informs us that Molly, her mother, was a servant of John Newman. And it suggests that Bana'ka and Molly were not as fortunate as earlier biographers had hoped. It seems that Molly had not been able to free her husband or her child, and was indeed subject to that Maryland law that sentenced her daughter Mary to servitude just because she was born of the union between a British woman and an African man.

This document indicates that Mary was publicly punished for being born as a mixed-race person herself and then for continuing to have her own mixed-race children out of wedlock, although legal marriage was denied to her as an indentured servant. As a servant, she could not fully protect herself from pregnancy or childbirth, so the situation was a setup that kept women like her in servitude throughout their lives and repeated this no-exit pattern for their daughters. Still, within these constraints, Mary lived and created. She worked in indenture, growing foods and herbs, treating people in her community. She may have done whatever she could to stay on the same plantation with her children so she could be there to raise them.

Then, in the very year she was granted her freedom, Mary summoned the courage to petition both the County Court of Baltimore and the Provincial Court—the most prestigious court in the region—for the freedom of her eldest daughter, Sarah. Mary was thirty-one and Sarah was sixteen at the time of this trial, which means that Mary would have been fifteen or sixteen when Sarah was born, a common age for a colonial first-time mother. Mary would have known firsthand the kind of vulnerability that Sarah would face if she were left behind in servitude. If Sarah became pregnant while she was indentured, it would only continue this multigenerational experience of enforced servitude. Mary's description of this indenture law as *repugnant* speaks to her sense of justice and her disgust with these rules that had already robbed her of free choice. It also foreshadows the fiery righteousness that her son Benjamin would later use in his writings to Thomas Jefferson.

In both 1715 and 1728, the Maryland General Assembly had doubled down on the laws that had forced Mary to spend her own first thirty-one years in indenture. The Assembly ruled that "mulatto" children like Mary, or like her children, Sarah, Zachariah, and Deborah Lett, should be bound until the age of thirty-one just for their mother's "crime" of having them with an African American man. If they were the offspring of an indentured woman and a *free* man of color, however, the women were commonly charged with the lesser offense of "fornication," and the children were bound until the age of twenty-one if they were boys and sixteen if they were girls. Mary's argument for these shorter terms, and her success in court, suggest that her offspring were, in fact, the children of a free Black man.

These are new wrinkles in the Banneker story and are not accepted by all Banneker-Lett descendants. But they do correspond remarkably with family members' DNA findings through 23andMe and Ancestry.com. Many of us with Banneker ancestry, including Edie and her brothers, can trace their DNA to Zachariah Lett as well as to Jemima Banneker, and family genealogists have long wondered how Zachariah connects to us biologically. It now seems that he was another of Mary's children, and the older half brother of Benjamin Banneker.

* * *

MARY'S NEW FREEDOM must have been a mixed blessing—a state she had longed for her entire life, made bitter because, in order to seize it, she would have to leave her children behind on the Rogers plantation. I can imagine Mary in the months before she was to leave, busying herself with tasks, putting up preserves, sewing the girls extra dresses and Zachariah new breeches. Their goodbyes would not be permanent—we know this from the way the family story unfolded—so they were not nearly as brutal as the separations endured by most enslaved mothers and their children. Mothers saying goodbye to sons in the morning, thinking the drivers were just taking them out to run an errand, but by evening, learning they had been sold away from them. Mothers hearing through the grapevine that the trader was coming down the road and having just five minutes to run and grab anything—a biscuit and some apples, a warm shawl or an apron, a favorite rag doll, to stash into a satchel for their daughters. Mothers hearing the "hiring list" read out on New Year's Eve and having just one day, supposedly a holiday, to say goodbye to their children forever. Slavery's violence to mothers and children was so extreme that it is impossible to comprehend how it was endured. For this reason, the maternal strength of Black women is one of the wonders of the world, and a source of profound wisdom.

Because she was indentured rather than enslaved, Mary enjoyed privileges unknown by most women of color. But she also faced special vulnerabilities as a mixed-race woman and the mother of three multiracial children whom she could not legally protect. Historian A. B. Wilkinson writes that Chesapeake laws of this time "effectively gave mixed children a legal status between freedom and slavery." Families with this in-between status used every tool available to them to insist on their freedom. Wilkinson adds that "these blended families and mixed-heritage people increasingly used the courts to fight for their independence." And since laws were designed to protect the property of white people, "the most successful mulattoes could prove a tie to European maternal lineage in court or had European mothers or family members who were active in preserving their freedom." This tie to a European mother was a way of turning the landowners' laws against them. When lawmakers decreed that the condition of the child "should follow the condition of the mother" to legalize the sexual assault and breeding of enslaved people by white landowning men, they hadn't banked on the British women who would dare to have children with African men. Certainly not the British women who would go on to argue for those children's civil rights. But some women did just that, and this "maternal tie to whiteness," Wilkinson explains, "literally meant the difference between bondage and freedom."

This would explain why Mary began her testimony by mentioning the whiteness of her mother, Molly. It also suggests why Molly's great-grandchildren continued to know of her and insist that she was, in fact, a white woman when they were interviewed for Benjamin's biography seventy years later. The consistency of their stories also suggests that Molly remained close to her children and grandchildren, even if she'd had to leave her eldest daughter, Mary, behind in indenture for thirty-one years. Even if she had not been able to free her beloved Bana'ka.

CHAPTER 14

Coincidences

Evanston, Illinois, and Arlington, Virginia, Summer 2020

AFTER SEVERAL YEARS of raising my daughter alone, I married a man named John McCarthy in November 2019. John and I had met six years earlier, when I went down to Springfield, Illinois, to give a reading at Edwards Place, the historic mansion that had belonged to Governor Edwards in the nineteenth century, where Abraham Lincoln had once courted Mary Todd. John and I both felt a layering of time on that day, a resonance with the past that held a vision of the future. We were married in the same room where we'd met.

I was on the phone with Edie, telling her about the wedding. Edie had grown up in Springfield, and Edwin still lived there in their family home. Springfield even had an Edwin Lee Elementary School, named after their father, who had been a beloved Black physician and community leader there. Edie and I chatted about Springfield, and when I told her that John had been living on Pasfield Avenue when I met him, Edie laughed. She had spent her childhood summers on that very block, three doors down, visiting the grandparents of her closest childhood friend.

"Here is another little anecdote that speaks to the synchronicity in all of this," Edie said. "Because my mother was adopted, and this is all from her line, I did not have much to go on. I had never seen my biological grandmother, and I had totally given up on getting any pictures of her.

"Well, right around the time that Carol Moseley Braun had been elected to the Senate, my husband and I came out here to Washington for her inauguration," Edie continued. "I had wanted to go to the National Archives because the Emancipation Proclamation was on display, so I asked my husband to drop me off there. But the line! The people were lined up all down the block, and around the corner. There were probably a thousand people just waiting to get in to see the Emancipation Proclamation that day.

"So I decided I would see that some other time, and walked around to the back entrance, so I could do some research of my own," Edie continued. "At that time, everything was on microfiche, and when it was busy, you lined up and they assigned you to a machine. I think I was at machine number ninety-nine that day. Anyway, I settled myself in to do some family research, and I'm there looking through old census documents, and there's a woman next to me wearing all African garb. I picked up that she was new to this kind of research because she called over a staff person for some help. And then she started asking about finding records for Benton Harbor, Michigan.

"Isn't that where your mom's family was from?" I asked.

"Exactly! That's where they moved when they left the Lett Settlement in Ohio. Finally, I couldn't restrain myself any longer, and I started talking to her. And, girl, it turns out she was a Lett from Michigan, sitting right there beside me! In all those crowds of people that day."

"'You gotta call my mom,' she said. So I did. Her mom was in her eighties at that point, but she was sharp as a tack. And before she died, she put me in touch with her sister who sent me those pictures of my grandmother."

"Wow," I said. "I saw those pictures on Facebook. Your grandmother was a beautiful girl."

"She was," Edie said. "And you know, I had just about given up the idea of ever getting to see my maternal grandmother. "You know, I have never been into any woo-woo stuff," Edie continued. "My father was a doctor and I am a lawyer, and so my whole life has been about doing research and compiling evidence. But some of the things that have happened while I have been researching these ancestors are almost too amazing to be believed."

"I believe them." I smiled.

"Sometimes it's hard to find the words to express what we know," Edie said. "There are so many ties that seem invisible to us. But if you're looking, if your eyes are open and you're digging, you start to see the connections.

"I have been doing this research since 1989," she went on. "Soon after our dad died in 1993, it was time for the Letts' Old Settlers Reunion. Edwin had been in touch with some other descendants, so we decided to go. There had to be fifty or sixty people there, of every color under the rainbow. It blew my mind. That was where I met Peggy Sawyer, one of several family griots. Peggy was funny because she was real matter-of-fact about history. And when she met me, she was just like, 'Here.' She shared all of her research with me. Peggy was instrumental in helping to establish the Fred Hart Williams Genealogical Society—for Black genealogy.

"Then a couple of years after I met Peggy, I was going up to Detroit to the jazz festival. I had gone with some friends and was really excited to hear the music and have a good time, so I'd decided that I was not going to see family on that trip. I'm sitting there at the concert, enjoying the jazz and the open air, and I got up to stretch, and there, just a couple rows behind me, was Peggy Sawyer!

"I said, 'Peggy, it's Edie!'

"And she said, 'I only know one Edie and she is my cousin in Springfield, Illinois.'

"I said, 'Peggy, It's *me*!'

"I think Peggy must have been a schoolteacher or something. She had that precise way of talking. We became really close. She looked over my research and she helped me straighten out all the different Aquillas. Since the family members all named their children after their siblings, doing genealogy can get really confusing because you have the same names repeating through the generations.

"You know, I had all your people mapped out on paper," Edie continued. "I had traced from Aquilla and Christina, to Peter and Polly, and then to all of their children who moved up into Lake County, Ohio. But I kept saying, 'Where are their descendants?' I was just waiting for one of you to get in touch."

"I am so glad we are connected now," I said, smiling. It was a wonderful feeling, to be a part of something so much larger than me.

"As a kid, I did not know that we had any family in Ohio," Edie said. "But whenever we would drive through that state on our summer road trips, I would relax, feel more comfortable all of a sudden. I always loved Ohio. I think it must be epigenetic or something."

We talked about all the long road trips our families would take. My parents would drive us to Florida every year, or to the East Coast to see my aunt and her family. Edie's parents would drive to different medical conferences across the country, or to visit her dad's friends from his army days, and other Black physicians who had been trained in the army.

"Sometimes we drove down to Mississippi, to see Dad's family," Edie said. "But because my mother was an only child, and adopted, and her parents were older when they adopted her, there was no one left in her family. By the time we came along, all we had were stories."

I thanked her for sharing her stories with me.

"Oh, I was helped by some griots before me," Edie said. "This is what this is, you know. It's griot work."

CHAPTER 15

Robert

Upper Patapsco, Maryland, 1730s

But farther still—I stop not here—I pursue this social interest, as far as I can trace my several relations. I pass from my own flock, my own neighbourhood, my own nation, to the whole race of mankind, as dispersed throughout the earth.—Am I not related to them all, by the mutual aids of commerce, by the general intercourse of arts and letters, by a common nature of which we all participate?

—Banneker's Almanac for 1794

ACCORDING TO THE oral histories compiled by Martha Tyson, "Mary married a native African. He had been purchased from a slave-ship by a planter living near her mother. His devotional turn of mind induced him early to become a member of the Church of England, and he received the name of Robert in baptism, upon which event the master gave him his freedom. It was subsequent to earning his freedom that he married Mary Banneker."

Robert's baptism and inclusion in the Anglican Church can give us a window into his sincere and devout personality, and into a larger shift in Chesapeake culture. From the late 1600s to the early 1700s, large planters resisted sharing the Christian faith with their enslaved people, because the rights of property ownership and legal protection were still tied to Christianity. According to historian Sylvia Frey, "Most of the gentry class were members of the Anglican church, and church membership usually overlapped with membership in the county court," making the exclusion of African Americans from Christianity a dual act of excluding them from political representation and from the fold of humans who were considered "saved" and worthy of eternal life. But in the 1720s, a group of missionaries came to Maryland and Virginia and began converting enslaved men and women to Christianity. In 1724, more than two hundred people of African descent were baptized by the Reverend William Black in Williamsburg, Virginia, and other ministers began spreading the gospel to African people in parishes throughout the Chesapeake. Robert may have been a part of this movement, and his devotion to Christianity probably facilitated his acceptance by wider Chesapeake society and influenced his "master's" agreement to free him.

We do not know the name of this enslaver who eventually manumitted Robert for his Christianity and good behavior, or allowed Robert to "hire himself out" and earn enough to purchase his freedom. But it is clear that Robert was affiliated with Richard Gist, and Gist may have facilitated Robert's earning of freedom. Richard Gist was a prominent member of Baltimore society. His father, Christopher Gist, was the first British person to settle on the banks of the Patapsco River in the 1690s. Richard himself surveyed the city of Baltimore and was eventually named both burgess and justice of the peace of the region. Although his parents were members of the Church of England, Gist was married in the Quaker Church and became part of the Quaker Society of Friends, who were becoming increasingly abolitionist. Later, in 1737, Gist sold Robert more than one hundred acres of land, indicating that he respected Robert and had much more progressive views on race than most elite white men of his time. Robert's connection with Richard Gist—who was one of the most respected and powerful landowners in Maryland—may have provided the credibility that allowed Mary and Robert to petition the prestigious Provincial Court for the freedom of Mary's daughter.

In any case, Robert's success speaks to his ability to impress and collaborate with people in power. He was able to appeal to the dominant culture enough to glean freedom, church membership, and land ownership. But we know from the way his son wrote about him later that Robert was also deeply proud of his African heritage, and fundamentally self-determined as a Black man.

* * *

I PICTURE ROBERT as a driven and intelligent young man who was determined to escape slavery or die trying. I see him stealing time to walk the woods around the plantation where he was enslaved, scoping out potential hiding places, and then, after months of planning, walking away from the fields through the woods, under the cover of darkness. I see him crouched in a hollowed-out log, listening to the patrollers as they galloped over the trails, calling him names and laughing to one another about what they would do to him when they caught him. Robert could hear the whiskey and excitement in their voices, the bloodlust, which was also a money lust for the reward they would be given when they dragged him back to the plantation. He thought surely one of those bloodhounds would smell his sweat and his fear, although he had tried to cover his scent with wild mint. His heartbeat was so loud in his ears that he thought surely they would hear it. But the patrollers kept heading north, looking for him, and he forced himself to delay walking onward. He knew a free Black man who was a cooper and had a cabin beside the river, where he soaked wood to make it pliable enough to make the casks so valuable for carting and selling tobacco. Robert went to this man and his family, who hid him for weeks under a trick board in the loft of the barn. He forced himself to stay close to the plantation much longer than seemed safe, and much longer than he wanted to. Finally, when he thought people had given up searching for him, he set off, walking many miles each night. But he was caught again, imprisoned, and put on a river barge to be sold.

But this time, Robert was bought by a farmer who read to his servants from the Bible in the evenings. For the first time, Robert felt that his life could have some dignity to it—some time to hire himself out for extra pay and experience a measure of independence unimaginable at the first, more brutal plantation. He was so hungry for the rhythms and words of the Bible that he memorized verses and recited them back to the household every evening. Robert became a casual preacher on the farm, and an honorary member of the Church of England. He hired himself out on the evenings and weekends, and stored up every extra coin. He always did a little more than was necessary, on every job, and he used his connections in the church and the community to eventually secure his own freedom.

*   *   *

I IMAGINE THAT, in 1730, the year before Mary's indenture was up, Robert started showing up at the Rogers plantation on Sundays to court her. He had to ride many miles to get there, with his papers on him to attest to his right to be out and about. He'd arrive in the afternoons with his wide smile, his work-calloused hands, and his lofty, biblical vocabulary. People on the plantation said that to hear him talk was like listening to the book itself.

It wasn't just Robert's words that got Mary, though, but his voice, the timbre of it when he spoke and sang. He laughed with a deep boom, and he could flail a hymn into feeling until she felt herself expanding somehow, something unlocking in her body. It made her think about the age-old braid of pain, faith, and wisdom, how rarely you could have one strand without the others. Robert had a deep voice, not just low, but the kind of voice that carried the waters in it—salt and brackish and fresh. Mary thought maybe it was Africa that gave his voice its depths, a tone that remembered the terror of the passage, the way her own father's had. Or maybe it was his insistence that gave Robert his edge, an endurance that never forgot the swamp waters where he'd crouched for hours, catching and eating fish and crawdads with his hands, the roots he'd chewed to stay alive when he'd run from the plantation once, twice, three times. Or maybe it was an anger so deep it came out as grief, a low bass note that remembered the grandmothers still sent out to plant the rows, their backs bent and aching, their hands stained and swollen from tying up tobacco. Robert never forgot what it felt like to be watched by cold eyes, knowing the overseer's wrist was just twitching to crack the whip at someone's back. Robert could not forget the people he'd left behind, the brethren who hovered at the edge of his consciousness. They were the reason he could never sit still, and why he vowed to make his own life a retribution, as if by being ambitious and successful enough he could somehow balance the ledger—free his offspring on behalf of those elders he could not free. That past was unspoken in Robert, but part of his presence. He had a buoyancy about him, and a simmering strength that lined up, hip to hip, with Mary's own.

One Sunday evening, Robert and Mary were walking down the lane at the back of the plantation. They always stayed to the back way so that William Rogers would not see them courting and become vindictive. The sweet smell of honeysuckle was in the air and cicadas were spiraling out the longing song of high summer. Everything was sleepy sweet and ripe to bursting, with blossoms calling out to one another on the wind.

Robert put his hand on Mary's lower back. "Just seven more months of this," he said.

Mary nodded. She had picked some chicory beside the lane, and now she shifted it to her left hand so she could interlink her fingers with his. Robert squeezed her hand, and the feel of his rough palm sent a current through her body, not just from the touch but from the fact that they were reaching for each other, *choosing* each other.

"Can't come soon enough," Mary said softly.

"Then what?" Robert's usually commanding voice cracked just a bit.

"Don't know. I need to look after my children."

"You need to come home with me," Robert said. His eyes were so confident that they startled Mary. It didn't seem safe for a Black man to want a thing with such clarity. She worried he was tempting fate.

"I'm working overtime now every evening, every Sunday too. Soon I'll have enough to buy our own land where we can raise *our* children," Robert said.

Mary couldn't trust her voice to hold steady. Nothing had ever been promised to her before.

"We can have a real life," Robert went on. They were getting up toward middle age but were going to have to think of themselves as younger, just to have the chance to begin again, to live a life that *they* had made, and not one they'd been locked into, the way they'd once been locked into stocks and irons.

Robert pulled Mary to him then, and she felt her heartbeat thrumming in her limbs. It was one of those moments when hope became physical, when the present pulsed with the future inside it. Later, Mary would think of that as the moment when she first felt their children, as if they were souls flickering on around them like fireflies in the clover.

Robert just about floated the twelve miles home that night. And Mary hardly slept at all. In the next months, they snuck off almost every Sunday, to walk deep in the woods, or to bar Mary's cabin door and lie with each other. Robert did not bring her trifles—ribbons and hats, candies, or wooden combs—as others had done. But he gave her something more solid, filling her mind with visions of what they would build together. Mary felt herself coming back to her old strength, a kind of dignity she hadn't felt since she was small and her father was still alive.

* * *

ROBERT CAME TO meet Mary on the day of her emancipation. She had packed herself a muslin bag, but most of her things—her wooden bowls and embroidered tablecloths, her aprons and best straw hat—she'd leave behind for her girls. She walked out of the cabin she had shared with her children, and they followed her into the yard. Her son Zachariah had gotten so tall. She did not have to stoop to him at all. Mary looked into his eyes. She hoped that the strength she was feeling—along with a turmoiled mix of guilt and freedom—could be passed into him so he could know the power of his own heart. She stilled her tears and willed them not to fall. It was not fair for her to cry in front of her children when they were the ones being left behind.

"You are the strongest man I know, Zachariah Lett," Mary said. Then she whispered, "Keep up with your reading—do it in secret, but do it. And take good care of your sisters."

Zachariah nodded, his eyes guarded. Then he pulled away and turned his back to her. He tried to walk away calmly, but Mary saw his shoulders shudder with a half sob just before he took off jogging toward the woods. The two of them had never needed language together but could just look into each other's eyes and know what the other was thinking. She knew he was going out to his favorite smooth-barked sycamore, where he would sit and break branches and stab his pocket-knife into a stump—anything, anything, to toss off some of his anger. Anger at this man Robert for stealing her away. Anger at his father for being unable to free him, although he *knew* he was his son. Anger at the laws that would keep him in indenture just so the magistrates on the courts could pay for their own silk robes. Anger at a colony that would treat him like a lesser person for no good reason at all.

Mary watched her son's retreating back and said a silent prayer for his safety. He was so grown that people would see him as a man now, a Black man, and that meant new dangers for him. She remembered when he was a baby, the way his eyes had fixed on hers when she nursed him, like he was afraid to look away from her, as if he knew he could find in her eyes everything he needed to understand this tangled, confusing life. Just yesterday, it seemed, he had ridden in a sling on her back while she topped tobacco and cut weeds, had stood beside her while she hung out laundry and boiled roots.

And her girls, Sarah and Deborah. Mary didn't know how to walk away from them without feeling like she was leaving behind a part of her own body. She drew them to her. Then she spat on her finger, smoothed back the stray hairs around their faces, and told them to stand up straight. "Pull your shoulders back and look people in the eye, and apologize to no one," she said, in the same clipped way her mother had once said it to her. "And stick together now, hear?"

They nodded back, their throats suddenly sore. Mary was like sunlight to them. She made their cabin into a haven, with wildflowers on the table, bright quilts on the bed, all manner of herbs and weeds strung up and drying from the rafters, and her laughter—their mother's very particular, too loud, embarrassing way of laughing.

Robert stood at the edge of the compound, watching this scene with his hat in his hands. He could feel his heart twisting in his chest like a fish on a hook. He remembered his own mother saying good-bye to him. He tried to recall her warm smell and the way when she bent down, the morning had lit up her hair in a blur of borrowed sun. She became that blur, and he couldn't see or remember her face afterward. His little knees had swayed, and like that, a white man had said,

"Boy, here," grabbed him under the arms, and tossed him like a flour sack into a wagon. The driver whipped the horses into action, and his mother began running after them, yelling his name. His old name, the one he lost when he lost her.

Was that really his mother, he wondered, *or another woman who had cared for him on the passage? The memory was so much a part of him that he wasn't sure it was a memory at all or an ache so deep it felt like the cold water of the quarry swimming hole, dropping down bottomless, numbing his limbs.* And here it was happening—almost—all over again.

Robert knew Mary would survive this. And her children were nearly grown. But he would have to make this up to her. He would have to give her land and a family right away. He would have to give her children with the freedom to remember their mother.

CHAPTER 16

Gwen

Baltimore, Maryland, and Evanston, Illinois, August 2020

ROBERT LETT REFERRED to Gwen Marable as the spiritual leader of the Banneker-Lett family and insisted that I talk to her next. Gwen lived outside Baltimore, not far from the Banneker Park and Museum. She had been instrumental in establishing the museum, protecting the Banneker artifacts, and sharing Benjamin's story with the public.

Gwen and I began talking over Zoom, every other Sunday afternoon during the COVID-19 quarantine. She was eighty-seven but looked much younger to me. When she told me stories about her early adulthood, about looking for housing in Manhattan, for instance, and being turned away time and time again because she and her physician husband were "colored," I could hardly believe it. It was not that I was surprised by the discrimination she'd faced. But I had to be reminded that she had already lived through so many chapters of history. James Baldwin was in Harlem writing his first books while she was looking for her first apartment just blocks away. She'd come of age before the civil rights movement, before the rise and assassinations of Martin Luther King and Malcolm X. But Gwen was still so engaged by life and by her deep processes of learning, spirituality, and creativity that she became a model for me of how to live with consciousness. Through these biweekly conversations, Gwen became one of my dearest friends, in addition to being my cousin and elder.

Sometimes when we talked, Gwen would just be finishing a virtual Qigong class. Sometimes she'd be logging off from a writing workshop or storytelling event. Once, we talked while her daughter Heather was visiting and pulling Gwen's dresses and sweaters from her closet.

"We are the same size and sometimes trade clothes for a while," Gwen explained. "I self-identify as a hoarder." She laughed. In truth, her apartment was decorated in the salon style, with art covering nearly every surface and African baskets and sculptures tucked into the corners of the rooms.

Occasionally, while we talked that day, Gwen would call out to her daughter, "That skirt goes with the little top I gave you last time. You know the one I mean, with the border on the edge? Take it! I want you to take it."

I smiled. Adele had just had a growth spurt and had begun borrowing my clothes. I hoped that when I was in my eighties and she was in her sixties, we would still be sharing dresses.

Gwen was ready to get down to business. She was happy I was writing a book about these ancestors and had been introducing me through email to other scholars and board members who had helped to establish the Banneker Park and Museum. "All these years we've been wanting another biography of Benjamin Banneker, and we've been wondering who was going to write it," Gwen said. "And now you're here!" She smiled.

I pushed the Record button on Zoom and asked her to tell me about her experience as a storyteller who had shared the Banneker histories herself.

"Well, I moved to Baltimore in 1988, just by invitation of my daughter, and not with any plan to stay here," Gwen began. "I was in my late fifties then, ready to retire from teaching, but not knowing what I was going to do next. Then after my daughter married and moved away, I received a phone call from my cousin Charles Weiker, in Ohio. He said that he had been doing genealogy in his mother's and my father's family line, and had discovered that we were descended from Jemima, who was the sister of Benjamin Banneker. So from the moment of that phone call, I felt, 'Oh, *this* is the reason why I moved to Baltimore.' I felt that it was a spiritual calling to be here and tell this story, and then I connected with other people at the museum, including descendants of the Ellicott family." Gwen smiled.

"Everyone who works on the Banneker story feels it as a spiritual calling, whether they are related to him or not," Gwen said. "There is a spiritual connection that I'm feeling now, as I speak with you."

"I feel it too," I said, smiling.

"When I began talking publicly about Benjamin Banneker," Gwen continued, "Baltimore County had advertised the fact that they were getting ready to build the Benjamin Banneker Historical Park and Museum, and even local people were saying, 'Who is Benjamin Banneker?' Then the park district would say, 'Oh, there's this woman who is a descendant who can come and make a speech about him.' And because I had been recently trained by the United Way to make fundraising speeches, I was in that mode. Then two women—one Black, one white—heard me make a speech and said, 'You are telling a story about a historic figure and there are so many layers to it. There's an organization of Black storytellers called the Griots' Circle of Maryland. We want to take you there so you can learn how to tell this story more fully.'

"So then I began to tell the story from the point of view of being a griot," Gwen continued, "which is a storyteller of Black history, African folktales, myths, and fables. That opened up a whole new way to tell the story of Benjamin Banneker, and it introduced me to the larger world of Black storytelling. The storyteller Mary Carter Smith was present when I first went to the Griots' Circle. I can still feel it. The meeting was held in the library, and I walked through the quietness to open the door to the community room . . . and it was like walking into a box of chocolates. It was warm and loving, and I immediately felt embraced."

I smiled.

"The Griots' Circle opened me to a whole new way to live while in retirement," Gwen went on. "All the stories that I crafted after that were done from the point of view of Black storytelling, which is very different from white storytelling. It is not about standing still and telling a story. It's using a lot of body language, a lot of facial expressions, and possibly a lot of Black English. Most of all, it's about expressing the *feelings* of what is taking place."

I nodded. Feelings were the most interesting part of a story for me too—the inner life, and not the outer plot. Not everyone has been able to chart the course of their lives, after all. But everyone has access to an inner life, and inner worlds are often most richly developed in people who do not have as much control in the outer world.

We went on talking about the stories of the Banneker family. "For me, the Banneker story has given me a sense of knowing my roots that I had not had since my father was alive," Gwen said. "He had done some research and had come up with a family tree. That family tree was done from a point of view of . . . ," Gwen took a breath, centering herself. "Well, it looks like we're descended from a Scottish man."

I knew what that meant.

"And it seemed to me that there were no connections that my father could make with the Black people of the family because there was nothing written about them," Gwen said. "So what he found was interesting in that it gave us something to start with, but it was incomplete.

"Then Chuck began to do his genealogy research," Gwen continued, "and subsequently Robert Lett began to do his work, and my cousin Anita Burden, who researched with Chuck for many years, and they all began to find things. Because my skin is lighter, and because other people in my family have light skin, there was always the question of where we came from in terms of our white ancestry. When I learned the Banneker story, I felt such a sense of relief, that I was not only this way because of a white 'massa.' I felt, 'Well, isn't this interesting that it's not just a white man that is making our family light-skinned. It is also a white woman.' Because Molly, of course, had her own story."

"She sure did," I said. Gwen and I had talked about Molly and had shared our sense of her wit and independence.

"So I'm finding that the Banneker story not only connects me to the Black origins of who I am," Gwen continued. "It also gives me the white piece that was missing too. This story relates to my personal journey of finding comfort with the color of my skin as I navigate the racial awakening that is going on today.

"I spoke about this just last week here at the senior development where I live," Gwen added. "We are a Quaker-sponsored retirement center and so we have a different way of doing things. Recently the CEO began holding conversations about diversity. So every Friday at one o'clock we have a structure for talking about these things, either in person or on Zoom.

"Last Friday, I was sitting outside with ten of my neighbors, and one woman who I don't know very well was also there. We got into a conversation about color, and she asked me why I had not chosen to pass for white."

"Wow." I raised my eyebrows. "That was rude." I felt unsteady in my chair suddenly.

"Yes, it kind of caught me off guard," Gwen said. "I don't know why I didn't say, 'Why are you asking me that question?' Later I realized it was really all about her. She was feeling like, 'Oh my God, I would never want to be Black.' She was essentially asking me, 'Why would you *choose* to be Black?'

"So I told her the story of my father who could have passed as a white man, as many of the people in our family did during World War II, in order to get work," Gwen continued. "There were good government jobs available to them in Washington, D.C., if they would just leave Ohio and become white. They did come back to Ohio for family reunions, but eventually, after they got married, they usually stopped visiting. Eventually, they kind of disappeared. Anyway, I got into telling that whole story, and then saying, 'Because my father was my model, I never would have passed.'

"You know, if my father had chosen to pass as white, then maybe I would have chosen to pass," Gwen went on. "Who knows, but there was never, ever a time when I would have wanted that. I would have been so nervous living with that as my choice. And in fact, because of growing up—I didn't tell the woman this at the time, but now I'm reflecting on it with you—because I grew up in the colored community of Cincinnati, I was surrounded by Black history and Black excellence. I grew up in a time of segregation—the Great Depression, World War II—and there was great pride in our history, and a lot of teaching in the community.

"From the time I stepped out of my front door and walked several blocks to the Black-owned drugstore to get my ice-cream cone, every porch along the way had people sitting on it who knew my name," Gwen said. "I knew that they would call my parents if anything was going on that shouldn't be. That's how safe the community was.

"We had so many programs and activities then that were not only nurturing but educational," Gwen added. "I guess that's what started my interest in speaking, because from the time I was four years old, I was standing up, reciting poems in church or on some stage or another."

It was quite easy to see Gwen as that bright and cherished little girl, reciting poems in church. "There had to be so many good things about growing up that community," I said. "Especially sensing your father's deep pride in being Black."

"Yes, he had that pride, but he was very discriminated against because of his skin color, for not being Black enough, and for not being white enough. My father was a race man. Do you know what a race man was?" Gwen asked.

"I've heard the term, but I don't know if I know exactly what it means," I answered.

"That meant that he was making a stand for his race, and a stand for equality," Gwen explained. "It was a way of saying, 'I am Black and this is what I am fighting and working for in my life.'"

I nodded.

"But he was never able to do everything he was capable of, and that pain went very, very deep for me," Gwen added. "I didn't even realize how deep it was, to witness that as a child. But he was not the only one. There were college-educated Black men who were working on the railroad, and glad to have that job. Even though there were lawyers and doctors, ministers, teachers, and principals, social workers, and many other college-educated people in the community, there were very few jobs for them. College was a possibility. You could get a scholarship. But getting a decent job . . . that was kind of beyond you."

"These stories are so important to share," I said.

"I can speak about them now, and hopefully somebody will read them," Gwen replied.

"But back to the Banneker story," she said. "I'm going to use the word 'solid.' It gave me solid proof. That there is a reason why I am where I am today, and why I am *who* I am today.

"For longer than I've ever lived anywhere," Gwen said, "I have been living in this story."

CHAPTER 17

Childhood

Baltimore County, Maryland, 1730s–1750s

It may be perhaps observed by the moralist . . . that our globe seems particularly fitted for the residence of a being, placed here only for a short time, whose task is to advance himself to a higher and happier state of existence, by unremitted vigilance of caution and activity of virtue.

—Banneker's Almanac of 1792

MARY AND ROBERT Banneker were married in 1730. This was the year recorded in the oral histories, and now affirmed by court documents, when Mary, already named Mary Beneca,* petitioned for the freedom of her daughter Sarah. She would have been newly pregnant with Benjamin when she stood before the Provincial Court and argued against the *repugnant* nature of these indenture laws for mixed-race children.

In Robert, Mary found an African man with an intelligence and determination that equaled her own. Mary felt about Robert the way Molly had felt about Bana'ka. But while Bana'ka was the deep well itself, Robert was an intellectual workingman, intensely practical and devoutly Christian.

---

* Because spelling was irregular then, the family name was spelled Bannaky, Banneky, Banneker, and Beneca, depending on the moment and the clerk who was handwriting the document.

Benjamin was their firstborn, arriving on November 9, 1731. A serious baby, wise beyond his years, he reminded his grandmother Molly of Bana'ka. Sometimes Molly—whom everyone called Little Ma—even went so far as to tell him the stories that Bana'ka had told, as if prodding him to remember an earlier lifetime. Two years later, a sister named Julian was born, and then three more girls—Minta, Molly, and our ancestor, Jemima.

In those years, Robert was absolutely untiring as a farmer and businessman. After securing his freedom, he first bought a twenty-five-acre parcel of land near Cooper's Branch of the Patapsco River, called "Timber Poynt." Then, on March 10, 1737, Robert purchased one hundred additional acres in Baltimore County, called "Stout," for 7,000 pounds of tobacco. Robert must have worked constantly, farming three times the amount of most men in order to accrue enough for this down payment on such a substantial tract of land. The land represented his vision for the family's future, as well as his good standing in the wider community. Robert hired a lawyer to have the deed written up in his name and in Benjamin's, although Benjamin was only six years old at the time. In legal language and beautiful script, the deed acknowledged Richard Gist's receipt of 7,000 pounds of tobacco in exchange for the property. It asserted that this receipt would

> aquit and discharge them the said Robert Bannaky and Benjamin Bannaky his son their heirs and assigns for ever from every part and parcel thereof hath given granted bargained and sold placed in escrow and confirmed unto them the said Robert Bannaky and Benjamin Bannaky his son their heirs and assigns for ever one hundred acres of land lying in the said country.

Robert secured this purchase in the elevated diction and elegant penmanship that would legitimate it in all corners of society. Later, his son Benjamin would use the same language and penmanship to legitimate his intellect in wider society. Freedom then was tied primarily to Christianity and to landownership. Robert had made the first move toward protecting his freedom by becoming a member of the Church of England. Now, by buying this land and putting the deed in his own name and his son's, Robert was aiming to secure his family's freedom for at least another generation, and ideally for many generations, as the land was assigned to them, in writing, "for ever."

Robert and Mary were deeply serious about freedom and always thinking about how to protect it for their children and *their* children. Without land, a man was just a servant to others, Robert would say. The family wanted to believe that slavery would be outlawed soon, and that more landowners would see slavery's fundamental immorality. But, despite landowners' increasing baptism of their enslaved people, the slave trade was only increasing. Large plantation owners, who were also the regional lawmakers, were passing more and more regulations that made it almost impossible for enslavers to free, or manumit, their enslaved people, and more difficult for free people of color to own land, keep weapons, hire servants, or marry. Many laws forced free people of color to leave the county or state within thirty days of achieving their freedom. Other laws targeted free people of color with discriminatory taxation, sending families into poverty or forcing them into indenture, almost as soon as they had earned their hard-won liberty.

Meanwhile, Enlightenment ideas were spreading across the globe, connecting whiteness to reason and Blackness to ignorance, and classifying humans into hierarchies and types. In 1735, the Swedish thinker Linnaeus classified the types of man in a racial hierarchy that put Europeans at the top of the ladder, because they were "Ruled by Law," and Africans at the bottom because they were "sluggish, lazy, careless" and "Covered by grease." This obsession with classification would lead to the popularization of the theory of polygenesis, which attested that different races evolved from separate human origins. These racist ideas were presented as objective science and were thereafter cited by enslavers as evidence for the "naturalness" of enslaving African people.

The Banneker family felt a new foreboding as these ideas became more prevalent and as Maryland increased its investments in slavery. They strived to achieve prosperity and learning, and they used their ingenuity, connections, and resources to protect the family. But like anyone, the Bannekers were not able to see into the future, which means that they could not have imagined how unjust things would actually become, how central slavery would become to the economy and culture of Maryland and later to that of the United States. They probably hoped that more and more people of color would achieve independence, as they had. They probably imagined that history would go an entirely different way.

*　*　*

THE FAMILY MUST have felt a new security after Robert purchased "Stout," the acreage that ensured their independence and provided the ground of their working lives. After clearing the underbrush, Robert girdled the trees—a process in which trees were wrapped with a tight belt until they died and fell. Then he planted his first crops of corn and tobacco among the stumps and felled logs, in little hillocks to prevent erosion. He selected the straightest, densest of these tree trunks and cut them into boards for the family's cabin. Mary and the children pitched in to build the cabin themselves, constructing the walls of strong logs and covering the roof with clapboards that Robert had chipped with an axe. He built a puncheon floor of split logs with one side sanded smooth and showed the children how to chink the walls with clay dug up from the Patapsco river bottom. One side of the cabin was almost entirely taken up with a large fireplace, made from stones carted from the riverbank that the children had helped to mortar into place. This fireplace heated the home and served as a kitchen hearth for Mary, who cooked their meals there in an iron pot.

They had a few hogs and chickens that grazed freely in the woods that ringed the fields, and they planted the acreage of corn required by law for their keeping. Then they planted squash and carrots, sugar beets, cucumbers, beans, parsley, tarragon, spinach, and potatoes for their kitchen garden and began an orchard with apple, pear, and peach saplings. Mary experimented with all the seeds she could gather. Each row of plants that did not take, each stand of fruit eaten by deer or lost to drought, hit her with a pang in the stomach, an awareness of the food they would go without. But they were eating much better than they ever had as servants, and living in relative abundance and plenty. In time, Robert even constructed beehives, and they had golden honey to bake into cakes and fruit pies.

Mary rose with Robert at dawn, warmed the hominy for breakfast, and walked with him beside the plow, humming and talking all the while. They taught their children to work that way too, rising with the sun and doing the arduous daily tasks uncomplaining and grateful for the chance to serve themselves. That was how the farm prospered, all of them pitching in and farming judiciously, changing the location of the fields, and allowing the land to rest between tobacco harvests. Mary and Robert understood that the health of the crops was dependent on the health of the soil. Robert tested the soil on his tongue and knew the smells and tastes of fertility and depletion. He knew to rotate the tobacco and corn crops. And sometimes he and Mary and the children went down to the Patapsco and carted up barrows of river grasses, mud, and reeds and spread them over the fields and kitchen gardens.

The Bannekers always had plenty of corn, herbs, greens, root vegetables, and eggs in their kitchen gardens and larder, and they drew more Orinoco tobacco from their fields than most of their neighbors. Some of the surrounding townspeople said that it was voodoo that let them glean so much from that land. Mary and Robert did pray over the land daily, saying their thanks for it, but it was not magic that allowed them to farm with such success, but intelligence. Historian Vera F. Rollo wrote that Robert used knowledge brought from Africa and "led the waters, by means of ditches and little dams, from the springs to irrigate the fields, so even in dry seasons the Bannakys usually raised good crops of tobacco."

Most of their time was spent with the tobacco, because it was their cash crop. Mary, Robert, and their children guarded the young plants closely and then tended to the leaves, inspecting them for worms, then topping them so the leaves grew thick before the picking. Then they hung the tobacco leaves by strings to air-cure. After the tobacco was cured, they packed the leaves in casks and brought them to sale in the port. Those casks then served as their currency in the colony.

Every day, Robert would work until darkness fell, until he could not see his hands in front of him. But at sunset, he would take a break from his labor to walk through the fields. He'd feel himself surrounded then, in a great glowing of gratitude—for his freedom, his family, for the chance to own and farm his land.

* * *

ORAL HISTORIES SAY that our ancestor, Jemima, was named after Mary's sister. The family had a tradition by then of naming the children after their siblings, so they would be tied together in a great braid of names. Many African-descended families did this at that time, as a way of denoting lineage in a world that denied them legalized kinship, and would wrench them apart at any opportunity.

Robert had a fence to mend, and some pickers to manage over in the far fields, but decided to let his daughter Jemima tag along with him. Jemima was a quiet, watching child. She was always asking him to tell her stories about Africa, or about the time when he was enslaved. He was too angry to think about Africa, which he'd left so young that remembering it was like a wisp of fog burning off, and he didn't like to tell his children about slavery either. Usually, he ignored Jemima's request for a story, or deflected it into a prayer for those still in bondage. They were always praying for those who were enslaved, always giving thanks that they were not. But sometimes, he complied. Usually that was when he was out on a task, with Jemima to help. Then he started moving fast as he talked, chopping wood, or stacking logs, or weeding a row, like he had to keep moving just to somehow shake off the fury of remembering and the guilt of escape. But Jemima listened to everything, even to what he did not say.

Once, he told her about his mother saying goodbye to him, her warm honey smell, and how when she bent down, the sunlight turned her hair into a blur and he couldn't remember her face afterward. Jemima listened to that story and understood that this grandmother was also part of her story. She mourned her, felt her absence in their cabin as acutely as she felt her other grandmother Molly's bustling presence. The anger gave her a slick iron taste in her mouth. Sometimes she bit her tongue until it bled, just to feel it. Jemima nursed a hidden urge for justice, for all the family still caught in that trap.

CHAPTER 18

I Can't Breathe

Pasadena, California, and Evanston, Illinois, Summer 2020

IN MAY 2020, George Floyd was stopped by four Minneapolis police officers who suspected him of using a counterfeit $20 bill at a convenience store. In the process of arresting him, one of the officers knelt on Floyd's neck and back for nine minutes and twenty-nine seconds, ignoring pleas from bystanders to release him, while Floyd gasped, "I can't breathe." He called out to his mother as he lay on the pavement, dying. Seventeen-year-old Darnella Frazier filmed this horrifying scene on her cell phone, and then millions viewed this video online, spreading outrage across the country and unleashing Black Lives Matter protests in large and small cities. People were already at home, on quarantine, and in lockdown. The COVID-19 epidemic had revealed long-standing inequities, and Americans had more time to acknowledge the racism that informs policing, law, and all other aspects of society. The movement galvanized people around issues of racial justice and brought the idea of generational trauma into mainstream consciousness.

Members of our extended Banneker-Lett family were posting on social media and keeping in close touch about the Black Lives Matter movement. Then Robert organized a group phone call to discuss the present moment, and to prepare a statement on behalf of the family. We felt compelled to speak out together, as people who ranged across cultures and colors, and as descendants of people who had been speaking out for racial justice since before the country's inception.

We were a talkative group, and our first phone call lasted four hours as we discussed the way the current movement for justice was helping us to reflect on our ancestors' activism, progress, and struggles.

We did not know it then, but while we were talking, the street and sanitation workers of Washington, D.C., were painting BLACK LIVES MATTER down the middle of Pennsylvania Avenue, one of the very streets that our ancestor Benjamin Banneker had helped to survey 229 years earlier.

* * *

THE DAY AFTER that group phone call, Robert called me again. We edited the family statement together, and he shared more stories from the Lett lineage. Then, later in the day, he messaged me to say that soon after we hung up, he had stopped breathing. He'd called the paramedics and was now in the hospital.

I saw his message, texted him healing wishes, and said I would be keeping him in my thoughts. My favorite great-aunt on my mother's side had died of COVID-19 two months earlier. I had called her the day before she died and had been fortunate to have that last conversation with her, as a nurse in hazmat gear held up the phone for us. But I hadn't been able to hold her hand or help her in any way as the virus tore through her body and she suffocated.

We were still in the first wave of COVID-19, when most people who went into the hospital did not return home again. And COVID-19 was killing Black and brown people at double the rate of white people because of underlying health conditions due to generations of stress, food scarcity, and economic injustice. Many people of color served as the nation's essential workers, and had not been able to stay home, work via Zoom, and quarantine. Robert, as a Black man in his seventies with severe asthma, was in the group most likely to die from the virus.

So the next morning, as I grabbed my phone to call Robert, I did not know if my call would go directly to voice mail, or if I would ever get to speak to him again. My finger shook as I pressed the call button on my cell phone.

Robert answered on the second ring, in his usual cheerful manner. "Hello!"

"Hi!" I said. "You're sounding great!" *You're there*, I thought with relief. I hadn't been aware that I was holding my breath, but I had been. I collapsed into my desk chair. "I'm so glad."

"Yes," Robert said. "I tested negative for COVID-19 and was diagnosed with having a severe asthma attack. But those were some of the most frightening few minutes of my life, when I was still struggling to breathe, and waiting on a hospital bed to get that test back."

"I can imagine," I said.

"You know, it was so strange," Robert began. He was already telling it like a story, I realized with a smile, already coming back to himself. "I got off the phone with you, and I called my daughter and talked to her for a while, and then my throat just started to close up. I grabbed my inhaler and when that didn't do anything, I had the presence of mind to call 911."

"I'm so glad you did that."

"Yes, in all my years as a coach, I learned how to read a situation and know when to take it seriously," Robert said. "I know that an asthma attack can usually be stopped unless they get to you too late. Once the heart starts shutting down, it is usually too late. So I was able to make it out to the porch and sit on a stool, and I was just trying to take breaths, as slow and deep as I could. But at that point I had pretty much resolved that this was maybe going to be the end."

"That must have been terrifying," I said. I had learned in my years as a caregiver to my terminally ill partner that death is terrifying, even for spiritual people, even for people who lived as we did, with some mysterious trust in our lives' deeper meaning. It was shocking to be out of control of your own body, to feel a downhill run of uncontrollable symptoms, a terrible tearing asunder of self from self.

"It really was," Robert said. "You know that state—apoplexy—when you lose control of your movements? That began happening to me. It was so odd to have no control of my body. As the ambulance pulled up, I was just barely able to raise my arm. But luckily, they saw me."

"I'm so glad they made it on time," I said.

"Me too. And that had been on my bucket list!" Robert began in a lighter, joking voice. "I had always wanted to ride in the back of an ambulance! But it's not what you think it will be, because if you're in an ambulance, you're distressed, so it doesn't have all the fun and excitement you'd expect."

I could hear a nurse coming in to give Robert his breakfast. He began to tease her and beg for some bacon to go with the watery oatmeal she'd brought. After she left, Robert turned his teasing to me.

"What did you do to me, girl?" he said. "You got all formal with me at the end of that last phone call, thanking me for sharing the family stories. And then the next thing I knew, I couldn't breathe. I was like, 'What? Is this the end?'"

"No, it can't be," I said, definitively. As if I could control such a thing.

We joked and talked for a while more. I knew Robert was just lightening the mood, but his question pained me. He must have wondered if sharing these long-held stories with me had robbed something from him or had meant that his work on earth was complete. It reminded me that our stories live in our bodies and become physically part of us, and that giving them into the air has its ramifications. COVID-19 had made us all realize that we were sharing one another's air, and that sharing held dangers.

I can't breathe, Eric Garner said, eleven times, as New York police officers suffocated him in a choke hold in 2014, even though he was unarmed. The phrase had been uttered by dozens more Black men in ensuing years during police stranglings, and had now become a rallying cry at Black Lives Matter protests. It was a reminder of the choke hold that racism still held on our people, and on the nation.

* * *

ROBERT WAS HOSPITALIZED two more times for not being able to breathe. He had several COVID-19 symptoms, but he kept testing negative for the virus.

During this time, we kept our phone conversations short and stayed in touch mostly through texts and Messenger. After Robert came home from the hospital the third time, I checked in to see how he was doing, and he sent me a series of long texts. We were living through our own chapter of history in the present, but we still connected most fully through our interest in the past.

> I'm doing well. Must be honest, I've kind of lost focus, but this week's plan is to share with a cousin (on my mother's side) my perspective of growing up within the community where my family had been held as slaves. What a contrast between my Banneker-Lett & Sleet families. I can only trace ancestry on my mother's Sleet family to 1800, which was the birth year of both my great great grandmother and grandfather. Whereas through the Banneker-Lett's Molly, we can trace her arrival to the late 1600's.
>
> My Sleet family's fifty years of life was lived within the bounds of slavery until my great great grandmother purchased her own freedom, and later in 1856 purchased her husband, delivering John Simon Sleet from slavery. At that point John Simon & Viney (Luevenia's) story includes their acquisition of a small farm before the Civil War and John Simon owning his own blacksmithing business and serving as a minister after the end of slavery. Two of their sons served in the Civil War in the United States Colored Troops Regiments. Both were present at Appomattox Court House for the surrender of Robert E. Lee. My own great grandfather was the son of the white slave master and Viney.
>
> These similarities in the family histories reflect the activism of strong women. A history which includes activism in regards to ending slavery. And deep traditions of religious faith.
>
> I am so blessed. WE are so blessed. Hugs!

"We *are* so blessed!" I responded. "And these two separate but connected histories are so interesting."

Robert responded:

> Yes, I have grown up with the awareness of family history, and these stories which motivated me to research further. But the truth is, while I have found my ancestors remarkable, I am remiss for not realizing their stories' significance to others. Of course, I will share

these stories with you. I too find it remarkable that my genealogy from both my mother and father each stem from owner and slave relationships. One story became a love relationship (Molly and Bana'ka), as an early free family of mixed ancestry and color. There is a trail left of their lives which we are able to document. The details of the other relationship (Luvenia and Weedon) are lost to history, but that was another owner and slave relationship. Their son, Robert Luevines Sleet, married another woman of Boone County Kentucky, Eva Mae Arnold Sheets Sleet, also of mixed-race ancestry.

Most remarkably, it is through the acts of the white Sleet family that the relationship between "Viney" and Weedon is confirmed. Weedon's will bequeaths property or money to each of his children. But it also includes Robert Luevines, without designation as a son, but following the gifts to his children. Robert is the only person of color included in the will, and Weedon gives him his watch.

The second confirming story of this ancestry is a collage of children's innocence and friendship in segregated schools. The grandchildren of Robert Luevines' son, also Robert, known as "Bud" Sleet, walked several miles to their Black schoolhouse in Beaver Lick, Kentucky. Often accompanying them were white children from neighboring farms who walked the same tobacco roads to their white school. There was an argument between the Sleet children that stemmed from the white Sleet children calling their Black Sleet friends "cousin." After a few days of the argument, my mother and her older brother asked their mother if they were related to those "white Sleet kids." My grandmother's response to her children's question was as follows, "You better go ask your daddy about that . . . those are his people."

So some white people did *know that they were related to their Black cousins across town*, I thought. I was grateful that Robert felt comfortable sharing these stories with me. And I noticed that his close encounter with death had made him even more reflective and eloquent than usual. "I've always framed myself as an eternal optimist," he wrote later that day.

Perhaps my perspective and patience were hewn within the solitary childhood I experienced in rural Boone County, Kentucky. I found answers, and if not answers, a resolution while lying upon my back amid tall grass and weeds or walking in tall corn and looking up where the appearance of the earth's greenery touched the sky.

As my very religious aunt would share, "We will have our answers in time."

Still within the Tall Grass,
Cousin Robert

CHAPTER 19

Keeping Time

Baltimore County, Maryland, 1730s–1760s

We meet those whom we left as children and can hardly persuade our-selves to treat them as men. The traveler visits in age those countries through which he rambled in his youth, and hopes for merriment at the old place.

—Banneker's Almanac of 1792

ROBERT BANNEKER WAS a brilliant farmer, a devoted husband to Mary, and a loyal son-in-law to Molly, but he took the greatest delight in the mind of his son. Robert would spend the morning making up a mathematical riddle, and then Benjamin would spend an hour or two solving it. The little boy would be out in a field, hoeing or weeding, and would run up to his father with the answer, rocking up on his toes with excitement. Robert was ever proud of that boy's mind. He cultivated it in endless questions, and bought him quills, an inkwell, and good writing paper when Benjamin was still a child.

Even as a small boy, Benjamin was passionate about learning. On Sundays, Grandmother Molly would read the Bible aloud to the family and then pass the book to Benjamin so he could work on his elocution. Martha Tyson wrote that Benjamin's "bright mind made him a great favorite with his grandmother, who found much pleasure in imparting to him all her small stock of knowledge in the department of letters. She much desired he should grow up a religious man, in furtherance of which view it was her delight to have him read to her from a large Bible which she had imported from England."

After Molly taught Benjamin to read, she paid for him to attend a small Quaker school that had been established in the area. In this school, white and Black children were taught side by side. Jacob Hall, another free person of color and Benjamin's lifelong friend, said that, as a boy, Benjamin was "never fond of play or any light amusement. All his delight was to dive into his books." Benjamin was only able to take a couple of winters away from the farm for this formal schooling, but the schoolmaster, William Heinrich, was so impressed with Benjamin's intelligence and curiosity that he went on meeting with his former pupil and lending him books. Benjamin continued to study, reading across subjects and practicing mathematical puzzles throughout his childhood and teens, until he had "advanced in arithmetic as far as Double Position," which is similar to algebra and was considered advanced mathematics at that time.

Benjamin's education was possible because the Bannekers were living in an area of Maryland that was being settled by Quakers. The Quakers were a society-within-a-society—a counterculture that believed in the equality of the sexes, education, pacifism, and, in many congregations, the abolition of slavery. Quakers believed in inner listening, in quaking before God, and taught that anyone could become a mouthpiece for morality and for the divine. For decades, the Quaker Church was engaged in internal debates about slavery, and by the 1750s, antislavery advocates within the church had convinced the Quakers to officially forbid congregants to purchase enslaved people.

These debates asked all Quakers to grapple with the immorality of slavery, and to see people of color as fellow human beings capable of good works, learning, and industry. The growing population of free people of color in the region, like the Banneker family, gave further credence to these ideas of Black potential. Their upstanding participation in the community, alongside their Quaker neighbors' abolitionist leanings, allowed them to live side by side with a safety and respect that would have been impossible in most counties.

Elsewhere in the South, dependence on slavery was increasing, plantations were becoming larger, and colonies were organizing militias to control the "enemy within"—which meant Black people, whether they were free or enslaved. These militias were made up of white men who policed people of color with brutal methods of surveillance, capture, torture, and lynching. Free people of color were often targeted by such patrollers, because they troubled the racial hierarchies that these militias were invested in maintaining. But the presence of powerful and respected Quakers around the Upper Patapsco neighborhood protected the Bannekers from most of these harassments.

* * *

WHEN BENJAMIN WAS in his early twenties, he borrowed a pocket watch from a friend of Robert's, and when everyone in the family was asleep, he took the watch entirely apart. Robert scolded him afterward, saying he was foolish to disrespect property in that way. Especially as an African man, he reminded him. Didn't he know what could happen to someone of their complexion who disrespected property? But Benjamin cared for property mostly to the extent that it preserved his freedom. What he loved most was the life of the mind.

Similarly, what fascinated Benjamin about the watch was not the face, with its Roman numerals and mother-of-pearl inlay, but the gears inside. When he was a boy, his father had put a stick in the ground and taught Benjamin to watch as the stick's shadow traveled in a smooth circle over the course of the day. Now, Benjamin marveled at a technology that could mechanize these natural rounds of time. He delighted in watching the way the clock's tiny notched gears moved the larger gears, the way the minutes moved the hours, and hours moved the days, eventually cycling into weeks and months. He had been observing the cycles of the moon and the sun throughout his life, and he appreciated how the circular logic of the clock resembled their movements. In it, he could see the regularization of what he observed in nature—the way everything moved forward through cycles and relationships, the way each notch was both delineated and specific, and part of an ongoing round.

Benjamin stayed up all that night, carefully dismantling the watch. He drew detailed sketches of its gears and noted the way that they were arranged and held in place. Then he used a mathematical extrapolation to determine the appropriate enlargement of each gear, keeping the ratios between them the same. He stared into the watch and memorized it, before carefully putting it back together again, screw by minuscule screw. Then, after he had returned the timepiece to his father's friend, he selected pieces of hard, cured wood and carved each of the gears to precision. Two gears cracked in the process, and he had to begin carving them all over again. He had to learn patience and focus, although his mind was always leaping ahead with intuition and enthusiasm. He learned that if he worked at something every day without distraction, even in the slender hours after his farm chores were finished, something meaningful would be accomplished.

In 1753, at twenty-two years old, Benjamin had carved a working wooden clock that successfully kept time and struck the hours. It was one of the first clocks in the region and represented the latest technology. His father had farmed hundreds of acres and had built them a home, but Benjamin had designed a clock. It hung in their cabin proudly as a symbol of the stature the family had achieved—not by birthright, inheritance, or formal education but by the grace of God, Robert said, and by the strength of their minds and efforts. Benjamin's parents delighted in the clock and marveled at him—this bright son of theirs. There was so much more they wished they could give him. Safety in a world that was growing even crueler to people who looked like them. An ironclad promise of freedom. More education. New laws were being passed that made lives like theirs more difficult, including laws confining all free people of color to their own counties. But Benjamin's mind would not be confined.

The clock and the young man who made it became the talk at outfitters and mills, in coffeeshops and taverns. People came to visit after that, traveling miles out of their way or stopping over on their journeys to get a look at the clock and to hear Benjamin explain how it worked. Benjamin always greeted his visitors warmly, serving them cider or peach melby and offering them a detailed description of the clock's creation. He was proud of what he had made, and he suspected that he was being examined alongside his clock. He understood that he was himself a curiosity—a well-read Black man who understood the latest technology, and who could hold forth on politics, history, poetry, and science.

This recognition changed Benjamin's life, and it changed the life of the family as well. They were already well known in the area because of Robert's thriving farm, the size and success of which were exceedingly rare in a time when only 40 percent of free white men in Maryland owned their own land. But now they became even more conspicuous— because someone in their family had been recognized for his intellect. It brought the Bannekers a little more safety as free people of color, and a little more danger too. Most small farmers and laborers, of any ethnicity, were unable to read or write at that time, and so a man of African descent with such learning attracted white envy, disbelief, and backlash. But Benjamin was obsessed with learning and generally too occupied with his scientific queries to be worried about such things. He went on studying, writing, and putting aside thoughts about who could or could not do what.

If Benjamin Banneker had been "of a different complexion," to use the phrasing he and Robert preferred, someone would have seen that clock and sent him off to Harvard or Oxford. But none of that transpired. Instead, he went on studying, reading, and solving mathematical equations in the dark hours after farming. He felt a burning need to read books by the thinkers of the day, to record what he had observed, and to compose riddles, equations, and poems. He sometimes received admiring letters from people who had heard about his clock, and he began corresponding with mathemeticians and other writers he admired.

But the intellectual conversation that meant the most to Benjamin was with his father, Robert. Robert and Benjamin had kindred minds marked by spiritual devotion, wide-ranging curiosity, and intellects that would not rest. Robert Banneker died on July 10, 1759, after he had achieved even more than he had set out to. He had been kidnapped as a boy from Africa, had been enslaved in the Americas, and had gone on to earn his freedom and farm more than one hundred acres, providing well for his wife and children. All of Mary and Robert's children were grown by the time of his death, and Benjamin was twenty-eight years old. According to Martha Tyson and the family stories, Robert Banneker left his widow, Mary, and his son, Benjamin, the dwelling in which they lived and seventy-two acres of land. The rest of his land he divided among his daughters.

But after Robert died, Benjamin was not the same. All the responsibilities of farm management fell to him and Mary, and he felt distracted and burdened by material matters. He stopped writing for a time, and everything he observed in nature only made him feel sad because his father was not there to share in his observations. Benjamin stopped recording ideas in his journal, and fell into an inarticulate depression. He had loved to make scientific observations and express his thoughts with an eloquent turn of phrase, which he knew would delight Robert. He had been his father's hopes incarnate. Now, with no one to share that hope with, and no one who would even believe the extent of his intelligence given the color of his skin, what would be the point?

In time, Benjamin's grief abated. His sisters all married, and he and his mother stayed on at the farm, developing a new closeness. Eventually, Benjamin realized that he would have to learn to make the most of his days as his father had done. Winters on the farm were dark months, marked by extra sleep, corn to grind, clothes to mend, and a bone-whittling cold that blew through the cracks in the cabin walls. Most folks talked about just getting through the winters, but Benjamin looked forward to them—for the solitude, and for the way that the cold kept the cloud cover down and made all the stars shine more brightly. He thought of winter as his season of thinking, the season when the outer world quieted down, and he could do his most important work of observing the cosmos, studying astronomy, and reflecting on what he'd learned.

Benjamin had gleaned much of his knowledge from reading English books, but his understandings also included African cosmology and an experiential awareness of the cycles of nature. He loved reading and study, but he also learned directly from his own observations. In his one surviving journal, Benjamin wrote about the seventeen-year cycle of the cicadas, years before this pattern was acknowledged by European naturalists. In April 1800, he observed the following:

The first great locust year that I can remember was 1749. I was then about seventeen years of age, when thousands of them came and were creeping up the trees and bushes. I then imagined they came to eat and destroy the fruit of the earth, and would occasion a famine in the land. I therefore began to kill and destroy them, but soon saw that my labour was in vain, and therefore gave over my pretension.

Again in the year 1766, which was seventeen years after their first appearance, they made a second, and appeared to me to be full and numerous as the first. I then, being about thirty-four years of age, had more sense than to endeavor to destroy them, knowing they were not so pernicious to the fruit of the earth as I imagined they would be. Again in the year 1783, which was seventeen years since their second appearance to me, they made their third; and they may be expected again in the year 1800, which is seventeen years since their third appearance, so that I may venture to express it, their periodical return is seventeen years.

Benjamin was never satisfied to simply make an observation, however. He described what he saw in detail and then reflected on its meaning in philosophical and poetic language, accessing the literal fact of a situation as well as its metaphors. "They, like the comets, make but a short stay with us," he went on, describing the locusts.

The female has a sting in her tail as sharp and hard as a thorn, with which she perforates the branches of the trees, and in the holes lays eggs. The branch soon dies and falls. Then the egg, by some occult cause immerges, [sic] a great depth into the earth, and there continues for the space of seventeen years as aforesaid. I like to forgot to inform, [sic] that if their lives are short they are merry. They begin to sing or make a noise from first they come out of the earth, 'til they die. The hindermost part rots off, and it does not appear to be any pain to them, for they still continue on singing 'til they die.

Benjamin's passion for learning—writing poems, studying astronomy, and recording naturalistic insights—was his way of singing, even if few people heard him. In the same journal, Benjamin observed the flashing light of the star Sirius and hypothesized that this meant that the star was actually two stars rotating around each other. It would be sixty years before German astronomer Friedrich Wilhelm Bessel would make this ingenious "discovery" in 1844. And yet the Dogon priests of Mali in Western Africa had long taught that Sirius flashed because an object circulated around it. The Dogon's ancient cosmology also took note of the rings around Saturn, the existence of Jupiter's four inner moons, and the fact that the planets, including Earth, make elliptical orbits around the sun. Whether this knowledge was passed down to him literally from his father, or passed down intuitively, as a hunch based on intergenerational remembrance, Benjamin Banneker's astronomy made ingenious use of both European and African systems of knowledge. We can only wonder what Banneker's other journals recorded about the natural world and can only guess at all that was lost in the fire that burned his papers.

Before the grandeur of nature and space, Benjamin was endlessly curious and deeply humble. His humility was not born out of any servile human shame but out of awe, out of his awareness of man's small part in the vast and marvelous universe. It was his feeling that to be human, to be alive at all, to be here on this earth under this sun instead of another, was statistically miraculous. When Benjamin lay on his back and looked up at the stars, he understood that each was a sun at the center of its own huge solar system. He peered into expanses of space that he understood were also expanses of time, and he felt the strife of human failings falling away. All those questions of wealth and poverty, race and power, seemed to him to be nothing more than the playthings of children, of beings that had a long way to go on their travels toward the sun.

* * *

WHEN BENJAMIN WAS in his forties, the Ellicott family moved to Elkridge Landing, which was just a few short miles from the Banneker farm. The Ellicotts were Quakers who hailed from Pennsylvania and had come to the banks of the Patapsco River in Maryland to set up a wheat-milling enterprise. The soil of the Chesapeake had been depleted from exclusive tobacco production, and tobacco farmers were losing money rapidly. The Ellicotts set out to convince local planters to turn to wheat, promising to construct mills that would store it, grind it, and provide it for sale in bulk markets. The Ellicott family were highly industrious and inventive, and in time they would develop new irrigation methods, a brake for wagons, lime fertilizer, and other innovations for surrounding farmers. As Quakers, they were far less hemmed in by prejudice than most white people. A few of the Ellicotts were enslavers, but most were abolitionists, and they lived and worked alongside people of color harmoniously, employing them in their stables and mills as wage earners.

Benjamin watched the construction of Ellicott's Mills with curiosity, fascinated by the state-of-the-art machinery of the gristmill and the new efficiencies of the mill's automation. He began to frequent the outfitters' shop that sprang up beside the mill and that functioned as a consignment store, a mail stop, and an informal meetinghouse. There he would sell his signature honey and preserves and stay on to read the newspapers and chat with the neighbors. Sometimes he would also cross the low stone bridge outside the outfitters and walk up the steep hill to the Quaker meetinghouse. Benjamin had an antique way of talking, much like the Quakers themselves, always using the biblical *thee* and *thou*, because he read the Bible daily.

"When he could be induced to lay aside the modest reserve for which he was conspicuous, all were pleased to listen to him," remembered Martha Tyson. "His mind was filled with volumes of traditionary lore, from which he would relate various anecdotes of the first occupation of the country by the emigrants; their disappointments and difficulties, and final successes; when, ceasing their own fruitless search for gold, they settled down to the cultivation of the soil." Benjamin understood himself to be a full citizen of that land, and he enjoyed telling stories and connecting current events with their historical underpinnings.

Soon his mother, Mary, was also recognizing new social and business opportunities in Ellicott's Mills. She and Benjamin rented out a few acres of their farmland to small farmers, and then converted much of their remaining land to orchards and vegetable plots, and they agreed to grow some wheat, as the Ellicotts suggested. Mary baked breads, made tinctures and salves, grew vegetables, and carted preserves, produce, and fresh eggs over to the outfitters and the mill to feed the men who worked there.

"The fame of Banneker's clock had been the cause of an early acquaintance between him and his miller neighbors," explained Martha Tyson, remembering how her family, the Ellicotts, first befriended the Bannekers. "They found him and his mother living together in great comfort and plenty. The boarding-houses for the workmen who erected the mills, and other buildings for Ellicott & Co., were largely supplied with provisions from the farm of Banneker. His mother, Mary Banneker, attended to the marketing, bringing for sale poultry, vegetables, fruit and honey."

After meeting Benjamin at the outfitters and conversing with him about politics, one of the younger members of the Ellicott family, George, came out to call on Benjamin at the farm. George Ellicott was just a child when his family first arrived in Maryland, and was, like Benjamin had been, a precocious and scientifically minded boy. When he was just seventeen, George surveyed the road that would become the National Turnpike between Frederick and Baltimore, Maryland, and was able to trim three miles from the old route. Although Benjamin was forty-seven and George was eighteen at the time of that first visit, they began their close friendship that afternoon. George began lending Benjamin books, and after they had both absorbed a volume, the two men would sit discussing its ideas late into the evening, unconcerned with their differences and brightly excited to be sharing their interests and intellects.

As he had known with his late father, Benjamin knew that he had met his mental match, although George Ellicott had the advantage of the wider white world of learning and access. George respected Benjamin's intellect, which seemed to him one of the most agile and observant he had known. The two men exchanged mathematical puzzles, poems, and naturalistic observations, and found the kind of kinetic friendship that happens when both mind and soul are advanced by another's.

CHAPTER 20

Letter Carriers

Baltimore, Maryland, and Evanston, Illinois, November 2020

GWEN AND I had both come to look forward to our biweekly visits on Zoom. It was a November Sunday, dully gray outside my window, and just slightly greener in Maryland. Gwen was on her sun porch, wearing a purple batik caftan, and I was drinking tea in my home office, wrapped in a fuzzy cardigan. There was a heaviness in the air as we headed into winter, still inside, still in quarantine. If it were not for COVID-19, I knew I would have traveled to meet these cousins, to sit with Gwen in her sunroom. Instead, the situation had forced us onto Zoom, but we probably talked more often, and more intimately, than we would have in person.

"I don't know if you want to return to any of the subjects that we were opening up last time we talked," I said to Gwen, "but I would love to hear more about your father. You painted such a vivid picture of growing up in Cincinnati. And I was moved by what you said about the men in your community being educated, but unable to find work or achieve their full potential because of racism."

"I will talk about it." Gwen smiled. "As usual, you and I are spiritually connected. I wrote about my father just this past week. His birthday is in November, and as we came into November, I started to feel his presence. Have you seen any pictures of the family at all?"

"I've seen a lot of pictures on Facebook, but I don't remember if I've seen your dad," I said.

"So the main thing about my father is that he absolutely looked white," Gwen began. "I mean, there was nothing about his physical features that would indicate that he was Black. He had very straight white men's hair."

I nodded, listening.

"He grew up on a farm outside of Lima," Gwen continued. "He was the oldest son, and his father died early, so my father became the head of the household. He left the farm at a very young age to make money to support his mother and the rest of the children. Do you know what a truck farm is?"

"Yes, I grew up around farms in rural Ohio," I said. I remembered my grandparents' yellow painted table, arranged with baskets of shining strawberries, stacks of sweet corn.

"Okay, so my father drove a horse and wagon into Lima, Ohio, and he sold the vegetables that they grew. He would tell stories about eating all of those fruits and vegetables and learning to cook with his mother. In the summer, breakfast was always a fruit pie with cream on it. Eventually, my father left the farm to make more money, and went to Detroit to work in a car factory. I'm assuming it was Ford. He lost part of his thumb at that factory. I think that was why he left and came back to Ohio."

"He worked at Ford just before you were born?" I asked. I was feeling a faint vibration moving from the top of my head down to my hands. This happened to me sometimes when I was talking with my cousins—a resonance in which something they said about their lives echoed in my own body. My father had worked at Ford too, just before I was born.

"Yes, my father worked at Ford before I was born in 1932," Gwen said. "I have pictures of those early cars. I also have a picture with him standing beside a very early airplane—you know, one of those biplanes that was open on the top."

"I'm sorry to interrupt, but I'm feeling the presence of my grandfather so powerfully right now," I said. I hated to intrude on Gwen's memories, and I felt weird about interjecting things about myself and my immediate family. In these conversations, I always tried to decenter myself and just listen. I figured we did not need more nostalgic stories about white people, but this one was my grandfather, and it was like I could feel him there in the room with me, standing just behind my right shoulder.

"My grandfather was one of the dearest people in my life," I began. My heart was beating. I was nervous, as if he were listening in on me or something. "He would have been your fourth cousin. He used to tell me a story of being a little boy and seeing the Wright brothers fly their first plane. He and his brothers and sisters all ran out into the field to see it, and it was astounding to them, to see a man up in the sky."

"When was your grandfather born?" Gwen asked.

"He was born in 1914," I answered. *And he passed away* this week, *twelve years ago*, I realized then, my eyes stinging.

"My father was born before the end of the nineteenth century," Gwen continued. "When he turned eighteen and left the farm, it was the 1920s. So his experiences all took place in the '20s, when everything was happening, before the Crash."

"That was the height of the Harlem Renaissance," I said, nodding. "An exciting time for your father."

"Yes, and my father was very popular, and had a good time," Gwen said, smiling. "But after he lost part of his thumb at the Ford plant, he came back to Ohio, and got a really good job working in Columbus at the Ohio State Capitol as the hatcheck person. He had to check the hats and coats in winter that belonged to the state representatives. I have a huge photograph of the Capitol workers. You know those old pictures that they took of like a hundred people that are two feet long?" She held out her hands.

"Yes, I've seen those," I said.

"Well, I have a picture of all of the government workers in Columbus, out in front of the Capitol building, with my father hidden in the photo because he looked white. There were no other Black people that did anything in those days at the Capitol. I don't even know if they were allowed to be janitors.

"I'm sure he got that job because he looked white and nobody would object to him being in the hatcheck room," Gwen continued.

"So my father worked doing many things, and over time, he picked up the knowledge of being an electrician. But he was not allowed to join the unions as a Black man, or to legally get an electrician's license. He did electrical work for neighbors and people in the colored community, but of course that was technically illegal because he didn't have a license. The reason we moved to Cincinnati from Columbus was because the Depression hit, and my father got a job as a sub on the mail truck at the Post Office."

"My dad and grandfather worked for the Post Office too," I said. There it was again, a feeling of vibration, of resonance.

"My father got that job the minute I was born," Gwen said. "We moved to Cincinnati and we lived with a family that my father had met through the Post Office. That Black Post Office community was such a huge source of support. And to this day, my oldest childhood friend is the daughter of the Post Office clerk that my father worked with. So when Trump was trying to do away with the Post Office this year, my friend and I were on the phone saying, our fathers must be turning over in their graves because they never, ever dreamed that the Post Office would be . . ."

"Threatened! It's a central institution," I said. "I know what you mean. My grandfather was the postmaster in our area, and then—just to give you a sense of all the echoes here—my dad's first job was at Ford. But then he lost that job, and the week my mom got pregnant with me, he went to work for the Post Office. My dad was the first generation to go to college in his family. He and his sisters graduated from Kent State, and his first jobs were in offices at Ford and U.S. Steel. It was one of his first weeks on the job when the shooting happened, just outside his dorm at Kent."

"My cousin went to Kent State, and he was never the same after that shooting," Gwen said.

"It changed everything for my dad too," I said. "The news came over the radio while he was at work. First they heard that there had been a protest and some people had been shot and killed, and the entire office went silent. Then they announced that the National Guardsmen were unharmed and that the protesters had been shot, and my dad's boss stood up and cheered. This man had a cup of little American flags on his desk, and he started waving one of those flags, saying that those kids got what they deserved for protesting.

"My dad was very shaken up," I continued. "The shooting had happened just outside the dorm where he lived. He knew many people who were there that day. My dad and my grandfather got into huge arguments after that. They had always been really close, but my grandfather sided with the Republicans and said that the kids got what they deserved for protesting. 'Dad, that could have been me!' my dad would say to him. 'They weren't doing anything wrong.' That shooting and the war in Vietnam marked a generational divide in my family, and a loss of innocence for my dad. He could never fully believe in the industrial-military American myth after that. Just a few months later, the recession hit, and my dad lost that office job. He could not shake that image of his boss waving a little American flag, celebrating the killing and wounding of his classmates, and he felt repelled and intimidated by the corporate world. So when my mom got pregnant with me, he went and got a job at the Post Office."

Gwen was looking into my eyes, listening. It felt good to share some of my family's stories, after she had shared so much of herself with me.

"So, for me, growing up," I continued, "there was always a bit of a disconnect because my dad is one of the smartest people I know, but he had a job as a mailman and some of his friends who went on to white-collar careers looked down on that. There was a disappointment in him that I picked up on as a child, a sense that he hadn't gotten to live out his potential or ambitions. But he loved being outside walking all day, and he had lots of time for us. He loved being a parent and was very involved in our lives growing up."

"My father was around all the time too," Gwen said, nodding. "I realize this now, because my mother went to work. But my father was always there when I got home from school."

"My mom worked too," I said. "I was proud of her for that. And my dad would spend hours after he got home from his mail route, playing board games with us, or playing catch with my brother and his friends. My aunt would send her kids to Ohio for a few weeks in the summers, and my dad and my other aunt, Laurel, would watch us all."

Gwen nodded.

"So when all this happened with Trump wanting to get rid of the Post Office," I continued, "my dad called me and said, 'You should write an essay about the Post Office, because people don't know what we really do.'

"'Okay,' I said, 'what *do* you really do?' And he said, 'We are part of the community. A lot of times we're the only people who will see an elderly person all day or week, and we'll make sure they come to the door, or get their medication in the mail. We check up on people.'"

"I know what you mean," Gwen said excitedly. "My father knew everybody in our neighborhood. He knew everyone's business. And my father, who was able to be home with me, also served as a mentor to a friend of mine, whose father happened to be a doctor. He was a Black doctor who was never home. My friend used to say, 'Oh, I wish Mr. Jones was my father. I love him so much.'"

"He sounds wonderful," I said. "And the Post Office was important to the community."

"I mean, my God, you have opened up a whole bunch of memories. You've reminded me of that part of Black history," Gwen said. "The Post Office was an important part of Black history."

"Yes, I've heard the Postal Service described as a stepping-stone to the middle class for Black families," I said.

"That's exactly right," Gwen agreed, "because it was one of the only government jobs that Black people could have, and eventually postal workers were able to buy a house, to own a home on a street with a yard, and all that was a big deal."

"It's huge," I said. "My grandfather was so proud of his home and yard. He was your dad's cousin in this line, but I don't think he knew this history."

"My father didn't know he was related to Benjamin Banneker," Gwen said.

"But my grandfather did not even know that he had African American ancestry," I said. "The passing happened two generations before him. It started happening on paper with his great-grandmother Susan Lett, who was said to be a dark-skinned woman. After the Civil War, Susan and her siblings moved to Lake County, Ohio, where my family still lives. Two of the Letts married two of the Beebes, who were white. These brothers-in-law were both named Hiram and lived next door to each other, but one had fought in the "Colored Regiment" of the Civil War and the other had fought in the white regiment. On the censuses, Susan and her siblings were listed as 'mulatto,' until the last census of her life, when she was listed as white.

"My grandfather was a letter carrier, but he also farmed," I went on. "He had a few acres behind the house, where he grew all of our food. He did not know the history of the Lett family—how often they were driven from their land, how many times they had to start over, clear the fields, and begin again. But I do know that he never took for granted the chance to grow our food, on his own land."

"Yes, you know, even in Cincinnati, my father had a garden," Gwen remembered. "When we first moved to the house I was really young, but I do remember that he planted raspberries right away. So I was able to go out and pick raspberries, and put them on my cereal. And when the war came, he did a victory garden, and we always had plenty of vegetables. I was a vegetable eater. I didn't eat meat as a child."

"Me either." I smiled. I felt again that Gwen and I would have been friends at any time, in any place.

"What is happening with me," Gwen said, "is that my brain is being awakened. All this writing and talking with you and having to remember and then *wanting* to remember. I'm okay now with letting my mind daydream so that I can come up with these little snippets, like a fragrance or a slight memory, that makes it all real again."

"I love all the connections that are here," I said.

"Just think what it would be like if we could have a retreat with all of our cousins!" Gwen was smiling, widening her arms majestically.

"I want to picture it!" I said. "All of us having an in-person reunion. But I think my brain might explode!" I laughed. I was feeling an elatedness that often ended with a blinding tangle of tension in the center of my forehead. It felt like an attunement, like I was being expanded, harmonizing with something more than what I could rationally understand.

"It always feels like it is more than just us in the conversation," I said.

CHAPTER 21

Revolution

Chesapeake, 1760–1780s

Sir, suffer me to recall to your mind that time in which the Arms and tyranny of the British Crown were exerted with every powerful effort, in order to reduce you to a State of Servitude; look back I entreat you on the variety of dangers to which you were exposed, reflect on that time in which every human aid appeared unavailable . . . and you cannot but be led to a Serious and grateful Sense of your miraculous and providential preservation. . . . Here, Sir, was a time in which your tender feelings for your selves . . . impressed [you] with proper ideas of the great valuation of liberty.

—Banneker's letter to Thomas Jefferson, 1791

WHENEVER THE FAMILY got together for reunions, there were always some children who would run off and hide from their mothers, just to steal a little more time with their cousins. Some would go and sit by the creek, shoulder to shoulder, not even saying much, just tossing rocks and storing up a feeling until they could see each other the next time. Jemima and Samuel were like that, especially once they were close to being grown and knew how they felt about each other.

Jemima Banneker and Samuel Delaney Lett are the ancestors all of us in the Banneker-Lett family descend from. According to oral histories, Samuel's family name was originally Delaney and he was of "combined English, Irish, and Indian descent." His mother was a white woman who was widowed and married Zachariah Lett when

Samuel was a little boy. Samuel looked up to Zachariah so much that he took his stepfather's name, became known as Samuel Delaney Lett, and thereafter identified as a person of color. We now may assume that Zachariah was Mary's son from her first marriage, and so Samuel would have been a kind of step-cousin to Jemima—a relative not by birth, but part of the extended family. Marriages within and among allied families were common in free families of color, because there were relatively few people in the colonies whom they could legally marry, and few who enjoyed the same rights and liberties. For this reason, free families of color remained close-knit and became connected not only through their values and culture but through their marriages and descendants.

Jemima and Samuel's wedding may have taken place on Banneker land in the spring of 1757. Samuel's people would have been there—his mother, also named Mary, his stepfather Zachariah, and his siblings. Jemima's sisters, Minta and Molly, and their mother, Mary, had likely spent all week cooking for the guests—honeyed ham and sweet potatoes, baked chicken, greens, cornbread, rolls, preserves, and fruit pies. Minta was known to be a skilled seamstress, so she had probably sewn her sister's wedding dress, and perhaps Samuel had worked overtime at the mill for a serge greatcoat that made him look especially tall and dignified. I imagine the young couple hardly noticed all the pomp, although they were glad for it. They kept catching each other's eye, because they just could not wait to be married.

Maybe Robert officiated the service himself—tall, dignified, his voice a little thick as he smiled down at his daughter. Maybe Mary sat back on a bench fanning herself, her heart swelling with a cautious hope. She had known Samuel since he was a boy and trusted that he would take good care of Jemima. She hoped that Samuel's light skin would help secure their children's freedom, but she resented the fact that she had to think this way at all. She loved the darkness of her husband, and she was sick of living in a colony that dispensed laws to people according to this cruel and absurd ranking that had nothing to do with worth or beauty. She remembered her own early life, with Sarah, Zachariah, and Deborah as babies—and she rubbed her wrist distractedly, recalling the feel of the stocks, the way standing in that wooden entrapment had put such a bend in her neck she thought she'd never hold her head up straight again. How children could ever be considered crimes, she would never understand.

Mary raised her head high and pulled her shoulders back. She was here, all right, she thought to herself. And here was Zachariah, her boy, with gray hair salting his beard, standing up as the stepfather of the groom. And here were tall Samuel and sweet Jemima making eyes at each other. Mary didn't hear much of the homily, because she was looking over her family, at each one of those children who had come from her body, and who would go on to have more children. She was saying prayers for their protection and thinking of the struggles and how far they'd come. They were here, all right, and free, and there was nothing anyone on some court could say about it.

After the service, everyone ate too much, Zachariah offered the guests his homemade moonshine, and Benjamin played his fiddle. He hit some sour notes, but even so, he played the way he did everything—with unusual skill and earnest enthusiasm. Every leg was bouncing, fingers were snapping, hands were clapping, and there was dancing that spun everyone into the early hours of morning. The family ate their fill and told their funniest stories, laughing until tears ran from their eyes.

According to the oral histories of those who knew them, Samuel and Jemima Banneker Lett were known as people of "good manners and indomitable energy," traits that they passed on to their nine children, eight of whom lived to adulthood. Their first son, Aquilla, arrived in 1757, and Jemima and Samuel poured their hopes into him. This was true of all of the children, but Aquilla and Meshach were the eldest who helped to bring the others up. Samuel and Jemima were devout Christians, and their children were given biblical names; Aquilla, meaning Eagle; Meshach, meaning Guest of the King; Elijah, meaning Jehova is God; Samuel, meaning God Has Heard; Mary "Mollie," meaning Bitter; Keziah "Kizzie," meaning Fragrant Tree Resembling Cinnamon; Peter, meaning Rock; and Benjamin, meaning the Son of my Right Hand.

Today, all of us in the Banneker-Lett family can trace which of these Letts we descend from. But what do we know about Jemima— the woman who gave birth to them and raised them, the sister of the famous Benjamin Banneker through which we trace this ancestry? She is a little like the woman Virginia Woolf called Shakespeare's sister— not the genius everyone knows of but the sister of genius. She too had her extraordinary gifts, but because she was a woman of color, not many of them were recorded. Her contributions can be traced most clearly through the values that were passed down through her descendants. Jemima was described as "a modest person, devoid of all pretense. She lived a quiet and simple life, exerting a strong influence on her children."

* * *

JEMIMA AND SAMUEL's children were part of the Revolutionary generation. Maryland had declared itself a sovereign state of the Union in 1776, and that year, Baltimore was chosen as the site of the Second Continental Congress. Jemima and Samuel's eldest son, Aquilla, turned eighteen that year, reaching his own independence just as the Declaration of Independence was published.

The first draft of that document shamed England for importing slavery to American shores and cited the sin of slavery as one of the primary reasons that the colonies had to become independent. In a passage later removed from the Declaration, the young, fiery writer, Thomas Jefferson, made direct charges against George III's slave trade. Jefferson called it a "cruel war against human nature itself, violating its most sacred right of life and liberty in the persons of a distant people who never offended him, captivating them and carrying them into slavery in another hemisphere." But that passage became too controversial to include, because so many lawmakers at the Continental Congress were enslavers, including Jefferson himself. These men had opulent households and plantation economies entirely reliant on the labor of enslaved people. And yet, even the edited version of the Declaration of Independence was so attuned to freedom, so fervent in its language against bondage, that many insisted that it was just a thinly disguised call for the outlawing of slavery.

Like most free families of color, Jemima, Samuel, and their children discussed this issue almost endlessly. Samuel believed that they could not establish a new country on the ideals of freedom while perpetuating slavery. Something that hypocritical would not be possible because it took the wind out of the Patriots' sails, he insisted. By that time, more than half a million people of African ancestry were living in the thirteen colonies, and most of them were enslaved. The abolition movement had begun earlier in the century, with Quakers and a few New England ministers speaking out against slavery, through arguments framed entirely in moral and theological terms. But by the 1770s, colonists had begun to use Enlightenment ideas of natural human rights to argue for freedom from British rule, and this language also provided new, secular arguments against slavery. It was hard to overlook the hypocrisy of colonists complaining about their "bondage" and "enslavement" to a foreign power while continuing to enslave African people. As Abigail Adams wrote in a letter in 1774, "it always appeared a most iniquitous scheme to me to fight ourselves for what we are daily robbing and plundering from those who have as good a right to freedom as we have."

The Revolution was outwardly about independence from England, and covertly about slavery, as the fate of both enslaved and free people of color became part of the national debate. In the beginning of the war, several Northern colonies began accepting people of color in their militia units, but white people in both the North and the South were afraid of arming Black people and giving them the tools for insurrection. Northern lawmakers were also wary of alienating the Southern slaveholding colonies, which they needed to support the cause of Revolution. On November 12, 1775, the Continental Congress formally declared that all Black people, either enslaved or free, were ineligible for military service.

Then Virginia's Royal Governor, Lord Dunmore, issued his proclamation: that any "indentured servants, Negroes or others" who deserted from their plantations and fought on the side of England would be given their freedom. An all-Black "Ethiopian Regiment" resulted from this call, comprised of more than eight hundred men who escaped from their plantations. Enslaved people continued to join Dunmore until he was defeated and forced to leave Virginia in 1776. And the idea that the British would grant liberation to enslaved people persisted until the end of the long War of Independence, leading at least ten thousand Black soldiers to join the British side during the Revolution.

Delegates at the 1776 Continental Congress accused Dunmore's offer of freedom as "tearing up the foundations of civil authority and government." Southern states were so panicked about enslaved people's desertion that they finally allied with the North to support the war against England. Maryland's government barred all correspondence and communication with the neighboring colony of Virginia, in hopes that the enslaved people of Maryland would not hear about Dunmore's offer. Some counties, like Dorchester on Maryland's Eastern Shore, went even further and forcibly disarmed all people of color, whether they were free or enslaved, confiscating their guns, bayonets, and swords. But they could not control the power or efficiency of oral communication. Black people in Maryland learned of Dunmore's proclamation quickly. Domestics listened to table talk and then passed it along to porters, coach drivers, nannies, and traveling musicians, who spread the latest news in an oral network that spanned counties and colonies. As two of Georgia's delegates to the Continental Congress confided to John Adams, "the slave network could carry news 'several hundreds of miles in a week or fortnight.'"

Eventually, even General George Washington came to believe that the side to win the war would depend on "which side can arm the Negroes faster." By December 31, 1776, he was busy convincing Congress to agree to the enrollment of free Black men in the army while continuing to exclude enslaved people from military service. Around five thousand Black men, most of whom were already free like Samuel and Jemima's sons, joined the Continental army, mostly in Northern regiments.

A letter from Alexander Hamilton to John Jay on March 14, 1779, indicates that these questions of arming and emancipating enslaved people were still being debated well into the war. Hamilton proposed that the Patriots enlist two to four battalions of "negroes" from North Carolina, with support from that state's government. "I foresee that this project will have to combat some opposition from prejudice and self-interest . . . !" Hamilton admitted. "The contempt we have been taught to entertain for the blacks, makes us fancy many things that are founded neither in reason nor experience; and an unwillingness to part with property *of* so valuable a kind, will furnish a thousand arguments." Still, he insisted that it was essential to involve Black soldiers in the War of Independence. "It should be considered that if we do not make use of them in this way, the enemy probably will," Hamilton concluded. "An essential part of the plan is to give them their freedom with their muskets."

* * *

THE BANNEKER-LETT FAMILY would have known about these debates and wondered what they would mean for people like them—free people of color, whose citizenship and safety remained both uncommon and precarious. Their region of the Chesapeake was not at the center of Revolutionary fighting but provided the colonies' most valuable exports, making up nearly 50 percent of all exports to Britain. During the war, the British embargoed the tobacco trade in a strategy to destroy the Chesapeake's wealth and credit, but by that time, many small farmers like the Bannekers and Letts had diversified into other crops. The Banneker-Lett family was glad that they had gone from growing tobacco to wheat by then. Wheat was in dire need in the colonies, and it was a much less labor-intensive crop than tobacco. Tobacco required care at every stage of its cultivation, and its economic model relied upon cheap or enslaved labor. But it was possible to raise wheat on smaller, family farms. Oral histories say that the family grew wheat to feed the Continental army. And we know that corn and wheat from farms like theirs were sent to Annapolis and Philadelphia, to help feed the cities and the American troops.

During the war, Jemima and Samuel's family left Baltimore and moved forty miles west to Frederick County, Maryland. Land was scarce and becoming more expensive in and around Ellicott's Mills. Benjamin stayed on the original farmstead along with his mother and his sisters Minta and Molly and their families. But Samuel, Jemima, and their children headed farther west. They lived in a community with other mixed-race families—including the Calimans, the Stevens, the Normans, and the Browns, who would later migrate together to

Ohio. These families banded together to teach their children sewing, housekeeping, farming, blacksmithing, and construction—skills of artistry and self-sufficiency that were necessary for all, and doubly so in a world that continued to marginalize them. They grew their own food, and Samuel taught his sons blacksmithing to shod horses and make nails, hinges, chains, and bridle clips. They sawed their own logs and built their own houses, and the women did their own herbalism, treating, and midwifery.

On Sunday afternoons, Jemima and Samuel held school lessons, so all the children who wanted to could learn the basics of reading and writing. The families of the community helped one another and shared what they had, establishing a collective drive for excellence that was infused with a fierce form of hope. They knew they were next to invisible to the white world of cannon fire and brass buttons, but that did not mean they were invisible to one another. They raised one another's barns and houses. Raised one another's children too. They made quilts together, baked together, prayed and read the scripture together, and stayed up late on weekends playing music, dancing, and singing. They taught each other how important it was to live in community. You did it for survival. But also for joy.

On Sundays, they had the longest, most wonderful church services—first under the large oak tree, then later at the church they built themselves. On Wednesday evenings and all day Sunday, they would sing, feeling the Spirit moving their limbs, alighting on their heads, their chests flooding with light, casting out the clouds that had threatened them. Afterward, everyone gathered to eat sweet potato pie, collard greens, cornbread, venison spiced with pepper and sage. And sometimes a pig roasted for hours over the pit, the men taking turns sitting out the service to turn it while telling stories and smoking pipes. Everyone lived for those Sundays.

When talk of the war began, this community turned further inward, wary of sending their boys to fight for a colony that would just as soon enslave them as pay them. They knew what could happen, how even a free man of color could have his papers stolen so that he could not prove that he didn't belong to the white man who'd claimed him. Samuel was more hopeful, believing that if the Patriots won, they'd see slavery end in their lifetimes. They'd have long discussions at the Sunday gatherings, the men brainstorming about how new legislatures could work out the details of widespread manumission and reparations.

The women, meanwhile, would talk of more immediate things—children, recipes, and maladies—while piecing and quilting, or rolling out dough for pies. "I just don't know," Jemima would say when the men started arguing, shaking her head and pursing her lips. But secretly, she dreamed of it like a kind of rapture—the freeing of thousands of people, the reunification of families that had long been divided, the eradication of those ledgers that listed humans alongside property, as if a man were no more than a plow. She remembered how she'd longed to meet her father's mother, and wondered how many aunts or cousins she had whose names she didn't even know.

Aquilla and Meshach were caught up in the heady feeling of change, that heightened awareness that comes from knowing that history is being made in your very own lifetime. There was not enough glory in farming, some days, to satisfy these brothers, who daydreamed of winning valor in battle. "But those dreams are not ours anyway, as much as they are borrowed from others," Jemima would remind them. "There's a time to reap and a time to sow," she'd go on, "beat your swords into ploughshares, and be happy that you don't have blood on your hands. Be glad you only know the good kind of blood, the kind that comes from butchering hogs," she'd say softly.

Jemima would talk like this, her sons half listening but absorbing their mother's wisdom. Jemima was peaceful by nature and the bloodshed and waste of war sickened her. As a woman, she knew what it took to bring life into the world, so the thought of squandering it, boys upon boys falling to gunshots, cannon fire, and gangrene made her ill. She told her sons not to get caught up in the white man's battles. "Let them have it out with themselves," she'd say. But as the war dragged on one, two, three, on into seven years, she wondered how many would starve or go hungry for the privilege of "freedom" while so many went on laboring without it.

The Continental army, meanwhile, was crouching in ditches and sleeping in tents, sawing off boys' arms and legs where they'd been shot.

Just the stench of an army encampment could terrify a person. During the winter of Valley Forge, Aquilla was twenty and Meshach was nineteen. They heard the stories about it afterward—all those soldiers standing at attention in snow until their feet went dead, eating ash cakes made of nothing more than burnt sawdust. They weren't going through all that back on the farm. Currency had lost its value and there was always the worry that they would not be paid fairly for their work, but they were eating plenty, and working tirelessly, tending to their own acreage, and working as hired hands on the land of nearby white folks who were away fighting. Some of those men sent their enslaved men to die in their places, and some of those young men were the Lett brothers' friends.

One young man—Bazabeel Norman—came by one afternoon just after he had enlisted in place of his boss. He was proud, but frightened too, his dark eyes wide and wet with excitement. Jemima made a big fuss over him, sending him off with biscuits, hand pies, and a warm scarf. He was no more than a boy, she thought to herself. The family all walked with Bazabeel out to the yard and told him they'd be praying for his safety. Samuel took off his hat and said, "Come home to us, Son," and the boys made jokes about his aim. After he was safely out of earshot, Jemima looked at Aquilla with a stern look that meant "Don't go getting any ideas." They didn't know if they'd ever see Bazabeel again, but years later, they did. He came back from the war and was one of the few soldiers of color who was granted freedom in the new Northwest Territory of Ohio, as he'd been promised. It was partly on account of him that the Lett brothers decided to migrate to that county.

Jemima prayed more than she ever had during those long years of war, and she was someone who prayed all the time. She was forever quoting the Bible, bidding her children to remember the peace that passeth understanding. And although her conviction wasn't as strong as Samuel's, she had a little fledgling hope that the Revolution would mean freedom for her people. Her family and their community were proof of what would happen if people of color were simply given what white people were given—freedom, the chance to marry and have children, learn skills, and farm their own land.

* * *

THE BRITISH INVASION of the Chesapeake began with that blockade in 1777 that was intended to halt the delivery of wheat and other food to the rest of the colonies. The British then entered the region by water, with warships and private, armed vessels called "privateers" whose sailors came ashore and plundered houses, barns, storehouses, and shops. As the British ships moved into the bay and down the several rivers that make up the Chesapeake, they began to attract enslaved people who had heard Dunmore's promise of freedom. When the British battalion sailed into Maryland, along the Eastern Shore and Anne Arundel County, an onlooker noted, "Scarce a white person was to be seen, but 'negroes appeared in great abundance.'" These enslaved people had walked off their plantations, many of them taking canoes and rowboats to try to reach the ships. Others dove into the river and swam, being tossed and sometimes swallowed by the waters. Benjamin and his family would have known about this mass desertion, because the neighboring town of Elk Ferry, at the shallow mouth of the Patapsco, mobilized militias of people to watch for the wrecked canoes and boats of these fugitives. One scouting party discovered the bodies of five men, "drove ashore that was drowned going to the fleet."

The men had heard that the ships were coming closer and decided that, yes, that night, they had to make their escape. They had left under cover of darkness and followed the moonlight and stars to the river's edge. They carried their canoe over their heads, with provisions in flour sacks slung across their shoulders. Their women had packed those bags for them, filled them with cornbread, apples, and precious chestnuts. The men had flexed their hands with worry and impatience as they'd taken those bags, one kissing his wife goodbye, another bending to his children to tousle the tops of their heads, another making his face hard, looking into the distance, telling himself he was already gone from that place. They had set off for the river silently then, treading softly on the fallen leaves—a wild hope rising in them, as they stiffened at the sounds of the night and the hounds. Then they had done it, kicked off from the banks and into the current, rowing toward the British ships to offer their services in exchange for their liberty.

But something had gone wrong. Maybe the ship had cast them off, telling them they had no room for any more refugees, as the British ships sometimes did. Or maybe their canoe had cracked against the river rocks and taken on water before it could reach the ship. Either way, they had lost their bid for liberty and their very lives in the river where Benjamin and his father had loved to sit and fish.

Benjamin felt his stomach turn when he heard the news of the men, and thought of them, drowned and swollen, as the neighboring farmers pulled them roughly from the water. He was glad he had not been there to witness such a scene.

He walked away from the river now, across the fields, toward his favorite tree. He walked on his land most evenings, to bring some motion to his mind. But today his thoughts were dark and suffocating. He thought of the water swallowing the men, and of the war swallowing the region. The Revolution had arrived in the Chesapeake, and while officially it meant that the Americans were at war with the British, more immediately it meant that neighbors were distrusting neighbors, fighting one another. And people of color were, once again, snagged and entangled between them.

Benjamin walked until he felt his grief and anger sinking into the soil and his wonder returning. He lay down in the field and felt the calm of the earth soak into his back and tumble up and down along his spine. He could feel the pulse of the land moving like a heartbeat through his body, while he fiddled with a snail shell he had found in his pocket. He thought about how the spiral of the shell was repeated in the spiraling waves of stars in the galaxy.

Benjamin stayed like that until the sun went down and the sky deepened past indigo to a velvety black, illuminated by stars that were numberless and vast. Benjamin knew that every one of those stars was its own sun, a center of its own planetary realm. He knew that our universe was only one of many, and much older than the human species, much older than all the imperfect human systems that granted people privileges or stripped them away, that armed men or shackled them.

He stared so long at the sky that his perspective shifted and suddenly he felt himself to be of the stars and up among the forefathers, looking down to the little planet he lay upon. He saw from those distances our own earth, marbled with waters and crisscrossed with commerce, like the straps and shackles that cross a bound body. The tobacco trade, the rice trade, the sugar trade, and the trade in human cargo made the darkest crosses of all.

Benjamin knew that the same stars had been seen by his ancestors sitting around the fire in Africa, telling stories through their drums. He knew they would be seen by the descendants of those living looking up, centuries away in the future. He even understood that he would have to travel lifetimes to reach any of those other stars, those other solar systems that were complete unto themselves. He continued to expand his perspective out and out, watching the spiraling galaxies until early morning, until the sun rose to bless his brow with its age-old promise of constancy.

Then he got up, brushed himself off, and went home to read and write.

"To us, who dwell on its surface, the earth is by far the most extensive orb that our eyes can anywhere behold," he began reading, in his favorite essay by Joseph Addison—one he would later include in his first almanac. "Whereas to a spectator placed on one of the planets, it wears a uniform aspect, looks all luminous and no larger than a spot. To Beings who dwell at greater distances, it entirely disappears." The essay, and its reader, imagined life on other planets. It acknowledged the power and girth of our sun, but also knew that our own sun was still "a very little part of the grand machine of the universe; every star . . . is the centre of a magnificent system. . . . That the stars appear as so many diminutive and scarce distinguishable points, is owing to their immense and inconceivable distance."

In order to reach those stars, Benjamin posited, a cannonball would have to travel seven thousand years. Distance, in other words, was made up of both time and space, and to reflect on such an expanse was to feel a wondrous humility, a spaciousness that expanded the soul and made our own time-bound world seem small and flawed. "While beholding this vast expanse," Addison wrote, "I also discover the abject

littleness of all terrestrial things. What is the earth, with all her ostenta-
tiousness, compared with the astonishing grand furniture of the skies?
If then, not our globe only, but our whole system, be so very diminutive,
what is a kingdom or a country?"

What, Benjamin Banneker asked himself often in those years, is a
kingdom or a country?

* * *

AFTER THE REVOLUTION, people of color waited to see which promises
to them would be broken and which would be kept. Slavery was the
most contested issue at the country's first Continental Congress. But
as the votes came in, it became shockingly clear that Congress was not
going to outlaw slavery. Slavery had been depicted by many Patriots
as a moral aberration imported from England, and the new nation's
decision to legally continue it was a devastating blow to people of color.
Congress chose not to emancipate the country's existing enslaved people, and only agreed to outlaw the importation of newly enslaved people
beginning in 1800, which was later moved back to 1808.

This failure of the new government to live up to its ideals strained
the family's hope. When change did not come, it hurt Samuel and Jemima's sons. It hurt those who were enslaved far worse. It was a grievous
disappointment to Benjamin as well, who was in correspondence with
white scientists and thinkers, and who had wanted to believe that he
was included in their liberal, humanistic ideals. Like Jemima's husband
and sons, he had considered himself a Patriot. He had read the reprints
of the Declaration of Independence and the Constitution and had seen
in them a pattern of government that was better than all others, more
akin to the interlinking and harmonious patterns of nature, a system
able to check and balance itself, just as nature does.

The country's founders had created the most radical government
yet, one based on natural human rights rather than the divine right of
kings. They had stated that all men were created equal, and then suggested that government could create—like distributive properties—the
conditions to promote life, liberty, and the pursuit of happiness. But
Benjamin knew that there was a glaring hypocrisy in the Founders'

definition of equality. He had hoped that the government would not be laid atop this mistake, because, to him, it would be like failing to correct an error early in a mathematical equation, so all future outcomes are bound to be incorrect. In the same way he would want to correct a faulty equation, Benjamin burned to correct this flaw at the heart of the union.

There were three living generations of African Americans who had been prodded forward on a hope that now had been dashed. But the Revolution had given people a new, secular language for human rights and a new way to think about freedom, and after the war, Black Americans asserted that they deserved such freedoms themselves. The war gave African Americans a more cohesive identity as a people and furnished them with arguments about liberty that they would go on to use in their personal lives, in their communities, and in courtrooms. Sometimes this new awareness took the form of legal argument. Occasionally, it took the form of resistance on plantations. Most often, it took the form of cultural autonomy, as after the Revolution, Black Americans insisted on cultivating their own, distinct culture, establishing schools, gathering places, and churches, like the African Methodist Episcopal (AME) Church.

Meanwhile, one by one, states began to pass laws to free their enslaved people. The first state to free its enslaved people was Vermont in 1777. New York moved to gradually abolish slavery in 1799. By 1804, Pennsylvania, New Hampshire, Massachusetts, Connecticut, and Rhode Island had also outlawed slavery. Even the state of Maryland, one English traveler observed, was "rapidly giving way to emancipation," resulting in a growing population of free people of color like the Banneker and Lett families. Free people of color had comprised only 4 percent of Maryland's recorded population in 1755, but by 1810, they made up more than 20 percent of Maryland's population. Even Virginia—a state that had always made manumitting people legally almost impossible—began to ease its restrictions on liberation. Between 1782 and 1806, roughly ten thousand people of color were recorded as freed in that state, including many soldiers who had fought for the Continental army in the Revolution and had been granted freedom for their service, as promised.

As the numbers of free people of color increased, however, so did white legislative backlash. In Maryland, Black men who were landowners like Benjamin Banneker had long enjoyed provisional rights to vote and use the courts. But those rights were rescinded in 1783, when a new Maryland law stated that "no colored person freed thereafter, nor the issue of such, should be allowed to vote, or to hold any office, or to give evidence against any white, or to enjoy any other rights of a freeman than the possession of property, and redress at law, or equality for injury to person or property." This law not only removed the voting rights and rights to a fair trial for free people of color, it also stripped these people's offspring (their "issue") forever of those rights.

These laws influenced the Banneker-Lett family's decision to leave Maryland for the new Northwest Territory of Ohio. Samuel and Jemima's sons also noticed the presence of alarming new neighbors. In 1795, a French Catholic planter named Payen de Boisneuf moved to the Banneker-Letts' town of Frederick. Boisneuf was part of a family of sugar and coffee plantation owners who had fled Haiti after the country's enslaved people had revolted there and won their freedom. Boisneuf established a large plantation on a hill that occupied more than seven hundred acres in Frederick and exploited the labor of hundreds of enslaved people from both Haiti and the United States. His plantation used practices of torture and surveillance that were far more brutal than anything seen before in Maryland, even displaying the heads of lynched men as warning signs to other captives. The methods of this family were so violent that they were repeatedly brought to the Maryland courts and tried for the inhumane treatment of their enslaved people. The Polish traveler Julian Niemcewicz spent time in Frederick in June 1798 and recorded his driver's story about the plantation. "One can see on the home farm instruments of torture, stocks, whips, etc.," Niemcewicz wrote. "Two or three Negroes crippled with torture have brought legal action against [Payen Boisneuf], but the matter has not yet been settled."

The Banneker-Lett family would have heard of these horrific practices, and perhaps they worried—correctly—that these violent methods would soon come to characterize Southern plantations and large-scale American slavery. Maybe that was what convinced them that it was time to leave their beloved ancestral land of Maryland and travel to the new Northwest Territory of Ohio. The Banneker-Letts had raised five generations of people who had cultivated the land of the Chesapeake and had fed the Continental army. But it was going to become impossible to stay in the very state that they had helped to create.

CHAPTER 22

Toward the Setting Sun

Pasadena, California, and Evanston, Illinois, December 2020

"I REMEMBER BEING very young at a family reunion," Robert began, "and my dad lifting me up onto his shoulders and saying, 'Now, the old-timers are going to tell the story of the beginning of our family.'"

I was out for a quick walk, listening to Robert's warm, nostalgic voice on the phone. He had told me this story before, but the details changed a bit each time. Robert was the only one of us who had grown up going to Lett reunions and who had heard these stories as a child.

"This very old man walked out," Robert said. "He sat in a cane-back rocking chair and wore a caned hat, and he was smoking a pipe. 'They turned their faces toward the setting sun,' the elder began, 'and decided to go West for better opportunities.' And then he would tell the story of these families. They were the Calimans, the Guys . . .'"

"And the Simpsons?" I asked. These were the free families of color who had lived in community in Frederick and then migrated together to Ohio.

"Yes, the Simpsons and the Tates and the Earleys. That was funny, because the Earleys were the last to come to Ohio, so we always laughed that the Earleys came late."

I smiled. I could picture Robert's grandmother telling him that as a little boy.

"Then the elder would say a prayer and thank God for the riches that had been bestowed upon our family. And I'd kind of peek up through my bowed head and try to figure out who there was rich? Who had the family money?"

I laughed with him.

"Now from the perspective of someone who just turned seventy, I realize that the riches were the opportunities we have been given as a family. It is the fact that we can document our history, and the fact that our history is one we can treasure.

"These ancestors had opportunity," Robert went on. "The Lett group, and those they married, all had opportunities. They had been indentured people, some had been enslaved, some had become free people, and some had risen to the level where they were able to vote. Voting rights were tied to landownership then. Unless things were specifically spelled out otherwise, anyone who was a landowner could vote. So we had all of those things in our tradition—landownership, voting rights, and educational training.

"But after the Revolution, the ancestors saw the Freedmen Codes being instituted in the area and realized how those were going to limit their rights. At the same time, colonization societies were rising up and trying to round up aging Black folks to ship them out of the country. This was how Liberia was founded, by the American Colonization Society of white people who wanted to take African Americans back to Africa. Maryland had its own colony in Liberia, called the Maryland State Colonization Society of Africa.

"And this is interesting," Robert continued. "John Latrobe—you know, the guy who read Benjamin Banneker's history aloud before the Maryland Historical Society? He was the president of the Maryland Colonization Society. He was a main proponent of shipping African Americans back to Africa."

"I noticed that too!" I said. "It's telling that those who considered themselves the best advocates for Black people still could not imagine— or didn't want—their full integration into society. And most of those families that they were taking back to Africa had already been on this continent for three or four generations."

We continued to talk about the context of the times. It was freezing outside, and numbingly gray. But I was trying to look inward, to see what Robert was telling me.

"Our ancestors were more . . . I don't want to say more privileged," Robert said. "Let's just say they were the kind of people who could put their finger in the air and see which way the wind was blowing. And they could tell that things were not going their way down in Maryland. So they figured out a way to migrate.

"First they went to Frederick, Maryland," Robert continued. "They are there in the 1790 census, and you were right to notice that many of the families that went on to establish the Lett Settlement in Ohio were already part of that community in Frederick. We know that because they were listed as witnesses to one another's marriages.

"We know of only one of those community members who was in the Revolutionary War," Robert said. "Bazabeel Norman, who married Fortune Stevens. He served in the war, in lieu of who he was indentured to. And after the war, Bazabeel was freed of his indenture. By 1800, Bazabeel lived in Marietta, Ohio, which was then called Fort Harmar. But when it came time to receive his allotment of land—the land that the U.S. government was giving to all of the Revolutionary soldiers—the local townspeople protested that Bazabeel had already gotten enough by getting out of his indenture or enslavement, and he should not be entitled to land like the white soldiers. But the soldiers in his regiment insisted that he had served like anyone else and had saved their lives. Apparently, Bazabeel was a pretty good shot."

"And he got his land?" I asked.

"Yes, he did get his land, in Waterford, Ohio.

"You know, we were not raised, from the ground up, knowing about our kinship with Benjamin Banneker," Robert continued. "But we were raised knowing the multiethnic nature of our family. We were raised knowing about our resilience and self-sufficiency. The ancestors made everything themselves. They cut the trees, they made the shakes for their roofs, they baked their own bricks. We were raised to know we were Americans, because we knew our history and knew how to avoid getting locked into confines. And those of us who were born of color were taught never to deny our heritage.

"My mother, who was a teacher, introduced me to spirituality and faith," Robert added. "And my father, who was a principal, advised me of the value of introspection, planning, confidence, and the art of daring to dream things in perfection. He warned me that life will compel the application of reality to dreams, and will ultimately temper them. But he said that all people should embrace their dreams and should try to dream perfectly."

CHAPTER 23

The Dream

Oella, Maryland, 1790

The labors of the justly celebrated Banneker will likewise furnish you with a very important lesson, courteous reader, which you will not find in any other Almanac, namely that the maker of the universe is no respecter of colours; that the colour of the skin is in no way connected to the strength of mind or powers; that although the God of Nature has marked the face of the African with a darker shade than his brethren, he has given him a soul equally capable of refinement.

—from the Preface to Banneker's Almanac of 1796

BENJAMIN HAD ALWAYS worked best at night, after the world had quieted down, and no one could interrupt him with trifling thoughts about chickens and shovels, bridal clips, and whatnots. Life was too cluttered with those kinds of thoughts as far as he was concerned. He tried to leave space open in each day for real thinking and discovery. He took long walks and spent hours observing the workings of his bees or a line of carpenter ants, or the vascular patterns of a maple leaf. And through this patient, close attention, the world kept opening up to him, revealing its shapes and harmonies, its repetitions and intelligence. He loved to watch the moon rise and the stars brighten in their scatters and swaths. He mapped the planets' relations and positions to one another and memorized the circular zoo—the zodiac—as it marched its procession of seasons around the skies. He understood that those seasons were cycling into years, and years into epochs that sometimes he could sense the luminous echo of. And he felt intimately a part of this universal dance.

Benjamin watched the stars and planets with so much fascination and patience that many nights he fell asleep that way, faceup in the field. He would wake to cool dew on his cheeks and sunlight touching his upturned face. The best way to wake, he thought, the way the starlings and grasses woke. The hired farmers would be heading out to work at that time, and sometimes they'd see him lying in the field, or slowly making his way home, with a vague radiance on his face. That is how they got to calling him a drunk.

He wasn't a drunk. He was just strange in the way that all geniuses are strange. His mind was elaborate and often elsewhere, dreaming of planets or other solar systems, working out a mathematical puzzle, or ruminating on a pattern of avian or human behavior. At the same time, Benjamin was of the world, intensely interested in progress and technology. He loved to talk, and was known to spend hours in the Ellicott & Co. Store, discussing the news and holding forth on the issues of the day with his characteristic originality and biblical eloquence. He liked the company of other people, but he cherished the solitude that put him in the company of the living earth. In his journals, he noted the layers and relations of the plants, the way life hummed and intersected in webs of pollination and the vast commerce of communicating roots. He watched as the bees took to the flowers and made honey, and as the flowers plumped to fruit because of the bees. The interrelatedness of things was the world's greatest truth, as far as he could see.

Every year of his childhood, Benjamin's father, Robert, had purchased an almanac, consulting its ephemeris for its planting schedules, tide tables, moonrises, and sunrises. An ephemeris was the part of an almanac that included detailed astronomy and kept track of the cycles of the moon, sun, and stars—vital information that allowed seamen to navigate and farmers to determine when to plant and harvest. An accurate ephemeris linked the astronomical with the agricultural, the theoretical with the practical. An almanac, Benjamin knew, was the most useful book a family could own. It was often the *only* book a family owned—more popular and affordable than a Bible, and essential to the earthly keeping of a household, just as the Bible was essential to its spiritual keeping. Benjamin and Robert always jotted notes in the margins of their almanacs, marking where the ephemeris was accurate and where the weather had contradicted its predictions. Like many farmers, they used the blank pages in the back to keep track of their farm accounts and to plan for their planting times and harvests.

Almanacs had been introduced in the colonies in 1639, and for many years, they were the only contemporary reading material available to rural colonists because newspapers were only printed in large urban centers. Benjamin Franklin achieved fame through his *Poor Richard's Almanack*, which sold as many as 10,000 copies annually from 1732 to 1759, and included the essential ephemeris, alongside the aphorisms, folk wisdom, and entertaining essays for which American almanacs would become known. Compiling his own almanac may have been Benjamin Banneker's secret dream from the time he had first read *Poor Richard's Almanack* as a boy. I imagine him and Robert in the wagon, having just picked up the year's new copy in its brown paper cover. "Maybe you'll write one of these yourself someday," Robert said to his son, with a squinting smile and a confidence-inducing nod.

Through his adolescence and adulthood, Benjamin went on teaching himself science and mathematics, and he used his clock to keep time accurately enough to begin a casual study of astronomy. But it wasn't until 1788, when Benjamin was nearly fifty and living alone after his mother's death, that his friend George Ellicott lent him the books, telescope, and drafting instruments that allowed Benjamin to more seriously pursue his study of the cosmos. These books included Ferguson's *Introduction to Astronomy*, *The Tables of Tobias Mayer*, and Charles Leadbetter's *A Compleat System of Astronomy*. Benjamin absorbed their contents, reading and rereading them, and memorizing the formulas of their example equations. Mathematics was a language that just made sense to him, a language in which reality seemed to clarify and snap into place. He was comforted by the fact that numbers—unlike people—behaved the same way every time, regardless of their placement or context.

Benjamin enjoyed using the fine brass telescope, compass, and rulers to make detailed observations of the stars and to track their positions. He liked the idea of bringing the more orderly, consistent language of mathematics into conversation with the vast wonder of nature. He memorized the astrological houses and the way the planets moved through their various stations and influences, and began projecting upcoming astrological events for the coming year. He became so immersed in this new course of study that he began to neglect his chores through the late summer and early fall, the busiest times on the farm, leaving apples to rot beneath the trees and weeds to grow knee-high in his gardens.

In October 1789, Benjamin sent George a letter at the Ellicott Co. Store, including his astronomical calculations as well as a brief annotation of each of the books he had studied. George was staggered by the speed of Benjamin's learning, especially since he had undertaken it without any outside conversation or instruction. Benjamin detected one inconsistency between his computations and those of the texts. In his letter, he concluded, "Now Sir if I can overcome this difficulty I Doubt not being able to Calculate a Common Almanack—" revealing, for the first time, one of his life's ambitions.

Benjamin Banneker returned to the necessary work on his farm, but he remained obsessed with astronomy. While he weeded, picked, and shucked corn, he lined up the necessary equations in his mind and carefully planned the many calculations he would need to do to compile an ephemeris for the following year. He bought a new manuscript journal, imported from England, that had ledger-sized, watermarked pages, and he made a fresh batch of walnut ink, allowing the walnuts to soften and rot before boiling them down into a dark brown liquid. Then he filled the pages of the journal with straight grid lines. He wrote the name of each month in flourishing script at the top of the page, *January, the first month of the year*, and methodically recorded that month's astronomical information. His ephemeris tracked the movement and placement of the astrological houses, predicted the waxing and waning of the moon, noted the times of sunrise and sunset, and recorded major holidays.

Benjamin was passionately focused on astronomy during this time, and this focus had its own magnetism. Martha Tyson wrote of Benjamin's intellectual pursuits and his popularity as a thinker, even before he had published his almanacs. She told a story of her mother, Elizabeth Ellicott, calling on him with some of her friends in 1790:

> His door stood open and so closely was his mind engaged that they entered without being seen. Immediately upon observing them, he arose, and with much courtesy invited them in to be seated. The large oval table at which Banneker sat was strewn with works and astronomy and with scientific appurtenances. He alluded to his love of the study of astronomy and mathematics as quite unsuited to a man of his class, and regretted his slow advancement of them, owing to the laborious nature of his agricultural engagements, which obliged him to spend the greater part of his time in the fields.

Benjamin spent most of 1789 and the beginning of 1790 checking and rechecking his astrological equations. Finally, when those were complete, and supplemented with his neat drawings of the phases of the moon, Benjamin copied out the ephemeris, filling a page for each month. He titled the manuscript "Banneker's Almanac for 1791" and sent it out to potential publishers. He first sent it to the most prominent Baltimore printer, Goddard & Angell, but received a prompt rejection. Then he tried a second publisher, but again his manuscript was quickly returned to his postbox at the Ellicott and Co. Store. He may have been known in his county as a learned, well-read man who had designed the rural region's first wooden clock, but he was not formally educated or prominent enough for them to take on the project. And, of course, he was a Black man.

On his third attempt, Benjamin sent the manuscript to John Hayes, who was active in the Maryland Society for Promoting the Abolition of Slavery. Hayes was the publisher of the *Maryland Gazette*, the only newspaper in the area, and he printed a yearly almanac by George Ellicott's cousin, Andrew Ellicott. Hayes initially expressed interest in publishing the work but told Benjamin that he would have to forward it to astronomers in Philadelphia to double-check the accuracy of the computations. Hayes did so, but then he delayed in replying, so Benjamin was forced to write again and to send another copy of the ephemeris to Andrew Ellicott, along with a letter requesting his endorsement.

Hayes decided not to publish Banneker's almanac after all, because he was worried that it would compete with Ellicott's, and he sent Benjamin an official rejection. Hayes had held on to the work for so long, however, that it was now too late for Benjamin to get it to another printer in time for it to be released by 1791. Benjamin was frustrated and disappointed, because now he would have to do all the calculations again, for the following year. But he was determined to try once more. He knew that the almanac would be important, noting to his friends that it would be "the first attempt of the kind that ever was made in America by a person of my Complexion."

*　*　*

MEANWHILE, ON JULY 16, 1790, Congress had passed the Residence Act, calling for the new country's capital city to be constructed along the Potomac River, with land donated from both Maryland and Virginia. Congress appointed three commissioners to oversee its construction, and George's cousin, Andrew Ellicott, was brought on as the project's head surveyor and engineer. Andrew Ellicott had been a major in the Revolutionary War and was the new country's most prominent surveyor. Ellicott was responsible for charting the Mason-Dixon Line, the boundaries of Pennsylvania, and the New Northwest Territory. He first asked his cousin George to serve as his assistant, but George declined and recommended his friend Benjamin Banneker for the job. Andrew Ellicott had just seen Benjamin's work on the 1791 almanac, so he knew of Benjamin's mathematical talents and trusted that his exactitude would help him complete the surveying of the capital city. As abolitionist Quakers, the Ellicotts also wanted to promote Benjamin Banneker as an example of African American intelligence and capability. Major Ellicott asked President Washington and Secretary of State Thomas Jefferson if he could hire Benjamin Banneker as his assistant surveyor, and they agreed. Benjamin met with Major Ellicott in George's home, and humbly and gladly accepted the position.

*　*　*

As BENJAMIN BANNEKER prepared to leave for Alexandria, Virginia, for the most public and important opportunity of his lifetime, he could hardly believe his good fortune. Although Benjamin was locally known as a thinker and scientist, he had rarely left his farm or surrounding Quaker neighborhood. Whenever he was off his land, his body would ache with an undercurrent of fear. He was right to be cautious. Everyone knew of free Black men who had been beaten or murdered just for driving a wagon outside their county, just for looking at a white person directly, not bowing their head fast enough, or having patrollers assume that they had a gun. Every free person of color knew horror stories about friends and relatives who had traveled across towns or counties only to have their free papers snatched and their bodies sold into slavery, away from their families forever, sometimes by the police themselves. The laws of Maryland had made it increasingly difficult for people of color to leave the colony, and illegal to travel outside the bounds of their home counties. One such law stated that "any negro who might leave Maryland and remain away over thirty days, would be deemed a non-resident and liable to the law."

Still, Benjamin agreed to leave for Alexandria, knowing that this opportunity to assist Major Andrew Ellicott, the most prominent surveyor of the time, was an astounding privilege. Here he was, a self-taught astronomer and scholar, setting off to help with the design of the new country's capital. The opportunity was well worth the risk as it offered the kind of recognition and intellectual participation that Benjamin had been longing for his entire life.

Benjamin's friend George Ellicott was delighted that Benjamin had been hired for the role. He had marveled at Benjamin's intellect for years and thought it was only fair that Benjamin should get to exercise his intelligence in the wider world. He also knew that Benjamin's very presence on the commission would challenge widespread prejudice in the new government. Martha Ellicott remembered that her mother, Betsy Ellicott, "was careful to direct the appointments of [Benjamin's] wardrobe, in order that he might appear in a respectable guise" before the new country's most eminent statesmen and scientists. Benjamin's sister Minta was an expert seamstress. Betsy lent her some of George's waistcoats and vests and Minta deconstructed the clothing in her mind in order to copy the pattern and piece together a wardrobe for her brother. Benjamin would be working long hours in the cold and would need warmth, but he also needed urbane outfits that would announce him as a gentleman worthy of his presence on the survey. Minta was working long days for a local family, doing all of their mending and sewing, and was also the most in-demand midwife in the area. She prayed that no babies would be born during those rushed weeks of preparation. She'd work through the days, then stay up half the night, in candlelight, sewing her brother a red brocade vest with brass buttons, four new shirts, and a waistcoat. She reinforced all the seams, knowing that he'd be pulling at them, riding on horseback to Alexandria, and wearing them through rough weather. But it was all worth it. One of their own was on his way to survey the streets of the country's new capital. And she'd be there too, if only through her care and her creations.

CHAPTER 24

Griots

Baltimore, Maryland, and Evanston, Illinois, December 2020

COVID-19 WAS DRAGGING on and on, and we were all still cooped up. It was yet another Sunday afternoon during the quarantine, and Gwen and I had planned to talk. After three failed attempts, we finally got the Zoom link working and were very happy to see each other.

"I have been at a festival for the National Association of Black Storytellers," Gwen said. "And it really felt like I was flying! There was so much talk flying through the air. There's a lot of crosstalk, nobody waits for anyone else, nobody's polite . . . it was wonderful! Amazing, really. I felt like I got on a magic carpet and got out of here."

I smiled. I forgot sometimes that she lived in a retirement community, where she was one of the only people of color. Of course, she would want to get out of there once in a while.

Gwen began to tell me some of the griot stories she had heard that day. "One of the storytellers talked about a man who went to the plantations and taught the slaves how to escape through their imaginations," Gwen said. "He told them that through the imagination they could leave their bodies behind, so that the 'massa' would not know they were gone. And that's how they were able to survive.

"Of course, it wasn't a true story," Gwen added.

"But it *is* true," I said. "The only way to survive those horrors was through spirituality and imagination."

"Exactly."

"Imagination is seen as this frivolous thing," I said. "But it is also necessary for survival."

"That's exactly what my friend and I were talking about when she called me today," Gwen said. "We were talking about Black storytelling and Black spirituality and how different it is, how necessary. She spoke about enslaved Black people in the South who started their own church because they needed a place to go. It had to be *their* kind of spirituality. The white church was *too . . .*" Gwen tapped her forehead.

I nodded. "All up in the mind."

"Yes. My friend married a white guy in an old church here in Maryland that still has the balcony where the Black people had to sit," Gwen said. "It's a really old, beautiful church. When you come visit, I'll ask her to take us there. It's out in the country in a little town."

"I'd love that."

"The theme of the festival this week was 'In the Footsteps of Our Ancestors,'" Gwen went on. "Before the storytellers would perform, they would put these pictures of their parents and grandparents on the screen. And these were all people I *recognized*, by their hairdos and clothing and shoes. They were the people that I knew as a little girl. But of course these ancestors were from South Carolina, North Carolina, Atlanta. There are people in the Griot Collective from all over the country. Their locations have a lot to do with the slave trade, I guess.

"This call has been what I needed, to reflect," Gwen said. "After the conference, I just sat with it. I said to myself, 'I have nothing else to do today.' I mean, I did a lot, but I told myself, 'I can just vibrate with whatever comes up in my memory. I can just sit and remember.'"

I smiled. I liked thinking of memory as a vibratory and creative act. I told Gwen that I admired the fact that she was always learning, creating, and reflecting on meaning. I said I hoped that I would still be learning and writing when I was her age.

"Oh, years ago, I made the decision that I was going to keep living and learning every day of my life," she said. "And I am being led by Spirit."

CHAPTER 25

The Capital

Alexandria, Virginia, 1791

This projection I laid down for April the third 1791 when the sun arose centrally at the City of Washington. This is a back trial to see how my present method would agree with the former.

—Notes in Benjamin Banneker's Manuscript Journal, taken during the Federal Survey, 1791

BENJAMIN WAS THRUMMING with excitement and some nervousness when he mounted his horse and rode to Ellicott's Mills to meet Major Andrew Ellicott. The men set off for Jones Point, Virginia, in the first week of February 1791. Benjamin's saddlebags were packed, and he was wearing a beaver fur hat and one of the suits that Minta had made for him, as well as an oilcloth overcoat. He had packed his best quills, paper, a writing slate, and drafting instruments, but he suspected that these would look rather humble beside the equipment he was about to see. He was going to be working with the country's very latest technology. Andrew Ellicott had explained that Benjamin would be responsible for tending to the astrological clock and positioning the giant zenith sector—a telescope that precisely determined the positions of the stars. The measurements that Benjamin recorded through the clock and zenith sector would then be used to chart distances on the ground and plan the capital's city streets. This work of surveying, which measured land, was related to geodesy, which measured planets. Both mapped space and distances through a system of relation, and specifically through the use of the triangle. By drawing triangles from known points, surveyors and astronomers could calculate space and distance with unprecedented accuracy.

Benjamin understood the science and the process of surveying, although he had never done it before. He and Major Ellicott discussed the details of the project intermittently, in those rare hours when the riding was smooth and the skies were clear. For the most part, their trip was grueling, and the men spent two long days riding through cold, unrelenting rain. Finally, on February 7, 1791, they arrived in Alexandria, one of the largest cities in the country at that time, and a more bustling scene than Baltimore. They saw ships being loaded and unloaded in the harbor and heard people speaking several different languages. Soldiers and merchants crowded the streets, and old men still wearing their Revolutionary officers' coats sat playing chess and arguing in coffeeshops. Merchants sold Irish linen and Russian sheeting, rum, tobacco, shoes, and silver in shops crammed to the ceiling with imports. Andrew Ellicott found them lodging at Wise's Fountain Tavern on Cameron Street, and the men led their horses into the stables and carried their bags into the tavern. The sky was still overcast, and Ellicott worried aloud that the poor weather would delay their work on the survey, which depended on their ability to see the stars.

Over the next few days, Ellicott spent his time hiring laborers as woodcutters and linemen, purchasing horses, and gathering the provisions that the crew would need to set up camp and begin the survey. When Major Ellicott invited Benjamin to eat at the table with him and other members of the engineering corps, Benjamin politely declined, judiciously taking meals at a separate table, though dining at the same time. He chose this middle ground out of courtesy, self-respect, and a need for privacy. It was exhausting to be studied the way he was studied, as a kind of impossible curiosity. Benjamin did not want the color of his skin to be an inconvenience for Major Ellicott, who had respected him enough to hire him. And he did not need any trouble from those who did not share this same respect. He wanted to leave the commission with the highest possible recommendations from Major

Ellicott, President George Washington, and Secretary of State Thomas Jefferson.

As soon as he had a group of men under his employment, Ellicott set them to work assembling the surveyor's camp near Jones Point, above the city of Alexandria. Despite the persistent, icy rain, Ellicott ordered the men to clear trees, gather wood for fires, and set up tents. It was customary to establish the encampment at the highest point of an area being surveyed, which in this case was ten square miles. The observation tent needed to be on level ground, with at least one large tree in its vicinity. This tree was then cut down so its raised stump could serve as a stand for the regulator clock, the survey's most critical piece of equipment. The clock was used in conjunction with the zenith sector, which was at that time the largest and most accurate scientific instrument in America. Andrew Ellicott had designed the sector himself, with the help of his friend David Rittenhouse. It was five and a half feet long, with a five-and-a-half-foot lens that projected through the top of the observation tent, magnifying the stars to an unprecedented size.

Ellicott was only able to hire six untrained men for this survey, so he stayed in the field to supervise this reduced crew as they laid the lines for the city boundaries and streets. Benjamin was sixty years old, far too old to be in the field "running lines," so he was stationed in the observatory tent and put in charge of the astronomical clock and the zenith sector. It was Benjamin's job to observe seven stars as they crossed the meridian, and to use the clock and zenith sector to record the precise times of their passages each night. He made these observations over a number of consecutive nights—the accuracy of the work depending on his sleeplessness, vigilance, and meticulousness. Ellicott then used these computations to set his own timepiece, which allowed him to determine latitudes and to make his final measurements for the planning of the city.

On February 14, Andrew Ellicott made his first report to Thomas Jefferson. "I arrived this town on Friday last, but the cloudy weather prevented any observations being made until Friday which was very fine," he wrote. "On Saturday the two first lines were completed."

Ellicott and his crew worked seven days a week. Every morning,

Ellicott rose before dawn and rode into the encampment to review Benjamin's computations from the night before. Then the men walked through swamps and woods checking the placement of lines. They stood long hours in rain and snow, taking measurements to determine the meridians and placement of the future landmarks of Washington, D.C., including the sites of the Capitol, the White House, the Treasury, and other public buildings. Benjamin was paid $2 a day for this work, which was less than Ellicott's $5 per day, but was a fair salary for an assistant surveyor at that time.

On March 12, 1791, the presence of the surveyors was announced in the *Georgetown Weekly Ledger*:

> Some time last month arrived in this town Mr. Andrew Ellicott, a gentleman of superior astronomical abilities. He was employed by the President of the United States of America, to lay a tract of land, ten miles square, on the Potowmack, for the use of Congress. He is attended by Benjamin Banniker, an Ethiopian, whose abilities as a surveyor and astronomer, clearly prove that Mr. Jefferson's concluding that race of men were void of mental endowments, was without foundation.

This announcement conveys Benjamin's skill and prominence. It also positions him already as a challenge to Thomas Jefferson's ideas about race and Black inferiority, which Jefferson had presented seven years earlier in his book, *Notes on the State of Virginia*.

* * *

THE DESIGNERS OF the capital rejected the overall grid pattern, common to many cities, in favor of an aspirational radial design that included diagonal avenues and traffic circles. The French planner Pierre L'Enfant had designed the city to be laid out in response to meridians and to the twelve astrological houses. It was a rare work of city planning designed to reflect Enlightenment ideals of harmony between the earth and stars. Pennsylvania Avenue, which stretched a mile west from the Congress to the White House, was oriented to the movement across the sky of Sirius, Banneker's favorite star, the star he had long observed and had correctly guessed was actually two stars. Benjamin knew L'Enfant's design of the capital city intimately and understood its aspirational vision, even as he made the precise astrological observations that would make the vision work.

These men were mobilizing the latest tools of science and mathematics to plan something unprecedented. They had a disciplined trust in mathematical law and human reason, and they also had the imagination to see what did not yet exist. Benjamin stood on hillocks and in ditches that were destined to be streets, and walked through the wet wooded groves that would someday hold the chambers of Congress. He and Major Ellicott trudged over slushy, frozen mud and looked into oak forests and pictured buildings, streets, and bridges. Every one of those trees would have to be chopped down with a hand axe, and then the great stumps would have to be gouged out with mataxes, Benjamin knew. All of it would have to be done by hand, as they said, although Benjamin had worked hard enough on his farm to know that it took a man's entire body to do such work.

One evening, Benjamin walked from the observatory tent and stood on a hill in the frigid wind. Everything was blurred and gray. He was exhausted, and as he stood looking down into woods snaked by cold creeks—a bottomland soft with rotting branches and wet leaves—it seemed as though the trees were moving. Then he realized that a new group of axmen had been brought in to clear the woods. Their complexions were every shade of ebony, and their bodies were straining and sweating as they swung their axes with the whole of their broad and muscled shoulders. Benjamin knew what that felt like. He knew how difficult it was to cut those tall trees. First just nicking into them again and again with the axe, before breaking through resistance to the work until the body just becomes the work, arms and shoulders swinging round and round again to drive into the tree and chip it silver, white, its fragrant flesh coming off in chunks before the giant, booming crack, and the fall that always seemed to happen in slow motion, gathering momentum at the end. Benjamin watched the rhythmic way the men set to chopping, the way they called out one another's names and gruff directions, to keep the chopping steady and protect the man at the front. He saw them match their breaths to one another and to the swings of the axes. He saw, when one bent double with exhaustion, another walked over and put his broad hand on his shoulder and rubbed it quickly where he knew there was a knot. He knew there was a knot there because he could feel it in his own shoulder.

They were part of the strong-shouldered body of men who were making the wilderness into a country. He could see it in the way they untangled and held the ropes for the one who would shimmy up the trunk to the highest branches and tie himself in a sling before topping the tree. He could see it in the way the others teased him for his quick shimmying, and then fell silent all at once, watching, knowing that the man's life hung in the balance of the ropes and in the balance of their care.

To watch them was both breathtaking and maddening. It was to witness their beauty and power, and also to understand that the wigged white men in paneled rooms did not see them. They would use these men to build a city devoted to freedom while never looking them full in the face. Watching these Black men, Benjamin felt a great pride swell up in him, one that made him broaden and pull back his own shoulders. They did not watch Benjamin, though. They did not have the time or the inclination. One glanced up once and took in the color of his face and his greatcoat and brocade vest and then looked quickly away, and Benjamin felt in his avoidance a confusing kind of sting—his own shame or the man's, he did not know. He had wanted to nod at him, to say that they were both essential to what the new country was creating. But if Benjamin was part of the idea of the thing, he saw that these men were creating the capital in its actuality.

When the axmen walked back to their barracks together, Benjamin heard them humming low songs, and joking with backtalk and ribbing. It made Benjamin miss his father, who was the only man he had ever had that way with, joined with in the hard physical fellowship of work. He even missed his bees, how sometimes watching the hives, seeing how tirelessly the bees worked to please their queen, he thought he saw the natural instincts of human industry.

As the sky darkened and he checked the clock again, Benjamin could hear the men's music and laughter, harmonicas and thigh slapping, and the way they called out to the woman who brought them their soup, bread, and ham for dinner. This woman seemed so familiar to Benjamin—with her smooth brown skin and elegant hands, her no-nonsense capability, her grace. She reminded him of his sisters, the way she fed all the men and never seemed to stop moving, with her little girl at her apron strings clean and shod. Maybe her husband was among them. Or maybe he had been one of the men sent to the quarry, to cut the great white slabs of stone that would be used to build the Presidential Palace. When he saw her in passing, Benjamin always tipped his hat to that lady, and she smiled somewhat humorously but pleased, but he didn't know what else to say. He felt apart from them all, like he was looking at them through the wrong end of a telescope.

Benjamin would usually begin his work this way, listening to their music and low, rumbling talk, half wishing he was with them and half-grateful he was not, as he settled in for the night to do his equations. During those winter nights, the stars were the brightest and he could do his most accurate measurements of the stars as they passed the meridian. The huge telescope was so powerful that the cosmic expanse felt newly intimate to Benjamin. He had become so accustomed to looking up at the stars, in fact, that he often imagined the earth below from their vantage point. As he saw it, the stars were providing the measurements, the boundary lines, for what humans on earth could aspire to and create. It was as if the stars themselves were the watchers and we humans were merely the bees.

* * *

PIERRE L'ENFANT, AS a Frenchman, and Andrew Ellicott, as a Quaker, both refused to hire enslaved people to build the capital city and sought out free laborers for the work. But L'Enfant was released early in the project because he was a temperamental man who had numerous disagreements with the National Capital Planning Commission. Among other complaints, he had wanted to provide his laborers with fair pay and provisions, including a daily cup of hot chocolate. The other commissioners, enslavers themselves, did not see a problem with using enslaved people to build a capital city devoted to ideals of freedom. And there is no record of there ever being a debate about the ethics of this issue.

In April 1792, after Benjamin Banneker had finished his work on the survey, capital commissioners officially began using enslaved people for capital building projects. Plantation owners in nearby counties of Maryland and Virginia were made offers to "rent" their skilled enslaved men to build the city. These laborers worked as axmen to clear the land, quarrymen to cut the stone for the White House and Capitol, and carpenters and masons to construct the roads and buildings of what is now known as Washington, D.C. These men were listed in the Capital Commission records under their first names and the last names of their "masters." Edmund Plowden hired out Gerard, Tony, Jack, Moses, Lin, and Arnold Plowden. E. J. Millarde sent his men Tom and Joe Millarde. Valentine Reintzell sent Mike, George, Dick, Jacob, Will, Amos, and Charles Reintzell. Anne Digges sent Tom, Jack, and Dick Digges. The daughters of Robert Brent sent David, Charles, Sylvester, Gabe, Henry, and Nace Brent. And so on. History did not record their true names—the nicknames or pet names that they were called by their loved ones. We do know that their "masters" were paid roughly twenty-one pounds a year for their work. Meanwhile, the men themselves, whose labor and skills laid many of the streets and erected the buildings of the free nation's capital, were not paid at all.

In 1798, the Polish dignitary Julian Niemcewicz visited the site of the Capitol building, which was still being constructed. He noted the hundreds of workers climbing the scaffolding, raising the stones, and framing in the roof, observing that many were white laborers and many "were negroes working in large number." He described the grog shops and taverns that had sprung up around the white workers' cabins and added, "The negroes alone work." At first, he was told that all of the laborers earned "eight to ten dollars a week," but then he learned the truth, and he recorded his shock in his journal. "I am told that they were not working for themselves; their masters hire them out and retain all the money for themselves. What humanity! What a country of liberty. If at least they shared the earnings!"

* * *

MARTHA TYSON WROTE that Benjamin's elegance of manner, his attention to detail, and his humble bearing all did well to recommend him to George Washington, Thomas Jefferson, and the other men of the National Capital Planning Commission. "Banneker's deportment throughout the whole of this engagement secured their respect," she wrote, "and there is good authority for believing that these endowments led the commissioners to overlook the color of his skin to converse with him freely, and enjoy the clearness and originality of his remarks on various subjects." Again, these prominent white men *overlooked* the color of his skin, but did not see him as exemplary of wider African American potential.

The commissioners held a celebration in April 1791, after the first boundary stones were laid for the city. After the ceremony, Ellicott released Benjamin from his service. Benjamin's portion of the work had come to a close, and the cold had gotten into his bones. He had been both energized and challenged by being around so many people after his many years of quiet on the farm, and now he was ready to go home. He was proud that he had helped to design the seat of the new government. He suspected that those axmen—even unpaid, even laboring through fatigue and pain—felt the same way. He had seen them.

CHAPTER 26

Insurrection

January 6, 2021

ROBERT AND I had planned to talk the afternoon of January 6. That morning, we had been texting about Raphael Warnock's election as Georgia's first Black senator. In his speech, Warnock talked about his ancestors. "My roots are planted deeply in Georgia soil," Warnock began, describing himself as "a son of my late father, who was a pastor, a veteran . . . and my mother who, as a teenager growing up in Waycross, Georgia, used to pick somebody else's cotton." But then he framed that history in the context of hope and change, saying, "The other day, because this is America, the eighty-two-year-old hands that used to pick somebody else's cotton went to the polls and picked her youngest son to be a United States senator."

Robert and I were texting these quotes back and forth in anticipation of discussing the election. Then I sat down to research Banneker's role in the planning of Washington, D.C. Robert had sent me some articles about the design of the city, and I had been thinking about how unusual it was to plan a city in response to the astrological houses. It was such an aspirational design, in harmony with mathematics, mythology, and astronomy. Just as I was imagining the irony of Benjamin watching the enslaved men cutting down trees for a city devoted to liberty, a mob incited by President Trump stormed the Capitol.

I only knew what was happening because I heard my daughter's social studies teacher interrupt their Zoom class in an urgent voice.

"Go, turn on your TV," she said to the kids. "This is history happening, *right now*."

We put on CNN and saw the footage of a vigilante mob of people breaking windows to get into the Capitol. Someone was wearing a plastic Viking-style hat, people were smashing through windows, toppling American flags, and putting up Trump flags and Confederate flags in their place. An aide was crouched under a chair in the congressional chambers. She was wearing black nylons and little flat black shoes, her head covered with a rain bonnet. Her fear and vulnerability were terrible to see. It was a moment of great privacy, a person in a crouch, believing she was about to be killed, and it did not seem right for us to see her that way. Raiders pushed over statues, carrying American flags like barbaric spears. My phone vibrated nervously in my hand. Robert was calling me.

"Do you believe this?" he asked.

"No, this is madness," I said.

"Now let me ask you something," Robert said. "How are we supposed to let this guy stay in office now? Are we going to have Biden's inauguration on January twentieth, with the whole lawn lined with the National Guard? You know these people are going to try this again."

"I know," I said. I was pacing around my living room, my heart beating fast. I felt that we were watching the toppling of the democracy I had thought I lived in, in real time. I told Robert that just a day earlier, Trump had deployed hundreds of National Guard troops to my town and to Kenosha, Wisconsin, in expectation of the "riots" that were projected after the charges were dropped against the white police officer who had shot Jacob Blake seven times in the back, in front of his children.

"We had people in riot gear all along the streets in Kenosha," I said, "But there was no one guarding the Capitol as a mob of people shut down Congress? They knew they were coming.

"Jacob Blake grew up here in my town of Evanston," I continued. I was still pacing. "Adele's social studies teacher taught Jacob Blake and is close with his family. She is with them on Zoom now. I just heard her ask the class, 'What do you think would be happening if these were Black people storming the Capitol with weapons and pipe bombs?'

"I think they would have opened fire," I said, answering the teacher myself.

"Oh, sure they would have!" Robert said. "And this was supposed to be such a good day, with the election of Warnock. We were supposed to feel some relief today."

I looked back at the TV. They were showing the same clips over and over while reporters kept saying, "I've never seen anything like this." President-elect Biden was about to address the nation, so Robert and I got off the phone, deciding to talk again later in the day.

*　*　*

ROBERT CALLED BACK a few hours later. "I just feel really disappointed," he said. "You know, Trump really is as bad as we were afraid he was. There's no way to deny it now. The man is a racist. This event exposes him for exactly what he is. He's been talking about this for weeks with his followers."

"I know. He's convinced them that the election was stolen, although there's no evidence for that," I said.

"And they knew there was going to be a protest," Robert said. "They could have been prepared. What is so incredible to me is that he went and spoke to this group, telling them to walk down Pennsylvania Avenue. 'I'll be with you,' he said. 'You're going to have to do this, you're going to have to be strong.' They probably expected him to be marching alongside them, barging in. But the whole time he was hiding out in the White House. This has made me look back at everything in his administration differently and see it all in terms of racial inequality," Robert said. "After the Black Lives Matter movement and the death of George Floyd, there were police everywhere, all of that violence coming at the protesters."

"I know. I can't get over the disparity of it," I said. "The sight of National Guard troops guarding the Capitol during the Black Lives Matter Protest, versus the easy access that these people had today with their Trump flags and Confederate flags."

"But this is such a worn reality for people of color," Robert said, "because it exposes the pillars of lies on which the country was built. Those lies of equality. It all goes back to the Church, and the idea of Manifest Destiny, which says that man has dominion over all creatures and animals. The white man assumes that this means that *he* has dominion over the indigenous people and the people of color who were already here."

I agreed with Robert. He knew that I had spent time learning from indigenous elders, as well. We had talked about how this mindset of colonization extended to all people of color and even to the colonizers' exploitative relationship to the earth itself.

"I do believe that there are moral people who do not operate on that basis," Robert continued, "but our institutions are all based on this idea—our police departments, our prison system. Our jurisprudence is supposedly based on equal justice, blind justice. But there has never been equal justice. Justice has always gone back to what you can pay for. I see this entire Trump era and the events of today as having dredged up events that are familiar to Black Americans, but that I do not believe the average Euro-American has within their day-to-day psyches."

I thought about that. How familiar these scenes were in our national history—of plunder, of white people barging into houses that were not theirs and wrecking things, throwing things on the ground, defiling papers covered with other people's words. I felt sometimes that the past was erupting into the present, repeating unexamined trauma, as if we were all just recycling the same pain and injustices in different generations.

"This scene is all there in the white subconscious, though," I said. "When I saw that mob, storming in, waving their Confederate flags, it was very easy to see this as a pattern, to see the raids during Jim Crow, the patrollers of the South, all of that white fear and domination . . ."

"Right. It is being created all over again, right now, on live TV," Robert said wearily.

"There is a lot of white fear," Robert went on. "And there are always those in power that want to keep this fear alive. The guys who Donald Trump brought to the ballot box are not the same guys that he parties with. He's used poor whites to do his dirty work."

"It all goes back to the use of white supremacy as a way of dividing and conquering the working class," I said. "Those racist ideas would go to create this group of people—who would be the patrollers and overseers, who would burn down the houses of people of color, who would raid the houses of Congress . . ."

"We used to call it the redneck mentality. But it's also a neo-militia mentality," Robert said. "There is a mercenary, capitalistic psyche that drives this country and operates entirely on this level.

"It's like what happened after the Emancipation Proclamation," he went on. "You had many Black people elected to Congress in those first ten to fifteen years after Emancipation. Then people doubled down on segregation, then Jim Crow unleashed terror, and the people were driven out of office. It's a cyclical thing. But I'm not sure that our nation is currently in a place where we can survive this cycle without addressing it."

"I don't know if we can survive this cycle as a *democracy*," I said.

"The only way we can is if we can get our spiritual guides, our poets, and our theologians to lead us," Robert said.

"I think this was a completely manipulated and staged event," he added tiredly. "I know what would have happened to *me* if I was breaking in there and stealing things. My question is, What did these people think would happen to them?"

CHAPTER 27

The Correspondence

Oella, Maryland, 1792

*Sir, I freely and Chearfully acknowledge that I am of the African race,
and in that color that is natural to them of the deepest dye; and it is
under a Sense of the most profound gratitude to the Supreme Ruler of
the Universe, that I now confess to you, that I am not under that state
of tyrannical thralldom and inhuman captivity, to which too many
of my brethren are doomed; but that I have abundantly tasted of the
fruition of those blessings which proceed from that free and unequaled
liberty with which you are favored.*

— Benjamin Banneker in his letter to Thomas Jefferson,
August 19, 1791

BENJAMIN WAS GLAD to be home again, sleeping in his own bed, or in
his fields beneath the stars. After he finished his work on the federal
survey in April 1791, he returned to his farm and immediately began
compiling an almanac for the following year. As soon as he finished
his ephemeris for 1792, he mailed it to a printer in Georgetown, likely
the one who had published the *Georgetown Weekly Ledger* and had
announced his work on the survey alongside Andrew Ellicott. Then he
wrote out an additional copy of the almanac and delivered it to William Goddard, publisher of the *Maryland Journal* and the person who
had first proposed the U.S. Postal System to Congress. Haunted by the
previous years' rejections, this time Benjamin mounted his horse and

traveled to Baltimore to deliver the manuscript to Goddard in person. Goddard and Benjamin had a pleasant conversation, and Goddard found himself intrigued by the potential profits in marketing an almanac by a Black man when abolitionist sentiment was on the rise. He offered Banneker a sum of three pounds for the publication and made the verbal promise that this could increase to three guineas should the almanac sell successfully. Benjamin told him that he would be seeking out publishers in other cities, but Goddard did not believe or absorb this communication. William Goddard would later impede Benjamin's additional publications, arguing that he had been given exclusive rights to Banneker's almanac.

Andrew Ellicott went out of his way to support the project. He sent Benjamin's ephemeris to James Pemberton, the president of the Pennsylvania Society for Promoting the Abolition of Slavery and the Relief of Free Negroes Unlawfully Held in Bondage. Pemberton read the ephemeris, declared it accurate as far as he could tell, and then forwarded it to David Rittenhouse, the friend of Ellicott's who was himself a prominent surveyor, almanac author, and inventor of scientific instruments. Rittenhouse pronounced the ephemeris "a very extraordinary performance, considering the Colour of the Author." After concluding that he "had no doubt that the Calculations are sufficiently accurate for the purposes of a common Almanac," Rittenhouse reflected on the social good that could come from publishing Banneker's work. "Every instance of Genius amongst the Negroes is worthy of attention, because their suppressors seem to lay great stress on their supposed inferior mental abilities," he noted.

The timing was right for such a provocative document. Since the Revolution, numerous abolition societies had sprung up, eager for proof of African intelligence. Pemberton and the Ellicotts decided that they needed someone to write a preface to Banneker's almanac that would further legitimate the project, and they selected Senator James McHenry for the job. McHenry was a Maryland senator and a decorated Revolutionary War veteran. He had studied medicine under Dr. Benjamin Rush and later served on the medical staff of the Continental army, acting as General Washington's personal secretary. Because he was such a respected Southern senator, McHenry's endorsement would help Benjamin Banneker's almanac to reach its widest possible audience.

* * *

BENJAMIN APPRECIATED THESE recommendations and was eager to get his work into the world. Now he wrote out a final copy of his manuscript for someone else—someone he had met during the capital survey and whom he had wanted to correspond with for years, ever since he had read his *Notes on the State of Virginia*.

Notes on the State of Virginia was the best-selling nonfiction book of its time, and was made up of scientific queries and passages compiling Thomas Jefferson's descriptions of the region, including the native birds and wildlife and the people original to the continent. Reading the book, Benjamin felt that he had never encountered a mind so much like his own, with its catalogs and questions, its trust that close observation would yield practical insights into the workings of humans and governments, flora and fauna. But there was no easy way to read that book as a self-respecting African man, because Jefferson had not imagined a man like Banneker reading it. The Black man was not sitting beside Jefferson, learning over his shoulder, but was part of the natural world of fauna and flora that Jefferson coolly observed. To Jefferson, the Black man was one of the earth's specimens, a curiosity of nature, rather than one of the earth's thinkers and creators. And so for Benjamin to read Jefferson's writing was a complicated act. On the one hand, it was to feel his own mind quickened by Jefferson's probing and scientific intelligence. On the other hand, it was to be repeatedly confronted with the realization that Jefferson considered him a brute at worst, a curiosity at best, and not actually a man.

Jefferson was well acquainted with African American people, because he "owned" hundreds of them. He had inherited 175 enslaved people from his wife Martha Wayles's family, and those people continued to create people—and more wealth—for the Jeffersons. But the most famous sections of Jefferson's *Notes* detailed his conflicting feelings about slavery. "The whole commerce between master and slave is a perpetual exercise of the most boisterous passions, the most unremitting despotism on the one part, and degrading submissions on the other," Jefferson wrote. "The man must be a prodigy who can retain his manners and morals undepraved by such circumstances."

Jefferson admitted that he feared the wrath of God would come to those who held slaves. But he considered the integration and naturalization of Black people with pessimism and even terror. "Deep-rooted prejudices entertained by the whites; ten thousand recollections, by the blacks, of the injuries they have sustained; new provocations; the real distinctions which nature has made; and many other circumstances, will divide us into parties," Jefferson predicted, "and produce convulsions which will probably never end but in the extermination of the one or the other race."

Jefferson was haunted by the ways that white people had tortured enslaved Black people, but he held and perpetuated these "deep-rooted prejudices" himself and considered African Americans and Native Americans to be inferior humans. While the *Notes* acknowledged the poetic sensibility of Native Americans and admitted to the extraordinary musical talents of African Americans, the book also included long passages detailing Jefferson's "observations" of African inferiority.

"Comparing them by their faculties of memory, reason, and imagination, it appears to me, that in memory they are equal to the whites," Jefferson wrote, "in reason much inferior, as I think one could scarcely be found capable of tracing and comprehending the investigations of Euclid." He then added that "in imagination," Black people are "dull, tasteless, and anomalous . . . never yet could I find that a black had uttered a thought above the level of plain narration."

Jefferson failed to account for the fact that in a country that outlawed literacy for African Americans, uttering a thought more complex than "plain narration" in front of one's "master" could get a person killed. He very whitely did not imagine that Black people had thoughts, poetry, culture, and logic that remained unobserved by him.

While reading these passages, Benjamin must have bristled. I see him muttering back to the book, pacing around his cabin, his face flushed with anger and shame. He knew that he himself was the scientist and thinker—that African American who *could* comprehend Euclid—that Jefferson had not imagined.

Benjamin had tried, two or three times before, to write an angry, corrective letter to the author of the *Notes*. But he had discarded each one, deciding it too pleading or strident. For most of his life, Benjamin was painfully aware that he had too few external accomplishments to signify the reach of his mind. He had no access to the wider world, and no great laurels to recommend him to Jefferson, and he felt that his letter would have been too easily dismissed. But now Jefferson knew who he was. They had met at the ceremony celebrating the federal survey, when Andrew Ellicott had laid the first cornerstone of the District of Columbia. Jefferson had nodded to him in greeting and had himself signed off on Banneker's hiring and pay. Jefferson knew Benjamin to be someone talented and competent.

Now he wanted to share his almanac with Jefferson—as a way of connecting with a fellow scientific thinker, and indicating what was possible for a man of his "complexion." In sending him a copy of his almanac, Benjamin was upending the subject-object relationship that white people had always imposed on Black people. He was declaring that he was not an object of curiosity to be idly studied or, God forbid, to be "owned." He was not part of Jefferson's vast catalog of creatures, but a thinker in his own right, capable of making his own detailed observations of the world.

As Banneker began his letter, his sentences kept unspooling into a fervent and eloquent call for justice. First, he acknowledged the rarity of his own liberty and the widespread prejudice against African American people.

"I suppose it is a truth too well attested to you, to need a proof here, that we are a race of Beings who have long labored under the abuse and censure of the world," he wrote, "that we have long been looked upon with an eye of contempt, and that we have long been considered rather brutish than human, and Scarcely capable of mental endowments." The letter slyly referred to Jefferson's own writing, and reached out through flattery, citing the reports he'd heard that Jefferson was "measurably friendly and well-disposed towards us, and that you are willing to Lend your aid and assistance to our relief."

As the letter continued, Banneker quoted the Declaration back to Jefferson and asked him to recall the tender feelings he and the other

Founding Fathers had held for themselves during the Revolution, when they had understood the true value of liberty. He asked them to apply those feelings to his "brethren" who still labored in "groaning captivity," under "cruel oppression." Ultimately, he accused the Founding Fathers of committing the most criminal act by perpetuating slavery.

Benjamin dipped his quill back into the inkpot and took a deep breath. Having said what he needed to say about justice, he returned to the subject of his almanac. Benjamin recounted the self-study that led him to compute and compile the ephemeris and said that while he knew Jefferson could soon see a published version of the book, he wanted to send him the manuscript so he could "view it in my own handwriting." His elegant penmanship was another way for Benjamin to illustrate his intellect and legitimacy. It was inked proof that this work had come from his own hand, and had not been written by another on his behalf.

* * *

THOMAS JEFFERSON DID not take obvious offense at Banneker's letter but seemed to respect its forthrightness. Within four days of receiving the almanac, he wrote a quick note in reply, which included his usual answer to abolitionist critique:

Philadelphia, August 30, 1791

Sir,
I thank you sincerely for your letter of the 19th instant and for the Almanac it contained. No body wishes more than I do to see such proofs as you exhibit, that nature has given our black brethren, talents equal to those of the other colors of men, and that the appearance of want of them is owing merely to the degraded condition of their existence, both in Africa & America. I can add with truth, that no body wishes more ardently to see a good system commenced for raising the condition of both their

body & mind to what it ought to be, as fast as the imbecility of their present existence, and other circumstances which cannot be neglected, will admit.

In response to Banneker's pleas that Jefferson use his influence to change public opinion, he added:

> I have taken the liberty of sending your Almanac to Monsieur de Condorcet, Secretary of the Academy of Sciences at Paris, and member of the Philanthropic society, because I considered it as a document to which your whole colour had a right for their justification against the doubts which have been entertained of them.
>
> I am with great esteem, Sir, your most
> obedient and humble servant,
> Thomas Jefferson

Here, Jefferson conveniently used the passive verb tense to refer to "the doubts which have been entertained of them," failing to acknowledge that he himself was a primary publisher of those doubts through the *Notes*. But, true to his word, Jefferson did forward the book to the secretary of the Académie Royale des Sciences in Paris, the world's most respected institution of science. He enthusiastically wrote to the Marquis de Condorcet, Secretary of the Académie, that he was sending along an almanac by a "negro" and "very respectable mathematician," whom he had employed to help survey the new U.S. capital. Jefferson described Benjamin Banneker:

> I have seen very elegant solutions of Geometrical problems by him. Add to this that he is a very worthy and respectable member of society. He is a free man. I shall be delighted to see these instances of moral eminence so multiplied as to prove that the want of talents observed in them is merely the effect of their degraded condition and not proceeding from any difference in the structure of the parts on which intellect depends.

Although Banneker's almanac was sent to Condorcet, it arrived at an inopportune moment of political upheaval—the French Revolution. Condorcet was the secretary of the Legislative Assembly, and one of the first people to support the new Republic of France. He wrote the memo calling for the suspension of the king's powers, and then immediately went into hiding to prevent his own execution. Later, he tried to escape from his hiding place but was captured and imprisoned, then found dead from exhaustion or poisoning. Jefferson's letter and Banneker's almanac would have arrived just as Condorcet was fleeing Paris for his life. The letter and manuscript were understandably lost in this confusion and were most likely never presented to the Académie Royale des Sciences. Had the manuscript been presented to the Académie, it probably would have been publicized, especially among members of the French Société des Amis des Noirs, who, like American abolitionists, were actively seeking examples of African accomplishment.

But Benjamin Banneker still put this exchange to good use. He published this correspondence with Jefferson in the foreword to his 1793 almanac. By then, Banneker's 1792 almanac had been published with great success, and he had compiled another for the following year. Jefferson had been seen as a hypocrite by abolitionists since the publication of the *Notes*, and now these letters with Benjamin Banneker further complicated things for him politically. They also launched decades of response to Banneker's courage and Jefferson's shiftiness, as Black writers followed Banneker's lead and insisted that African Americans were not curiosities to be studied but themselves brilliant observers and thinkers.

Benjamin Banneker's legacy had begun—not just as a mathematician, a scientist, and a writer but as an abolitionist—a person who uses his own freedom to insist on freedom for others.

* * *

WHEN THOMAS JEFFERSON received Benjamin Banneker's almanac, he had just returned to Monticello from France, where he had been sent in 1784 as the American ambassador. His colleagues had found him the post just after his wife, Martha, died, when he was a deeply distraught widower. He brought his oldest daughter, Mary, with him, and when his middle daughter died shortly afterward in a fever, he became frantic not to lose any more loved ones and sent for his youngest daughter, Polly. In 1787, Polly arrived in Paris with her enslaved ladies' maid—fourteen-year-old Sally Hemings.

Sally Hemings was the youngest of Martha Jefferson's half siblings that their father, John Wayles, had fathered by his slave Betty Hemings. Thomas and Martha Jefferson had inherited Sally as an infant upon Wayles's death. Sally had three white grandparents, but because her mother was enslaved, she was enslaved, and, by law, she was owned by her half sister and her family. People said that Sally strongly resembled Martha, although she was twenty-five years younger and had slightly darker skin. Before arriving in France, Sally and her niece-as-master Polly visited Abigail Adams. Afterward, Adams noted in a letter to Jefferson that Sally was clearly not suited to service and seemed to need as much help as Polly, though she seemed "good natur'd" and "very fond of Polly."

Slavery had been outlawed in France under their new constitution, and, understanding this, Thomas Jefferson paid Sally and her older brother James (his half brother-in-law, who was also his "property"), for their service while the family was abroad. James apprenticed with French chefs and ended up supervising the white kitchen help in Paris, while Sally wore couture gowns, attended lavish events, and served Jefferson's daughters as a lady's maid. Perhaps in Paris, Jefferson felt shame about enslaving these half siblings of his late wife, or perhaps he was able to see them with more respect on French soil, where they were granted legal human rights. Maybe he half imagined that he was with Martha again, Martha as Sally, as a beautiful young girl.

In any case, by the time Sally Hemings was sixteen, forty-four-year-old Thomas Jefferson had begun a sexual coercion with her. When Jefferson was called back to the United States in 1789, Sally threatened to go to the National Registry and stay in France. Sally knew that she and her brother James had the legal right to remain in France as free people. According to the oral history of her son Madison, Sally understood her rights and only agreed to return to Monticello with Jefferson—where she knew she would be enslaved—on the condition that all of their children would be freed. Sally was smart, and a good negotiator, and must have been aware of what she would gain from a life with Jefferson, and of what she would lose. Maybe he had impregnated her before she realized that she could be free on French soil. Maybe she knew that she was sacrificing her freedom for the freedom of the next generation. In any case, she was carrying Jefferson's child, and she seemed sure enough of Jefferson's infatuation with her that she negotiated on behalf of future offspring.

Back at home, Sally was installed in the main house of Monticello, where she went on to have six children by Jefferson, four of whom survived to adulthood. Jefferson's political opponents began accusing him of fathering these children as early as 1802, and Jefferson himself never publicly denied these allegations. But his white descendants did so for generations—and vehemently.

It was common for plantation owners to take enslaved woman as their mistresses, although it was expected that they would be discreet about it, far more so than Jefferson was with Sally and their children. The Hemings children lived in Monticello and were not forced to labor, but were taught to read and play the violin and were apprenticed with artisans. We may wonder if this was something of an experiment on Jefferson's part, or if he knew, at this point in his life, that people with African ancestry were also capable of learning, logic, and reason. The two oldest Hemings children, Beverly and Harriet, "escaped" from Monticello when they reached adulthood. The groundskeeper, who described Harriet as "very beautiful" and "nearly white," gave her money from Jefferson to join her brother Beverly in Washington, D.C. Both of them changed their names, married into society, and lived away from the family, passing as white people.

Two more of Sally and Jefferson's sons stayed in the South and married free Black women. Thomas Jefferson kept his word to Sally and freed all of the Hemings children at the end of his life. And his daughter Polly "gave Sally her time," allowing her to spend her last days in a home in Baltimore that her son Madison owned.

The Hemings family passed the knowledge of their parentage down through the generations, but it wasn't until DNA testing in 1998 corroborated this heritage that their story became part of our official

United States history. In fact, this was one of the first public uses of DNA as a force of narrative reparations, thanks to the Hemings family griots and historian Annette Gordon-Reed. It is notable that this correction centered on the family of one of our Founding Fathers, writer of the Declaration of Independence, and the man who best represents the contradictions and hypocrisies at the heart of American freedom.

* * *

As THE YEARS passed and their correspondence was made public, both Benjamin Banneker's and Thomas Jefferson's feelings about their exchange shifted. In 1809, Jefferson wrote to his friend Joel Barlow in an especially foul mood. He was piqued by how his writings in the *Notes* had been continually used against him by abolitionists and political opponents, as if he were "the champion of a fixed opinion," rather than a scientific observer engaged in learning and open-ended inquiry. Then he vented his ire at Benjamin Banneker himself, writing, "to what we know ourselves of Banneker, we know he had spherical trigonometry enough to make Almanacs, but not without the suspicion of aid from Ellicott, who was his neighbor & friend, & never missed an opportunity of puffing him. I have a long letter from Banneker which shews him to have had a mind of very common stature indeed."

In fact, the letter was far from common. It was a brilliant attack on hypocrisy within a hopeful call for justice. Benjamin was proud of that letter and the way his most intense thoughts had come into clear articulation. As he was writing his letter to Jefferson, he had felt that he was not merely himself, but his people—a channel connecting to his father and his father before him, and even to those "brethren" to come.

CHAPTER 28

The Rift

Summer 2021

As GWEN, EDIE, Robert, and I continued to collaborate and share our research, things began to go very well. We established new partnerships between the Banneker-Lett descendants, Morgan State University, and the Baltimore County Parks, with the aim of preserving the artifacts at the Banneker Park and Museum. We set up a filming date with a producer at Maryland Public Television to record oral histories. The project seemed to have a life of its own, and I began to experience this process of getting to know my ancestors and fellow descendants as one of the most profound chapters of my life.

Often, I would be thinking or writing about some aspect of this history, and Robert, Edie, or Gwen would send an email or text about that same idea or research question. "Weird, I was just texting you," we'd laugh. It happened so often that we got used to it. I had the sense that we were each different branches of the same intention. I also felt like we had always known each other, like I had been missing them my whole life, and I was happier and more grounded because I was with my cousins.

"This story is much bigger than us and will go on longer than any of us," Gwen said one afternoon on a group phone call. We had just wrapped up a successful meeting with Baltimore County, in which we had invoked the participation of our ancestors. "And this process is all unfolding in Divine Order. We hardly even need to *do* anything."

"But that's where I disagree," Robert said. "I think we need to show up and do the work, and then the process can happen through us."

"I feel like I am a conduit for something much larger than me, but also a necessary participant," I said in agreement. "That's why I would call this a spiritual experience. The other reason is because this process is leading me to do so much self-reflection. I keep hitting moments when I am unsure about my role. Or moments when I make mistakes." I was constantly navigating how much I should keep quiet and decenter myself and how much I should contribute. I was well aware that white people often take over or talk too much in meetings, and I was trying not to do this. But being too silent and retiring also felt inauthentic.

"Yes, it is not exactly easy," Robert said. "I've been so overwhelmed at times, trying to harmonize different people in the family, different ways of thinking and working. I keep having to learn what parts of this are mine to do and what parts are not."

We were all learning to trust in the collaborative process, that paradox in which we were each vitally necessary and also just part of a much larger whole.

*　*　*

THEN SOMETHING HAPPENED. We had a cousin who did not like that I was writing this book, and saw it as just another white exploitation of a Black story. I had anticipated this critique of me and the project, and I found her point of view important. I reached out to her and asked if we could talk and invited her to be part of the process. I understood the long and ugly legacy of white people profiting from Black contributions and creativity and I wanted the book to be reparative in any way it could be. But again, this cousin wanted no part of my white privileged project.

Robert also talked with a scholar of African American studies—a man whom he had worked with in the past and long admired—who also expressed his skepticism and disapproval that I would be writing a book about Benjamin Banneker. I tried to introduce myself to him, and also told this cousin again that I respected her point of view and asked if she wanted to talk one-on-one. Then, when I did not hear back, I realized that it was time to let go. I stopped reaching out and just focused on my research and writing. But Robert, who was collaborating with this cousin on another project, kept trying to defend me and harmonize everyone. Our cousin's suspicion of me eventually got to him, and he too started to distrust my methods.

It was late summer, the weather warm and lush, and I would take long walks beside the lake, in a state of distraction and anxiety. Months earlier, a strong windstorm had brought a huge silver maple tree down onto our house's roof, nearly hitting me and falling into the ceiling of Adele's bedroom. We had waited for our insurance money to get approved, and then when summer came, we'd moved out of our house while contractors made repairs and improvements. In July, we stayed a few weeks with my parents in Ohio, and in August, we stayed at our friends' house while they were out of town. Then, as the construction dragged on toward fall, we rented a small apartment across town. The experience was destabilizing, and during this time, my absorption in the Banneker project had given me a feeling of groundedness. Now, to have the project in peril felt frightening and further destabilizing in the already unsettling time of COVID-19.

To make things even trickier, in these same weeks, the researcher Paul Heinegg, who maintains the historical database of *Free African Americans in Maryland and Delaware*, emailed Robert to tell him that he had located new documents relating to our Banneker-Lett family. One of these was the Provincial Court Record in which Mary Beneca argues for her daughter Sarah's right to freedom. The others were wills from Mary Welsh—possibly our Molly—which another genealogical researcher interpreted to mean that Molly was the family's *owner* rather than the family's grandmother. These documents changed the family story from how it had been told for centuries, and this change was triggering to my African American cousins. Pride in our documentable history was being replaced by anxiety and anger about the ways that the family oral histories were potentially being undermined.

"Why would Heinegg want to upset the apple cart?" Robert said.

"Why would he want to hang a whole new story on a new coatrack, when we had a perfectly good one before?"

I disagreed with Heinegg's sweeping new interpretation of the story, and I still thought that Molly was the grandmother, as generations of family oral histories had attested. I had been doing contextual research into mixed-race families in the Chesapeake, and I also felt that the new documentation had the potential to make our family's story even more remarkable, now that some of the main features in the oral histories were supported on paper. In these documents, we see Mary Beneca arguing in court to free her Lett children from indenture. We also see a Molly Welsh freeing "her people" and making one of them executor of her estate.

But for Robert and many other Black family members, the new information was unconfirmed, irritating, and all too familiar. Their own intimate history was being reconfigured by white researchers who were disregarding oral histories to base everything on documents. And documentation is always white by nature since white people controlled the courts, the police, and colonial churches. Archives—of court and marriage records, land deeds, letters, journals, and ship manifests— masquerade as objective spaces, but they are far from it. Archives always indicate who had power in a society and who did not. The only people who show up in colonial land deeds and marriage records, for instance, are white people. Most people of color were not legally allowed to marry and were not even recorded *as people* in early American archives, but were listed as property. They are denoted by first names, or even colder markers like "negroe boy, 6 yrs old," in ledgers alongside livestock and plows. And this historical trauma of being treated as the property of white people is reignited every time a white person treats a Black story as their property, as well.

The only other place where people of color show up in early American archives is in court records chronicling their criminality. These records often finished the work that racist police forces and patrollers had begun, by framing people of color as criminals more permanently and historically, on paper. Just as such inequities persist in the courts and prison complex of the present, the archives prime us to read the history of people of color through the lens of criminality.

Although the new documents show Mary bravely petitioning the courts for the freedom of her children, for instance, they also let us know that she was found guilty of "bastardy," for having these children out of wedlock. Out of the many ancestral histories that my Black cousins were connected to, the Banneker-Letts' was the most triumphant. The Bannekers and Letts had enjoyed the earliest freedom and respect, so to read their history through lenses of white ownership and criminality made this history painfully more typical for my cousins. And to have *me*, as a white woman, reading it this way only compounded the pain.

"These new documents are all about the women, anyway, and I'm not as interested in them," Robert said at one point. "They do not change the fact that Benjamin was a genius, or the fact that Robert was a large landowner."

"Well, I care about the women!" I said back. I had been treated with condescension by most of the male researchers I had contacted. They often explained things to me in a rudimentary way, as if assuming I had not read anything yet or done my own research. And I was tired of the old idea that we had all unwittingly absorbed—that the "official" histories were told by men, through the accomplishments of men. "That's why I am writing the book this way," I said to Robert, realizing that I was no longer disguising my impatience. "As far as I'm concerned, the women are as much a part of the story as the men. Molly and Mary, Jemima and Minta, are as interesting to me as Benjamin and Robert."

At the same time, I understood why Robert was upset and wanted nothing to do with the new findings, and part of my impatience was fear. I was nervous to tell him that I had to look into these documents. I knew I could not write about our ancestors responsibly without returning to the archives and looking at all the wills and court records myself. But my willingness to consider these new documents as potential additions to the story felt to Robert like a breach of trust and a break with the larger family. He wrote to a large group of family members, quoting out of context a private email I had written and saying that I was aligned with Heinegg and thought his research may clear up some "questionable" parts of the family's oral histories. I was angry and embarrassed because the last thing I wanted to do was hurt feelings or disrespect our Black family history. I wrote back that I was going to go to Maryland to see the documents myself and said that I would love to have a family phone call to discuss it all when I returned. I rented an Airbnb big enough for all of us, and asked Edie and Robert to join me.

But when I felt Robert's anger at me and worried that the whole group of Banneker-Lett descendants now resented me, I fell into a depression. The pain lasted for two long weeks that felt like slow-passing months. Whenever I talked during those weeks, my voice sounded awkward and unsure, or defensive and strident. It did not sound like my voice. And in those two weeks, this ancestral history moved from something that was more conceptual, or something that I had *thought* was more conceptual, to something that I felt very deeply, physically, and emotionally. I began to understand in a new way that I was also part of this story, that the cells of my body were also a part of this story.

Mostly what I felt was homesickness. I missed my family. I wanted to be with my grandparents, my cousins, with people who knew me and trusted my intentions. I had thought that these more distant cousins had known me too. I missed my weekly talks with Robert, and I found myself wishing that I could sit with my grandfather, who was the person in my family most closely related to the other Banneker-Letts but who had never met them. I didn't want to work on the book with him. I just wanted to hang out, to spend the day with someone who had known me since I was a baby, or maybe even before that. My grandfather could always make me laugh and would always deliver a little instigating wisdom when he thought I was getting too serious about something. He had always helped me to just lighten up and *enjoy* my life.

On two of the days when I felt the loneliest, I thought I saw my grandfather. Once was in front of the post office, in the tall, long-legged stoop of a letter carrier just beginning his route. Another time was at a coffee shop. An older man who had his crinkly, mischievous eyes looked across the room at me. I sat in the booth wiping my eyes with a napkin after that, hoping that no one would notice that I was crying. It wasn't that I thought those men *were* my grandfather. I just missed him, and I wondered if sometimes the ancestors can borrow the bodies of the living, to connect with us in quick necessary moments of reassurance. If you believe that human love is a thread twisting down through the ages, like those twists of protein turning and turning in the DNA helix, then why couldn't such a thing be possible?

One thing that became obvious was that I began to feel this story most viscerally when I was *excluded* from it. That exclusion *was* my inheritance, as someone descended from the family members who had left their cousins to pass into whiteness. And that feeling of exclusion opened a loneliness in me that was so deep, it seemed to stem from more than one situation, more than one lifetime. It was a feeling of being in-between. It was a feeling of deeply wanting to be trusted, but being seen as someone untrustworthy. It was a feeling of having found my people, just to lose them. And it was connected to another feeling of guilt.

"You're with the high-rollers now," my grandpa had said to me years ago when I first moved to Chicago and began working with Mayor Daley and his wife, Maggie. "We can't help you anymore." He did not say it bitterly—just matter-of-factly. I had left our small town for a fast-paced city life that he would not have chosen for me. There is a divide in America between city and country. And there are cultures in which upward mobility is not only distrusted but subtly punished. My grand-parents were quietly proud of my accomplishments, but suspicious of my ambition, as if ambition, by its very nature, takes us away from our humanity. I do not know if that is true, but ambition does take us away from our homes. I left home at eighteen and never came back again. And now, after I had been welcomed into the fold of my Black cousins, I had decided to go my own way in pursuing the archival research. In considering these documents, I was validating the *white* way of think-ing, and I was afraid I could never live in the fold, or the family, or the story, again.

My grief was also twisted up with defeat because I had already written a full draft of this book, and I thought I would have to scrap it. When you are obsessed with a story, it is as if you are living inside of it. The book becomes your dominant relationship, and for a time, everything signals back to it. It had been my central obsession for years, and I had loved it more than anything else I'd worked on because I hadn't worked on it alone. I knew that without the voices and insights of my cousins, without their consent and our present-day conversations, the story would lose its necessary form. And so my grief was also for all the work I had done, and for what I had hoped our book could become.

But if I had spent years on the project, Robert had spent decades researching and sharing these family histories. He and our cousin Marsha Stewart had helped to create a network of hundreds of Banneker-Lett descendants, who shared their talents and came together for reunions and restorative projects—like getting grave markers for the ancestors who had fought in the "Colored Regiment" of the Civil War. I could only imagine what Robert felt when I insisted on researching documents that no other biographer of Benjamin Banneker had seen. This story was Robert's life's work and legacy. It was also his identity. And as he had told me before, and I had known myself, Black people needed the Banneker story more than white people did. White people had plenty of ancestors who could be documented back to the 1700s. But Benjamin Banneker was one of a very small handful of Black people who had been recorded and remembered *as people*, let alone geniuses, and they deserved his story.

There is also an intense and natural fear that arises whenever a sacred, private story is on the brink of being made public. These were our family members, and because I was writing a book about them, that meant that soon they would be in the hands of strangers, and who knew how they would be cared for? What evidence did Black people ever have that their loved ones would be treated with reverence in the hands of the wider white world?

* * *

IN THOSE WEEKS when I felt left out of the family, I couldn't write anything. I was just processing. I kept thinking about the blocks and traumas that make intimacy between white women and women of color so difficult, those repeating patterns in our familial and national history that had led this cousin to intensely dislike me after just one phone meeting.

One afternoon, I was out walking along the lake with my friend Stephanie, who is also a white woman.

"I think I need to write a paragraph about white women," I said.

"A paragraph?" she asked, her eyebrows raised.

"Yeah, you're right," I said. "Maybe a whole page."

* * *

I HAD WANTED to decenter myself. I had also wanted to decenter the Ellicott family, who had played a starring role in Benjamin Banneker's earlier biographies. The abolitionist Ellicotts had given Benjamin Banneker the access to survey Washington, D.C., and to publish his almanacs. But they were always positioned as benevolent patrons rather than admiring friends, as if the Ellicotts had *granted* Benjamin his intelligence. Benjamin was in his forties by the time he met the Ellicotts. He had already designed his clock, and had been writing, inventing, and thinking for years before that. The Ellicotts had had plenty of time to be part of this story, I figured. Now it was time to make Benjamin's context that of his own family, his own parents and grandparents, and other free people of color who had found ways to survive and thrive in colonial and Revolutionary America.

But I couldn't quite get rid of the white women, because we were there all along, with our good intentions and our ill intentions, with our occasional resistance and our more common complicity and cruelty in an increasingly racist patriarchy. White women were legally unable to own land in early America, and could only own "moveable property"—china and armoires, petticoats, dining chairs, and *people*. This means that all over the colonies and then the United States, white women amassed wealth through the ownership of Black human beings. White girl babies were given enslaved people when they were born. White women gave their daughters entire enslaved families, or broken-off parts of families, as wedding gifts. Owning and controlling every aspect of the lives of these people became the proof and experience of wealth for these white women. White women also had control over Black women's offspring, and those children made even more wealth for white women.

If all this were not awful enough, "the tangled genealogies of slavery," as Harriet Jacobs called them, only amplified the pain and dysfunction between white "mistresses" and their enslaved people. White women's husbands and sons often coerced their enslaved women into sexual relations, leading to mixed offspring. These entanglements caused white wives intense jealousy and pain, and facilitated a level of denial and anger that made white women some of the most vindictive and violent enslavers of all. After escaping slavery in Maryland, Harriet Jacobs wrote about white women whose nerves were "too delicate" to dress or bathe themselves but could watch as their female slaves were whipped until they were crippled, lying in a pool of blood. And Frederick Douglass remarked that the offspring of "masters" and slaves "invariably suffer greater hardships, and have more to contend with, than others. They are, in the first place, a constant offence to their mistress. She is ever disposed to find fault with them; they can seldom do any thing to please her; she is never better pleased than when she sees them under the lash."

But if slavery is the central multigenerational trauma between white women and Black women, it is one that still needs to be publicly recognized for its massive destruction and its ongoing echoes in contemporary life. It is a trauma that awakens every time white women assume they are speaking for all women, or fail to listen to Black women, or neglect to acknowledge their own privileges and blind spots. It is a trauma that awakens every time white women choose their alliance with white men over an alliance with other women, including women of color. White women made that choice when 53 percent of them voted for Donald Trump in 2016, even after he bragged about sexual assault, and they made it again in 2020. White women did not want to elect a woman to the presidency or the vice presidency. Instead, they chose white male privilege, because this model was more familiar to them. They had been banking on that brand of security for generations.

*　*　*

THINKERS FROM JAMES Baldwin, to Martin Luther King, to Ta-Nehisi Coates have all written about their disappointment with white liberals, those "good white people" who congratulate themselves on their open-mindedness but do nothing to change unjust distributions of wealth or racist societal structures. These are the people who put a Black Lives Matter sign in their yard but have never had a Black person over for dinner. These are people who live in a house in a gentrified neighborhood that they bought with cash—with their multigenerational white wealth—that had gone into foreclosure after the bank seized it from a Black family. I know these people. I live in their neighborhood. And I respect Black people's exhaustion and disgust with those of us who want to *look* progressive more than we want anything to actually change.

But I have to believe that there are good white people, and good white women, and that more of us can become this as we wake up from the collective delusion of white supremacy. The fact is, there have always been a few good white women in terms of race, although America's racist history has been so brutal that this goodness often appears later to have not been good enough. Our ancestor Molly was one of these good white women. So was Mary Williams, a Quaker woman who owned the land beside the Banneker property. When Mary Williams's husband died, she inherited his land and thirteen enslaved people. In her last will and testament of August 23, 1786, she bequeathed to the "Quarterly Meeting of the Society of Friends of Baltimore all my right of thirteen negroes," whom she then named individually. She willed "also ten acres of Land, where James and Margaret now live, being part of a tract of land called Mt. Gilboa, laying in Baltimore County for the use of the aforesaid Thirteen Negroes."

By willing her enslaved people to the Society of Friends—abolitionist Quakers—Mary was effectively freeing them without engaging in the legal quagmire of manumission. The Quakers' guardianship of James, Margaret, and their offspring may have protected them more than free papers, because it shielded them from abduction by other whites. But Mary Williams knew that even this kind of custodial freedom remained precarious. So she left the remainder of her land to her brother-in-law, John Teale, with specific instructions that if her heirs came to "claim any part of the aforesaid negroes as his or their property," Teale was to sell the land to buy the people's freedom back again. In other words, Mary knew that the only way to free Margaret, James,

and their families was to free them *twice*, with a backup insurance pol-
icy against her own descendants who may come to rob these people of
their liberty.

That was one way to be a good white woman in the late 1700s. It
was legally convoluted, countercultural, and necessarily *insistent*. Mary
Williams's heirs did not come to claim the land or the people. And that
tract that she left to James, Margaret, and their families became the
town of Mt. Gilboa—a free Black community that thrived well into
the twentieth century. It was in this context, beside a self-sustaining
community of people of color and among abolitionist Quakers, that
the Banneker family's own freedom was able to take root and flourish.

* * *

YET WHITE WOMEN have always posed problems for the Banneker
story. In the beginning, there was Molly, a white woman. Then there
were the white women who tried to record Benjamin's biography for
posterity.

The first person who tried to write a book-length biography of Benjamin Banneker was Rachel Mason. Rachel was the daughter of the
writer Susanna Mason, who was one of Benjamin Banneker's admirers,
correspondents, and friends. After her mother died, Rachel published
her memoirs, which included a description of Susanna Mason's visit
to the "aged astronomer" and a poem she had written for Benjamin.
"There lived a man called Banneker, An African astronomer . . . will
stand exposed from age to age, Extant on some historian's page,"
Susanna's poem grandly intoned. Rachel decided that she herself would
secure Banneker's place in history by writing his biography.

Rachel Mason enlisted her distant cousin, Martha Ellicott Tyson, to
interview Benjamin's remaining family members and record oral histories about him and the family. Of all the children in the Ellicott family,
Martha had been the one most interested in history and politics. She
had seen Benjamin Banneker talking with her father, George Ellicott,
late into the evenings about government, history, and science, and had
grown up surrounded by Benjamin's almanacs. She agreed with Rachel

that publishing a biography of Benjamin Banneker "would have a useful influence on his brethren, both in the United States, and in the African Colonies."

When I was telling my husband this story, he interrupted me to say, "Wait, Benjamin's first biographer was named *Rachel*? And she worked with her distant cousin to gather oral histories and write it?"

"Yes." I laughed.

"This is all starting to sound like a computer simulation," he said

"It's weird," I agreed. "The way names repeat, the way *we* seem to repeat."

At first, Rachel was struck by how much she did not know and felt confused about her role in the project. "I have not materials to complete anything worth giving to the public," she wrote to her cousin Martha. "I think if I had, I should not feel competent to do it."

But Martha took a more pragmatic approach, based on research. She continued interviewing family members who lived in the area and had known Benjamin Banneker personally, including his nephew John Hendon and his childhood friend Jacob Hall. Hendon and other family members told Martha that they had a white grandmother named Molly Welsh. Could such a thing be true? Martha confirmed that, yes, everyone in the family had talked of their great-grandmother, "Little Ma," or Molly, who had children with their African great-grandfather.

When Rachel learned about this "admixture" of whiteness in Benjamin's ancestry, she did not know how to continue with the book. She wrote to Martha nervously about the findings, noting that the value of Banneker's story would be reduced if he could not be proven to be "of strictly African parentage." This insertion of a white woman in the story was problematic, she said, and now she worried that the book would harm rather than help the cause of abolition. Then, in 1849, Rachel Mason died suddenly, without having seriously begun the biography.

After Rachel's death, Martha decided to fashion her notes into a biography of Banneker herself. When her nephew offered to read excerpts of Banneker's biography aloud at the Maryland Historical Society in 1851, Martha returned to her notes and sought out other Banneker relatives to double-check those tricky parts about his ancestry. In December, she wrote in her journal:

Just before completing the "Sketch" which had been presented to the Historical Society, I sent for a niece of Banneker, named Harriet Henderson, in order to find if her account of her Mother's grandmother would coincide with John Henden's statement. Her account of Molly Welsh was similar to that I have given above with a few additional particulars, respecting the case of her leaving England.

According to her great-granddaughter Harriet, Molly *was* the white woman who had come from England and worked through her indenture before becoming Mary's mother and Benjamin's grandmother—an unusual, independent woman a little like Martha Tyson herself. Martha was interested in government, politics, and history, but, as a woman, she was not allowed to study those subjects or pursue law. She married Nathaniel Tyson, who was the son of a prominent abolitionist, and became an ordained minister in the Quaker church—the only denomination in America that would permit a woman to speak before a congregation. Martha felt so strongly about women's fundamental right to an education that she cofounded Swarthmore College. But because she was a woman—even an illustrious one—her writings and intellectual contributions were often sidelined, put into the service of others, or left unpublished. Excerpts of her biography of Benjamin Banneker were read before the Maryland Historical Society twice during Martha Tyson's lifetime, but the men reading from the biography never said the name of the author. Instead, they praised the "modesty" of the lady who did not put her name on her work. Although she continued to work on Benjamin's biography, Martha Ellicott Tyson was never granted credit for the book and was not able to publish it in her lifetime.

After Martha's death in 1873, her daughter, Anne Tyson Kirk, decided to edit and publish the biography of Benjamin Banneker as a way of honoring both his and her mother's legacy. While she was preparing the manuscript for publication, Kirk reached out to Frederick Douglass for advice. In response to her first letter, of March 4, 1878, Douglass replied that he was "greatly obliged" to her for her note about the *Sketch of the Life of Benjamin Banneker*. He added that if the book were short and "not made to cost more than fifty cents per copy," it would sell well among "my newly emancipated people."

"We as a people are especially in need of just such examples of mental industry and success as I believe the life of Bannecker furnish," Douglass wrote. "The sooner you give us the work the better and more timely it will be."

Anne Tyson Kirk continued to edit the material, but whether it was due to her own insecurity and internal censor, or to her many female duties, or to the fact that she was trying to publish as a woman, the book was met with several delays. When she contacted Frederick Douglass again, two years had passed, and he had begun to qualify his enthusiasm for the project.

"I can speak for myself," Douglass wrote, "for one I believe that a full narrative of the life of so exceptional a character as Bannecker will find a ready sale both in the North and in the South among colored and among white readers." Then he hedged a bit, writing, "I wish I could see the manuscript before you publish it. . . . There has been an attempt lately to make him a son of a white woman by a black father, and thus to credit the white race with whatever ability he possessed. I confess that my interest in him would be measurably diminished if this should turn out to be true."

Douglass knew firsthand how Black genius could be undermined. And he had his own complicated feelings about a white "admixture" of blood. In the very first chapter of his 1854 autobiography, *Narrative of the Life of Frederick Douglass*, he delved into this pain. "My father was a white man," he began. "The opinion was also whispered that my master was my father; but of the correctness of this opinion, I know nothing; the means of knowing was withheld from me." He went on to explain that he and his mother were separated when he was an infant, in a method commonly employed by plantation owners to strip people of their families and attachments. He remembered seeing his mother only four or five times in his life, in the middle of the night, when she snuck back from the far plantation where she'd been sent to work. "She would lie down with me; and get me to sleep. But long before I waked she was gone." Then he wrote:

> She died when I was about seven years old, on one of my master's farms, near's Lee's Mill. I was not allowed to be present during her

illness, at her death, or burial . . . The whisper that my master was my father, may or may not be true; and, true or false, it is of but little consequence to my purpose whilst the fact remains, in all its glorious odiousness, that slaveholders have ordained, and by law established, that the children of slave women shall in all cases follow the condition of their mothers; and this is done too obviously to administer to their own lusts, and make a gratification of their wicked desires profitable as well as pleasurable.

* * *

ANNE KIRK CONTINUED to wrestle with the manuscript about Benjamin Banneker. It was not until 1882 that she wrote to Frederick Douglass again to say that the little book was ready for publication.

Once again, Douglass expressed his happiness that the biography existed and generously offered to buy fifty copies of the first edition for free circulation in Black communities. "If a few others will do the same," he wrote helpfully, "the Book can easily be set well afloat."

But in 1884, just after Anne Kirk submitted the manuscript to publishers in Philadelphia, she, too, suddenly died, and the book was never properly distributed. Banneker's biography was given a few impressive reviews in abolitionist newspapers but remained largely unknown by the reading public.

It had taken almost eighty years, and three well-meaning white women, to write and publish a slim biography of Benjamin Banneker. We do not know which of these female authors' obstructions were external and which were internal. The blocks were there because they were writing about the genius and humanity of a Black man and his family. And because they were women. Their serious writing and research was treated like a hobby to be done in the margins of their lives—the center being about giving to others, teaching, parenting, hostessing, and serving as a wife.

It is still a little this way. Judgments abound whenever a woman takes up serious work, and we women can feel self-conscious and wobbly as we walk the line between caring for others and actualizing our own talents. As one of my male colleagues asked me, "Why would you write about this, as a *white woman*?" Perhaps that was a genuine question, a prod for me to find my own way to the story. But it was delivered in a tone meant to shame and intimidate me. It was a dig around cultural appropriation, and an unsaid suggestion that as a white woman I should be primarily concerned with myself.

In those weeks, when I was grappling with white womanhood and its history of being both oppressor and oppressed, I felt unsteady and confused. Ashamed in an inarticulate way. I still did not know how much of this story was about me, and how much of it was not.

Gwen Marable during the construction of the replica of Banneker's cabin, Benjamin Banneker Historical Park and Museum, 2009.

Rachel's daughter, Adele, and niece Gwyneth, in front of a replica of Banneker's cabin at the Benjamin Banneker Historical Park and Museum in Oella, MD, 2017.

Edie Lee Harris (left) and Gwen Marable (right) reconnecting at the Benjamin Banneker Historical Park and Museum, 2021.

Gwen Marable and Rachel
meeting in the woods, 202

Gwen Marable and
Edie Lee Harris looking
at the ledger from the
Ellicott & Co. Store,
Benjamin Banneker
Historical Park and
Museum, 2021.

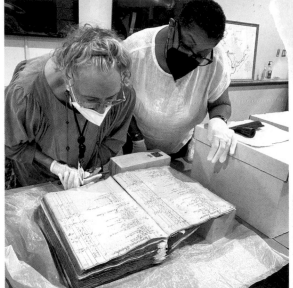

The reunion of Edie Lee Harris,
Gwen Marable, and Rachel Webster,
Benjamin Banneker Historical Park
and Museum, September 2021.

Rachel and Edie Lee Harris in the Maryland State Archives, searching for documentation of their ancestors, Annapolis, MD, September 2021.

(Left) Robert Lett at home in Pasadena, CA, 2022.

(Above) Edwin Lee and Rachel Webster meeting in person in Springfield, IL, November 2021.

(Left) Edie Lee Harris with an original copy of Benjamin Banneker's Almanac at the Maryland Center for History and Culture in Baltimore, MD, September 2021.

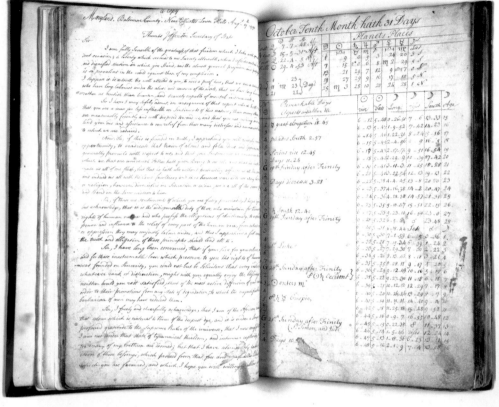

Page-spread of Benjamin Banneker's manuscript journal, showing a copy of his letter to Jefferson on the left, and his ephemeris for October 1792 on the right.

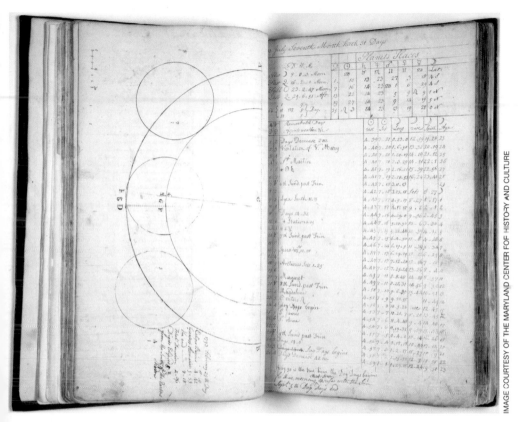

Page-spread of Benjamin Banneker's manuscript journal, showing his drawings of an eclipse on the left and his ephemeris for July 1793 on the right.

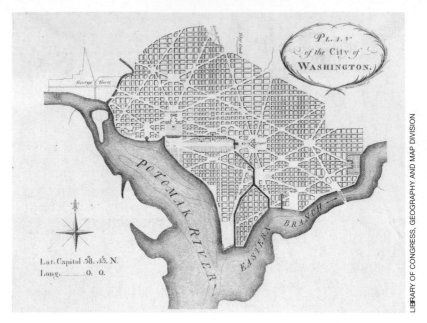

Plan of the city of Washington, drawn by Pierre L'Enfant and first published in the *Columbian Magazine*, Philadelphia, March 1792. Benjamin Banneker helped Andrew Ellicott to survey this urban plan.

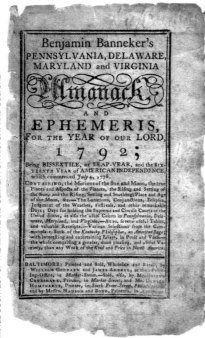

Cover of Benjamin Banneker's first Almanac of 1792.

Cover of Benjamin Banneker's 1795 Almanac with his woodcut portrait.

Geraldine Dubisson, Edie Lee Harris and Edwin Lee's mother, 1921.

Elzy Jones, Gwen Marable's father, with his twin brothers, Leonard and Roy Jones, 1920s.

Robert Lett's parents, Charles Loren Lett and Anna Mae Sleet Lett, on their wedding day, August 1949.

Edie Lee Harris and Edwin Lee's ancestor William Lett, a free person of color, around 1870.

Rachel and her dad, Jim Webster, in Madison, OH, on Lake Erie, 1995.

Rachel's grandfather Philip Webster, holding her daughter, Adele, 2007.

CHAPTER 29

Publication

Maryland, 1792–1806

Benjamin Banneker's Pennsylvania, Delaware, Maryland and Virginia Almanack and Ephemeris For the Year of our Lord, 1792, Being Bisextile, or Leap Year, and the Sixteenth Year of American Independence, which commenced, July 4, 1776. CONTAINING the motions of the Sun and Moon; the true Places and Aspects of the Planets; The Rising and Setting of the Sun; Place and Age of the Moon, &c.—the Lunations, Conjunctions, Eclipses, Judgement of the Weather, Festivals and Other Remarkable Days; Days for Holding the Supreme Court and Circuit Courts of the United States. . . . Also several useful Tables and valuable Receipts.

—From the cover of Benjamin Banneker's Almanac of 1792

BENJAMIN'S FIRST ALMANAC, *Benjamin Banneker's Pennsylvania, Delaware, Maryland and Virginia Almanack and Ephemeris, for the Year of Our Lord, 1792,* was a great success whose sales outpaced even Major Ellicott's popular almanac. It began with the introduction by Senator James McHenry, informing readers of the author's race and attesting to his gifts. It also included an essay on the cosmos titled "Planetary and Terrestrial Worlds, Comparatively Considered"; an essay titled "Remarks on the Swiftness of Time," imploring people to cast aside procrastination and live their lives with purpose; and an abolitionist essay by David Rittenhouse.

The almanac's ephemeris brought together Benjamin's astronomical computations of moon cycles, tides, and eclipses. It also listed holidays, court meeting days, directions to major cities, and exchange rates for coins, because at that time Americans were still using pounds, doubloons, francs, and other currency from Europe. Banneker's almanac was praised for its accuracy, its practicality, and its readability. It was so successful that several firms rushed to issue Banneker's later editions, and Benjamin immediately began compiling an ephemeris for the following year.

That next year—1793—Banneker published editions of his almanac in both Maryland and Pennsylvania, and printers included several more essays in the book. The Maryland edition of Banneker's almanac praised the "ingenious self-taught astronomer" and noted that Benjamin's 1792 almanac had been presented in the House of Commons by British antislavery advocates who wanted to put an end to "the diabolical Traffic in human Flesh." This version of the almanac also featured an essay proposing "A Plan of a Peace Office for the United States" that was later attributed to Benjamin Rush, the Philadelphia physician who had signed the Declaration of Independence and had become increasingly outspoken against slavery.

The Pennsylvania edition of the 1793 almanac included excerpts from the Parliamentary debates in England against slavery and a passage condemning slavery from Jefferson's own *Notes on the State of Virginia*. Most controversially, in it were published the letters between Banneker and Jefferson. These contents made this edition of Benjamin Banneker's almanac one of the most important publications of its time. It was distributed widely and discussed in all political circles, making considerable trouble for Jefferson, who was still secretary of state under President George Washington but preparing a run for president. The Pennsylvania Society for the Relief of Free Negroes Unlawfully Held in Bondage stayed in close touch with Benjamin and made plans to produce another of Banneker's almanacs for 1794.

Benjamin was delighted. He spent the first part of every spring making projections of eclipses and calculations for the next year's ephemeris, double-checking his observations and equations. He also began penning more poems and short essays and observations that he hoped to include in future almanacs. Finally, it seemed, his mind and curiosity, observations and eloquence would be known beyond the realm of his family and neighborhood. He stopped drinking altogether and began taking regular long walks around his property, determined to keep his mind clear and his body fit so that he could continue his intellectual pursuits as he aged.

But in 1793, Benjamin fell into a terrible, lingering illness. He was so sick that he could barely sit up in bed some days and could not take his customary walks. He used every hour he was well enough to complete his astronomical observations. But he lost track of his correspondence with publishers and missed several deadlines. His notes from this year also show that he had begun calculating an ephemeris for the latitude of London, probably because the British antislavery movement had also wanted to publish one of Banneker's almanacs. Still feverish and weak, his usually perfect handwriting wavering, Benjamin was eventually able to complete the Maryland ephemeris for the following year, but he never completed the computations necessary for England. Several American editions of Banneker's almanac for 1794 went to press, however, and Benjamin was deeply relieved that he had come through the illness and continued with his series.

The Maryland edition of the 1794 almanac began with a poem by Phillis Wheatley, bringing Banneker and Wheatley together as the era's primary examples of African American brilliance. This edition sold more copies than the publisher's wildest expectations. Arguments ensued among readers about whether Wheatley and Banneker had written their own work or had others write it for them. People were either threatened or curious about the poet Wheatley and the scientist Banneker, because they contradicted the current "science" that said that African American people were incapable of reason, artistry, and complex human feeling. If African American people could write poetry and do higher mathematics, then slavery was even more of a problem than it seemed. Banneker's next almanac of 1795 reached its widest-ever distribution when it was published by six different companies in several editions. Some of these editions were less lofty than those of earlier years, replacing long essays with shorter folk aphorisms and humorous stories, but they were still abolitionist by nature. In one of these 1795 almanacs, the usual drawing of the Vitruvian Man, showing which astrological houses influenced which parts of the body, was replaced with a drawing of a Black man, positioning an African American figure as emblematic of humanity.

And so it went. Banneker's almanacs continued to be published in several states and cities for two more years, and he and Wheatley became the first Black best-selling authors in America. Benjamin Banneker was a household name and part of the national conversation in those first years after the Revolution. Those postwar years were heady with the relief of peace and survival, and marked by a lofty patriotism that touted American liberty and opportunity. But if Benjamin Banneker was a beacon of achievement for other people of color and a promising symbol for abolitionists, he was also a thorn in the side of the national narrative. If America was so free, his presence reminded, why were so many people who looked like him still cruelly enslaved?

* * *

BENJAMIN BANNEKER HIMSELF was said to be heavyset and dignified, resembling that more well-known thinker and inventor, Benjamin Franklin. Charles W. Dorsey, a planter from Elkridge Landing, who worked as a clerk in the store of Ellicott & Co., remembered meeting Banneker during these later years of Benjamin's life. "In the year 1800 I commenced my engagements in the store at Ellicott's Mills, where my first acquaintance with Benjamin Banneker began," Dorsey said.

> He was a large man and inclined to be fleshy. He was far advanced in years when I first saw him. He often came to the store to purchase articles for his own use, and, after hearing him converse, I was always anxious to wait upon him. After making his purchases, he usually went to the part of the store where George Ellicott was in the habit of sitting, to converse with him about the affairs of our government, and other matters. He was very precise in conversation and exhibited deep reflection. His deportment, whenever I saw him, was perfectly upright and correct, and he seemed to be acquainted with everything of importance that was passing in the country.

Dorsey went on. "I recollect to have seen his Almanacs in my father's house, and believe they were the only ones used in the neighborhood at the time."

During these years, Benjamin prioritized his astronomical work and found ways to lease or sell parts of his farm so he could focus on his almanacs. In 1792, Benjamin sold a portion of his land on the river to John Nimiy, probably a nephew-in-law, who was a cooper and wanted access to the waterway to soak the wood to make hogshead barrels for tobacco. He sold another tract of land to his nephew Greenbury Morton. Soon after that, Benjamin found a way to devise a kind of retirement plan for himself. According to the Ellicott family, he contracted his land to George Ellicott and Ellicott & Co., in exchange for a pension that would carry him through the last years of his life. He drew up a contract by way of a letter: "I believe I should live fifteen years, and consider my land worth 180 pounds Maryland currency. By receiving 12 pounds a year for fifteen years, I shall, in the contemplated time, receive its full value; if, on the contrary, I die before that day, you will be at liberty to take possession," he wrote. He then explained his thinking, saying that he wanted to "increase his knowledge on subjects to which his attention had been directed from his youth, and to his inability from physical infirmities, to perform much laborious exercise; his land would thus be poorly cultivated, and poverty, an evil he much dreaded, increase upon him." He defended the idea—to himself as well as to the Ellicotts—writing that if he were to divide his land among all of his family members, the parcels would be too small to be of service to anybody. If he gave it all to one or two, however, he worried that "they would become objects of envy" and create strife within the family.

Benjamin's sisters Minta Black and Molly Morton lived nearby. They cooked, cleaned, and sewed for him, while he devoted himself to writing, mathematics, and astronomy. "Still cultivating sufficient ground to give him needful exercise, he might be seen hoeing his corn, cultivating his garden, or trimming his fruit trees," Martha Tyson wrote of Benjamin's later years. "Sometimes he would be found watching the habits of his bees." He would often take a break from his studies at the twilight hour, when he liked to sit beneath a large chestnut tree that stood near to his house. There he would play the violin or flute, alone but with the brightening stars for company.

CHAPTER 30

Reckoning

Evanston, Illinois, and Pasadena, California, Summer 2021

IN THOSE WEEKS when I was out of my home and out of touch with the family, I was harried and overly busy, not at my best. Every time Robert and I would attempt to talk, we would just tick each other off again. We agreed with each other conceptually, but we kept getting into arguments so entangled that afterward we could hardly remember what we had been at odds about.

During one conversation, he told me that the Smithsonian had rejected Banneker's writing table for their exhibits.

"That was stupid of them," I said. I was loading the dishwasher and trying to find a container to put my daughter's sandwich in. I was also trying to show my support of him, to remind him that I was on his side. It seemed to be another case of the old guard not realizing who needed to be included in history.

"Really?" he said. "You think the Smithsonian is *stupid*? And isn't that just a white way of thinking anyway? Who cares about a desk? Aren't white people always a little too obsessed with objects?"

I leaned back against the counter. It was amazing—how similarly Robert and I thought sometimes. I had just been journaling about the same idea, something about how whiteness—itself an invention of capitalism—had become the culture of consumerism, and how our fixation with objects keeps people from addressing underlying structural inequities. I was looking for a lid for this little metal snack tin. And I was so bored with my culture's fixation on *things*.

"I agree!" I said. "I just think that Benjamin deserves more regard at the Smithsonian, and in history in general." I was about to continue with this line of thought, but I could feel that Robert was bracing for a battle, and I was so tired.

"Robert, I don't want to do this today," I said. "I don't want to argue."

"When you go away and say you can't talk right now, isn't that you just retreating into your whiteness?" he said.

"No, that's not it. It's just that I can tell that we are both defensive today and could say things to hurt each other. I am at a place in my life when I want to notice those moments and walk away. Let's wait and try to talk next week."

The feelings that Robert and I were experiencing were bigger and sloppier than either of us. All along, we had acknowledged that this story and process were larger than us as individuals. But that spacious sense of collaboration that we had experienced in earlier months had now expanded to include pain as well as wonder. Strife as well as harmony. Any real healing would have to come through pain, it seemed. We would eventually have to arrive at the rift that had gotten us here.

I had been writing about systems of power and structural racism, including the economic and legal setup that had led to the privileging of whiteness, the oppression of people of color, and the establishment of racial hierarchies that still existed today. But it was not just structures of power that had done this to us. It was also individual people, making individual choices—some for survival and some for self-interest.

My ancestors who first passed as white had done so as a group of siblings, but the next generation moved across town and denied this family altogether. What must that have felt like to the Black family members who were not acknowledged by their white-passing cousins at the hardware store, or who had to step aside on the sidewalk for those cousins to walk by, not looking at them in the eye? My family had been those *not* saying hello, denying their kin, saying horrible things about Black people behind their backs, making racial jokes—all to appeal to the white world they were passing into. That disregard—that disavowal of family—was in my DNA. And now I was feeling an echo of the rejection from my cousins that my ancestors had perpetuated on theirs.

I was also feeling something of what my family had lost when they left—a feeling of connection and wholeness, that soft nod of implicit recognition, a rhythm that combines mind, heart, and soul. I was being reminded that Black culture was not my culture. And I was not going to be invited in.

But I did know that these cousins were my own, because they *felt* like family. All through those weeks, I would think to myself about Robert, "You may not be claiming me, but I'm claiming you! You're my cousin. I can tell you are my cousin because we are both so stubborn and openhearted and intellectually elaborate and *alike*. I *know* you." I was feeling a loyalty to Robert even while he acted like I was some kind of stranger or white parasite. *How often had the Black relatives felt this about the white ones who passed?* I wondered. You may not be admitting we're kin, but I *know* who you are. You are of the other culture now, a culture that has so sold its soul it thinks it's okay to *own* human beings. Oh, I know who you are.

"I feel like I've been in a war," Robert said when we tried to talk again the next week. "There is so much going on. California is burning again, and I'm so afraid I'm going to have another one of those asthma attacks I had last year and not be able to breathe."

There we were—in the broken, burning present of our divided country. We were still caught in a pandemic, and Robert was at the highest risk of us all for contracting the deadly virus. There was COVID-19, and then there was the plague of racism that had infected America from its very beginning and would still permit a white policeman to kneel on the neck of a Black man and suffocate him to death. And there I was, sucking the wind out of his story—the story he had spent his life telling and sharing with family members.

Later, I would think that we had not actually been at war with each other as much as in a battle between our aspirational selves that wanted to honor everyone's particular viewpoint, and our embodied selves that were still carrying the traumas, disappointments, and fears of this life-time and our forebears' lifetimes.

Finally, something shifted. The season changed.

Email from Robert Lett, September 2, 2021

Good Morning,

I want to take a moment to share with you how much I do appreciate the work you are doing. The recent ripples which we have experienced should not be in anyway be considered as threatening as river rapids.

Our differences are rooted in my lifetime awareness of my Lett surname and being raised with the knowledge of family exceptionalism as African Americans. I had the good fortune of having been raised by parents—graduates of Historically Black Universities who took great pride in African American History and our families' role as early landowners, activists, and abolitionists. What you seek to learn and share has been well-integrated within my every breath since birth, along with a knowledge of lynchings and biased accounts to denigrate and revise African American history. I thank God every day for being raised in a family which acknowledged the inequity and brutality of racism but also believed in the freedom of the individual soul and adventure.

I want to remind you that unlike Edie who learned of her Lett ancestry as she approached mid-life, or your similar discovery of Lett & multi-ethnic history, my Lett ancestry has been shared for seven generations. So when the revisionists arrive I believe it only fitting and proper that I hold them to the standard by which I should be held accountable.

I believe that I am justified to be suspect of those who will alter that which they will only visit, but yet I am to live.

Hang in there Sloopy,
Cousin Robert

*　*　*

I THANKED ROBERT for his email, and we set a time to talk the following week. "I feel like you and I kept triggering each other," I said, "making each other mad and bringing up pain that had generational echoes to it."

"I don't know about that," Robert said. "I just think that if you're really in it, really committed, you are going to have to hang in there for the good, the bad, and the ugly."

"True," I said. "And the difficult moments have at least as much to teach us as the harmonious moments."

"Of course they do," Robert said.

"What happened with me in these last weeks is that I began to understand how deeply I care about this project," I said. "It was as if the process reached more levels of my being. I had to experience your rejection of me in order to understand my part in these family stories. The grief I felt when you were angry at me and no longer wanted to be in the book was so intense that I felt like it connected me to an ancestral grief."

Robert listened. I was amazed, not for the first time, at the level on which we could communicate. In many aspects of my life, I can communicate on one register—the intellectual at work, the emotional with many friends. When my cousins and I spoke, we mixed it all together. We got each other.

"What happened to me is that I had to go back to your intentions and acknowledge the positivity that has always resulted from our conversations," Robert said. "But I do have to say that I never imagined all of this would get so out of hand. I thought this would be more of an intellectual exercise, just to introduce more people into the mix and hear their points of view. I had no idea it would all get so tangled up and emotional. So *intense.*"

In harmonizing with our cousin and trying to get us all into one conversation, Robert had been riding the waves and was experiencing an emotional whiplash. In continuing to work with me, as a white woman, he was also risking losing respect from Black people he admired.

"But I don't think we can talk and write about race without bringing up a whole lot of pain," I said.

"I guess not," Robert agreed. "The other thing that happened was that Edie gave me a talking to. She said I was being too hard on you."

"She did?" I had not known this, and it made me smile. I had never had to defend myself with Edie or Gwen.

"Yes, she said that you are just as much a descendant as any of us, and that you have the intuition and sensibility to write about our family. But I said that it was going to take more than intuition to get it right!"

"Of course," I said. "It is also research, lots of study and drafting."

"I know it is an enormous amount of work," Robert replied. "That's why I never wrote the book.

"And I had to go back to your original intentions," he went on. "I had to accept that we have different perspectives, but that your intentions are sound and good. I had to return to the spirit in which Benjamin Banneker did things. I'm sure white people pissed him off all the time, but he had to keep finding a way to work with them. After I realized all that, that's when I wrote that email wishing you well and saying that these rough patches we've hit are not rapids that are going to capsize the vessel."

I thought about how much he had shared with me over the last year. "You've been so generous with me, Robert," I said. "To share your research, your family histories, your personal stories, and your perspective. Thank you."

"Well, I've had to realize that this is just what we do," Robert said. "As Cousin Charles Henry Lett used to say when I was your age and he would share the stories with me, 'If I don't share them with you, they will end with me and then what good will they do?' Oh, I used to love the way he would tell a story, all the time he'd take to set it up. It was just wonderful. And, you know, he never wrote any of it down."

"I know it changes things to write it down," I said. *It puts it in the realm of objects*, I thought. *It makes it a* thing. "The part of your email that really resonated with me was when you said, 'Permit me to be protective of a story that I have been told my whole life, and that you are only visiting.' I want you to know that I heard that, Robert."

"Yes, you white writers just dip in and visit. You will write this book and then go away, but I am compelled to live here."

"I know that there's a truth to that. I know I cannot have the Black experience. I do not move through the world as a Black man. But I can tell you that I am not going away from this family," I said.

"Okay," he said. There was a thread of vulnerability in his voice that pained me. I realized that I should have said this in the very beginning. Hadn't he known that I felt that way? Didn't he know that all this talking and getting to know each other was much more than just a project for me?

"But you know, if we didn't have all this pain, and these misunderstandings and conflicts, it wouldn't be real," Robert said. "It would be like this whole thing had been too Pollyanna."

"Yes, like some kind of post-racial American fairy tale." I agreed. "I was so sad when I thought that you no longer wanted to participate in the book because I never wanted this story to be told from my perspective. I think that is the main spiritual mistake that is made around ancestry. Ancestry is not an individual acquisition but a collective inheritance, a shared process of awareness."

"Oh, I agree," Robert said. There was more openness in his voice. Like he was beginning to trust me again, to remember who I was.

"I also felt like, if *we* can't talk and work across the color line," I continued, "because we have been doing this our entire lives, and because our ancestors did this through *their* entire lives—then who can?"

"Now I think you're being a little melodramatic," Robert said. "You are putting too much on them. For our ancestors, it wasn't always about changing the world. Sometimes it was just about finding a way to survive in it. We were survivalists."

"Yes, that's more realistic," I said.

"And we all knew family members who crossed the color line, not because they thought being white was better than being Black," Robert said. "But because not being 'colored' gave them opportunities to live their lives and to actualize the talents and the dreams they had as individuals.

"But when I think of Peter Lett's line, and all those children of his that passed over," Robert went on, "I do wonder what he did that was so bad that none of them came back to bury him. Was he just a terrible guy? Or was it more like they moved on, and then they thought, 'I'm in a place now where no one knows who I really am, and I want no part of my father anymore.'"

"Maybe," I said. "You are right about passing. Passing is a denial of family and a falsification of history. Ultimately, it is a denial within the self that is not healthy."

"Well, that part is *your* story," Robert said. "That is the part of this story that you have to grapple with. Because you've entered a world now that you did not grow up in."

"I know," I said. "And you were right when you said that I have to come to terms with my own point of view. I always wanted this book to be more of a chorus of people and perspectives, but I will have to take responsibility for my part in it."

"And even though you are not speaking *for* the family," Robert said, "you can't do the family a disservice by ignoring the part of the family that is not happy that you are writing this book. There is a subset of Afrocentric thought in our family that does not like that you are a new comer and a white woman who is going ahead and writing this book. That perspective is, 'You enslaved me, you rejected me, you exploited me, and now you want to tell me who I am?' You know, this family member who is so upset with you right now, that is her perspective."

"I know it is. You know I reached out to her to see if she wanted to be part of these conversations, but I realize that was asking her to participate in something that she did not agree with."

"Right," Robert said. "But you still have to share her perspective through my telling you about it. She would have the entire Banneker story aligned with the Black Nationalists, and would like to see no collaboration with white people. And I keep saying to her, 'Here you are attempting to remake the family through your eyes and identity, but the family doesn't have a Black Nationalist identity. You have to be mindful of the collaborative spirit in which Benjamin Banneker did things.'

"The fact is, there are those in our family who do not feel comfortable interacting with you as a white female," Robert went on. "And that is not to punish you, or to punish white people. That is because of the long history of exploitation by white people. That is because they do not believe that they can be granted any respect or dignity within a white construct. This cousin of ours is Afrocentric, because that is where she has found her sense of community and respect, and that is where she has had her growth experiences.

"So that anger also has to be part of the story," Robert said. "You have to include this point of view without asking those family members to participate. That cousin did not feel comfortable talking with you. That may have had to do with you personally or with her idea of you as a white woman. In any case, it gave you a new awareness of things."

"I anticipated this critique, and that is why I have been trying to write this book differently," I said. "Ethically, if such a thing is possible. And I respect that point of view because I know that it stems from the injustices of history and of the present. It also comes from an awareness of the power and sacredness of stories, especially ancestral stories."

Robert was quiet, listening.

"But in these weeks, while I was so sad," I went on, "I also realized that I believe I *do* have a place in this. I feel nervous saying this. But there is a legacy of passing that is all about hiding. I have always been most comfortable when I am hiding—behind my students as a teacher, or behind others' stories or voices as a writer. In these weeks, I realized I would have to find the courage to be here, to admit that I am *choosing* to write this book, and that I am actually in it. I don't think we will solve anything unless white people realize that we are also part of the story of race.

"And back to our cousin's anger and the Black Nationalist identity," I added, "I also see that righteous anger as another part of the family tradition. Because as good as Benjamin Banneker was at working with white people, he was also a fierce activist. That letter to Jefferson was so bold!"

"Talk about an intellectual excoriation of someone!" Robert agreed.

"You know, that activism continued," Robert said. I could hear the tone of his voice lift as he launched into another story. "Benjamin's nephew Greenbury Morton went to vote in 1807, a year after Benjamin died. Years earlier, Benjamin had sold Greenbury twenty acres of his land, and, as a landowner, Greenbury had always voted. But when he got to the polls that day, they said, 'Oh, we changed the laws. Black men can't vote anymore, even if they do own land.' Well, Greenbury carried out such a stir that they took him before the court and put him in indenture. And here he had always been a free, landowning man."

"Oh no," I said. I had imagined Greenbury vividly. "That's terrible."

"The Maryland Archives has a copy of that transaction between Greenbury Morton and Benjamin," Robert continued. "And then there is a big gap until George Ellicott dies, and the trust of the land goes into infinitum. There is no written record of that letter the Ellicotts claimed to have from Benjamin, giving them the land."

"Oh," I said. "That's why this cousin calls it the first reverse mortgage in history."

"Exactly," Robert answered. "Somehow the Banneker property remained in a wild state until years later, in the 1980s, and that's how it was able to be acquired by Baltimore County for the Park and Museum.

"Now how did that happen?" Robert continued. "How did it remain a nature preserve, while everything around it was developed? Was that some kind of magical coincidence, or was there an issue in which there was no clear title to the land? Did the Ellicotts not actually have the deed, but acted like they did, just as they assumed that they were so central to Benjamin's story?

"See, there are so many examples of land and histories being stolen that there is a distrust of white historians among Black people," Robert added. "They come in and take the information and mold it into the stories that *they* want to tell. And those stories are usually very patriarchal. That's where the disdain comes in, and that is part of the whole cycle that feeds the Afrocentric perspective."

"It makes sense," I said.

"Your work, though, is much more dear to me. With you, I've shared the pain and awkwardness of all of this."

"The pain and awkwardness are important, aren't they?"

We laughed.

"Well," Robert said, "pain is definitely part of the story."

CHAPTER 31

The Final Years

Oella, Maryland, 1797–1806

Among the colored people of the country generally, few names are more honored than that of Benjamin Banneker, of Ellicott's Mills, Baltimore County.

—Newspaper article noting the November 9, 1860, celebration of the Banneker Institute, a literary society for young African American men in Philadelphia

BENJAMIN COMPILED AND published almanacs in Maryland and several other states until 1797. His publications attracted fame and respect throughout the colonies. But they also attracted harassment—especially from those who incorrectly assumed that his almanacs had amassed him great wealth.

Martha Tyson wrote that Benjamin's "remarkably mild and philosophic temperament" was most apparent in "his forbearance to his ignorant neighbors, who trespassed on his private rights and to the boys of his vicinity who were in the constant habit of robbing his orchard." She explained that Banneker's fruit was the tastiest in the area, especially his cherries and pears. Local teens "would call respectfully at his door, ask and obtain permission to partake of some of his fruit." But then, "when he was shut up in his house immersed in calculations, they would return and strip his trees; thus he was often deprived of his fruit, sometimes even before it had reached maturity."

A friend remembered Benjamin expressing regret about this plunder. "I have no influence on the rising generation," he said sadly. "All my arguments have failed to induce them to set bounds to their wants." He then mused upon a question that had interested him for many years. "If evil communications corrupt good manners, could it be that good communications could correct bad manners?" Was there any way to teach these boys respect, just by talking with them and engaging with them kindly?

Benjamin continued to record scientific and naturalistic observations in his journal, along with dreams he'd had, poems and mathematical riddles, and lists of monthly expenses. In those final years, after he had become a famous almanac author, he listed his usual purchases of buttons, chocolate, and cloth, as well as a new monthly payment to the sheriff. It is unclear whether he was paying for police protection, or whether he was paying off the police themselves so they would not seize some aspect of his property or safety, as law enforcement sometimes did with free people of color. It is clear from his journal, however, that in those last years of his life, Benjamin Banneker felt increasingly under threat.

And yet, even elderly and under duress, Benjamin was endlessly curious. In one entry in his single surviving journal, he made an observation about the speed of sound.

August 27, 1797
Standing at my door, I heard the discharge of a gun, and in four or five seconds of time, after the discharge, the small shots came rattling about me, one or two of which struck the house, which plainly demonstrates that the velocity of sound is greater than that of a cannon bullet.

He had been shot at, and had used that terrifying experience to make an accurate observation about sound's velocity. The passage suggests Benjamin's wry sense of humor and indicates that his curiosity was an irrepressible tool of survival. He used his intellect and wonder to pull himself up out of the pain and fear of living as a Black man in the early days of this country. I picture him dodging the bullets that flew at him, then sitting down to write afterward, his cheeks flushed and his heart fluttering from adrenaline. He comforted himself by observing those laws of nature that were more just and impartial than the laws of man.

Soon after that, Benjamin had to admit that he was growing too old to spend entire nights outside, observing the stars. He continued to make calculations for almanacs up to the year 1804, but he stopped publishing them. The tone of public discourse had changed. Jefferson had become president, and the idealism and abolitionism of the post-revolutionary years had been replaced with ideas of Western expansion that led to the Louisiana Purchase, the Lewis and Clark Expedition, the forced removal of Native Americans from their lands, and the extension of slavery into the West.

Benjamin continued to read and write in his journal. His sisters went on cooking for him and cleaning his cabin, and he maintained a daily schedule of gardening, beekeeping, and walking around his property. On Sunday, October 9, 1806, Benjamin took a walk with a friend, invigorated by the sunshine and the changing leaves. As he and his friend talked, he told him that he felt suddenly unwell and graciously excused himself. The friend walked him home and made sure he was laid out comfortably on his bed. That evening, Benjamin passed away in his sleep. He had lived just a month short of his seventy-fifth birthday.

* * *

BENJAMIN BANNEKER HAD looked far beyond the boundaries his society had set for him. In a time when almost all Black men were enslaved, he had dared to become a public intellectual, a Black man who uttered thoughts well beyond "plain narration." In a time when liberty was being propagandized, he had exemplified both external and internal liberty. In a time when the average life expectancy was forty years, Benjamin had lived three-quarters of a century, achieving the most in the last decade of his life. In a time of life when most people were winding down, he had continued learning, creating, wondering, and writing. He had illustrated that African Americans were capable of self-directed study, actualization of talent, and even genius.

CHAPTER 32

Legacies

Pasadena, California, and Evanston, Illinois, 2020

ROBERT AND I were on the phone again. I had him on speakerphone because I was trying to organize my desk while we talked. There were books piled everywhere and stacks of papers—documents from the founding of the Benjamin Banneker Park and Museum that Gwen had sent to me, transcripts from our conversations, photographs and news articles about the Lett ancestors. I was trying to sort it all into piles.

"I keep thinking about the burning of Banneker's cabin," I said. "And wondering about all the journals, letters, and manuscripts he must have had. Maybe if those had been preserved, he would be more known to history."

"I appreciate your empathy," Robert said, "but I imagine that he got about as much recognition as a strident Black man could have at that moment in history."

I sat down. I wasn't going to be able to sort it that day. "Maybe that's true," I said.

"But, you know, to hear his biographers tell it," Robert continued, "Benjamin Banneker had no family members. But he had aunts who resided in the vicinity and who worked on the farm. He had sisters and nieces and nephews, lots of relatives. The museum in Oella has a copy of the ledger book from the Ellicott and Co. Store, where the family used to do their buying and selling. There were transactions recorded with Samuel Delaney Lett and many others in the family. That tells me that Banneker had family all around but his biographers never mention that. They act like he existed in a vacuum, solely through the patronage of the Ellicotts. Most of his family was there for his funeral. And even though Benjamin did not have any children, he had sisters and aunts, nieces and nephews, and he lives on in all of these descendants."

I smiled, thinking of the thousands of descendants that Edie had traced, and the many thousands more yet to be connected.

"But as you know, our branch of the Banneker-Lett family moved to Ohio," Robert said. "And from the branches that stayed in Maryland, no one has ever officially claimed this heritage. That makes me ask, what did they go on to experience back in Maryland that made them detach from the Banneker story?"

"Racial injustice got much worse in those years, long before it would get better," I said.

"Elkridge Landing is the city beside Oella. One side of Elkridge Landing connects to the Banneker property," Robert continued. "And there's a big AME church there with a memorial to Benjamin Banneker. I don't think you'd have that memorial there if there wasn't some kind of family connection."

"Do you think his nieces and nephews put that memorial up?"

"Yes, that's what I'm thinking," Robert said. "There was a large community of free people of color there in Mount Gilboa. We know that his nephew Greenbury Morton lived there, and at least three other people who were part of the family."

"It is amazing to me that the land where the family farmed and lived still exists as a memorial to them," I said. "Especially since Benjamin was such a naturalist. I think that the Park and Museum is the perfect tribute to him as a learning center and nature preserve."

"I told you about the reunion we had there on the opening of the Park and Museum, right?"

"Yes," I said. "But tell me again."

"Well, I was so excited that I couldn't really sleep, so I arrived really early that morning. And you know how you drive down the long gravel road, and there's that little ridge? I drove over the ridge and the mists were burning off the fields and the woods were kind of glowing with the rising sun, and I felt it. It was the most amazing feeling. I felt like my ancestors were there with me, surrounding me, and they were celebrating.

"Then when the program started, Gwen came up to the podium and made a speech, and she said she wanted to thank Robert Lett for bringing the family together. That was touching, because I did not know she was going to acknowledge me like that. And then she began speaking on behalf of Molly and Bana'ka, Mary and Robert, Benjamin and his sisters. She said, 'Children, grandchildren, children of grandchildren, welcome home. We have not all been here together since they laid Benjamin to rest all those years ago. . . . And we have been waiting for you.'

"When I am on that land," Robert added, "I feel it so strongly. That part of my DNA comes from this place. That part of my embodiment begins *here*."

CHAPTER 33

Burning

Oella, Maryland, 1806

*The Letters, from which this facsimile is taken, are in the handwrit-
ing of Banneker, who copied them into a volume of manuscripts. His
house and manuscripts were burnt soon after his decease, except this
book which was at a neighbor's at the time.*

Inscription on the Banneker-Jefferson letters
published as a broadside by Moses Sheppard in 1852

THE DAMPNESS IN the air made it hard to start the fire. A pearly rain
mixed with wind, and the trees peeked out of the mist in a high green
froth. In all that dawn fog, the boys felt cloaked. They figured they
would not be caught or tried. The taller boy kicked at the wooden
door, fortified with an iron lock, then brought his axe to it until it
swung from the hinges. Both boys stepped into the cabin to search for
the loot—money, letters, maybe even the famous clock the old man
had built. No matter that they wouldn't have been able to read the
letters if they found them.

As long as the boys had remembered, they had hated Benjamin
Banneker, hated him as a pastime nursed by their parents in odd hours
of boredom. Their father had cursed him and the Banneker family as
he chopped wood or drove back from the town. Whenever he'd passed
the Banneker land, he'd spat on the ground. Their mother had said

nothing much more than, "It ain't natural, *them* living like that," pursing her lips as if that was the end of it. The boys had made a game of stealing fruit from his orchard whenever they passed the old man's cabin. Once, they smeared cow dung over Banneker's window, just for the fun of it, knowing he'd have to scrub it off with boiled water and would probably scratch the glass. Who did he think he was, a Black man—to have glass?

The boys scoured the cabin. The taller one swept books off the shelf, tearing pages and tugging at bindings to see if they hid any paper money. The other boy pulled the ticking mattress from the bed and sliced it open with his knife, spitting and cursing when a couple feathers stuck to his lips. They threw down sugar and coffee jars and kicked them around until the contents spilled across the floor. They took what they figured was worth something, tucked it into large flour sacks tied to their waists—a bag of coins, a pair of good leather shoes, a pot of ink and stack of fine paper, an iron fire poker. The man's plates and steins were much finer than anything they had at home, but there was no way they would drink from a cup a Black man had put his lips to, so they threw them against the wall, breaking them to shards. They didn't notice the loose floorboard off to the left of the loft ladder. Underneath it, Benjamin had constructed a strongbox. He'd filled that box with his journals and commonplace books, drafts of astronomical computations, riddles and poems, as well as forty years' worth of letters from his sister and brother-in-law, Jemima and Samuel, over in Frederick.

The boys laughed a high, nervous laugh and their hands shook as they doused the mattress and piles of books with moonshine. Then they lit matches, swearing and cursing, and jumped back out of the doorway. They saw a huge, bright burst of light before the fire began to burn more steadily, licking at the old, smoothed wood of the cabin floor. Then, when it reached all those letters and manuscripts under the floorboards, the flame flared up again, expelling a darker, more pungent smoke to replace the mist that was burning off with the morning. They'd have just enough time to hightail it home and climb into bed so no one could prove they'd done it. They'd sleep off some of the moonshine they'd drunk to give them courage, and maybe they'd even dream.

But even dreaming, they could not have imagined what was happening. The way those poems and computations of the stars were taking to the air like little lunar moth wings. The way those letters were curling back their smoldering lips, their long flowing sentences. Ashes, thin as skin, were gusting up on the air, dispersing into bitterness, loss, injustice, transmutation. They were planting themselves in the earth as fertilizer to the trees, to the descendants who may as well be ancestors, so complete would be the return, the rounds of time that Banneker had watched through the seasons and had mapped in the stories of the skies.

Those boys slept their shallow sleep, their feet kicking while they dreamed. They would sleep a long drunken time before they'd wake to what they'd done.

*   *   *

DURING ONE OF their evening conversations, Benjamin had told his nephew Greenbury that after he died, he wanted the gateleg table and brass instruments that he had borrowed to be returned to George Ellicott. He wanted to give his books to George, as well. On the very evening that Benjamin passed away, Greenbury had carried out his uncle's wishes. He brought over his cart and filled it up, expecting to return for the rest of Benjamin's belongings after the funeral. Among that first load of books was one of Benjamin's manuscript journals—the newest one that had described the seventeen-year cycle of the cicadas and the dual nature of the star of Sirius. It is only because Greenbury picked up this book that we have any indication of the kind of thinking and writing that Benjamin had been doing throughout his life.

The family had a service for Benjamin and buried him on his favorite part of the land, under the chestnut tree where he had loved to sit and think. They read psalms and sang, and then they all came back to Minta's house for the wake. She and the other women of the community were bustling around, setting out pies, cornbread, and sweet rolls, baked chicken, ham hocks, and beans. Every surface in the cabin seemed to be covered with platters of food. The men were standing about in the yard, smoking. They had all smelled fire on the wind after the service but had thought nothing of it, but then Greenbury, stepping out past the clothesline, saw smoke rising in a puff of gray over the distant trees. His first foggy thought was that it looked like his Uncle Benjamin's hair, that full gray head of it he'd had until the very end. Then he realized that the fire was on his uncle's land, and bigger than somebody just burning off garbage or brush. He walked back into the yard, smiled, clapped the backs of some of the men, and nodded politely to the few white folks, Ellicotts mostly, who were standing around, acting like they were more comfortable than they actually were.

Then he mounted his horse and rode out to his uncle's cabin. As he got closer, his heart started to *clop, clop, clop* down to his stomach, because what he'd most feared did, in fact, seem to be the case. Benjamin's cabin was on fire, a fire that someone must have started knowing that the family would be busy at the funeral, doing the man his honors. It must have happened fast because here it was, already almost burnt to the ground, a heap of char still smoldering, the walls and floorboards, beds and books reduced to no more than knuckled, glowing charcoal and an ashen hole where once the great man had lived and slept and written. Greenbury swore and kicked at the embers and burnt the toe of his boot in the process. He saw the shattered glass of the window and the stone hearth and chimney, still in place. And just a single rake and hoe that had been tossed a ways away from the cabin and looked to be unscathed. Otherwise, it all seemed to be stolen, burnt, or gone.

Greenbury was glad that he'd gone back just after his uncle's passing, late that very day, to load up the cart with the astronomical instruments, the gateleg table, and so many books. His mother had teased him, said it was almost disrespectful to cart off the belongings of a man so fast. But he wanted to do well by his uncle, and if he hadn't done that, there would be nothing left at all. As it was, there was so much that was lost. Other journals, Banneker's box of correspondence, paper money, and the carved wooden clock. It pained Greenbury most of all to think of the clock, which had continued to operate and strike the hours through more than half a century. It must have been stolen by the ones who started the fire, Greenbury thought, or maybe they were so ignorant they let it burn up like nothing more than kindling. It had been a fascinating thing, evidence of his uncle's brilliance and also of the reassuring continuation of time. In that same evening conversation, Benjamin had told Greenbury that he wanted him to have the clock after he died. Greenbury tried to remember now if he had said it clearly enough, what he had been thinking, which was, "Thank you, Uncle Ben. It'd be my honor." He had pictured that clock on his own cabin wall, had seen himself standing tall as he explained the workings to his children and grandchildren, teaching them how to wind it so it went on keeping perfect time, the way Benjamin had shown him when he was a boy.

Greenbury looked down at the smoking char. He rubbed his eyes. The smoke had gotten into them and he was crying.

* * *

GREENBURY RODE BACK to the wake and returned with his sons and his cousin John Hendon to put out the smoldering fire. Hendon was a gentle soul, a healer type who worked in the Ellicott stables and had a way with horses. He could usually say something that took you up out of the pain and confusion of a situation. But that day, he was pretty quiet.

It was always haunting to see a chimney still standing, alone in the rubble that had been its house. When Greenbury saw it, he thought it looked like a monument—not just to Benjamin, but to the whole family. To his grandfather Robert, who had carted those stones up from the river bottom, filling the wheelbarrow over and over again with the heavy round ones. To Benjamin and Jemima, Minta and Molly, who had helped Robert to chink them with mud, even though they were just children then. To grandmother Mary, who had bent to light the fire countless times, who had set the pot of water to boil over it, who had sat rocking her children and grandchildren before its warmth. It hadn't just been their uncle's home, but the family's homeplace, and it had been filled with their memories. He hadn't just been a famous African American scientist. He had also been *one of theirs.*

The men had brought a cart filled with buckets of water and shovels. They planned to make sure all the embers had stopped smoldering and then dig through the ash to see if anything could be salvaged. Greenbury felt choked by the smell of smoke and furious at the fragility of paper. He could not stop picturing his uncle's perfect penmanship, all those lines of poetry and equations, observations, and letters curling up like nothing more than sawdust or chicken feathers. His stomach sloshed with sickness at the thought of those men—neighbors, he was sure, white people he'd run into at the Outfitters and have to tip his hat to—putting their torches to a lifetime of writing and study.

Greenbury, Hendon, and their sons threw water on the fire, shoveled and dug, but the only things they found in all that char were a couple of fragments of Benjamin's speckled earthenware painted with a blue leaf pattern. One piece was from the handle of a stein and one was from the rim of a plate. But they were so broken, there was no sense in saving them.

They all had the bleak thought that at least their uncle hadn't been inside when the vandals burned the place. At least they had waited until he had gone to burial, as if that were a kind of grace, and not just a lesser crime.

"It must have made quite a conflagration," Hendon said sadly. "Bright as one a them comets he was always looking up at."

It was almost a pretty thought, and Greenbury realized that he should look up from his shoveling to nod at his cousin. But it wasn't like the fire had just *happened*. No, the fire had been started by people, people they would have to keep living and working alongside.

"It was done *to* him, Hendon," Greenbury said. "Don't forget. *They* did it." He kept on shoveling, letting his muscles burn through some of his anger, letting his sweat do some of the work of his tears.

CHAPTER 34

Fragments

St. Leonard, Maryland, September 10, 2021

I HAD BEEN waiting all through COVID-19 to get back to Maryland. Finally, in September 2021, COVID-19 numbers dropped, and I decided it was safe enough the travel. Robert was still at risk, so he declined to come. But Edie, Gwen, and I made plans to visit for a week in Baltimore and Annapolis. Edie and I would rent an Airbnb in Baltimore, and we would all get together at the Banneker Park and Museum to help secure the artifacts there.

Edie was set to arrive on a Saturday. On the Thursday beforehand, I drove down through the state, watching the terrain become gradually more windswept and coastal, until I arrived at the Maryland Archaeological Conservation Laboratory in St. Leonard. Baltimore County had done an archaeological dig on the Banneker homestead in 1985 and 1986, at the sites of Benjamin's cabin and an older family cabin. The dig had unearthed more than twenty-eight thousand objects and fragments, the most significant of which were housed at the Archaeology Lab.

A curator named Becky Morehouse had reserved a room for me to see the findings. She greeted me at the door and walked me down a long hallway. We entered a small room with bright lighting.

The artifacts were set up on plain white tables, in pale blue cardboard trays. The trays were filled with individual pieces of pottery, metal, and glass—fragments, mostly, officially termed "sherds." Each tray was labeled with its contents—*coarse earthenware, stoneware, pearlware, tin glazed earthenware, metal objects yet to be conserved.* And each fragment was in a tiny Ziploc bag further labeled with a number and the exact location where it had been found.

"The most iconic object from the entire dig," Becky explained, "was a glass lens from some kind of scientific instrument."

I was amazed by how much they had discovered, although Becky explained that there was still much more to be excavated, and classified most of the artifacts as "small finds."

"But even the fragments give us information," I said.

"Yes," she answered. "Once you have a tiny fragment, you can know exactly what the vessel was."

It was one of those sentences that seem to rise up out of a conversation and echo with metaphorical meaning. I wondered if each one of us *was* the same, some fragment of a family, a history, that could suggest the whole. It was a little like DNA itself, the way once we have one cell, we can access entire histories of genealogical information.

As I walked up to the trays to begin looking at the artifacts, I felt tears welling up, a pressure in my chest and behind my eyes. I took a deep breath. "I can hardly explain what this feels like," I said to Becky. "I have studied and written about these ancestors for years, and now I'll get to see and hold objects that *they* saw and held."

Had I actually just believed them to be stories *all this time?* I had to ask myself. That was not quite it, but there was something so intimate about seeing their things that I felt myself entering a new atmosphere somehow, the fragments becoming emissaries between time periods. I had had this experience with intuitive work and with ritual. As a college student, I had found resonance in the ideas of Mircea Eliade, an anthropologist who studied shamanism, and explained that a ritual drops us through time and allows us to enter sacred time in which past, present, and future are sutured together, revealed as simultaneous. Now I was feeling a similar, dizzying drop through time. And before that moment I had not believed that the material realm could really facilitate such a thing.

But the feeling of wonder did not hold. Becky left me alone to do my research, and I sat down in front of the trays. The room was brightly lit, white, cold, and unadorned. It felt like a morgue, and I realized that a morgue is probably the worst place to connect with the essence of a loved one.

I remembered when my partner Richard died. I went to visit him, laid out just before cremation. He was dressed in the outfit I had chosen for him and lying in a sturdy cardboard box, much like the boxes that held the shards. I realized that I did not know the Kaddish by heart, and I wanted to say it for him. I looked it up on my phone and read it aloud and cried and smoothed his brow. I could not believe that I was seeing him in physical form for the last time. I didn't know how that could be possible. His feet were under a wool blanket I had sent with him, one his own mother had used, and suddenly I wanted to see his feet just one more time. I had loved his long, slender feet. I pulled the blanket back and took off his sock and there was a paper tag with a number on it tied around his toe. The number was big and dark, written in Sharpie. A chill shot through me that would not leave. I realized that to the undertakers he was a number, an intake, a body to be logged and cataloged. He was Jewish, and so to see a number on his body carried the historical trauma of the way Jews were branded with numbers after all their belongings had been stripped from them in the camps. Kidnapped African people had been similarly branded with the name and logo of the ship that would carry them on the Middle Passage. This branding was a strategic step in the process of suggesting that they were not full humans. The chill that shot through me would never leave. It was the truth of mortality and, more than that, the staggering fact of what humans will do to one another.

* * *

BECKY HAD TOLD me that I could take the objects out of their baggies and touch and hold them. I did not know where to begin, so I decided to begin intuitively, which is to say, anywhere. The first box I grabbed contained coins, lead shot, bullets, toys, and Benjamin's jaw harp. I held the lead shot in my hand. The round bullet's surface was gray with cream veining like a mottled stone, or like our own planet when seen from a great distance, marbled by the clouds and waters. It was small but heavy, with lead's strange, concentrated weight. I could see the tiny seams where it had been pulled from the mold. I thought of those teenagers who shot at Benjamin when he was an old man, standing in the doorway of his cabin. I wondered if that lead shot had belonged to the same people who burnt down his cabin on the day of his funeral. I thought of the boys' mother, melting the lead over the fire, pouring it molten into a mold. Those little globes would glow, before darkening to something solid and beholden to our old, divisive notions of power. It was a heavy reminder of the fear and suspicion that has always been concentrated here, a piece of lead shot embedded in the heart of America, poisoning the blood.

It seemed odd that the bullets would share a tray with the jaw harp, an early harmonica, although when hasn't music—all art—arisen inventively from hardship? Benjamin was shot at, and afterward he dipped his quill into the ink and wrote in his journal. He steadied himself with the strength of his own mind, his wonder and curiosity lifting him up over his fear. It was the same resilience that allowed him to stand in his doorway in the evenings and play his jaw harp, turning his breath into music on the wind. "If you are still alive and breathing after this year of COVID," I had heard a Black preacher say on the radio that morning, "then you'd better be using every breath you have left to work for justice and peace. Hate is a state of being," he said, "and you'd better learn to hate anything in yourself that stops you from loving."

I do not believe Benjamin wrote his letter to Jefferson out of a feeling of hatred or huntedness, although I think he knew the kind of clarifying anger that burns away falsities to uncover the truth. I think that letter was about love. I believe he stood in his cabin doorway in the evenings and played his violin or his jaw harp and watched the sunset flush his fields and trees a range of lilac, pink, and peach, and his heart opened in the same swelling spectrum, in a kind of crescendo of energy that made him *need* to add the notes of his singular life to the wider, rising air. I think he had so much insight and inspiration coming into him that he had to find ways to give it back to the world again.

The next tray I grabbed was one I called the woman's tray, which consisted of straight pins, thimbles, buckles, and buttons. It felt very familiar to me and made the past seem not that far back. As a girl,

I had sat beside my grandmother as she sewed. I had played in her button box, which was a biscuit tin filled with buttons that I would sift my hands through, loving the way they drifted and clicked against my fingers, holding them up one by one. They were like little bright coins I could tender to go back in time with her. "What was this one for?" I'd ask. Each button recalled a time before I was born—a dress she had sewn for Easter, a school pinafore for one of my aunts, a shirt my grandpa had worn.

"What was this one for?" I tried asking the air.

I got no answer but a sudden upwelling of grief. My fingers had come upon a baggie labeled "thimble interior, encrusted dirt." Even those who lived a long time ago are not quite comfortable with it, it seems, this pinpricking trick of mortality. The fact that her finger became the dust in the thimble, the fact that the thimble outlasted the woman who used it.

There were so many buttons, I could not possibly hold or consider them all. What was this one for? Dozens were made of pewter. Some were carved from bone. Many were brass, and a few were silver. Some of the pewter buttons had been stamped with a basketweave pattern, and when I saw that, I understood that the buttons were not just functional, but were signalers of style, beauty, class. The bone buttons would have been used for lighter cloth, undergarments, and the linings of vests. I held one bone button that was smooth, solid, perfectly intact, and wondered if this could have been sewn on Mary's bodice, covered by a fabric placket. In the mornings, she would button them up, then pause at one button—and ask Robert to do it for her. He'd rub his thumb across the inside of her wrist before buttoning it closed. She liked asking things like this of him because she knew he liked to be asked. Most people of their complexion were forced to wear clothes like prison garb, made of the same coarse linsey-woolsey or indigo stripes, so they could be identified as unfree. Enslaved people didn't get their own clothes as much as too-short hand-me-downs that never quite fit and that itched against the skin. Even free people of color were hemmed in by sumptuary laws that made it illegal for them to wear hats, fancy trimmings, or elaborate suits that would compete with white folks, though most people of color found ingenious ways to break those rules. Robert fluttered his fingers a little teasingly down Mary's spine because, didn't she know, there was something to it. Being free enough to wear whatever you wanted, and to ask your man to come on over and do up your buttons.

Some of the heavier pewter and brass buttons must have been for heavier clothes—the vests, waistcoats, and jackets that Robert and Benjamin wore. One in particular was calling to me to take it out of its suffocating plastic baggie. It was flat brass and marked with the feel of the hand. It had been smoothed down by the particular press of the thumb and forefinger that had buttoned and unbuttoned it, that had grabbed that favorite coat over and over for his long walk across the fields. It was rubbed thin, and the brass—a burnished, earthy brown now—grew warm against my fingers, so warm that it felt like touching the hand that had touched it. Fingers that had lived more than two hundred years ago, I had to remind myself.

There were shards of pale green bottle glass. And clods of dirt I didn't know how to interpret. A whole tray of gun flints. The stem of a pipe made of pale clay. A sparkling white quartz arrowhead. Two-tined forks and several knives. Horses' bits. Swivels from stirrups. Tiny blue glass beads, like you see in the handwork of Native Americans. Shards of black slate from the writing slates Benjamin used to sketch out his equations before committing them to expensive paper. Several bits of slate pencils, and that did not surprise me but made me feel an affinity with Benjamin that I had been too shy to admit to before then. I too have pens and pencils stashed everywhere—in pockets and purses for fear that I will have a thought and no way to write it down. I imagined Benjamin's favorite jacket, the one with the smoothed brass button, with an inner pocket filled with slate pencils that faintly rattled while he walked across the fields.

And the dishes. Someone had loved beautiful dishes. The farm was not simply the dwelling of a brainy bachelor, I remembered, but a homeplace where feminine taste had space to reign. There were pieces of creamware, Staffordshire, and blue transfer-printed earthenware. There was the Rhenish stoneware—gray with a blue stripe and leaf pattern around the edge—that Benjamin had used for his everyday dishes. He was known to be a little absentminded, and his sisters didn't need him knocking over their china. The Rhenish stoneware had been imported from Germany and was nothing to scoff at. Now it had been reduced by fire, time, and plows to the handles of tankards and the rims of plates, but it was still remarkable. Somehow, I was holding the handle of a stein that Benjamin Banneker himself had held.

I know that this catalog has gone on a bit long. I think we Americans tend to put too much stock in things. It is part of our American mythology to believe that things make the man or woman, so to be without objects in this culture is to be precariously close to being without an identity. We all participate in this idea—consciously or otherwise—as consumers, through which we construct a set of signals, a kind of visible personality. When enslavers forced their enslaved people to all wear the same thing, they were stripping them of an opportunity to express their individual identities, and this stripping was something that enslaved people constantly and brilliantly resisted—fashioning styles by their own hands, making combs and hats from feathers and flowers, salvaging scraps of fabric and sewing them into dresses.

By the time the Banneker family had their land, they were free and able to purchase and keep all of these objects. So even though the collection before me was made up of thousands of fragments, I still felt a vibrant pride shining through them, a pride in being able to buy and own buttons and china, horses' bits and writing slates. "The most glaring thing about all of these possessions is that they possessed *themselves*," writes historian Tiya Miles in her book, *All That She Carried*, an illuminating meditation on a sack given by an enslaved mother to her daughter. "They lived in a world that would count people of color as objects, but they possessed objects."

Even in their broken forms, these objects were giving the ancestors' lives a new veracity for me, a common quality that I could hold in my hand. They suggested specificities and personalities in ways I had not quite anticipated. I now could imagine that Benjamin was a clotheshorse with a thing for shiny buttons. (Later, when I read the ledger from the Ellicott Co. Store, I saw how frequently he bought "a dozen buttons.") I now could deduce that Minta or Molly had a thing for pretty dishes. And they all favored—like me—blue patterns with a repeating leaf motif along the edges. I could imagine John Hendon saving up some of his earnings from Ellicott and Co. stables and buying his mother this blue-patterned platter. He knew she would heap it with butter beans or sweet potatoes, and she would love carrying it out to folks when they came to supper.

My reverie was interrupted when another archaeologist walked into the room. Her name was Sara Rivers-Cofield, and Becky introduced her as the curator of Federal Collections in Maryland, specializing in what they call "small finds," particularly buttons. I asked Sara to walk me through the collection, and she pointed out the buttons made in the eighteenth century versus the nineteenth century and verified that the smoothed button that I had been holding was in fact brass and from around 1780, when companies began rolling out sheets of brass and stamping them into buttons. "The size suggests that it would have been worn on a men's jacket," she said.

"Was it unusual for a family of color to have this many buttons?" I asked.

"Not necessarily," she answered. "People who were aspirational would always use buttons, and pretty much everyone in a capitalist culture is aspirational. The Banneker family certainly was. They were a very successful family.

"And buttons would signal how much money you had to spend," Sara continued. "People were very aware of the particular metal of their buttons. If you had real gold, silver, or pewter buttons, people could tell that they were real, and that would let them know where you stood. Buttons were mostly a male thing, though. Women typically only wore metal buttons in styles meant to mimic male attire, like riding clothes.

"We make a mistake when we think that people back then did not have things," she went on. "We do digs at sites of slavery, and digs at emancipation sites, and we find all kinds of buttons. If people of color wanted buttons, they could find a way to get them. Sometimes they would get them secondhand. Sometimes they would work on the side and save their earnings to purchase their possessions. All people of color at that time knew what was and was not fashionable, and they would always try to be part of the times.

"At the same time, people make other mistakes when they find all of these objects at the sites of enslaved people," Sara said. "Sometimes archaeologists will find fine china or a tea set and think, 'Oh their lives weren't that bad,' as if having tea with a china set somehow made up for not having autonomy over your own body or life."

* * *

I DID MY last little meditation while holding the heavy shard of an eighteenth-century cast-iron pot. The fragment was almost as large as my hand, slightly curved with a ribbed edge, which Sara had explained meant that it was from a pot and not a kettle. I held it and thought about how I was somehow touching a pot that my female ancestors had touched, probably every day, boiling water, stirring the hominy. Mary had placed her hand just there as she hung it on its hook over the fire. It was so heavy. It reminded me of how strong their arms had been.

CHAPTER 35

The Archive

Maryland, September 2021

THAT SATURDAY, I drove up to Baltimore and waited at the train station for Edie, who was coming in from Arlington. I felt a little fluttery and nervous, like I was waiting for a first date or something. I put on more deodorant and smiled at myself in my rearview mirror, to make sure I had nothing in my teeth, then put on more lipstick. Edie and I had talked for hours on the phone, but we had never met in person.

I saw Edie as soon as she stepped off the train, wearing her shiny black glasses and stylish whites and grays. My eyes went to her, magnetically, like I could find her in a crowd anywhere.

We hugged, and I said something about how it was brave of us to spend a week together in an Airbnb, even though we had never met.

"Oh, I haven't been nervous at all," she said. "I *know* you."

"I know you too." I smiled. We hugged again.

"Isn't it weird that it hasn't even been two years since we first started talking?" I said.

"That's what 2020 did to us!" Edie laughed. "It warped time."

*   *   *

OUR AIRBNB WAS an old house in a peaceful little neighborhood on the edge of Baltimore that felt like going back in time. When we first walked into the house, Edie called out, "Thank you, Aquilla and Christina!

"You know, it was Aquilla who brought us together," she said. "I sat down and I really didn't know what I was going to work on that day, so I just said to myself, 'I'm going to Google Aquilla Lett and see if anything new comes up about him. And there you were with your article about him and the family in Ohio. I was like, 'Who dis woman, Harpo? Who dis woman writing about my family?'"

I laughed.

"And then I realized that you're one of ours!" she said.

"Thank you, Aquilla and Christina!" I called into the empty rooms. "Thank you for bringing me back to the family!"

We unpacked in our bedrooms and met back in the kitchen for a glass of wine. It felt like we had years to catch up on, so many stories to tell. "Isn't it cool that this was all only possible with technology?" Edie said. "The internet, and then the technology of DNA testing, and then all this Zooming we've been doing all year. I think Benjamin would have loved that, because he was always interested in the latest technology."

"And it's amazing that all of these technologies are based on the stars—GPS, our ability to talk to one another from anywhere. They are all based on astronomy," I said.

"Yes, Ben would *really* love that," Edie said.

*   *   *

IN THE MIDDLE of the week, Edie and I drove from Baltimore to Annapolis and settled in to do our research in the Maryland Archives. I had already contacted the librarians with a list of the documents we wanted to see, and they had filled two carts with huge bound volumes of court records and land deeds from the colonial and Revolutionary eras. First, we went to look for Mary Beneca's testimony in the Provincial Courts, and it was Edie who confirmed that, yes, this seemed to be our Mary. Her first children, Sarah, Deborah, and Zachariah, had been held in indenture just for being mixed-race. And Mary had summoned the courage to fight against those "repugnant" laws.

Then we began searching for the 1752 will of Mary Welsh that Paul Heinegg was newly attributing to our Molly. We looked for the will through the usual databases, and when we found nothing, we solicited an archivist's assistance. When she finally found it online, the scans were not clear enough to read.

"We do have the paper copy of the will here, on-site. Would you like to see it?" she asked.

"Yes!" we responded in unison, looking at each other with wide eyes.

The librarian brought it out to us—a stained and fragile piece of paper in a manila folder that she told us we could touch and hold. I held it in my hand and tried to comprehend that this was perhaps the very paper that Molly had signed with her own hand. She would have been seventy-four or seventy-five then—an old woman, who, inside, was still that brave girl who had crossed the pitching sea determined to survive. I pictured her—pale and wan, under quilts, as a Quaker lawyer sat beside the bed, his quill scratching at the paper, beginning the will:

> I, Mary Welsh, of Prince George's County, Widow, being very sick and weak in body but of perfect mind and memory, Thanks be to God, and therefore calling to mind the mortality of my Body, and knowing it is appointed for all men to die, I do make and ordain this my last will and testament . . . and recommend my soul into the hands of God.

Her mouth was dry and her voice was frail, but it was still Molly. She still had that fiery insistence about her. She told the lawyer exactly what she wanted to say. First, she discharged "My Molatto" Samuel Molton as the sole executor of her estate. Then she made sure to "set free and discharge all my negroes, Solomon and Juday and his wife, and their children. I also set free my negroes [and here a word is crossed out, and over it is written Benjamin] and Aleck."

Wait, *was* this our Molly? Or was she just another common enslaver?

The truth is, the people mentioned in this will were already free. John Welsh had registered a will with Prince George's County four years earlier, in 1748, that left his entire estate to "Mary, my wife," and declared that all of his "negroes" were to be freed at the time of his death. He also bequeathed his "mulatto Samuel Molton" all of his movable property, making Molton executor of his estate. In repeating this information, Mary Welsh seemed to be putting in writing—again—the freedom of those individuals she later referred to as "my people." And the Mary Welsh of this will was a literate woman, evidenced in the fact that she signed the document herself, which was quite rare at that time. So *was* this our Molly?

Martha Tyson and all of Banneker's subsequent biographers had assumed that Molly raised her daughters alone as a widow after Bana'ka died, never remarrying. But if this was our Molly/Mary, this will suggested that she had remarried a white man named John Welsh several years after Bana'ka's death. If such a thing seems unlikely, again, it is because we are seeing the story through the lens of American racism. Historians record evidence of many British women from the colonial era who had children with African men and then married British men afterward, indicating that this choice was not as stigmatized as one may assume. John Welsh, moreover, bought his land in the same year as Robert Banneker, suggesting that this marriage between Molly and John was a late-in-life union that included grown children from each of their earlier partnerships.

There were thousands of women named Mary in Maryland at this time, and so this may be a different Mary/Molly. The only reasons to suspect that this Mary was Benjamin's grandmother Molly are the fact that her grandchildren had always referred to her as Molly Welsh, and the fact that the names Molton and Banneker continue to show up in records pertaining to this Welsh family. This "Samuel Molton," who was made executor of the Welsh estate, was probably the Samuel Morton who later married one of Mary Banneker's daughters, Molly's granddaughter, and then became the father of Greenbury Morton. Spelling was highly irregular then, based on the hearing and variable handwriting of whoever penned the document, and the names Molton, Morton, Beneca, Banneky, Banicker, and Banneker were continually intertwined with the Welsh family in the historical records.

In a later document dated February 27, 1757, another Mary Welsh assigned to *Mary Banicker* her right to "a mealato servant called Samuel Morter" and fulfilled the assignment in Prince George's County on March 31, 1757. This would have been right around the time that

Mary and Robert's children were marrying. Mary and Robert Banneker were large landholders by this time, and the fact that Mary Welsh would "assign" Samuel Morton to "Mary Banicker" suggests that the family may have been protecting one another's freedom by assigning "mulatto" and African American family members to one another in writing. By then, Mary Banneker was free and prosperous enough to help secure a marriage for her daughter, who was called Molly after her grandmother, to this Samuel Morton. By having Morton "assigned" to her—his mother-in-law—Samuel was less likely to be kidnapped into servitude by someone else, and the free Banneker family could help to protect his liberty on paper.

There are many similar examples in history of free African American people assigning family members to one another, legally holding them in slavery, not as a way of actually enslaving them but as a way of protecting them from the purchase or kidnapping by white enslavers. In her memoir, *Incidents in the Life of a Slave Girl*, Harriet Jacobs recounts spending considerable time and effort trying to secure the purchase of her children by her brother—so they can be safely removed from enslavement to her cruel "master." To be owned or "assigned" to a family member was often safer than being freed, since free people of color could be targets for kidnapping by white people who would then sell them farther south. When white members of the Welsh family assigned people of color in their wills, it may have been a sidelong way of stating their family connections under the law, in a country that made multiracial families like theirs technically illegal.

Sixteen years later, a will in the name of another Mary Welsh also mentioned several members of the Banneker family. In December 1773, this Mary Welsh of Prince George's County reasserted the freedom of "negro Ben, born free, age 43; negro Alik, born free, age 45; Moses Adams, age 27; Robert Adams, age 29; Jane Adams, age 21; Henry Adams, age 32; Juday Adams, age 4; and Solemon Adams, age 22 months." This Mary Welsh also bound herself "for 200 pounds sterling to be paid to Ben." This was probably not our Molly, who would have been nearly one hundred years old by this time and had most likely died twenty years earlier. But it could have been the daughter of John Welsh from an earlier marriage, making her an aunt of Benjamin, who was, indeed, forty-three in that year. If Molly and John Welsh were both widowed parents when they married, they would've created a blended family with their own grown children. A close reading of the wills of this time, and my own study of the ways that mixed-race families were using any tools in their power to protect their offspring, suggests to me that this Benjamin could, in fact, be Benjamin Banneker. And this Mary Welsh was using her will to reassert his freedom in writing and to leave him money in the form of silver.

Still, these documents complicate the Banneker-Lett family oral histories and are overwhelming to confront. In these documents, Mary/Molly Welsh does not refer to these people as her offspring but calls them, alternately, "my molattos," "my "negroes," and "my people." She comes close to claiming them, in other words, even as she manumits the family and insists on repeatedly putting their freedom into writing. These findings are not accepted by all of the Black family members in the Banneker-Lett line, because, as Robert explained to me, "This removes a sentimental feeling that we had for Molly. It potentially turns her from being a mother of mulatto children, to being an *owner* of mulatto children."

But, although these newly discovered documents put new wrinkles in the Banneker family histories, they do not completely oppose the stories as remembered by the family. Molly could have loved and had children with Bana'ka, and years later, married John Welsh. The Mary Welsh of the documents does seem like our legendary Molly in that she was literate, and she used her privileges to subvert the usual power dynamics and free as many people as possible before she died. Her landowning white husband also freed his enslaved people and protected Molly's children and grandchildren with legal statements of their liberty and financial credit. Their repeated written insistence that Samuel Morton was free and financially trustworthy as the executor of their estate, for instance, secured a more certain future for Molly's granddaughter—her namesake, Molly, who then married and had a family with Samuel.

Still, it is not surprising that family lore would have omitted this part of the story. John Welsh would have been the white stepfather rather than a biological father, and his presence as a white man who enslaved people—at least at one time—would have troubled the family's triumphant history. After all, oral histories were concerned with preserving the African lineage of Benjamin Banneker. The white line would be documented as part of the dominant culture that had the court system and church records on their side. The African line, on the other hand, had to be preserved orally, through family stories and griot memory as a form of protection, memory, and affirmation.

When I consider these documents along with the family oral histories that insist on the family's mixed-race ancestry and claim Molly Welsh as the grandmother, I see a portrait of a blended, multiracial family that was committed to abolition. Or perhaps it is more accurate to say that they were a blended, multiracial family that was committed to their continued survival in an increasingly racist society.

With these new findings, Paul Heinegg, who compiles the database *Free African Americans of Maryland and Virginia*, has written that our Banneker-Lett family is now the most documented family of color in colonial times. The most recent version of Paul Heinegg's database states, "Although it is evident that [Molly] Mary Welsh was the wife of a white man named John Welsh, it is still quite possible that she was Benjamin Banneker's grandmother and the mother of Robert Banneker's wife."

* * *

IT WAS EVENING. Edie and I had been in the Maryland Archives all day and we were exhausted, feeling the papery, thin-headed fatigue that results from staring for hours at historical records, straining to decipher their antiquated language and handwriting. Now we were out on the porch of our Airbnb, drinking wine. We were listening to the music of Elliott Skinner, a young old soul who seemed to be doing some deep healing with his tunes and lyrics. I kept taking long breaths of fresh air. My skin felt thirsty after the false indoor lighting of the archives.

What we had seen that day was amazing, but it was also confusing. And while we had read the wills of the Welshes freeing their "people," we had only found them after scanning through hundreds of the more common wills that listed people of color alongside livestock and farm implements, as if they were objects.

"I find it so exhausting to do this research," I admitted to Edie. "And it must be even more draining for you."

"Yes, it is," Edie said. "Sometimes it just levels me, to see the utter disregard people were shown. But if you want to avoid finding uncomfortable information, you really don't want to do genealogical research. Especially as a Black person. Because you need to look at all of it. The good, the bad, and the ugly. That is the crucible you were formed in. That is the crucible we are *all* formed in."

I nodded. I admired her courage to face whatever we were going to find.

"If you're going to study history, it's painful for everybody, but especially for any marginalized group," Edie went on. "And Black people, we seem to have gotten a huge dose of that pain. Especially here in this country that we love but that doesn't seem to love us.

"Even the Founding Fathers were perpetuating it all," Edie said. "Oh yes, 'that freedom-loving slaveholder,' my mother used to say about Jefferson."

We laughed.

"That's good," I said.

"Oh, my mother knew her history," Edie said. "Whenever my brothers and I would start asking her about something, she'd say, 'Well, go look it up.' We had a shelf in the living room with the complete set of the *Encyclopaedia Britannica* that we were always looking through and reading. She wouldn't just give us an answer but taught us to find the information for ourselves. Every Christmas, my brother Edwin wanted an almanac, so he could write down his long lists of figures. He's a facts and figures kind of guy. Even now, when you ask him, he can tell you the racial breakdown of any American city, and he'll know it from memory.

"Now why was Edwin always wanting an *almanac*?" Edie laughed. "It all makes more sense to me now."

We kept listening to the music and talking. We were on the porch, looking out over the gravel road in front of our rental, which looked like a memory, which looked like a lane our ancestors could have looked out on.

"I think the people who do this work must be guided by the ancestors," Edie said after a while. "Because otherwise how could these things keep showing up?

"It's like those rocks all around us on the path." She laughed. "The rocks are everywhere, but you have to know when to look down and turn over that particular rock."

I knew what she meant. We had taken a long walk down the lane and through the woods together that morning before we left for the archives. And her comment had reminded me of a Zora Neale Hurston quote that I loved: "Like the deadseeming cold rocks, I have memories within that came out of the material that went to make me."

"Did I tell you that a couple of months ago I came across one of the boundary stones laid by the capital survey?" Edie asked.

"What! You just stumbled upon it?"

"Yeah, I didn't even know it was there. Here I was strolling right by it every day on my afternoon walk. Now I go there and say, 'Hi Uncle Ben, I know you are around here checking on your work.' Someone said to me, 'Well, he didn't lay that actual stone.' And I said, 'No, but he did the math to show where it should go!' How cool is that? Of all the people to be related to!"

"He was brilliant," I said. The fact that we were indirectly related to such a figure still felt almost impossible to me.

"Here he was this really smart dude living in the woods, trying to survive and looking up at the stars to figure out what it all meant," Edie said. "He was a scholar. And he actually got to express his brilliance, just through an accident of where he was born and who he was born to. It's a very unique American story."

I nodded.

"But I've been doing all this research since 1989, and sometimes I wonder why I haven't done more," Edie added wearily.

"More! How could you do more? How many do you have in the family tree now?"

"Twenty-five thousand people. And I have another tree just for the DNA matches. It's like this big, giant puzzle. And names come up and you have to know where and how they connect to the family."

"I feel like we each have an essential role to play in all of this," I said.

"You are the thorough genealogist. You can keep the whole huge tree of us in mind, and then for me, it's like the stories light up like fireflies in the branches."

"Well, when you come from a branch of the family that's been disconnected, you have to be the one to reconnect it," Edie said. "And sometimes you have a hunch and you follow it and things just start to fall into place."

I nodded.

"But sometimes you feel like you're being manipulated!" She laughed. "Like they're just leading us all around—saying, 'This one, you need to meet this one.' Like they're going, 'They need to be working together down there, or each one of 'em'll be working in the dark.'"

CHAPTER 36

On Banneker Land

Oella, Maryland, September 2021

AFTER A WEEK of exploring and researching, talking, laughing, eating, and shopping, I dropped Edie off at the train station. I missed her already.

As I drove away, I called my parents. Over the course of the project, they had also become interested in the Banneker-Lett story, and that interest had spread throughout our more immediate family. Earlier that summer, my aunt and uncle had taken a road trip to see the Lett Settlement. And my parents and I had driven to Crawford County, Pennsylvania, to see the site of John Brown's tannery. The caretakers there had invited us into their home, and told us stories of John Brown as a young abolitionist. They had even recognized the Lett name from the lists of laborers at the tannery.

"It will be interesting," my dad said that day, as I drove west from Baltimore, "what you feel when you're on the Banneker land."

"You're right," I said. "I've scheduled all this time for visiting and doing research, but I also need more time on the land."

"Make sure you take some time to be alone today," my dad said, "to walk the land and pay attention to how you feel there."

We talked about the sense of connection that we feel in nature, especially in certain wooded landscapes. "It seems like a mystical thing," I said, "but it is also probably scientific. What must happen chemically when we breathe the same smells and walk among the same plants and mycelium that our ancestors knew? If our ancestors, who share our DNA, lived on that land, worked that land, and were fed by that land, and now are buried there, it should not be that surprising if our bodies respond with a feeling of recognition."

"But there are people who are never going to understand this way of relating," my dad said. "Historians who don't believe that anything is true unless it can be separated out and documented on paper are not going to respect this kind of knowledge. You are going to have to stop trying to convince them."

My dad knew of the argument about Heinegg's findings, and like Robert, he felt defensive about the family's oral histories and aware of how written documentation can hide or omit the full truth.

"Maybe my work is to bring together what can be documented and what has to be intuited," I said.

"Maybe," my dad said skeptically. "Just remember that those intuitive skills are real skills that would have been familiar to our ancestors. Our culture has caused people to repress them and to say that they're not real, but we still have those instincts. Most people know if someone is looking at them from across the room. That is the kind of awareness that our ancestors were using all the time just to survive.

"There are lots of ways to listen and communicate," my dad added. "Just make sure you make time to be in communication with the land."

* * *

So I SPENT the afternoon on the Banneker land. I walked the trails, and I let the land instruct me. The Banneker Park is part meadow and largely wooded and home to thousands of species of plants, fungi, animals, and insects. I realized that the land has an ornate intelligence and endless webs of relationships that I could spend my whole life observing and still only graze the surface of. Benjamin Banneker had known that too.

On my first step into the woods, I found a feather—black with white spots, and perfectly intact. It felt like a gift. I took three or four steps more and realized I was standing directly in front of a family of deer, just watching me. I chose another trail and kept walking. I was looking for the largest trees, wondering if any of them could have been alive when the Banneker family was living there. When I saw a few huge elm trees, I thought maybe they could have been around then. Then I realized that all of the trees I was walking among were the descendants of the trees that had been there in Benjamin's time, and how was that any less wondrous? They had grown from the seeds of those ancestor trees, had shot up strong and stubborn from the mulch of their stumps.

I started walking toward the sound of the water then and found what was once the creek, which was now just a long sunken arc of mud and stones. Back then, it ran with cool, clear water, and Benjamin and his sisters would wade out onto the flat, slippery rocks and let their feet prickle and go numb in the cold. On the hottest days of summer, their mother Mary would let them walk right into the creek in their underclothes, and they'd stay cool that way for hours, the water wicking away from their bodies as they worked at their chores.

Farther along the bend of the creek was the remnant of the old stone well, its sides broken down now and rocks mossed over with spots of green. It had taken Robert and Benjamin a whole long weekend to build it. Benjamin's job was to wedge the stones up from the mud of the creek bed. Robert had decided that the best stones were roughly ten inches across and slightly blocky, so Benjamin looked for these, calling out to his father excitedly when he found them. They were of the granite local to the area, with the glitter of mica in their veins. Robert had lifted the stones and positioned them in a perfect arc at the bend in the creek. Mary had wanted the well placed precisely there, and Robert had to admit that, as usual, she had been right. It was a well and a cistern at once, and it never failed to yield good clean water for the family's cooking and bathing.

Fetching the water had been Mary's job as long as she could remember, and she kept at it even after she could have asked her daughters to do it. She loved the act of drawing water from their own land. There was something ancient and purifying about it. As the sun lightened the sky and she walked the path toward the well, she used the time to clear her mind, thank God, and set her intentions for the day. She took long strides over the roots and bent her neck this way then that, fluttering her fingers and stretching her arms toward the rising sun, to get out the stiffness that had crept in overnight. Then she sank the bucket into the cold, clear water. The early morning light stippled green and yellow through the trees and swam shadows on the surface of the water. She always let one dipper spill onto the ground, tipping it into a nearby fern or a parched patch of leaves. That was Mary's way of saying thanks to the earth and the ancestors.

I kept walking, looking for a spot to sit. The creek led down to the river, and I waded across it, my bare feet balancing on dark granite slabs. On the other bank, I sat leaning against a tree. It was a sycamore, the kind with marks on the trunk that look like hieroglyphic writing, and I imagined Jemima carving her future initials into a sycamore— J.L. for Jemima Lett. She knew when she was a girl that she loved her step cousin Samuel and had resolved to marry him when they both were old enough. Their relation wasn't by blood, so she did not worry. But when Robert saw his daughter's initials carved into the tree's flesh, he thought of the brands on the ship, and admonished her, saying she ought to have more respect for nature than that.

I heard the hounds then, barking and barking, those dogs owned by the white folks who lived around the rear of the property. It wasn't that the dogs themselves were evil, Robert explained to his children, but you never knew what their owners had trained them to do. Sometimes the hounds would bark all day and night and it made a person won- der what they were being deprived of to make them sound so anxious. Their barking spread the sound of threat on the air.

At the edge of the property were broken shards of brown bottles— remnants of the local boys' partying. Robert had warned his children never to play over there at the edge of the lot line because they would cut their feet on the garbage those people had left. All those shards of glass, set jagged-side up, just barely glinting from the leaves. The chil- dren knew that the warning was not just about the glass but about the danger of wandering past the edge of their land.

Sometimes Robert woke up in the night in a cold sweat thinking it had happened, that one of the girls had gotten distracted gathering sassafras or blackberries, and a catcher had seen her. She was just a lit- tle humming brown girl with ribbons on her braids, and that man had thrown her onto the back of his horse like no more than a sack of pelts, gagging her with a sour bandana before she could so much as scream. "No!" he'd cry out, thrashing at the quilts, his feet kicking up to run.

"You had a bad dream," Mary would say softly, resting her hand on Robert's chest. But he'd lie awake the rest of the night, thanking God it hadn't happened, that his children were all still with them. He could make out the particular rhythm of each one's breathing there in the cabin. He'd try to shoo away the grim thoughts by feeling grateful, or planning out everything he had to do that day, but the fear had stiffened his jaw. He vowed that none of his children would ever have to know what he had to know.

A bird flies very differently when it is free and unhunted than when it is frightened. When I first sat down against the sycamore on the riverbank, I saw a heron watching me from just below, standing in the water. He was slender and silver with long, elegant legs. Heron was one of Bana'ka's nicknames, seeing as he was so tall. Molly used to tease him, calling him heron, water bird. He was solitary like the heron too, and a little otherworldly. *Hi Bana'ka*, I said to the heron in my mind. I went on writing, and he went on doing his work, which was dipping into the water for algae and tadpoles. Then some walkers came down the path, very loudly. The heron was afraid of the hikers and their colonizing voices. He wanted to stay at the river, but how could he, with the child yelling "NO NO NO," and the mother calling out loudly, "JUST KEEP WALKING." The heron took off clumsily, rapidly. "Look, a heron!" the mother yelled, and everyone in the group said "Ooh," causing the heron to fly with no joy away from its place. Now they could say they saw a heron. But they had only seen one aspect of the heron, which was its fear. The heron knew in its straw-hollow bones and deep species memory what it was to live on a quieter planet, with safe skies in which to fly.

There were bits of silica and fine granite ground down in the dirt, so when the sun caught it, it glowed as if it were glittering with gold. "This here is gold," Robert would say, lifting the dark, moist soil in his hand. He'd known it was good land as soon as he'd come out here with Richard Gist. He'd bent down and picked up a pinch of the soil and placed it on his tongue like the eucharist. He knew that this rich, hydrated land would be perfect for growing tobacco, corn, and vegetables.

Brown gold, he called it, because he was the kind of man who could feel where the waters ran into the earth and kept it fertile, could sense where many generations of leaves had fallen and fed the mycelium that thickened the loam.

My grandfather, too, was a diviner, which meant that he could feel where the rivers ran under the land, the way I can feel the past running in tributaries under the present. Most of the men between Robert and my grandfather in this family line could take a handful of soil and tell you if it was worth planting on and what exactly you could grow. "We know, we know," his children would say, when Robert went on about that brown gold and how they were wealthier than barons because they had their own land and, more than that, they knew enough to know that they didn't own the land any more than the white man who claimed to own a brown man's body. "The land owns itself," his grandson Aquilla would later tell his children. "Knows more about itself than we will ever know."

One part of the riverbank ran down to a smooth beach overgrown with weeds and wildflowers. A tree had fallen there, making a children's bridge for crossing the water. They all got very fast at running across the trunk barefoot and not falling off. On one end was where Minta liked to sit and braid her sisters' hair. She'd lean back against the smooth trunk and splay out her legs and pat her skirt down, then pull Jemima into her lap. "If I'm going to be doing your braids," she'd say, "then I get the good sitting place." Jemima loved to lean against her sister. She loved her sweet smell of clover and sweat, the soft sound of her wetting her lips, and the way her breath made a pretty pattern against her neck when she started breathing in rhythm with the braiding. She pulled so hard that Jemima's scalp stung and tears leapt involuntarily to her eyes, but she knew to sit still. And how Minta loved to braid. She could hardly walk through a field without stuffing the longest, strongest strands of grass into her apron pockets. At night, she'd sit by the fire, listening to her parents talking and Benjamin playing the fiddle or reading from the Bible, and braid those long grasses into little sweet-smelling baskets.

Robert's favorite place on the plot was beyond the fields and across the river, on the highest ridge of the property. He would stand on the ridge and look as far as he could see in every direction. He knew the names of all the neighbors. He knew who envied him, who despised him, who respected him, and who wanted him to succeed, because they were themselves free people of color, or Quakers who had a moral disdain for slavery. He wished sometimes that he believed in hexes, but he was a God-fearing man. He imagined a fence around all the neighbors who wished him ill and said prayers for all the neighbors he thought well of, who he hoped would help Mary and the children if he should die too soon. He said prayers for those families and, above all, for his own—that they should all grow to be healthy, prosperous, and still free. Then he did the closest thing he had to a ritual—drawing his eyes all along the perimeter of the property in a circle of protection. Sometimes a heron came to join him, flying along the line of his gaze.

They all lived on the land and within it. They were in relationship to the land in ways I cannot even imagine.

I sat there all afternoon. The most powerful insight I had is one that I did not write down because I knew that words would fail it. It was something like the feeling of the whole matrix of time coming to rest in the present moment. It was a celebratory feeling, both grounded and expansive, as if the ancestors were there with me in the present and simultaneously back in the full lives they had lived in that place. They were so glad that I was there, so glad that we all existed. I felt the undeniable *reality* of them all. And simultaneously, I felt my own reality, the wonder and sacredness of my life *now*.

The science of DNA had opened up new narratives to me. But all of this had been about more than the stories, I knew now. It had been about relationships. It had given me a new way of existing in the world—a way that was both more connected to others and more rooted in myself. It had given me a present that was much fuller for being connected to the past.

Later in the day, the heron came back. He flew to the place on the river just below where I was sitting. He fished. I wrote. He looked up at me. We appreciated each other's quietude. Eventually, he lifted off again, and I saw it—the grace of a departure when it is chosen. He took to the air, and I saw the great tribal marks of the heron—iridescent blue and pink spread in a glorious fan across his open wings.

*　*　*

I REALIZED THEN that I was late for a visit to Gwen. I called her on my cell phone, feeling weirdly like I was calling from centuries away. But I was close, roughly a half-hour drive from her apartment.

"Can you bring me some water?" she asked.

"Sure," I said. "I can stop at the store on my way over."

"No, water from the river," she said. "I want to use it in my sacred ceremony this Sunday."

So I stepped into the stream. I stood barefoot on the rocks where our ancestors had stood, and dipped my bottle in the current until it bubbled over with cold, clear water. It was more than one vessel could carry. I took a long deep gulp of it, then brought it back to Gwen.

CHAPTER 37

The End

Oella, Maryland, 1806

I thought I was dead and Beheld my Body lay like a corpse, there seemed to be a person in the form of a Man his rainment somewhat of a sheep skin or bright fawn color, who said, follow me. He ascended a Hill on top of which was a Large Building, the outside appeared strongly built, of large, rough Stone. It seemed white and Bright, and a Large Company sitting, such a number as I never beheld. The farther we went in, the Brighter it appeared and more like the reflection of the Sun . . . there appeared a sweetness & composure in every countenance, far beyond what I had seen in any person, while in the Body, and the luster reflected from the light . . . I looked to see if I could distinguish Men from Women, but could not.

—from Benjamin Banneker's journal, October 1762,
titled "A Remarkable Dream"

BY THE TIME Benjamin Banneker had entered the winter of his life, he had achieved more than anyone had believed possible for an African American man living in the late eighteenth century. When a person fulfills his destiny, as Benjamin Banneker did, his story enters the great constellation of stories differently and becomes a much wider inheritance. When a person's fulfillment has not been through his offspring, but through the work of the mind, and when that mind has been taken up by others, then the idea of inheritance shifts. Inheritance is no longer a familial, biological concept but is widened to include everyone whom that mind has influenced, illuminated, and touched. In this way, Benjamin Banneker's story belongs to everyone who feels a connection to it.

Benjamin still had family in the area—sisters, nieces, and nephews who remembered him, and their descendants, who would share pride and wonder over his achievements. But he had many more offspring who were not biological—Black people who would use his talents and writings to inspire their own. When Benjamin Banneker wrote about his "brethren" to Thomas Jefferson, he claimed this family and lineage as all African American people.

In the decades after Benjamin's death, Banneker Societies sprang up all over the new nation, providing education and opportunities for young African American men. Black writers like William Wells Brown, Carter Woodson, Shirley Graham, and Charles Cerami told his story. Even today, there are hundreds of parks and schools named after Benjamin Banneker scattered throughout the country, including Banneker High School in the Englewood neighborhood of Chicago. There are the Banneker-Douglass Museum in Annapolis, Maryland, and the Benjamin Banneker Historical Park and Museum in Oella, Maryland. And a statue of Benjamin Banneker welcomes visitors to the Smithsonian's National Museum of African American History and Culture.

On October 28, 1806, an obituary ran in the *Federal Gazette* commemorating Banneker and presenting him as an example of African American brilliance:

> On Sunday, the 9th instant, departed this life at his residence in Baltimore County, in the 73rd year of his age, BENJAMIN BANNEKER, a black man, and immediate descendant of an African father. He was well-known in his neighborhood for his quiet and peacable demeanor, and among scientific men as an astronomer and mathematician. In early life he was instructed in the most common rules of arithmetic, and thereafter, with the assistance of different authors, he was enabled to acquire perfect knowledge of all the higher branches of learning. Mr. B. was the calculator of several almanacs which were published in this, as well as some of the neighboring states, and although in later years none of his almanacs were published, yet

he never failed to calculate one every year, and left them among his papers, preferring solitude to mixing with society, and devoted the greatest part of his time in reading and contemplation, and to no books was he more attached than the scriptures. At his decease he bequeathed all his astronomical and philosophical books and papers to a friend. Mr. Banneker is a prominent instance to prove that a descendant of Africa is susceptible of as great mental improvement and deep knowledge into the mysteries of nature as any other nation.

It was said that Benjamin was buried beneath his favorite tree on his property, but a stone was never erected over his grave, and we do not know where it is exactly. This makes me think of the tomb of the unknown soldier, in which one soldier's remains stand for all the soldiers who were lost. We could consider Benjamin Banneker a similar model for Black genius. We have the story of this brilliant Black thinker and naturalist, astronomer, and writer from the Revolutionary era. But his story can stand as a monument to all of the brilliant African Americans whose stories, inventions, observations, and even names are lost to us. Benjamin Banneker was the most documented and acclaimed Black scientist of his time, but he was certainly not the only Black thinker, observer, and inventor of the Revolutionary era.

Benjamin's legacy is also one of liberation—a reminder of the creative possibility in each brief lifetime, of the sustenance of learning and wonder, and of the decision to use one's own freedom to promote freedom for others. His legacy lives whenever someone sees past the limitations society would put on them, in favor of invention, discovery, spirituality, and study. His legacy lives on whenever anyone fights for racial justice or writes what they did not know they could write, because love of their brethren has "enlarged" their mission.

I like to imagine that Benjamin and all of these ancestors are watching from the cosmos and embedded in the land, present in the interconnectedness of things, in the plants and moon cycles and sunrises. Maybe even in the sudden presence of a red cardinal out my window as I write this.

* * *

WHENEVER THE FAMILY got together for reunions, the mothers would let the children convince them to stay a little later, just to give them more time with their cousins. There were always those who'd go off together and sit talking by the creek. Others who would run and hide in the stables. Others who would get into mischief, letting a cart roll into the pond or jumping from the barn loft.

Then they'd hear their mother's laughter—a loud, unbuckled sound because she was with her sisters. And the kids would realize that the adults were having just as hard a time leaving.

Finally, it was time to go. You had to tell yourself that you'd be back again, that you'd see everyone again. Otherwise, you'd be too sad to even get in the wagon.

Afterword

I DID NOT meet my great-grandmother Mildred—of the Banneker-Lett line—during her lifetime. As a baby I lived in her old home, a small blue farmhouse in Grand River, Ohio. My parents wanted it to stay in the family, and it was the only house they could afford anyway, so they bought it just after Great-Grandpa Webster passed away. My nursery was in the front room where years before they had laid out family members for their wakes. My dad was only four years old at one of those funerals, but he remembered it. There was a pale lady lying there, very still, and she was covered with flowers.

"I didn't understand," he told me. "Somehow I thought that the flowers had been pinned to her and were suffocating her."

"It was strange," my aunt Marla agreed.

The last place that Mildred would sleep would be the first place that I would wake. Once, soon after I was born, my cousin Melissa and her twin sister, Elisabeth, were sleeping on the living room couch. A woman came walking by in the middle of the night in a long white nightgown, pacing from the back of the house toward my crib at the front. She seemed to be checking on me, the baby. She stopped in front of my cousins.

"Who are you?" she asked.

"I'm Lisa, one of the twins," Elisabeth said.

"The twins?" the woman said, confused, because she too had twin girls, our grandfather's youngest sisters.

In the morning, Elisabeth and Melissa said to my mother, "Wow, you were really confused last night. You were sleepwalking or something."

But my mother did not own a long white nightgown and had not been walking through the house at midnight. They all decided it was Great-Grandma Webster, still roaming around in her home. Great-Grandpa Webster had smoked cigars, and whenever my parents went away for the weekend, they'd return and the house would be filled with cigar smoke. Like he had been back again, visiting.

*　*　*

THE NEXT TIME I met my ancestors, it was in the form of flowers. My grandmother grew beautiful gardens—wisteria climbing the lattice at the back door, mums planted in front of the porch, and a side flower bed running all along the street, filled with roses, peonies, marigolds, and black-eyed Susans. She loved the black-eyed Susans best of all because her father had given them to her as a wedding gift. He was a first-generation Hungarian immigrant who ran a fish house and became mayor of the tiny town of Grand River, Ohio. He intensely disliked the Webster family because Great-Grandpa Webster had opened a tavern across the street from his fish house, and then had dared to purchase a pool table. Grandpa Evans thought that was low-class and said that the Webster family were poor and lazy, were too friendly, and were not good enough for his daughter. He told my grandmother that if she proceeded to marry Philip Webster, he would refuse to speak to her ever again, and would not come to the wedding.

But my grandmother persisted. She sewed her own wedding suit, of pale blue wool. She saved her money from working overtime at the restaurant to buy a hat to match, with a little netting veil. I knew that hat well. It sat in a trunk in the basement, and sometimes I would secretly pull it out and try it on. I could imagine her in it, elegant and shy, holding her bouquet of white mums as she walked toward my grandfather, tall and handsome, at the altar. I could not imagine a world in which they had not been married. What would have happened if she had been a more obedient girl? What if she had not had the courage or spunk to defy her father and marry the man she loved? I couldn't imagine it, because it meant that none of this—the garden with its strawberry patch and hundreds of flowers, the house with its dim basement, its rows of canning on the shelves, and its sunny, golden kitchen—none of this, and more importantly, none of *us*, would even exist.

"I was so nervous," my grandmother told me. "I kept hoping that my dad would get over his stubbornness and come. I kept looking at the back of the church, but true to his word, my father never showed up. So Philip's dad had to walk me down the aisle." I could tell by the way she said it that this had been an embarrassment for her.

"My father didn't speak to me for months afterward. Then, finally, he gave me this black-eyed Susan plant as a belated wedding gift. It was for my middle name, Susan."

My grandfather was playing catch with my brother in the side yard. As she talked, my grandmother was cutting flowers to put into little vases to take to the graves for Memorial Day. I loved the way the sunlight filtered through her curled hair, which looked like the color of sunlight to me, and the way her wrinkled, veined hands knew how to make everything—from soups to pies to knitted sweaters and smocked dresses. I wanted to be by her side all day, whether we were cutting out a pattern, or shelling peas, or taking flowers to a grave—anything— that was okay. The cemetery seemed too far to walk to when I was a little girl. But I know now that it was close, almost visible from the house. She cleaned the graves and put the flowers in front of some of Grandpa's relatives. His grandmother, and his grandfather, and his parents, as well as her own. Those ancestors felt very remote to me then, impossible to even imagine. But my grandmother was initiating me in a ritual of connection.

The black-eyed Susans came back every year, with roots strong and resilient enough that my grandmother could dig them up and separate them and give them to her own daughters for their gardens. How foolish her father's judgment seemed from there, how petty his decision not to bless that marriage, with children and blooms all around, and with him in the ground now. Black-eyed Susans are said to symbolize justice. Giving her those flowers was her father's way of saying he was sorry, and also that she had won. She had won the right to love who she wanted to love.

For their honeymoon, she and my grandfather borrowed his brother Guy's Model T Ford—the first car any of their siblings owned—and all of their brothers and sisters pitched in to buy them gas. They drove down through the state of Ohio not knowing where they would end up. They just knew that they had to stop when half of the gas money was through. They drove four hours south to Marietta, and got a room at an inn. It was a little upstairs room, and it felt odd to be so far from home, in a town among strangers. They had grown up across the street from each other and had eighteen siblings between them, so they had probably not had much time alone before then. They had barely any money left and could not afford dinner, knowing they would have to buy gas to drive home again. So they bought a watermelon from someone selling produce from the back of a truck. They brought it up to the room, and my grandfather split it open with his knife. When that red fruit rocked open, my grandmother started to cry. She was afraid. She had never slept in a room without her sisters. She had never been alone with this man—her friend from childhood, someone she had loved since she was a girl—who was now her husband. She said that she wanted to go home because she missed her sisters.

"Then Philip made up a game," she told me, "of spitting the seeds into a hole in the floorboards." She was fiercely competitive and determined to beat him. "After that, I stopped crying and we began to have fun."

They woke up the next morning and drove the four hours home again, and all of their sisters and brothers came over for dinner that evening. She told me that story as a way of telling me that they were their happiest when they were with family. But that story was about family in more ways than they knew. My grandpa had driven all afternoon of his wedding day, his first time leaving Northeastern Ohio, back to the township where his ancestors had first entered the state, had first bought and farmed land, had fought time and time again for the education and safety of their children. They had taken their honeymoon just a few miles away from the Lett Homestead. My grandfather had dozens of cousins in that town that he didn't even know about.

Sometimes I have wondered if this book has been a way for my grandfather to get home again. My grandfather loved this country as both a land and an ideal, and above all, he loved his family. Maybe he's been wanting to get us all back to a reunion somehow. Those reunions were the high point of the summer for my grandparents—with children doing three-legged and potato sack races, and everyone eating off of paper plates in wicker trays, heaped with three bean salad, apple pie, bread-and-butter pickles, pulled pork, potato salad, and sliced tomatoes. But now we need a different kind of reunion, a truer kind, one where we can enjoy being together but also look at our denials square in the face. One where we can look at race and racism in an honest way. And then, if we're lucky, after some time spent listening to stories and looking in one another's eyes, learning something and laughing, we can feel it. The reunification with parts of our family and parts of ourselves that we lost. In other words, a real American reunion.

"I think that your grandpa, for most of his life, would have denied his Black ancestry," my dad said at one point.

"Maybe not at the end of his life," I answered. "And you know I would have talked to him about all of this."

I had grown up with my grandparents, seeing them almost every day in the summers. I adored them, but I also knew them as people—wonderful, fallible people who were products of their time and place. We stayed in conversation, we disagreed, and we knew how to be imperfect together. And I saw this writing as a continuation of that love. The kind of love that believes that a person can change, and knows that we need one another in order to evolve.

When I became a parent and took my newborn daughter Adele home to meet my family, my grandfather could not wait to hold her. He adored babies. He held Adele for a long time, looking down into her face. She was only two weeks old, but she looked up at him and held his eyes with hers. It was her first month of life and one of his last months of life, and I wondered what strength her little body was storing up from his arms, what love or knowledge was passing between them.

In those years, I always tried to say goodbye to my grandparents with intention because I did not know which visit would be our last. Finally, it was time to go. "Thank you," I said, taking my daughter from my grandfather's arms. "Thank you for helping to raise me."

"Well, you raised us too," my grandpa said. It was a wise thing to say. And it was true. We are raised by our elders as well as our descendants, our children who urge us forward into more awareness, and our ancestors, whose wisdom, pain, joy, and resilience filter down to us.

I tend to think that the forward-marching linearity of time is a lie. I tend to think that narrative time is just the narrow column of time that our human minds can understand, the way our sun is both necessary to life—the light that we see and grow by—and also just a tiny star in a much larger universe. This was something that Benjamin Banneker thought about constantly, the vast mysteries of space and time. He knew that it is here on earth where we get to *experience* time, to survive its challenges and embody its lessons, in all of our life's seasons.

And what a strange season this has been, when we all rode out a pandemic, when Black Lives Matter became a rallying cry and elicited a new national reckoning with racism, when my cousins and I called each other again and again, to share the stories of our ancestors, to list their names for one another. It reminds me of pointing out stars in the sky. Like we know that soon they are going to be the light we steer by.

This book was written in honor of Benjamin Banneker and in memory and gratitude for all of our ancestors. To those whose stories we told, and to the many more, whose stories live in us, told and untold.

GRATITUDE

This book would not be possible without the Banneker-Lett cousins who shared their stories, research, and hearts with me—Edith Lee Harris, Robert Lett, Gwen Marable, and Edwin Lee. Thank you for trusting me, and trusting in ancestral connection enough to embark on the collaboration that became this book. Thank you also to the griots and family researchers who came before us and preserved and shared these ancestral stories—including Chuck Weiker, George Simpson, Vandhalia Lett Gee, Peggy Sawyer, Rosemary Clifford McDaniels, Marsha Stewart, and Sherman Lett. Thanks to the additional DNA cousins I talked with while working on this book, including Charles Calaman, Patricia Calaman, and Ron Mosher. The collective memory of this family is extraordinary.

This book begins with the idea that families can talk, listen, laugh, learn, disagree, and grow together. I learned this first in my immediate family, and I thank them for their love and example: my dad, James Webster, my mom, Cynthia Webster, and my brother, Douglas Webster. Mom, because this book is about Dad's family line, you are not in it much, but your compassion shaped our worldview and kept us fiercely alert to narrow-mindedness and bigotry. Douglas—thank you for always making me laugh and making me think. Dad—thank you for your wisdom, for connecting me to the earth, and to embodied happiness. When I was a child, you answered my unending questions, and you helped me to be comfortable in my skin.

I also thank my grandparents, Martha and Philip Webster, who were unfailingly loving and attentive to me in their lifetimes, and who were with me in spirit as I wrote this book. You connected me to the gardens and to growing things. You gave me a rooted sense of family and a daily practice of creating sustenance for others. Because I was with you so much as a child, I developed a comfort with my elders and a longer relationship to time.

I thank the next generation, as well—especially my daughter, Adele Fammeree. Adele, thank you for all the author photos, career encouragement, and patience as I toiled away at my writing. You have been with me since the beginning, and my understandings as an author are shaped by my understandings as a mother. I also thank my niece, Gwyneth Webster, for your enthusiasm for history and your deep way of understanding stories. Thanks to both of you for going on that research trip disguised as a family vacation when you were nine! You never doubted that these ancestors' stories *needed* to be in the wider world, and you were this book's first champions.

Thank you to my aunts, Marla, Laurel, and Janice, who gave me multiple examples of how to be strong women. Thank you to Laurel Webster, who believed in my imagination enough to build me a playhouse—a Room of One's Own—when I was just a girl. Thanks to my Webster-Major-Martin cousins for each of your examples of brilliance, activism, and artistry. Thanks especially to Melissa Major, for finding these ancestors, reconnecting our branch of the tree, and generously sharing your research and insights with me throughout this long process. And thanks to our cousin Nathan Martin, who first told me about the Bannekers and Letts.

Thanks to my agent, Marcy Posner, who believed in this book even before I did. Marcy, your clarity and advocacy have changed the arc of my career, and my life. Thank you for being such a fierce protector of truth, and of your authors, and for staying in constant conversation with me. And thank you for leading me to the perfect publishing team in Henry Holt. What a group of brilliant, visionary women! Amy Einhorn, Sarah Crichton, Maggie Richards, Shannon Criss, Julia Ortiz, and Hannah Campbell. I have not stopped pinching myself since we got the first email from you, and I have loved learning from your intelligence and expertise through every stage of this process. Thanks also to Henry R. Kaufman, for your warm conversation and incisive legal read of the manuscript.

Shannon Criss, I was meditating and asking the ancestors to lead this book to the perfect editor when you acquired this project. Thank you for the intuitive brilliance that you bring to everything you do, for understanding that aesthetics are also ethics. You agreed that this had to be a conversation between the present and the past, myself and my cousins. When you joined us on our research trip in Maryland, and I saw you holding Benjamin Banneker's almanac, I understood that you, Shannon, are an essential part of this legacy of Black publishing, of Black genius, and of this family. Thank you for all your work and care with this project.

To research and write a book like this takes enormous amounts of time. I thank Northwestern University for being my intellectual home, and the Alice Kaplan Institute of the Humanities for awarding me my first-ever teaching leave to work on my writing. I thank Thomas Burke, Jill Manor, and Wendy Wall for their advocacy in allowing me to accept this opportunity, although it was without precedent for someone in a non–tenure track position. Thanks and admiration to my cohort, and especially to my mentor in the group, historian Ken Alder. Ken, your questions, brilliance, conversation, and early encouragement were deeply appreciated and formative for this project. Thanks also to Natasha Trethewey—for the example of your beautiful writing and your early encouragement.

Thanks to my research assistants: Olivia Behr, C. Chen, May Dugas, and Min-Li Chan, who provided help with my endnotes, editing, and promotion around the book. Thank you to the Dean's Office for the Baker Faculty Grant that allowed me to employ these brilliant young people. Thanks also to the students in my 2016 class, The Situation of Writing, and my 2021 class, Writing Ancestry, for sharing your stories and questions with me. Your candor and our conversations helped to evolve my thinking.

I also thank the Op Ed Public Voices fellowship, and Michele Weldon and Katie Orenstein, for your visionary work to get more women's and BIPOC voices into the public forum. Your fellowship changed the way I thought about my own writing. It became less about creating a polished, "perfect" product and more about listening and contributing something to the public conversation. Thank you to my cohort, and especially Viorica Marian, who celebrated this story when it first appeared in an Op-Ed and later provided encouraging feedback on this manuscript. Her book, *The Power of Language*, is coming out at the same time as this one, and it has been a joy to share this experience of writing and publishing.

Thanks also to the Mycelium Collective—and my dear friend, Geeta Maker-Clark, who brought us together to talk about our work for racial justice and our own hearts. You changed my understanding of justice work into something more organic, sustainable, and collaborative. Our Mycelium conversations are intimately a part of this book. I especially want to thank Erika Allen, Dr. Gilo Kwesi Cornell Logan, and Reverend Michael Nabors for telling the stories of your ancestors in a way that allowed me to better understand the Great Migration, Black genius, and multigenerational resistance. Thank you also to Rahul Swarma, who asked this question: "Does healing begin with understanding that we *belong* to each other?" In these precarious times, you all give me hope.

I am grateful to my friends and co-teachers from my early days of teaching at the Urban League and Gallery 37: Derwin Boyd and Keturah Show-Poulos. Thank you for trusting me, for teaching me, for letting me see and understand your lives as Black folks. You and our students deeply enriched my life and changed my way of being in the world. Thank you also to my professors at Lewis & Clark, including Rishona Zimring, who encouraged me to do the project at the Urban League, and to my mentor in teaching as a whole and present person, Kurt Fosso.

I have talked about this project—and almost nothing else—for the last few years, and I thank the friends who have stayed in the conversation with me and read early drafts of this. Julianna Vermeys, for your daily wisdom and touchstone in the depths. Vanessa Filley, for being my first reader of this manuscript, for your gentle yet incisive questions, your own deep work for justice, and your excellent book and podcast recommendations. Stephanie Smith, for your insights on ethics and collaboration. Lucy Doyle, for your energy clearings and understanding of channeling. Ariel Barbick, for your enthusiasm and sisterhood. Karen Behm, for your extraordinary example of being present and loving with elders. Michelle Colledge, for our expansive cosmic conversation. Martha Arnett, for your understanding of wider support, and your insight about male and female balance in the book. My sister-in-law, Lindsey Dalrymple Webster, for your very early, astute reading of this manuscript and your ethical and scientific mind. Rachael Gates Bergan, for reading the manuscript and providing much-needed encouragement and suggestions at the end of this process. Once upon a time, you pretended the past with me in that same small town in Ohio. Thank you for being a kindred spirit. And thanks to your parents, Karen Gates and Geof Gates, for listening to my ideas and helping me believe that I could someday make an intellectual contribution.

For their intellectual contributions, I thank the many scholars who are cited in the notes and who helped me to understand the contexts of these ancestors' lives. Jacqueline Battalora's scholarship on the invention of whiteness in colonial America shaped my thinking and gave me the permission and responsibility as a white woman to reexamine racialized U.S. history. Jacqueline and I are neighbors, and the synchronicities in our research provided early encouragement, that sense that this *was* what I needed to be doing, and offered opportunities to collaborate. It is always difficult when such collaborations shift, and Jacqueline was generous and respectful as this process turned into a collaboration with my cousins. Thank you to Paul Heinegg, as well, for his database of *Free African Americans in Maryland and Delaware*. Although we disagreed with some of his interpretations, Paul continued to find documents about our ancestors even as I wrote and revised this, and he shared his findings with Robert, who then shared them with me. Thank you to Tiya Miles and Saidiya Hartman, who have inspired me with their scholarship, their ways of imagining into history, reading the archive with humanity and insight for what has *not* been said, and collaging contexts to tell Black women's intimate and essential stories.

I thank Kim Holcomb at Maryland Public Television for joining us at the Banneker Park and Museum and filming me in conversation with Gwen and Edie in September 2021. I thank Rebecca Morehouse and Sara Rivers-Cofield, curators at the Maryland Archaeological Conservation Lab, for allowing me to sift through the artifacts found at the excavation of Banneker's cabin. I thank Catherine Mayfield, at the Maryland Center for History and Culture, who allowed Edie, Shannon Criss, and me to spend time with Benjamin Banneker's almanacs and manuscript journal. Thank you also to Rachel Frazier at the Maryland Archives in Annapolis, and Breena Doyle, who worked with the entire family and allowed us to see the artifacts at the Benjamin Banneker Historical Park and Museum. Thanks also to Willa Banks for the early conversation.

I also thank some of my favorite authors, who have helped to teach me what it means to be human: Toni Morrison, James Baldwin, Alice Walker, Audre Lorde, Jamaica Kincaid, Lucille Clifton, Jesmyn Ward, Jean Toomer, Robert Jones Jr., Edward P. Jones, Ralph Ellison, Ta-Nehisi Coates. Your books are a part of me now. Thank you also to Daniel Foor and his profound and timely book *Ancestral Medicine*, for helping me to establish an authentic ritual practice for connecting with my ancestors.

Last but not least, I thank my husband, John McCarthy. We married in November 2019, just before a global pandemic, and I was grateful every day to be stuck at home with him. Thank you for making me laugh, John, for meeting me in the place of soul and of poetry, and for respecting my seriousness and studiousness. After years of struggle, your love and support of me and Adele means that we can finally be more at home in the world. We love you forever, and we thank you.

Above all, I thank the Ancestors and forces of Spirit that accompanied this book. I know that you *were* real. Working on this book, I began to understand that you *are* real, that the past is participant in the present, and that any healing and work for justice that we do moves both forward and back.

SOURCES

ARCHIVAL COLLECTIONS

Banneker's Almanacs, Special Collections, H. Furlong Baldwin Library, Maryland Center for History and Culture, Baltimore, MD.

Banneker Astronomical Journal, Special Collections, H. Furlong Baldwin Library, Maryland Center for History and Culture, Baltimore, MD. https://www.mdhistory.org/resources/benjamin-banneker-astronomical-journal/.

Banneker/Tyson Archive, Benjamin Banneker Historical Park and Museum, Oella, MD.

Provincial Court Records, Land Records, and Wills, Maryland State Archives, Annapolis, MD.

Banneker Homestead Archaeological Dig, Archaeological Collections of Maryland, Maryland Archaeological Conservation Lab, St. Leonard, MD.

ONLINE ARCHIVES

Adams, Abigail. "Letter from Abigail Adams to John Adams, 22 September 1744." *Adams Family Papers: An Electronic Archive*, Massachusetts Historical Society. https://www.masshist.org/digitaladams/archive/doc?id=L17740922aa.

Addison, Joseph. "The Planetary and Terrestrial Worlds Comparatively Considered." Evans Early American Imprint Collection. https://quod.lib.umich.edu/e/evans/n26929.0001.001/247:5?page=root;size=100;view=text;q1=Juvenile+literature+—+Poetry+—+1799.

Ancestry. https://www.ancestry.com.

Banneker, 18BA282. Archaeological Collections in Maryland. https://apps.jefpat.maryland.gov/neh/18BA282-%20Banneker%20Finding%20Aid.aspx.

Banneker, Benjamin. Benjamin Banneker Astronomical Journal. H. Furlong Baldwin Library, Maryland Center for History and Culture. https://www.mdhistory.org/resources/benjamin-banneker-astronomical-journal/.

———. *Banneker's Almanack and Ephemeris for the Year of Our Lord 1793*. Collection of the Smithsonian National Museum of African American History and Culture. Smithsonian Digital Volunteers: Transcription Center, Smithsonian Institution. http://n2t.net/ark:/65665/fd542a4090e-a9f0-447f-8654-148c6c9a9ad4.

———. "To Thomas Jefferson from Benjamin Banneker, 19 August 1791." Founders Online, National Archives https://founders.archives.gov/documents/Jefferson /01-22-02-0049.

———, and American Almanac Collection. *Benjamin Banneker's Pennsylvania, Delaware, Maryland, and Virginia almanack and ephemeris, for the year of Our Lord*. Baltimore: Printed and sold . . . by William Goddard and James Angell, 1792. Periodical. https://www.loc.gov/item/98650590/.

Benjamin Banneker Homestead, Site. Architectural Survey File, BA-1141, Maryland Historical Trust, Inventory. https://mht.maryland.gov/secure/Medusa/PDF /BaltimoreCounty/BA-1141.pdf.

Burke, Henry, and Robert Lett. Lett Families Settlement, History and Genealogy. https://henryburke1010.tripod.com/lettsettlementreunion/id6.html.

Gibb, Carson. *The New Early Settlers of Maryland*. Gibb Collection. Maryland State Archives. http://earlysettlers.msa.maryland.gov/.

Griot's Circle of Maryland, Baltimore https://www.griotscircleofmarylandinc.org /more-about-me.

Heinegg, Paul. *Free African Americans of Maryland and Delaware from the Colonial Period to 1810*. Digital archive. http://freeafricanamericans.com/maryland .htm.

Jefferson, Thomas. "Thomas Jefferson to Benjamin Banneker, August 30, 1791." Thomas Jefferson Exhibition, Library of Congress. https://www.loc.gov/exhibits /jefferson/79.html.

———. "Thomas Jefferson to Joel Barlow, 8 October 1809." National Archives: Founders Online. Annotations by Princeton University Press. https://founders .archives.gov/documents/Jefferson/03-01-02-0461.

National Association of Black Storytellers, Inc., Baltimore, MD. https://www .nabsinc.org.

Stewart-Sanders, Marsha. "Lett Families." *Old Settlers Reunion Collections*. https:// www.oldsettlersreunion.com/index.php/old-settler-family-pages/2 -uncategorised/63-lett-family.

BOOKS

Abbott, Mary. *Life Cycles in England 1560–1720: Cradle to Grave*. London: Routledge, 1996.

Alder, Ken. *The Measure of All Things: The Seven-Year Odyssey and the Hidden Error That Transformed the World*. New York: The Free Press, 2002.

Allen, Danielle. *Our Declaration: A Reading of the Declaration of Independence in Defense of Equity*. New York: Liveright, 2014.

Arnebeck, Bob. *Slave Labor in the Capital: Building Washington's Iconic Federal Landmarks*. Charleston, SC: History Press, 2014.

Ashbridge, Elizabeth. *Some Account of the Forepart of the Life of Elizabeth Ashbridge*. n.p.: Franklin Classics Trade Press, 2018.

Audlin, James David (Distant Eagle). *Circle of Life: Traditional Teachings of Native American Elders*. Santa Fe: Clear Light Publishing, 2006.

Baldwin, James. *The Cross of Redemption: Uncollected Writings*. New York: Vintage International, 2010.

———. *The Fire Next Time*. New York: Vintage International, 1993.

Banneker, Benjamin. *Benjamin Banneker Astronomical Journal*. Baltimore: Maryland Center for History and Culture, 1790–1802. https://www.mdhistory.org/resources/benjamin-banneker-astronomical-journal/.

Battalora, Jacqueline M. *Birth of a White Nation: The Invention of White People and Its Relevance Today*, 2nd ed. New York: Routledge, 2021.

Bedini, Silvio A. *The Life of Benjamin Banneker: The First African-American Man of Science*. Rancho Cordova, CA: Landmark Enterprises, 1972.

———. *The Life of Benjamin Banneker: The First African-American Man of Science*. 2nd ed., revised and expanded. Baltimore: Maryland Historical Society, 1999.

Behn, Aphra. *Oroonoko*. London: Penguin, 2003.

Brathwaite, Kamau. *Ancestors*. New York: New Directions, 2001.

Breen, T. H., and Stephen Innes. *"Myne Owne Ground": Race and Freedom on Virginia's Eastern Shore, 1640–1676*. New York: Oxford University Press, 2005.

Briggs, Harrison, et al. *Crime and Punishment in England: An Introductory History*. London: University College London Press, 1996.

Brown, Adrienne Maree. *Emergent Strategy*. Chico, CA: AK Press, 2017.

Brown, Kathleen M. *Good Wives, Nasty Wenches, and Anxious Patriarchs: Gender, Race and Power in Colonial Virginia*. Chapel Hill: University of North Carolina Press, 1996.

Buel, Joy Day, and Richard Buel Jr. *The Way of Duty: A Woman and Her Family in Revolutionary America*. New York: W. W. Norton, 1995.

Butler, Octavia E. *Kindred*. Boston: Beacon Press, 2003.

Calder, Isabel, and J. F. Jamison. *Colonial Captivities, Marches and Journeys*. New York: Macmillan, 1935.

Cerami, Charles. *Benjamin Banneker: Surveyor, Astronomer, Publisher, Patriot*. New York: John Wiley & Sons, 2002.

Chase, Portland, and Charles Cleveland. *Anti-Slavery Addresses of 1844 and 1845*. New York: Negro Universities Press, 1969.

Clark, Margaret Goff. *Benjamin Banneker: Astronomer and Scientist*. Illus. Russell Hoover. Champaign, IL: Garrard, 1971.

Clifton, Lucille. *Generations: A Memoir*. New York: New York Review Books, 2021.

Coates, Ta-Nehisi. *Between the World and Me*. New York: Spiegel & Grau, 2015.

Coldham, Peter Wilson. *Settlers of Maryland 1679–1700*. Surrey, England: Genealogical Publishing Company, 1995.

Condé, Maryse. *I, Tituba, Black Witch of Salem: A Novel*. Charlottesville: University of Virginia Press, 1992.

Cooper, T. *The Statutes at Large in Maryland*. New York: Viking Press, 1902.

Cox, Anna-Lisa. *The Bone and Sinew of the Land: America's Forgotten Black Pioneers and the Struggle for Equality*. New York: PublicAffairs, 2018.

Davis, David Brion. *Slavery in the Colonial Chesapeake*. Williamsburg, VA: Colonial Williamsburg Foundation, 1984.

Defoe, Daniel. *Moll Flanders*. New York: W. W. Norton, 2004.

Douglass, Frederick. *Narrative of the Life of Frederick Douglass, an American Slave, Written by Himself*. New York: Signet Classics, 1997.

Dove, Rita. *Thomas and Beulah*. Pittsburgh: Carnegie Mellon University Press, 1986.

Du Bois, Shirley Graham. *Your Most Humble Servant*. New York: Messner, 1949.

Du Bois, W. E. B. *The Souls of Black Folk*. New York: Millennium Publications, 2014.

Equiano, Olaudah. *The Interesting Narrative of the Life of Olaudah Equiano, or Gustavus Vassa, the African: Written by Himself*. New York: Modern Library, 2004.

Foner, Eric. *Gateway to Freedom: The Hidden History of the Underground Railroad*. New York: W. W. Norton, 2015.

Foner, Philip Sheldon. *Blacks in the American Revolution*. Westport, CT: Greenwood Press, 1976.

Foor, Daniel. *Ancestral Medicine: Rituals for Personal and Family Healing*. Rochester, VT: Inner Traditions International, 2017.

Frey, Sylvia. *Water from the Rock: Black Resistance in a Revolutionary Age*. Princeton, NJ: Princeton University Press, 1991.

Gamble, David, Linda K. Salmon, and Ajhaji Hassan Nije. *Peoples of the Gambia: The Wolof*. San Francisco: San Francisco State University Press, 1985.

Garrett, J. T. *The Cherokee Herbal: Native Plant Medicine from the Four Directions*. Rochester, VT: Bear & Co., Inner Traditions, 2003.

Glave, Diane B. *Rooted in the Earth: Reclaiming African American Environmental Heritage*. Chicago: Lawrence Hill Books, 2010.

Gordon-Reed, Annette. *The Hemingses of Monticello: An American Family*. New York: W. W. Norton, 2008.

Haley, Alex. *Roots: The Saga of an American Family*. Los Angeles: Da Capo Press, 2007.

Hartman, Saidiya. *Lose Your Mother: A Journey Along the Atlantic Slave Route*. New York: Farrar, Straus and Giroux, 2008.

———. *Wayward Lives, Beautiful Experiment: Intimate Histories of Riotous Black Girls, Troublesome Women, and Queer Radicals*. New York: W. W. Norton, 2019.

Heinegg, Paul. *Free African Americans of Maryland and Delaware: From the Colonial Period to 1810*. Baltimore: Clearfield, 2000.

Holliday, Carl. *Women's Life in Colonial Days*. New York: Frederick Ungar, 1960.

Holloway, Jonathan Scott. *Jim Crow Wisdom: Memory & Identity in Black America Since 1940*. Chapel Hill: University of North Carolina Press, 2013.

Holt, Keri. *Reading These United States: Federal Literacy in the Early Republic, 1776–1830*. Athens: University of Georgia Press, 2019.

Hurston, Zora Neale. *Barracoon: The Story of the Last "Black Cargo."* New York: Amistad, 2019.

Irving, Debby. *Waking Up White and Finding Myself in the Story of Race*. Cambridge, MA: Elephant Room Press, 2014.

Jacobs, Harriet. *Incidents in the Life of a Slave Girl*. Garden City, NY: Dover Publications, 2001.

Jefferson, Thomas. *Notes on the State of Virginia*. New York: Penguin Group, 1999.

Jones, Edward P. *The Known World: A Novel*. New York: HarperCollins, 2004.

Jones, Robert, Jr. *The Prophets: A Novel.* New York: G. P. Putnam's Sons, 2021.

Jung, Carl. *The Spirit in Man, Art, and Literature.* Trans. R. F. C. Hull. New York: Princeton/Bollingen Paperbacks, 1966.

———. *Synchronicity: An Acausal Connecting Principle.* Trans. R. F. C. Hull. New York: Princeton/Bollingen Paperbacks, 1973.

Kearse, Bettye. *The Other Madisons: The Lost History of a President's Black Family.* New York: Harcourt, 2020.

Kendi, Ibram X. *Stamped from the Beginning: The Definitive History of Racist Ideas in America.* New York: Nation Books, 2016.

Kenneally, Christine. *The Invisible History of the Human Race: How DNA and History Shape Our Identities and Our Futures.* New York: Penguin Group, 2014.

King, Martin Luther, Jr. *Strength to Love.* Philadelphia: Fortress Press, 1981.

Kingston, Maxine Hong. *The Woman Warrior: Memoirs of a Girlhood Among Ghosts.* New York: Random House, 1989.

Larsen, Nella. *Passing.* New York: Oshun, 2013.

Latrobe, John H. *Memoir of Benjamin Banneker, Read Before the Maryland Historical Society at the Monthly Meeting, May 1, 1845.* Published under the direction of the Society. Baltimore: John D. Toy, 1845.

Menakem, Resmaa. *My Grandmother's Hands: Racialized Trauma and the Pathway to Mending Our Hearts and Bodies.* Las Vegas: Central Recovery Press, 2017.

Michael, John. *Identity and the Failure of America: From Thomas Jefferson to the War on Terror.* Minneapolis: University of Minnesota Press, 2008.

Miles, Tiya. *All That She Carried: The Journey of Ashley's Sack, a Black Family Keepsake.* New York: Random House, 2021.

Milne, Anne. *Lactilla Tends Her Fav'rite Cow: Ecocritical Readings of Animals and Women in Eighteenth-Century British Labouring-Class Poetry.* Lewisburg, PA: Bucknell University Press, 2008.

Milteer, Warren Eugene, Jr. *Beyond Slavery's Shadow: Free People of Color in the South.* Chapel Hill: University of North Carolina Press, 2021.

Mittelberger, Gottlieb. *Journey to Pennsylvania.* Cambridge, MA: Belknap Press of Harvard University Press, 1960.

———. *On the Misfortune of Indentured Servants.* Philadelphia: John Jos McVey, 1898.

Morgan, Edmund S. *American Slavery, American Freedom: The Ordeal of Colonial Virginia.* New York: W. W. Norton, 1975.

Morgan, Kenneth. *Slavery and Servitude in North America, 1607–1800.* Edinburgh: Edinburgh University Press, 2000.

Morrison, Toni. *Beloved.* New York: New American Library, 1987.

———. *A Mercy.* New York: Alfred A. Knopf, 2008.

———. *Paradise.* New York: Alfred A. Knopf, 1998.

Murray, Lindley. *The English reader: or, Pieces in prose and poetry, selected from the best writers. Designed to assist young persons to read with propriety and effect; to improve their language and sentiments; and to inculcate some of the most important principles of piety and virtue. With a few preliminary observations on the principles of good reading.* New York: Isaac Collins, 1799.

Nash, Gary B. *Forbidden Love: The Secret History of Mixed-Race America*. New York: Henry Holt, 1999.

Nell, William C. *The Colored Patriots of the American Revolution*. Boston: R. F. Wallcut, 1855.

Nelson, Alondra. *The Social Life of DNA: Race, Reparations, and Reconciliation After the Genome*. Boston: Beacon Press, 2016.

Northup, Solomon. *Twelve Years a Slave*. Los Angeles: Graymalkin Media, 2014.

Painter, Nell Irvin. *The History of White People*. New York: W. W. Norton, 2011.

Pennington, James. *The Fugitive Blacksmith, or Events in the History of James W. C. Pennington*. Westport, CT: Negro Universities Press, 1971.

Postman, Neil. *Building a Bridge to the 18th Century: How the Past Can Improve Our Future*. New York: Alfred A. Knopf, 1999.

Rankine, Claudia. *Citizen: An American Lyric*. Minneapolis: Graywolf Press, 2014.

Rollo, Vera. *The Black Experience in Maryland*. Lanham: Maryland Historical Press, 1980.

Rusert, Britt. *Fugitive Science: Empiricism and Freedom in Early African American Culture*. New York: New York University Press, 2017.

Smallwood, Stephanie E. *Saltwater Slavery: A Middle Passage from Africa to American Diaspora*. Cambridge, MA: Harvard University Press, 2008.

Stowell, Marion Barber. *Early American Almanacs: The Colonial Weekday Bible*. New York: Burt Franklin, 1977.

Strickland, William. *Journal of a Tour of the United States of America, 1794–1795*. New York: New-York Historical Society, 1971.

Thompson, John. *The Life of John Thompson, a Fugitive Slave*. New York: Penguin Books, 2011. First published in the United States of America in 1856.

Tichy, Susan. *Trafficke*. Boise, ID: Ahsahta Press, 2015.

Tubbs, Anna Malaika. *The Three Mothers: How the Mothers of Martin Luther King, Jr., Malcolm X, and James Baldwin Shaped a Nation*. New York: Flatiron Books, 2021.

Tyson, Martha Ellicott. *Banneker, the Afric-American Astronomer*. Philadelphia: Friends' Book Association, 1884.

Ulrich, Laurel Thatcher. *A Midwife's Tale: The Life of Martha Ballard, Based on Her Diary, 1785–1812*. New York: Alfred A. Knopf, 1990.

Wadsworth, Ginger. *Benjamin Banneker: Pioneering Scientist*. Illustrated by Craig Orback. Minneapolis: Millbrook Press, 2003.

Walker, Alice. *In Search of Our Mothers' Gardens*. New York: Harcourt, 1983.

Ward, Jesmyn, ed. *The Fire This Time: A New Generation Speaks About Race*. New York: Scribner, 2016.

Wilkinson, A. B. *Blurring the Lines of Race and Freedom: Mulattos and Mixed Bloods in English Colonial America*. Chapel Hill: University of North Carolina Press, 2020.

Woloch, Nancy. *Early American Women: A Documentary History, 1600–1900*. Belmont, CA: Wadsworth, 1992.

BOOK CHAPTERS

Anderson, Carol. "White Rage." In Jesmyn Ward, ed., *The Fire This Time: A New Generation Speaks About Race*. New York: Scribner, 2017, 83–89.

Burke, Edmond. "Speech to Parliament, March 22, 1775, collected at Edmund Burke Urges Reconciliation with the Colonies." In Michael P. Johnson, ed., *Reading the American Past: Selected Historical Documents*, 5th ed. Boston: Bedford/ St. Martin's, 2012, 114–18.

Milteer, Warren Eugene, Jr. "Liberty in the Colonial South." In Milteer, *Beyond Slavery's Shadow: Free People of Color in the South*. Chapel Hill: University of North Carolina Press, 2021.

Morrison, Toni. "The Site of Memory." In William Zinsser, ed., *Inventing the Truth: The Art and Craft of Memoir*, 2nd ed. Boston: Houghton Mifflin, 1995, 83–102. https://blogs.umass.edu/brusert/files/2013/03/Morrison_Site-of-Memory.pdf.

Oldendorp, Christian George Andreas. "History of the Evangelical Brethren's Mission on the Caribbean Islands, 1777." "Document 5-5, A Moravian Missionary Interviews Slaves in the West Indies, 1767–1768." In Johnson, ed., *Reading the American Past*, 94–97.

Sprigs, Elizabeth. "Letter to Mr. John Sprigs in White Cross Street near Cripple Gate, London, September 22, 1756." In Isabel M. Calder and J. F. Jameson, *Colonial Captivities, Marches and Journeys*. New York: Macmillan, 1935, 151–52.

Wilkinson, A. B. "Children of Mixed Lineage in the Colonial Chesapeake." In A. B. Wilkinson, *Blurring the Lines of Race and Freedom: Mulattoes and Mixed Bloods in English Colonial America*. Chapel Hill: University of North Carolina Press, 2020, 59–92.

ARTICLES

Atkinson, David. "An Introduction to English Sea Songs and Shanties." English Folk Dance and Song Society, 2016. https://media.efdss.org/resourcebank/docs/An _Introduction_To_English_Sea_Songs_and_Shanties_2016.pdf.

Baker, Henry E. "Benjamin Banneker, the Negro Mathematician and Astronomer." *Journal of Negro History* 3, no. 2 (April 1918): 99–118.

"Bazabeel Norman." Wikipedia. https://en.wikipedia.org/wiki/Bazabeel_Norman.

"Benjamin Banneker Historical Park and Museum." Baltimore County Government. Last modified April 14, 2022. https://www.baltimorecountymd.gov/departments /recreation/countyparks/mostpopular/banneker/.

"Blacks Before the Law in Colonial Maryland," chapter 3, "Freedom or Bondage— The Legislative Record." Maryland State Archives. https://msa.maryland.gov /msa/speccol/sc5300/sc5348/html/chap3.html.

Burke, Henry, and Robert Lett. "Lett Settlement School House Meigs Twp"— History. https://henryburke1010.tripod.com/lettsettlementreunion/id23.html.

———. "Lett Settlement Marker!" https://henryburke1010.tripod.com/lettsettlemen treunion/id30.html.

Doolittle, I. G. "The Effects of the Plague on a Provincial Town in the Sixteenth and Seventeenth Centuries." *Medical History* 19, no. 4 (October 1975): 333–41. https:// pubmed.ncbi.nlm.nih.gov/1102817/.

Eglash, Ron. "The African Heritage of Benjamin Banneker." *Social Studies of Science* 27, no. 2 (April 1997): 307–15. https://doi.org/10.1177/030631297027002004.

Fayer, Joan M. "African Interpreters in the Atlantic Slave Trade." *Anthropological Linguistics* 45, no. 3 (2003): 281–95. http://www.jstor.org/stable/30028896.

Galenson, David W. "Literacy and Age in Preindustrial England: Quantitative Evidence and Implications." *Economic Development and Cultural Change* 29, no. 4 (1981): 813–29. http://www.jstor.org/stable/1153465.

Ganev, Robin. "Milkmaids, Ploughmen, and Sex in Eighteenth-Century Britain." *Journal of the History of Sexuality* 16, no. 1 (2007): 40–67. http://www.jstor.org/stable/30114201.

Gates, Henry Louis, Jr. "Exactly How Black Is Black America?" *The Root*, February 11, 2013. https://www.theroot.com/exactly-how-black-is-black-america-1790895185.

———. "How Many Africans Were Really Taken to the U.S. During the Slave Trade?" America's Black Holocaust Museum, January 6, 2014. https://www.abhmuseum.org/how-many-africans-were-really-taken-to-the-u-s-during-the-slave-trade/.

Glawe, Eddie. "Feature: Benjamin Banneker." *Xyht Magazine*, Professional Surveyor Archives, February 13, 2014. https://www.xyht.com/professional-surveyor-archives/feature-benjamin-banneker/.

Gowing, Laura. "Women's Bodies and the Making of Sex in Seventeenth-Century England." *Signs* 37, no. 4 (2012): 813–22. http://www.jstor.org/stable/10.1086/664469.

Grubb, Farley. "Fatherless and Friendless: Factors Influencing the Flow of English Emigrant Servants." *Journal of Economic History* 52, no. 1 (March 1992): 85–108. http://www.jstor.org/stable/2123346.

"A Guide to the History of Slavery in Maryland." Maryland State Archives, 2007. https://msa.maryland.gov/msa/intromsa/pdf/slavery_pamphlet.pdf.

"Historical and Biographical Abstract of the Lett Family." Old Settlers Reunion Association. https://www.osra1977.org/lett-settlement-history.

Keene, Louis. "Benjamin Banneker: The Black Tobacco Farmer Who the Presidents Couldn't Ignore." White House Historical Association. https://www.whitehousehistory.org/benjamin-banneker?%20#footnote-14Keene,%20footnote-13.

King, Julia A. "Tobacco, Innovation, and Economic Persistence in Nineteenth-Century Southern Maryland." *Agricultural History* 71, no. 2 (1997): 207–36. http://www.jstor.org/stable/3744247.

Kulikoff, Allan. "The Origins of Afro-American Society in Tidewater Maryland and Virginia, 1700 to 1790." *William and Mary Quarterly* 35, no. 2 (April 1978): 226–59. https://doi.org/10.2307/1921834.

Lenz, Lyz. "White Women Vote Republican: Get Used to It, Democrats." *Washington Post*. https://www.washingtonpost.com/opinions/2020/11/27/white-women-vote-republican-get-used-it-democrats/.

Levine, Sam. "Trump Admits He Is Undermining USPS to Make It Harder to Vote by Mail." *Guardian*, August 13, 2020. https://www.theguardian.com/us-news/2020/aug/13/donald-trump-usps-post-office-election-funding.

Lodine-Chaffey, Jennifer. *From Newgate to the New World: A Study of London's Transported Female Convicts, 1718–1775.* Varsity Tutors. https://www.varsitytutors.com/earlyamerica/early-america-review/volume-14/newgate-new-world.

Magel, Emil. "The Role of the *Gewel* in Wolof Society: The Professional Image of

Lamin Jeng." *Journal of Anthropological Research* 37, no. 2 (Summer 1981): 183–91. https://www.jstor.org/stable/3629709?seq=1.

Mancera-Saavedra, Valeria. "Fiction Lover Keturah Shaw-Poulos Spread Her Passion for Writing Until the Last Day." *Columbia Chronicle*, March 6, 2020. https://columbiachronicle.com/fiction-lover-keturah-shaw-poulos-spread-her-passion-for-writing-until-the-last-day.

Muskin, Adena. "Unionville Tavern." *Cleveland Historical*. https://clevelandhistorical.org/items/show/570.

Phelen, Elaine Paulionis. "How Did Freemasonry Influence the Design of Washington, D.C.?" Masonic Philosophical Society. Last modified November 29, 2019. https://blog.philosophicalsociety.org/2019/11/29/freemasonry-design-washington-dc/.

Pointer, Thomas, and Maria Pointer. "Thanksgiving at Hopedale." In *Antislavery Bugle*, January 26, 1861. Black Abolitionist Archives. https://henryburke1010.tripod.com/lettsettlementreunion/id41.html.

Reed, Paula S. "The Hermitage, a French-Caribbean Plantation in Central Maryland." *Material Culture* 38, no. 1 (2006): 1–35. http://www.jstor.org/stable/29764311.

Rogers, Katie. "White Women Helped Elect Donald Trump." *New York Times*, November 9, 2016. https://www.nytimes.com/2016/12/01/us/politics/white-women-helped-elect-donald-trump.html.

Rush, Benjamin. "A Plan for the Peace Office for the United States." Included in *Banneker's Almanac for the Year 1793*. Special Collections in the Maryland Center for History and Culture.

Russell, George Ely. "Molly Welsh: Alleged Grandmother of Benjamin Banneker." *National Genealogical Society Quarterly* 94, no. 4 (December 2006): 305–14.

Salmon, Emily Jones. "Convict Labor During the Colonial Period." Encyclopedia Virginia: Virginia Humanities, December 14, 2020. https://encyclopediavirginia.org/entries/convict-labor-during-the-colonial-period.

Schuba, Tom, et al. "'Our Kids Are Becoming Extinct': Chicago Children Are Being Killed by Guns at Far Faster Rates Than Years Past." *Chicago Sun Times*, June 8, 2021. https://chicago.suntimes.com/crime/2021/6/8/22523157/chicago-gun-violence-children-kids-killed-shootings.

Shelley, Terry. "Slavery in Ohio." *Star Beacon*, December 14, 2019. https://www.starbeacon.com/news/slavery-in-ohio/article_b0335730-1854-11ea-aca3-9fa5261b80d2.html.

Skaggs, David Curtis. "Maryland's Impulse Toward Social Revolution: 1750–1776." *Journal of American History* 54, no. 4 (March 1968): 771–86.

Sullivan, Walter. "6th-Century Manuscript Adds to Mystery of Star." *New York Times*, November 18, 1985. https://www.nytimes.com/1985/11/18/us/6th-century-manuscript-adds-to-mystery-of-star.html.

"Transportation of Felons to the Colonies." *Maryland Historical Magazine* 27, no. 4 (December 1932): 263–74.

Webster, Rachel Jamison. "White Lies and Fiction." *Pacific Standard*, March 21, 2018. https://psmag.com/social-justice/white-lies-and-fiction.

GENEALOGY

"Jemima (Banneker) Lett (abt. 1737–abt. 1800)." WikiTree: Where Genealogists Collaborate. Last modified April 18, 2022. https://www.wikitree.com/wiki/Banneker-1.

"Richard Gist." *Geni*. Last modified April 28, 2022. https://www.geni.com/people/Richard-Gist/6000000006348265291.

LECTURES/SPEECHES

Clark, Sonya. "The Flag We Should Know." Presented at Block Museum of Art, Northwestern University, February 6, 2020.

Morrison, Toni. "Wellesley College Commencement Address." Video accessed C-span .org, 2004. https://www.c-span.org/video/?182148–1/wellesley-college-commen cement-address.

Warnock, Raphael. "May My Story Be an Inspiration." Victory Speech for the Georgia Senate, January 6, 2021. https://www.youtube.com/watch?v =2wPPWJIsOvs.

Wrightson, Keith E. "England, Britain, and the World: Economic Development, 1660–1720." Lecture 23, History 251, "Early Modern England: Politics, Religion, and Society Under the Tudors and Stuarts." Open Yale Courses, 2009. https:// oyc.yale.edu/history/hist-251.

DOCUMENTARIES/NEWS

"Benjamin Banneker." PBS: *Africans in America*. Accessed August 14, 2021. https:// www.pbs.org/wgbh/aia/part2/2p84.html.

"January 6 Insurrection of the U.S. Capitol." CNN Politics. Accessed June 20, 2022. https://www.cnn.com/specials/politics/january-6-insurrection.

"The Revolutionary War." PBS: *Africans in America*. Accessed March 20, 2021. https:// www.pbs.org/wgbh/aia/part2/2narr4.html.

EXHIBITS/ARTWORKS

Caravans of Gold. Block Museum of Art. Chicago: Northwestern University, Fall 2019.

Clark, Sonya. *Black Hair Flag*. Virginia Museum of Fine Arts, 2014. https://www .culturetype.com/2014/07/22/a-tale-of-two-flags-sonya-clark-at-virginia -museum-of-fine-arts/.

PODCASTS

Bailey, Radcliffe, and Tyler Green. "No. 471: Radcliffe Bailey." Produced by Tyler Green. *The Modern Art Notes Podcast*. November 12, 2020. Soundcloud. https:// manpodcast.com/portfolio/no-471-radcliffe-bailey/.

Butler, Bisa, and Tyler Green. "No. 472: Bisa Butler, Malcolm Daniel." Produced by Tyler Green. *The Modern Art Notes Podcast*. November 19, 2020. Soundcloud. https://manpodcast.com/portfolio/no-472-bisa-butler-malcolm-daniel/.

Butler, Nic. "Private Manumission: An Intimate Path to Freedom." Produced by Charleston County Public Library. *Charleston Time Machine*. February 21, 2020.

Soundcloud. https://www.ccpl.org/charleston-time-machine/private-manumission
-intimate-path-freedom.

Hemphill, Prentis. *Finding Our Way.* Podcast series, Spotify. https://open.spotify
.com/show/3uuNl7k4lUjk9UaSkjvf4W.

DISSERTATIONS

Crawford, Julma B. "The Writings of Benjamin Banneker: Their Effect upon Concepts Regarding the Negro in America, 1750–1800." Master's thesis, Loyola University of Chicago, 1947.

Foster, Tess Bass. "Felonious Women & Familial Bonds: Convict Transportation to
the Maryland Colony, 1718–1739." PhD. diss, University of Maryland, Baltimore County, 2018.

Perot, Sandra. "Reconstructing Molly Welsh: Race, Memory and the Story of Benjamin Banneker's Grandmother." Master's thesis, University of Massachusetts
Amherst, 2008.

NOTES

EPIGRAPH

    All epigraph quotes at the beginning of chapters are taken from Benjamin Banneker's almanacs and his astronomical journal, available in the Special Collections, H. Furlong Baldwin Library, Maryland Center for History and Culture, Baltimore, MD.

    All the conversations in the present-day chapters are reprinted with participants' permission.

vii   Toni Morrison, "Commencement Address to Wellesley Class of 2004," https://www.wellesley.edu/events/commencement/archives/2004commencement/commencementaddress.

vii   James Baldwin, "Mass Culture and the Creative Artist: Some Personal Notes," from *The Cross of Redemption: Uncollected Writings* (New York: Vintage International, 2010), 7.

AUTHOR'S NOTE

xii   **our position of power and relationship to the story being told:** Jess Row, talk, February 8, 2022, Northwestern University English Department.

xii   **ancestry is as much about cultivating healthy relationships:** The idea of "right relationship" is a Native American concept that I learned when studying with Lakota elders in Pine Ridge, South Dakota, from 2013 to 2019. To be in "right relationship" with another is to be in a relationship of balance and respect. These elders kept their family stories alive and were in relationship to their own ancestors. They became a model for my own reverence and process with my own elders and ancestors.

xiii   **We need our imaginations to "feel with" one another:** I took to heart statements on this by the somatic healer and scholar of racialized trauma, Resmaa Menakem. Resmaa Menakem, *My Grandmother's Hands: Racialized Trauma* *and the Pathway to Mending Our Hearts and Bodies* (Las Vegas: Central Recovery Press, 2017), 61.

xiii   **far less documentation:** Saidiya Hartman writes brilliantly about the limits of the archive. I have been guided by her scholarship and by that of Tiya Miles, as they read between the lines of the archive, and vivify the stories of Black women's lives. Saidiya Hartman, *Wayward Lives, Beautiful Experiment: Intimate Histories of Riotous Black Girls, Troublesome Women, and Queer Radicals* (New York: W. W. Norton, 2019); Tiya Miles, *All That She Carried: The Journey of Ashley's Sack, a Black Family Keepsake* (New York: Random House, 2021).

CHAPTER 1: LETTER TO THE FUTURE

2   **"Sir, I am fully sensible of the greatness":** "To Thomas Jefferson from Benjamin Banneker, 19 August 1791," Founders Online, National Archives.

CHAPTER 2: DENIAL IN THE BLOODLINE

6   **Shame creates shut-down rather than openness to transformation:** This insight comes from my friend, author Selah Saterstrom, who says that "no transformation can happen in the space of shame." She gives workshops in Divinatory Poetics at https://www.fourqueens.org/.

6   **My creative writing students:** I thank the students who were in my fall 2016 section of The Situation of Writing, especially those quoted here: J.D. Amick, Zining Mok, Mackenzie Broderick, and Mahalia Sobhani. In the years since, J.D. has written and published poems about his *abuelo*, and Zining has published a genre-defying book called *The Orchid Folios* about the hybrid that is Singapore.

15   **We share 99.9 percent of our DNA with all other humans:** Alondra Nelson, *The Social Life of DNA: Race, Reparations, and Reconciliation After the Genome* (Boston: Beacon Press, 2016), 13.

16   **"a technology of power":** Kathleen M. Brown, *Good Wives, Nasty Wenches, and Anxious Patriarchs: Gender, Race and Power in Colonial Virginia* (Chapel Hill: University of North Carolina Press, 1996), 110.

16   **Keturah Shaw-Poulos:** Keturah passed away during the writing of this book. I will never forget her depth, gentleness, and kindness to students. For more on her: Valeria Mancera-Saavedra, "Fiction Lover Keturah Shaw-Poulos Spread Her Passion for Writing Until the Last Day," *Columbia Chronicle*, March 6, 2020, https://columbiachronicle.com/fiction-lover-keturah-shaw-poulos-spread-her-passion-for-writing-until-the-last-day.

17   **a Chicago Public School student was shot and killed:** At the time of this writing, in June 2021, fifty-two CPS school children under fifteen have been shot in this year alone. This atrocity remains underreported in the news: Tom Schuba et al., "'Our Kids Are Becoming Extinct': Chicago Children Are Being Killed by Guns at Far Faster Rates Than Years Past," *Chicago Sun Times*, June 8, 2021, https://chicago.suntimes.com/crime/2021/6/8/22523157/chicago-gun-violence-children-kids-killed-shootings.

19 **"No sir, I am as white as you are":** Oral history included in the papers of Vandhalia "Vandy" Lett Gee, recorded by George Simpson. Henry Burke and Robert Lett, "Lett Settlement School House Meigs Twp.—History," Henry Burke 1010, https://henryburke1010.tripod.com/lettsettlementreunion/id23 .html.

20 **schoolhouse:** The schoolhouse was built on land donated by James Lett. Generations of children proudly etched their names into its walls. Oral histories provided by Burke and Lett, "Lett Settlement School House Meigs Twp.—History."

CHAPTER 3: THE MILKMAID

23 **"escaping a heavier penalty because she could read":** Martha Ellicott Tyson, *Banneker, the Afric-American Astronomer* (Philadelphia: Friends' Book Association, 1884), 10.

23 **She was literate and owned her own Bible:** Literacy for girls and women was still quite rare at this time. Carl Holliday, *Women's Life in Colonial Days* (New York: Frederick Ungar, 1960), 70–71. Oral histories recorded by Martha Ellicott Tyson recall Molly's mother's Bible back in England: Tyson-Banneker Archive, Banneker Park and Museum.

23 **sitting with her mother:** Economist David Galenson explains that literary instruction would have occurred at home, within the family, in poor families in England in the 1670s and 1680s. David W. Galenson, "Literacy and Age in Preindustrial England: Quantitative Evidence and Implications," *Economic Development and Cultural Change* 29, no. 4 (1981): 824, http://www.jstor.org /stable/1153465.

25 **a girl could not just read and write for a living:** Kathleen M. Brown, *Good Wives, Nasty Wenches, and Anxious Patriarchs: Gender, Race and Power in Colonial Virginia* (Chapel Hill: University of North Carolina Press, 1996), 27, 29.

25 **a lusty sort of slut:** Dairymaids were depicted as sexual objects in eighteenth-century songs, poems, and jokes, and "milking" was used as a euphemism for sex. See Robin Ganev, "Milkmaids, Ploughmen, and Sex in Eighteenth-Century Britain," *Journal of the History of Sexuality* 16, no. 1 (2007): 40–67, www.jstor.org/stable/30114201.

27 **extract even more of a ladies' payment:** Historian Laura Gowing calls "harassment and abuse a frequent risk at this time." She writes of one servant woman commenting in court that she wore extra drawers to "protect herself from her master's hands." Another recalls her "master" telling her, "Thou art my servant and I may do with thee what I please." Laura Gowing, "Women's Bodies and the Making of Sex in Seventeenth-Century England," *Signs* 37, no. 4 (2012): 819, www.jstor.org/stable/10.1086/664469.

28 **committed out of dire necessity:** Kenneth Morgan, *Slavery and Servitude in North America, 1607–1800* (Edinburgh: Edinburgh University Press, 2000), 55.

28 **"stealing property worth a shilling or more":** Harrison Briggs et al., *Crime and Punishment in England: An Introductory History* (London: University College London Press, 1996), 73.

29 **"benefit of clergy"**: Briggs, *Crime and Punishment in England*, 74.

30 **England became overrun with vagrants and gig laborers**: Keith E. Wrightson, "England, Britain, and the World: Economic Development, 1660–1720" (Lecture, 23, History 251: "Early Modern England: Politics, Religion and Society Under the Tudors and Stuarts," Open Yale Courses, 2009), https://oyc.yale.edu/history/hist-251.

30 **"youth crime was a constant worry to the authorities"**: Briggs, *Crime and Punishment in England*, 21.

31 **women . . . a subject of increasing debate among clergymen and lawmakers**: Brown, *Good Wives, Nasty Wenches, and Anxious Patriarchs*, 27.

31 **"yeild a profitable service to the Common wealth in parts abroade"**: Emily Jones Salmon, "Convict Labor During the Colonial Period," Encyclopedia Virginia: Virginia Humanities, December 14, 2020, https://encyclopediavirginia.org/entries/convict-labor-during-the-colonial-period.

32 **people were much more likely to survive their indentures there**: Kenneth Morgan, *Slavery and Servitude in North America*, 66.

32 **In the seventeenth century, two hundred thousand people left England**: Kenneth Morgan, *Slavery and Servitude in North America*, 8.

CHAPTER 4: REVERSE MIGRATION

33 **They named that cooperative the Lett Settlement**: Henry Burke and Robert Lett, "The Lett Settlement!," https://henryburke1010.tripod.com/lettsettlementreunion/id30.html.

34 **Lett Settlement historical marker**: "The Lett Settlement Marker," Google Maps, https://www.google.com/maps/place/The+Lett+Settlement+Marker/@39.7909304,-81.7568253,15z/data=!4m5!3m4!1s0x0:0xbf1b92bb98a0d-12f!8m2!3d39.7909304!4d-81.7568253.

34 **"The Wilds"**: "The Wilds," Columbus Zoo, https://thewilds.columbuszoo.org/.

35 **absurd prolonging of childhood**: James Baldwin, *The Cross of Redemption: Uncollected Writings* (New York: Vintage International, 2010), 78.

CHAPTER 5: AT SEA

38 **a thousand Marys arriving in Maryland between 1670 and 1690**: Peter Wilson Coldham, *Settlers of Maryland 1679–1700* (Surrey, England: Genealogical Publishing Company, 1995).

38 **names of indentured and convict servants are lost**: Kenneth Morgan, *Slavery and Servitude in North America, 1607–1800* (Edinburgh: Edinburgh University Press, 2000), 11, 16.

38 **English courts sent approximately twenty-three hundred**: Emily Jones Salmon, "Convict Labor During the Colonial Period," Encyclopedia Virginia: Virginia Humanities, December 14, 2020, https://encyclopediavirginia.org/entries/convict-labor-during-the-colonial-period.

40 **"pled the belly"**: The editors of *Crime and Punishment in England* write, "One of the most interesting devices used to circumvent the death penalty was the so-called 'benefit of the belly.' A woman would claim to be pregnant so the sentence of death would be respited until after the innocent child had

been born." Harrison Briggs et al., *Crime and Punishment in England: An Introductory History* (London: University College London Press, 1996), 75.

40   **just to arrive there as a woman:** T. H. Breen and Stephen Innes, *"Myne Owne Ground": Race and Freedom on Virginia's Eastern Shore, 1640–1676* (New York: Oxford University Press, 2005), 60.

40   **maybe her first husband could come over:** Inspired by the 1722 novel by Daniel Defoe, *Moll Flanders*. Daniel Defoe, *Moll Flanders* (New York: W. W. Norton, 2004).

40   **The women had a bawdy sense of humor:** Jennifer Lodine-Chaffey, *From Newgate to the New World: A Study of London's Transported Female Convicts, 1718–1775*, Varsity Tutors, https://www.varsitytutors.com/earlyamerica/early-america-review/volume-14/newgate-new-world.

41   **"Oh they calls me Hanging Johnny / Away, boys, away":** David Atkinson, *An Introduction to English Sea Songs and Shanties*, English Folk Dance and Song Society, 2016, https://media.efdss.org/resourcebank/docs/An_Introduction_To_English_Sea_Songs_and_Shanties_2016.pdf.

42   **lived to see the end of their contracts:** David Brion Davis, *Slavery in the Colonial Chesapeake* (Williamsburg, VA: Colonial Williamsburg Foundation, 1984), 6.

42   **dead before the age of forty:** Historians Innes and Breen write, "Before 1680, the life expectancy in the Chesapeake colonies for a migrant was only about forty years. Seventy percent of the males who transferred from England to Maryland, for example, died before celebrating their fiftieth birthday. Approximately half of the children born in this region were dead before age twenty, a quarter before age one. A majority of the marriages recorded in seventeenth-century Maryland were broken within seven years by the death of one of the partners." Breen and Innes, *"Myne Owne Ground,"* 45.

42   **"so that many die miserably":** Gottlieb Mittelberger, *Journey to Pennsylvania* (Cambridge, MA: Belknap Press of Harvard University Press, 1960), 26.

42   **hoisted them off the ship's deck:** Gottlieb Mittelberger wrote, "No one can have an idea of the sufferings which women in confinement have to bear with their innocent children on board these ships. Few of this class escape with their lives; many a mother is cast into the water with her child as soon as she is dead. One day, just as we had a heavy gale, a woman in our ship, who was to give birth and could not give birth under the circumstances, was pushed through a loop-hole [porthole] in the ship and dropped into the sea, because she was far in the rear of the ship and could not be brought forward." Mittelberger, *Journey to Pennsylvania*, 25–31.

42   **people kept dying:** Carl Holliday, *Women's Life in Colonial Days* (New York: Frederick Ungar, 1960), 3.

43   **"His Majesty's Seven Years Passengers, who had too much Ingenuity to be suffer'd to live in England":** "Transportation of Felons to the Colonies," *Maryland Historical Magazine* 27, no. 4 (December 1932): 263–74, http://mdhs.msa.maryland.gov/pages/Viewer.aspx?speccol=5881&Series=1&Item=108.

44 **"the rolling roads":** Silvio A. Bedini, *The Life of Benjamin Banneker: The First African-American Man of Science* (Rancho Cordova, CA: Landmark Enterprises, 1972), 8.

CHAPTER 6: THE PARK AND MUSEUM

45 **Park and Museum:** "Benjamin Banneker Historical Park and Museum," Baltimore County Government, last modified April 14, 2022, https:// www.baltimorecountymd.gov/departments/recreation/countyparks /mostpopular/banneker.

46 **architectural dig that they had conducted on the site:** *Banneker, 18BA282*, Archaeological Collections in Maryland, https://apps.jefpat.maryland.gov /neh/18BA282-%20Banneker%20Finding%20Aid.aspx.

46 **"of the deepest dye":** These word choices are taken from Benjamin Banneker's letter to Thomas Jefferson. He wrote, "Sir, I freely and Chearfully acknowledge, that I am of the African race, and in that colour which is natural to them of the deepest dye.*" His asterisk footnote then reads, "My Father was brought here a Slave from Africa." "To Thomas Jefferson from Benjamin Banneker, 19 August 1791," Founders Online, National Archives.

48 **not "strictly of African parentage":** Silvio A. Bedini, *The Life of Benjamin Banneker: The First African-American Man of Science* (Rancho Cordova, CA: Landmark Enterprises, 1972), 339.

CHAPTER 7: THE COMPANY OF MARYLAND

51 **Molly was "a white woman servant of John Newman":** Provincial Court Judgments, R.B. #1, 426–26, Maryland State Archives, Annapolis.

51 **John Newman bought three tracts of land in Maryland:** Peter Wilson Coldham, *Settlers of Maryland 1679–1700* (Surrey, England: Genealogical Publishing Company, 1995), 122.

51 **the African people whom Molly would have met . . . would have come from Brazil or Saint Domingue:** Allan Kulikoff, "The Origins of Afro-American Society in Tidewater Maryland and Virginia, 1700 to 1790," *William and Mary Quarterly* 35, no. 2 (1978): 229, https://doi.org/10.2307 /1921834.

51 **they would have slept and worked alongside the European servants:** Kathleen M. Brown, *Good Wives, Nasty Wenches, and Anxious Patriarchs: Gender, Race and Power in Colonial Virginia* (Chapel Hill: University of North Carolina Press, 1996), 110.

51 **regardless of their skin tone or nationality:** David Brion Davis, *Slavery in the Colonial Chesapeake* (Williamsburg, VA: Colonial Williamsburg Foundation, 1984), 9.

51 **Staple agriculture was dependent on a large, cheap labor force:** Sylvia Frey, *Water from the Rock: Black Resistance in a Revolutionary Age* (Princeton, NJ: Princeton University Press, 1991), 10.

52 ***A Character of the Province of Maryland:*** Kenneth Morgan, *Slavery and Servitude in North America, 1607–1800* (Edinburgh: Edinburgh University Press, 2000), 16.

53 **"What we unfortunate English People suffer here":** Elizabeth Sprigs, "Letter to Mr. John Sprigs in White Cross Street near Cripple Gate, London, September 22, 1756," in *Colonial Captivities, Marches and Journeys* by Isabel M. Calder and J. F. Jameson (New York: Macmillan, 1935), 151–52.

53 **"masters" withholding food and extending their terms of work at the littlest provocation:** At the same time, "masters" were required by law to provide their indentured servants with food, lodging, and clothing. Kenneth Morgan, *Slavery and Servitude in North America, 1607–1800*, 20.

54 **they were unable to read their own contracts:** When Virginia deeds up to 1697 were examined, it was found that 75 percent of the women signing could not write their names. "If the condition was so bad among those prosperous to own property, what must it have been among the poor and so-called lower classes?" asks historian Carl Holliday. Carl Holliday, *Women's Life in Colonial Days* (New York: Frederick Ungar, 1960), 71.

54 **Servant women were legally forbidden to marry:** A. B. Wilkinson, *Blurring the Lines of Race and Freedom: Mulattoes and Mixed Bloods in English Colonial America* (Chapel Hill: University of North Carolina Press, 2020), 59.

54 **"particularly vulnerable to sexual exploitation":** Jacqueline M. Battalora, *Birth of a White Nation: The Invention of White People and Its Relevance Today* (New York: Routledge, 2021), 11.

54 **"masters" extended the women's contracts:** Wilkinson, *Blurring the Lines of Race and Freedom*, 84.

54 **physical, psychological, and sexual abuse:** Wilkinson, *Blurring the Lines of Race and Freedom*, 7.

54 **a new type of capitalism:** Battalora, *Birth of a White Nation*, 25.

54 **120,000 indentured and convict servants:** Kenneth Morgan, *Slavery and Servitude in North America*, 8.

55 **belongings to their children in their wills:** T. H. Breen and Stephen Innes, *"Myne Owne Ground": Race and Freedom on Virginia's Eastern Shore, 1640–1676* (New York: Oxford University Press, 2005), 145.

55 **Europeans and Africans of the lower classes accepted:** Battalora, *Birth of a White Nation*, 8.

55 **"follow the condition of the mother":** Frederick Douglass, *Narrative of the Life of Frederick Douglass, an American Slave, Written by Himself* (New York: Signet Classics, 1997), 21.

56 **Bacon's Rebellion united European laborers and laborers of color:** The most influential interpreter of Bacon's Rebellion is historian Edmund S. Morgan, who called the rebellion an "instinctive attempt to subdue class conflict by racism." Ibram X. Kendi, *Stamped from the Beginning: The Definitive History of Racist Ideas in America* (New York: Nation Books, 2016), 53.

56 **The first of these laws naming whiteness:** Battalora, *Birth of a White Nation*, 27, 33.

57 **four hundred thousand kidnapped African people:** Henry Louis Gates Jr., "How Many Africans Were Really Taken to the U.S. During the Slave Trade?," America's Black History Museum, https://www.abhmuseum.org/how-many-africans-were-really-taken-to-the-u-s-during-the-slave-trade/.

57   **"single-minded emphasis of blackness and inferiority":** Brown, *Good Wives, Nasty Wenches, and Anxious Patriarchs*, 110.

CHAPTER 8: THE UNTANGLING

60   **Erika Allen:** Erika Allen is the founder of Urban Growers Collective. And this group of friends is called the Mycelium Collective, and it was inspired by ideas shared in *Emergent Strategy* by Adrienne Maree Brown. The mycelium represents a natural nervous system of the earth, and we represent the fruitings of those ideas through our lives and work. From our very first meeting, we marveled at the previously unknown (subterranean) connections between us. Urban Growers Collective, https://urbangrowerscollective.org.

61   **The Op-Ed had been published two years earlier:** Rachel Jamison Webster, "White Lies and Fiction," *Pacific Standard*, March 21, 2018, https://psmag .com/social-justice/white-lies-and-fiction.

67   **Sonya Clark [and] the use of human hair in her work:** Sonya Clark, "The Flag We Should Know," Block Museum of Art, Northwestern University, February 6, 2020. For an image of *Black Hair Flag*, see here: https://www .culturetype.com/2014/07/22/a-tale-of-two-flags-sonya-clark-at-virginia -museum-of-fine-arts.

CHAPTER 9: STOLEN

69   ***The Book of Routes and Realms*:** I saw this book, alongside a fifteenth-century astrolabe from the Gold Coast of Africa, in the exhibit *Caravans of Gold*, at Northwestern University's Block Museum of Art in fall 2019.

70   **"The first that is known of the name of Banneker is that it was borne by an African prince":** Martha Ellicott Tyson, *Banneker, the Afric-American Astronomer* (Philadelphia: Friends' Book Association, 1884), 9.

70   **walls made of mud-millet adobe, and a conical thatched roof:** David Gamble, Linda K. Salmon, and Ajhaji Hassan Nije, *Peoples of the Gambia: The Wolof* (San Francisco: San Francisco State University Press, 1985), 3–5.

70   **the quincunx—a four-pointed star:** Ron Eglash, "The African Heritage of Benjamin Banneker," *Social Studies of Science* 27, no. 2 (April 1997): 307–15.

71   **voluntary and involuntary kinds of slavery in Africa:** Sylvia Frey, *Water from the Rock: Black Resistance in a Revolutionary Age* (Princeton, NJ: Princeton University Press, 1991), 47.

71   **linked institutions of church, courts, and trade:** White command of the courts continues, with dire consequences for people of color. As Carol Anderson wrote, "White rage doesn't have to take to the streets and face rubber bullets to be heard. Instead, white rage has access to the courts, police, legislatures, and governors." Carol Anderson, "White Rage," in *The Fire This Time: A New Generation Speaks About Race*, ed. Jesmyn Ward (New York: Scribner, 2017), 83.

71   **These departed were thought of as "the living dead":** Stephanie E. Smallwood, *Saltwater Slavery: A Middle Passage from Africa to American Diaspora* (Cambridge, MA: Harvard University Press, 2008), 130.

72 **"*tumbeiros*":** *Tumbeiros* is a term historians have translated as "floating tombs" or "undertakers." Smallwood, *Saltwater Slavery*, 137.

76 **speaking in Wolof, Ashanti, and Mandinka:** Stephanie Smallwood writes, "The Wolof-speaking peoples of the Jolof kingdom, a coastal state situated in the well-watered lands just south of the Senegal River, were important partners in Afro-European commercial networks throughout the slave-trading era, and as such they never figured prominently in slave exports after that region's contribution to the Atlantic traffic peaked in the sixteenth century." Smallwood, *Saltwater Slavery*, 103.

78 **He noted the many times his "masters" changed his name:** Olaudah Equiano, *The Interesting Narrative of the Life of Olaudah Equiano, or Gustavus Vassa, the African. Written by Himself* (New York: Modern Library, 2004), 45–46.

78 **"Thus by repeated cruelties":** Equiano, *The Interesting Narrative*, 60.

78 **These notes were not made to protect the captives:** Smallwood, *Saltwater Slavery*, 35.

79 **There were twelve different languages there in the boat:** Joan M. Fayer, "African Interpreters in the Atlantic Slave Trade," *Anthropological Linguistics* 45, no. 3 (2003): 281, http://www.jstor.org/stable/30028896.

81 **Statistically, a third of those confined to the slave ships died at sea:** Smallwood, *Saltwater Slavery*, 164.

81 **described not really as people but as tools:** Smallwood, *Saltwater Slavery*, 52.

81 **they invited buyers on deck and served them brandy, wine, and pastries:** Smallwood, *Saltwater Slavery*, 160.

81 **outward resistance would be futile or deadly:** Smallwood, *Saltwater Slavery*, 179.

82 **sold to separate bidders:** "Most Africans arrived alone off shipboard at the end of the Middle Passage," wrote Kenneth Morgan. "They had been torn from their roots in Africa, often leaving complex family and kinship ties behind them." Kenneth Morgan, *Slavery and Servitude in North America, 1607–1800* (Edinburgh: Edinburgh University Press, 2000), 81.

CHAPTER 10: THE WHITE HORSE

83 **a long list of the ancestors and living cousins:** These relatives include George C. Simpson, Vandhalia Lett Gee, Ruth Caliman Brown, Sherman Lett, Charles Henry Lett, Peggy Sawyer Williams, Wilbur Norman, Charles Weiker, Anita Burden, Louis Earley, Edie Lee Harris, Robert Lett, Marsha Stewart, Diana Todd Green, and Peter Byrd. At the 2003 Lett family reunion, Robert Lett presented a certificate to Ruth Caliman Brown for her work to preserve family history. The mayor who gave the award, Charles McIntyre, was a descendant of the superintendent of Meigs Township Schools who removed the Lett children from their schoolhouse in the 1840s. Oral history with Robert Lett, March 2022.

87 **"'What about Aquilla? Wasn't he Native American? Didn't he live on Native land?'":** This reference is to our ancestor Aquilla McClelland Lett,

who was living in Cherokee territory, in Cherokee County, Oklahoma. Oral history with Robert Lett, August 2021.

87 **"a tendency among white-passing people"**: Henry Louis Gates Jr., "Exactly How Black Is Black America?," *The Root*, February 11, 2013, https://www.theroot.com/exactly-how-black-is-black-america-1790895185.

89 **"John Brown's tannery"**: We did not solve that question that day, but at the end of the summer, I traveled with my parents and daughter to Crawford County, Pennsylvania, and the site of the old tannery. We were looking at it when the caretakers invited us into their home for the afternoon. They told stories about John Brown, and when they asked the name of our ancestor, Peter Lett, they recognized his name from the laborers' roster. Then they mentioned another name—David G. Lett, who had been a barber in the neighboring town of Meadville. Edie had, coincidentally, told me about David G. Lett just the day before. David Lett worked as a barber in Ohio, Michigan, and Pennsylvania. But then he went down to the Deep South, sometime in the 1850s, and worked as a barber in New Orleans and Alabama. At another point, he shows up working as a barber in Ontario, Canada, just across Lake Erie from Crawford County. The custodians of the old tannery told us about the way the fugitives would be put in wagons, hidden under tanned hides, and then hidden again in the holds of the ships, to be taken across to Canada. This is another story that remains to be written.

CHAPTER 11: THE ELDERS

92 **she purchased two enslaved men "from a ship anchored in the Bay"**: Silvio A. Bedini, *The Life of Benjamin Banneker* (Rancho Cordova, CA: Landmark Enterprises, 1972), 16.

92 **"one good Cloth suite of kersey or broad cloth"**: Kenneth Morgan, *Slavery and Servitude in North America, 1607–1800* (Edinburgh: Edinburgh University Press, 2000), 9.

92 **"freedom dues"**: Kenneth Morgan, *Slavery and Servitude in North America, 1607–1800*, 9.

93 **slavery became much more common in Virginia and Maryland**: Kenneth Morgan, *Slavery and Servitude in North America, 1607–1800*, 36.

93 **African people now outnumbering European servants four to one**: David Brion Davis, *Slavery in the Colonial Chesapeake* (Williamsburg, VA: Colonial Williamsburg Foundation, 1984), 8.

93 **Molly would have worked alongside the men**: Sylvia Frey writes of slavery in the Chesapeake, "On smaller farms, masters worked side by side with their slaves on every step of the production cycle." Sylvia Frey, *Water from the Rock: Black Resistance in a Revolutionary Age* (Princeton, NJ: Princeton University Press, 1991), 10.

95 **"They hold their morning and evening prayers very punctually"**: Christian George Andreas Oldendorp, "History of the Evangelical Brethren's Mission on the Caribbean Islands, 1777," "Document 5-5, A Moravian Missionary Interviews Slaves in the West Indies, 1767–1768." In *Reading the American*

Past: Selected Historical Documents, 5th ed., ed. Michael P. Johnson (Boston: Bedford/St. Martin's, 2012), 95.

95 **Eglash writes that African and Islamic systems of numerology . . . shaped Benjamin Banneker's complex mathematical thinking:** Ron Eglash, "The African Heritage of Benjamin Banneker," *Social Studies of Science* 27, no. 2 (April 1997): 308.

95 **"a man of bright intelligence, fine temper, with a very agreeable presence":** Martha Ellicott Tyson, *Banneker, the Afric-American Astronomer* (Philadelphia: Friends' Book Association, 1884), 10–11.

95 **Other scholars have traced the name "Banakas":** Silvio A. Bedini, *The Life of Benjamin Banneker: The First African-American Man of Science*, 2nd ed., rev. and expanded (Baltimore: Maryland Historical Society, 1999), 14.

96 **He sat with a drum in his lap that he had made from a giant dried gourd:** Historian Sylvia Frey writes of West African spirituality and enslaved people's insistence on keeping their spiritual traditions. "Evidence is found in the complaints of Maryland colonial authorities about the use of 'Negroe Drums' that called slaves together for gatherings and religious rituals." Frey, *Water from the Rock*, 36.

98 **Newly freed British and European women of the lower classes:** Jacqueline Battalora writes, "Records from one county show that in the 1660s, one-fourth of all children born to European female servants were of joint African and European ancestry." Jacqueline M. Battalora, *Birth of a White Nation: The Invention of White People and Its Relevance Today* (New York: Routledge, 2021), 7.

98 *Free African Americans of Maryland and Delaware from the Colonial Period to 1810*: Paul Heinegg, *Free African Americans of Maryland and Delaware: From the Colonial Period to 1810* (Baltimore: Clearfield, 2000).

98 **"Over two hundred and fifty British women were prosecuted in Maryland":** Heinegg, *Free African Americans of Maryland and Delaware from the Colonial Period to 1810*, digital archive, http://freeafricanamericans.com /maryland.htm.

98 **thousands of people resulted from marriages:** A. B. Wilkinson, *Blurring the Lines of Race and Freedom: Mulattos and Mixed Bloods in English Colonial America* (Chapel Hill: University of North Carolina Press, 2020), 76.

98 **a racist rant by Virginia governor William Gooch:** Warren Eugene Milteer Jr. "Liberty in the Colonial South," in Milteer, *Beyond Slavery's Shadow: Free People of Color in the South* (Chapel Hill: University of North Carolina Press, 2021), 15.

98 **"Forasmuch as diverse freeborn English women":** "Blacks Before the Law in Colonial Maryland, Chapter III, Freedom or Bondage—The Legislative Record," Maryland State Archives, https://msa.maryland.gov/msa/speccol /sc5300/sc5348/html/chap3.html.

99 **pilloried or put in the stocks—common punishments for women:** Harrison Briggs et al., *Crime and Punishment in England: An Introductory History* (London: University College London Press, 1996), 77.

99 **sexual crimes . . . positioned as a threat to the very identity of the "Nation"**: Milteer, *Beyond Slavery's Shadow*, 26.

100 **made servitude an "inherited status for many free children of color"**: Milteer, *Beyond Slavery's Shadow*, 26.

100 **"magistrates in Virginia and Maryland consciously engineered legal systems"**: Wilkinson, *Blurring the Lines of Race and Freedom*: 61.

100 **"When a Black woman is able to choose"**: Anna Malaika Tubbs, *The Three Mothers: How the Mothers of Martin Luther King, Jr., Malcolm X, and James Baldwin Shaped a Nation* (New York: Flatiron, 2021), 83.

100 **"Within the Black communities themselves, the family was the central institution"**: T. H. Breen and Stephen Innes, *"Myne Owne Ground": Race and Freedom on Virginia's Eastern Shore, 1640–1676* (New York: Oxford University Press, 2005), 83.

CHAPTER 12: JUNETEENTH

107 **"seventy percent African and thirty percent European"**: Henry Louis Gates Jr., "Exactly How Black Is Black America?," *The Root*, February 11, 2013, https://www.theroot.com/exactly-how-black-is-black-america-1790895185.

108 **"The Northwest Territory of Ohio . . . was seen as such a hopeful place"**: Anna-Lisa Cox writes that "a particularly terrible form of this backlash against equality arose in the Northwest Territory as the region settled, its territories became states, and more people of African descent moved onto that frontier. Whites decided to take away equal voting rights." Anna-Lisa Cox, *The Bone and Sinew of the Land: America's Forgotten Black Pioneers and the Struggle for Equality* (New York: PublicAffairs, 2018), 39.

CHAPTER 13: MARY

111 **Bana'ka "died early, leaving his wife with four young children"**: Martha Ellicott Tyson, *Banneker, the Afric-American Astronomer* (Philadelphia: Friends' Book Association, 1884), 11.

111 **"She had a knowledge of the properties and uses of herbs"**: Tyson, *Banneker, the Afric-American Astronomer*, 25.

112 **to gather healing leaves, roots, and barks from the woods:** Some of these insights around Mary's work as a healer and midwife are derived from studying Laurel Thatcher Ulrich, *A Midwife's Tale: The Life of Martha Ballard, Based on Her Diary, 1785–1812* (New York: Alfred A. Knopf, 1990).

112 **"she sought out woodland plants that had medicinal value"**: Silvio A. Bedini, *The Life of Benjamin Banneker* (Rancho Cordova, CA: Landmark Enterprises, 1972), 32.

113 **Maryland Provincial Court Records from May 1731:** Provincial Court Judgments, R.B. #1, 426–26, Maryland State Archives, Annapolis.

113 **a "mulatto" woman, Mary Beneca:** Because of the connection of the Lett and Banneker names, as well as the date and location of this trial, Paul Heinegg and I believe that this "Beneca" is what we later spell "Banneker" or was locally known as "Bannaky." Again, name spellings were highly irregular

then, and dependent on who was clerking the courts or writing the ledger. Paul Heinegg, *Free African Americans of Maryland and Delaware from the Colonial Period to 1810*, digital archive, http://freeafricanamericans.com /maryland.htm.

114 **Mary Beneca did, in fact, win her case:** Provincial Court Judgments, R.B. #1, 426–26, Maryland State Archives, Annapolis.

115 **women were commonly charged with the lesser offense of "fornication":** *Archives of Maryland*, 30:289–90; 36:275–76; *Laws of Maryland*, 1715, chapter 44, section 25; Heinegg, *Free African Americans of Maryland and Delaware*.

116 **a satchel for their daughters:** Tiya Miles, *All That She Carried: The Journey of Ashley's Sack, a Black Family Keepsake* (New York: Random House, 2021).

116 **Mothers hearing the "hiring list" read out on New Year's Eve:** Harriet Jacobs, *Incidents in the Life of a Slave Girl* (Garden City, NY: Dover Publications, 2001), 16.

116 **this "maternal tie to whiteness," Wilkinson explains, "literally meant the difference between bondage and freedom":** A. B. Wilkinson, *Blurring the Lines of Race and Freedom: Mulattoes and Mixed Bloods in English Colonial America* (Chapel Hill: University of North Carolina Press, 2020), 61.

117 **Even if she had not been able to free her beloved Bana'ka:** Historian Warren Eugene Milteer Jr. explains that "the significant number of children of color born to white mothers were among those most greatly affected by the lack of privileges granted to them by colonial lawmakers. The laws punishing white mothers and their children of color indeed influenced the life trajectories of innumerable free people of color." From Warren Eugene Milteer Jr., "Liberty in the Colonial South," in *Beyond Slavery's Shadow: Free People of Color in the South* (Chapel Hill: University of North Carolina Press, 2021), 15.

CHAPTER 14: COINCIDENCES

120 **"But if you're looking . . . you start to see the connections":** This recalls Matthew, Chapter 13, in the King James Bible: "Therefore speak I to them in parables: because they seeing see not; and hearing they hear not, neither do they understand. . . . But blessed are your eyes, for they see: and your ears, for they hear (Matthew 13:13, 16). For more on synchronicity and acausal relationships, see Carl Jung, *Synchronicity: An Acausal Connecting Principle*, trans. R. F. C. Hull (New York: Princeton/Bollingen, 1973).

CHAPTER 15: ROBERT

122 **"Mary married a native African":** Martha Ellicott Tyson, *Banneker, the Afric-American Astronomer* (Philadelphia: Friends' Book Association, 1884), 1.

123 **In 1724, more than two hundred people of African descent were baptized:** Sylvia Frey, *Water from the Rock: Black Resistance in a Revolutionary Age* (Princeton, NJ: Princeton University Press, 1991), 19.

123 **it is clear that Robert was affiliated with Richard Gist:** "Richard Gist," *Geni*, last modified April 28, 2022, https://www.geni.com/people/Richard-Gist /6000000006348265291. See also Silvio A. Bedini, *The Life of Benjamin Banneker: The First African-American Man of Science*, 2nd ed., rev. and expanded (Baltimore: Maryland Historical Society, 1999), 25.

124 **crouched in a hollowed-out log, listening to the patrollers:** We do not know if or how Robert actually escaped or was manumitted from enslavement. These details are all taken from factual first-person narratives by people who escaped enslavement. This note comes from John Thompson, *The Life of John Thompson, a Fugitive Slave* (New York: Penguin Books, 2011).

124 **Robert went to this man and his family, who hid him for weeks:** Almost all successful runaways from slavery were helped by other people of color, revealing that even an individual bid for freedom was dependent on community ties, shared risk, and cooperation. Allan Kulikoff, "The Origins of Afro-American Society in Tidewater Maryland and Virginia, 1700 to 1790," *William and Mary Quarterly* 35, no. 2 (1978): 253, https://dol.org/10.2307 /1921834.

125 **he used his connections in the church and the community to eventually secure his own freedom:** Two more Bannekers show up in the records that attest to the standing of the Banneker family at this time. On May 22, 1735, Katherine Banneker was married to James Boston, recorded as a "Free Negro" in St. Paul's Parish. And nine years later, on September 22, 1744, Esther Banneker married William Black, also recorded as a "Free Negro" in St. Paul's Parish. Researchers have always assumed that these were Mary's younger sisters, Molly's other daughters with Bana'ka. But another recently discovered document shows Robert petitioning to not have to pay taxes on two daughters, and researcher Paul Heinegg has suggested that these were Robert's daughters from an earlier marriage. They were all using some form of the name Banneker, all living as free people of color, and all respected and integrated enough in Chesapeake society to be listed on the official registers in the Anglican Church of St. Paul's, St. Paul's Parish in Baltimore, Maryland. Parish Register Folio 102, No. 27, listed the marriage of "James Boston to Katherine Banneker, May 22, 1735, Negroes." Folio 111 read "William Black and Esther Banneker was married September 22, 1744." Cited in Silvio A. Bedini, *The Life of Benjamin Banneker: The First African-American Man of Science* (Rancho Cordova, CA: Landmark Enterprises, 1972), 346. When I contacted St. Paul's Parish in September 2021 to see the records, I was told that a fire at the church had destroyed all of the old records.

CHAPTER 16: GWEN

132 **"'Griots' Circle of Maryland'":** https://www.griotscircleofmarylandinc.org /more-about-me.

132 **"storyteller Mary Carter Smith":** https://www.griotscircleofmarylandinc.org /mary-carter-smith.

135 **"You could get a scholarship":** Anna Malaika Tubbs explains, "Keeping Black

people from advancing by restricting their ability to become educated has long been a strategy of oppression. During times of slavery well through the 1800s, it was against the law to teach Black people to read and write. Once the law allowed it, Black people who pursued education were still met with attacks, intimidation, withholding, shortened school years, and more. It was an act of resistance every time a Black family was able to prioritize education, but it was not an easy feat. According to the National Center for Education Statistics, in 1910, 5 percent of whites over the age of fourteen were able to read at the most fundamental levels, as compared to 30 percent of Blacks." Anna Malaika Tubbs, *The Three Mothers: How the Mothers of Martin Luther King, Jr., Malcolm X, and James Baldwin Shaped a Nation* (New York: Flatiron Books, 2021), 50.

CHAPTER 17: CHILDHOOD

137 **Mary, already named Mary Beneca, petitioned for the freedom of her daughter Sarah:** Provincial Court Judgments, R.B. #1, 426–26, Maryland State Archives, Annapolis.

138 **"Timber Poynt":** Silvio A. Bedini, *The Life of Benjamin Banneker: The First African-American Man of Science*, 2nd ed., rev. and expanded (Baltimore: Maryland Historical Society, 1999), 24.

138 **Robert purchased one hundred additional acres in Baltimore County, called "Stout," for 7,000 pounds of tobacco:** Robert was called "Robert Bannaky, a Negro Free" on November 1, 1743, when the Baltimore County Court ordered that his daughter Julian be levy free for the future. Silvio A. Bedini, *The Life of Benjamin Banneker: The First African-American Man of Science* (Rancho Cordova, CA: Landmark Enterprises, 1972), 27.

138 **"Robert Bannaky and Benjamin Bannaky his son their heirs":** Bedini, *The Life of Benjamin Banneker*, 27.

139 **despite landowners' increasing baptism of their enslaved people, the slave trade was only increasing:** Allan Kulikoff, "The Origins of Afro-American Society in Tidewater Maryland and Virginia, 1700 to 1790," *William and Mary Quarterly* 35, no. 2 (1978): 250, https://doi.org/10.2307/1921834.

139 **Many laws forced free people of color to leave:** Warren Eugene Milteer Jr., "Liberty in the Colonial South," in Milteer, *Beyond Slavery's Shadow: Free People of Color in the South* (Chapel Hill: University of North Carolina Press, 2021), 24.

139 **Other laws targeted free people of color with discriminatory taxation:** Milteer, "Liberty in the Colonial South," 66.

139 **Africans . . . were "sluggish, lazy, careless" and "Covered by grease":** Ibram X. Kendi, *Stamped from the Beginning: The Definitive History of Racist Ideas in America* (New York: Nation Books, 2016), 92.

140 **After clearing the underbrush, Robert girdled the trees:** Bedini, *The Life of Benjamin Banneker*, 31.

141 **"led the waters, by means of ditches and little dams":** Vera F. Rollo, *The Black Experience in Maryland* (Lanham: Maryland Historical Press, 1980), 11.

142 **Those casks then served as their currency in the colony:** Martha Ellicott Tyson, *Banneker, the Afric-American Astronomer* (Philadelphia: Friends' Book Association, 1884), 12. For more on tobacco cultivation, see Julia A. King, "Tobacco, Innovation, and Economic Persistence in Nineteenth-Century Southern Maryland," *Agricultural History* 71, no. 2 (1997): 207–36, http://www .jstor.org/stable/3744247.

142 **Naming as a way of denoting lineage:** Sylvia Frey, *Water from the Rock: Black Resistance in a Revolutionary Age* (Princeton, NJ: Princeton University Press, 1991), 33.

CHAPTER 18: *I CAN'T BREATHE*

144 **Robert organized a group phone call:** The people on the phone call were Robert Lett, Charles and Pat Calaman, Rachel McDaniels, Jessica Perry, Gwen Marable, Marsha Stewart, Ron Mercer, Edwin Lee, Edie Lee Harris, Belinda Sheppard, Joseph Blair, and Rachel Jamison Webster.

149 **"Boone County Kentucky":** Toni Morrison's book *Beloved* is set in Boone County, Kentucky, and is based on the true story of Margaret Garner. In 1856, the very year that Margaret Garner escaped from the Gaines plantation with her husband, Robert, Luvenia Sleets was on a neighboring farm, purchasing her husband John Simon's freedom from enslavement. Oral history of Robert Lett, March 2022. Toni Morrison, *Beloved* (New York: New American Library, 1987).

CHAPTER 19: KEEPING TIME

151 **Benjamin's "bright mind made him a great favorite with his grandmother":** Martha Ellicott Tyson, *Banneker, the Afric-American Astronomer* (Philadelphia: Friends' Book Association, 1884), 13.

152 **"All his delight was to dive into his books":** Tyson, *Banneker, the Afric-American Astronomer*, 13–14.

152 **"advanced in arithmetic as far as Double Position":** Silvio A. Bedini, *The Life of Benjamin Banneker: The First African-American Man of Science* (Rancho Cordova, CA: Landmark Enterprises, 1972), 41.

152 **antislavery advocates within the church had convinced the Quakers to officially forbid congregants to purchase enslaved people:** Ibram X. Kendi notes that 30 percent of Quakers found ways to free their enslaved people, while 70 percent failed to free their captives. Ibram X. Kendi, *Stamped from the Beginning: The Definitive History of Racist Ideas in America* (New York: Nation Books, 2016), 88–89.

152 **colonies were organizing militias to control the "enemy within":** Sylvia Frey, *Water from the Rock: Black Resistance in a Revolutionary Age* (Princeton, NJ: Princeton University Press, 1991), 33.

153 **he borrowed a pocket watch from a friend of Robert's:** Silvio Bedini writes that "the fact that a borrowed watch served as a model for the clock he subsequently constructed is based on Banneker's own statement which he made to neighbors." Bedini, *The Life of Benjamin Banneker*, 43.

154 **Benjamin's mind would not be confined:** Charles Cerami, *Benjamin Banneker: Surveyor, Astronomer, Publisher, Patriot* (New York: John Wiley & Sons, 2002), 100.

154 **The clock and the young man who made it:** Bedini writes, "His fame spread rapidly through the valley. Those who had known nothing about Benjamin Banneker the farmer learned about him as a maker of a fascinating timepiece." Bedini, *The Life of Benjamin Banneker: The First African-American Man of Science,* 2nd ed., rev. and expanded (Baltimore: Maryland Historical Society, 1999), 43.

155 **only 40 percent of free white men living in Maryland owned their own land:** David Curtis Skaggs, "Maryland's Impulse Toward Social Revolution: 1750–1776," *Journal of American History* 54, no. 4 (1968): 772.

155 **But now they became even more conspicuous:** Kendi, *Stamped from the Beginning,* 125.

155 **Most small farmers and laborers . . . were unable to read or write:** Bedini, *The Life of Benjamin Banneker,* 2nd ed., 49.

155 **a man of African descent with such learning attracted white envy, disbelief, and backlash:** For laws on literacy and writing on the risk and experience of learning to read while in enslavement, see Frederick Douglass, *Narrative of the Life of Frederick Douglass, an American Slave, Written by Himself* (New York: Signet Classics, 1997), 48.

155 **he began corresponding with mathematicians and other writers he admired:** Britt Rusert notes that "comments from Tyson's sketch reveal that Banneker's writing was embedded in a network of poetical composition and letter exchange with white women, as well as the circulation of mathematical problems and answers in verse by white men." Britt Rusert, *Fugitive Science: Empiricism and Freedom in Early African American Culture* (New York: New York University Press, 2017), 39.

156 **Robert Banneker left his widow, Mary, and his son, Benjamin:** Tyson, *Banneker, the Afric-American Astronomer,* 14.

156 **his father was not there:** Robert Banneker died on July 10, 1759, according to the entry in Benjamin Banneker's Bible. Cerami, *Benjamin Banneker: Surveyor, Astronomer, Publisher, Patriot,* 100.

156 **He stopped writing for a time:** Cerami, *Benjamin Banneker: Surveyor, Astronomer, Publisher, Patriot,* 58.

156 **Benjamin's knowledge . . . included African cosmology:** Ron Eglash, "The African Heritage of Benjamin Banneker," *Social Studies of Science* 27, no. 2 (April 1997): 308, https://doi.org/10.1177/030631297027002004.

157 **"The first great locust year that I can remember was 1749":** "Banneker Astronomical Journal," Special Collections, H. Furlong Baldwin Library, Maryland Center for History and Culture, Baltimore.

158 **the Dogon priests of Mali in Western Africa had long taught:** Walter Sullivan, "6th-Century Manuscript Adds to Mystery of Star," *New York Times,* November 18, 1985, https://www.nytimes.com/1985/11/18/us/6th-century-manuscript-adds-to-mystery-of-star.html.

159   **The Ellicott family were highly industrious and inventive:** Vera F. Rollo, *The Black Experience in Maryland* (Lanham: Maryland Historical Press, 1980), 8.

159   **"His mind was filled with volumes of traditationary lore":** Tyson, *Banneker, the Afric-American Astronomer,* 27.

160   **"They found him and his mother living together in great comfort and plenty":** Tyson, *Banneker, the Afric-American Astronomer,* 24.

160   **George surveyed the road that would become the National Turnpike between Frederick and Baltimore, Maryland:** Bedini, *The Life of Benjamin Banneker,* 69.

CHAPTER 20: LETTER CARRIERS

166   **"Trump wanting to get rid of the Post Office":** Sam Levine, "Trump Admits He Is Undermining USPS to Make It Harder to Vote by Mail," *Guardian,* August 13, 2020.

CHAPTER 21: REVOLUTION

168   **Jemima Banneker and Samuel Delaney Lett:** "Jemima (Banneker) Lett (abt. 1737–abt. 1800)," WikiTree: Where Genealogists Collaborate, https://www.wikitree.com/wiki/Banneker-1.

169   **Jemima and Samuel's wedding may have taken place on Banneker land:** Samuel Delaney Lett and Mary and Benjamin Banneker all signed the ledgers at the Ellicott & Co. Store during these years, so we know that they were living nearby, in Ellicott's Mills, Oella, or Elkridge Landing. "Ledger from the Ellicott & Co. Store," Banneker/Tyson Archives of the Banneker Park and Museum, Oella, MD.

169   **[Mary] rubbed her wrist distractedly, recalling the feel of the stocks:** Interview with Edith Lee Harris, November 2021: "Zachariah Lett's story is documented by Henry Pedens in a book on Colonial Maryland. Mary Lett (probably a single white woman of German ancestry) living in Baltimore was charged with the crime of Bastardy and I believe sentenced to the stocks. Peden's book names her two children as Zachariah and Sarah. Her crime was giving birth to two mulatto children out of wedlock."

170   **their children were given biblical names:** "Historical and Biographical Abstract of the Lett Family," Old Settlers Reunion Association, https://www.osra1977.org/lett-settlement-history. Information was taken from oral history recorded and thereafter researched by George Simpson in the early 1900s. This oral history was passed on in manuscript form to Amanda Lett, who in turn passed the documents on to Charles Henry Lett, son of Judson Lett and a descendant of Aquilla Lett Sr. Old Settlers site authored and maintained by Marsha Stewart.

171   **Jemima was described as "a modest person, devoid of all pretense":** "Jemima (Banneker) Lett," WikiTree.

171   **a "cruel war against human nature itself":** Anna-Lisa Cox, *The Bone and*

Sinew of the Land: America's Forgotten Black Pioneers and the Struggle for Equality (New York: PublicAffairs, 2018), 28.

172 **As Abigail Adams wrote in a letter in 1774:** Abigail Adams, "Letter from Abigail Adams to John Adams, 22 September 1744," *Adams Family Papers: An Electronic Archive*, Massachusetts Historical Society, https://www.masshist .org/digitaladams/archive/doc?id=L17740922aa.

172 **On November 12, 1775, the Continental Congress formally declared:** Philip Sheldon Foner, *Blacks in the American Revolution* (Westport, CT: Greenwood Press, 1976), 46.

173 **ten thousand Black soldiers to join the British side during the Revolution:** "The Revolutionary War," PBS: *Africans in America*, accessed March 20, 2021, https://www.pbs.org/wgbh/aia/part2/2narr4.html.

173 **"tearing up the foundations of civil authority and government":** Sylvia Frey, *Water from the Rock: Black Resistance in a Revolutionary Age* (Princeton, NJ: Princeton University Press, 1991), 63.

173 **Maryland's Eastern Shore . . . forcibly disarmed all people of color:** Frey, *Water from the Rock*, 64.

173 **"the slave network could carry news 'several hundreds of miles'":** Frey, *Water from the Rock*, 50.

173 **George Washington came to believe:** Frey, *Water from the Rock*, 78.

173 **the enrollment of free Black men in the army:** Frey, *Water from the Rock*, 78.

174 **"An essential part of the plan is to give them their freedom with their muskets":** "From Alexander Hamilton to John Jay, [14 March 1779]," Founders Online, National Archives, https://founders.archives.gov/documents/Hamilton /01-02-02-0051. [Original source: *The Papers of Alexander Hamilton*, vol. 2, 1779–1781, ed. Harold C. Syrett, New York: Columbia University Press, 1961, 17–19.]

174 **Wheat was in dire need in the colonies:** Historian Paula Reed writes, "Frederick County . . . along with adjacent Washington County were the leading wheat- and flour-producing counties in Maryland," and "traders in the Caribbean regarded 'Baltimore Flour' as among the best in the world." Paula S. Reed, "The Hermitage, a French-Caribbean Plantation in Central Maryland," *Material Culture* 38, no. 1 (2006): 12, http://www.jstor.org/stable /29764311.

174 **corn and wheat from farms like theirs were sent to Annapolis and Philadelphia:** Frey, *Water from the Rock*, 143–44.

175 **how important it was to live in community:** "Lett Settlement Reunion," Henry Burke 1010, https://henryburke1010.tripod.com/lettsettlementreunion /index.html. These allied families have continued to get together for reunions. This excerpt of a poem, "Resume," by Gertrude Brown, written in the 1930s, captures the feeling:

> The Letts and the Calimans came by the score
> With Guys and Simpsons and Cliffords galore,
> The Tates and Browns and Pointers were there

While the in-laws and Cousins made up a large share,
The Pritchetts, the Reynolds, the Jackson's, Normans and Greens,
The Barnetts, Carlisles, all came in machines.
And there were the Crostons, the Toneys,
the Earleys and all of the families that our family marries.
I can not begin to call each one by name
The point I am making is, every one came
We'll never forget that day in the woods,
It made our hearts glad and it did our souls good.
The bumps and the scratches, the uneven roads,
The mosquitoes and spiders, the snakes and the toads,
The dinners spread out for the starved inner man,
All seem to recall that first meet of the clan.
Good wholesome lives, lived kindly and true,
This is the heritage they left to you,
Not riches, not titles, but pride in your race
And the right to look God and all men in the face.

177   **Bazabeel Norman:** "Bazabeel Norman," Wikipedia, https://en.wikipedia.org /wiki/Bazabeel_Norman.

178   **enslaved people who had heard Dunmore's promise of freedom:** Frey, *Water from the Rock*, 145.

178   **"Scarce a white person was to be seen":** Frey, *Water from the Rock*, 147.

178   **five men, "drove ashore that was drowned going to the fleet":** Frey, *Water from the Rock*, 147.

181   **"what is a kingdom or a country?":** This essay is unattributed in the Almanac, but can be seen there, *Banneker's Almanac of 1792*, Special Collections, Maryland Center of History and Culture, Evans Early American Imprint Collection, https://quod.lib.umich.edu/e/evans/n26929.0001.001/247:5?page =root;size=100;view=text;q1=Juvenile+literature+—+Poetry+—+1799. The essay was written by the English essayist Joseph Addison. Lindley Murray, *The English reader: or, Pieces in prose and poetry, selected from the best writers. Designed to assist young persons to read with propriety and effect; to improve their language and sentiments; and to inculcate some of the most important principles of piety and virtue. With a few preliminary observations on the principles of good reading* (New York: Isaac Collins, 1799).

182   **The war gave African Americans a more cohesive identity as a people:** Frey, *Water from the Rock*, 218.

182   **Maryland . . . was "rapidly giving way to emancipation":** Frey, *Water from the Rock*, 218.

182   **Free people of color had comprised:** William Strickland, *Journal of a Tour of the United States of America, 1794–1795* (New York: New-York Historical Society, 1971), 19.

183   **landowners like Benjamin Banneker had long enjoyed provisional rights:** Keri Holt, *Reading These United States: Federal Literacy in the Early Republic, 1776–1830* (Athens: University of Georgia Press, 2019), 92.

183   **a new Maryland law stated that:** T. Cooper, *The Statutes at Large in Mary-land* (New York: Viking Press, 1902), 59.

183   **"instruments of torture, stocks, whips, etc.":** Reed, "The Hermitage, a French-Caribbean Plantation in Central Maryland," 17.

CHAPTER 22: TOWARD THE SETTING SUN

185   **"They were the Calimans, the Guys . . . the Simpsons and the Tates and the Earleys":** Henry Burke and Robert Lett, "Lett Families Settlement, History and Genealogy," https://henryburke1010.tripod.com/lettsettlementreunion /id6.html.

186   **"Maryland State Colonization Society of Africa":** Jennifer Davis, "The Constitution of the Colony of Maryland in Liberia," in *Custodia Legis*, Law Librarians of Congress blog, https://blogs.loc.gov/law/2021/03/the-constitution-of -the-colony-of-maryland-in-liberia/.

186   **"John Latrobe . . . president of the Maryland Colonization Society":** John H. Latrobe, *Memoir of Benjamin Banneker, Read Before the Maryland Historical Society at the Monthly Meeting, May 1, 1845* (Published under the direction of the Society. Baltimore: John D. Toy, 1845).

CHAPTER 23: THE DREAM

189   **He mapped the planets' relations and positions to one another:** Benjamin Banneker, "Projection of a Solar Eclipse Made by Banneker, from his Manuscript Journal," page facing calculations for 1792, "Banneker Astronomical Journal," Special Collections, H. Furlong Baldwin Library, Maryland Center for History and Culture, Baltimore.

190   **He wasn't a drunk:** In the opening entries in the ledger for the Ellicott Co. Store, available in the archives of the Benjamin Banneker Historical Park and Museum, Benjamin purchases rum, but later in life, he stopped purchasing alcohol altogether. Martha Tyson wrote that when he returned from Washington, D.C., he discussed the trip with her family. "One matter, personal to himself, gave him great pleasure in the retrospect. *He had not, in his absence, tasted either wine or spiritous liquors.* He had experienced the fact that it was unwise for him to indulge, ever so slightly, in stimulating drinks. . . . He was a noble example of what may be accomplished by a firm resolve." Martha Ellicott Tyson, *Banneker, the Afric-American Astronomer* (Philadelphia: Friends' Book Association, 1884), 38.

190   **He loved to talk:** Silvio A. Bedini, *The Life of Benjamin Banneker: The First African-American Man of Science* (Rancho Cordova, CA: Landmark Enterprises, 1972), 72.

190   **An accurate ephemeris linked the astronomical with the agricultural:** Marion Barber Stowell, *Early American Almanacs: The Colonial Weekday Bible* (New York: Burt Franklin, 1977), 15.

191   **Almanacs had been introduced in the colonies in 1639:** Silvio A. Bedini, *The Life of Benjamin Banneker: The First African-American Man of Science,*

2nd ed., rev. and expanded (Baltimore: Maryland Historical Society, 1999), 93.

191 *Poor Richard's Almanack* . . . **sold as many as 10,000 copies annually:** Bedini, *The Life of Benjamin Banneker*, 2nd ed., 94.

191 **These books included:** Bedini, *The Life of Benjamin Banneker* 2nd ed., 84–86.

192 **In October 1789, Benjamin sent George a letter:** Bedini, *The Life of Benjamin Banneker*, 2nd ed., 91.

192 **"Now Sir if I can overcome this difficulty":** Letter from Benjamin Banneker to George Ellicott, dated October 13, 1789, Special Collections, Maryland Center for History and Culture; Bedini, *The Life of Benjamin Banneker*, 2nd ed., 89.

193 **"His door stood open and so closely was his mind engaged":** Tyson, *Banneker, the Afric-American Astronomer*, 32.

194 **it was now too late for Benjamin to get it to another printer:** Bedini, *The Life of Benjamin Banneker*, 2nd ed., 90–92.

194 **"the first attempt of the kind that ever was made in America by a person of my Complexion":** Bedini, *The Life of Benjamin Banneker*, 2nd ed., 93–94.

194 **asked President Washington and Secretary of State Thomas Jefferson:** Tyson, *Banneker, the Afric-American Astronomer*, 36–37.

195 **"any negro who might leave Maryland and remain away over thirty days":** Julma B. Crawford, "The Writings of Benjamin Banneker: Their Effect upon Concepts Regarding the Negro in America, 1750–1800" (master's thesis, Loyola University of Chicago, 1947), 20.

195 **Betsy Ellicott, "was careful to direct the appointments of [Benjamin's] wardrobe":** Bedini, *The Life of Benjamin Banneker*, 2nd ed., 114.

195 **Minta deconstructed the clothing in her mind:** Bedini, *The Life of Benjamin Banneker*, 2nd ed., 114.

CHAPTER 24: GRIOTS

197 **"I have been at a festival for the National Association of Black Storytellers":** "In the Footsteps of the Ancestors, 2021 Festival," https://www.nabsinc.org/past-festivals.

CHAPTER 25: THE CAPITAL

200 **By drawing triangles from known points:** Ken Alder, *The Measure of All Things: The Seven-Year Odyssey and the Hidden Error That Transformed the World* (New York: The Free Press, 2002), 28.

200 **Ellicott worried aloud:** Silvio A. Bedini, *The Life of Benjamin Banneker: The First African-American Man of Science*, 2nd ed., rev. and expanded (Baltimore: Maryland Historical Society, 1999), 115.

200 **Benjamin politely . . . taking meals at a separate table, though dining at the same time:** Martha Ellicott Tyson, *Banneker, the Afric-American Astronomer* (Philadelphia: Friends' Book Association, 1884), 37.

201 **It was Benjamin's job to observe seven stars as they crossed the meridian:** Bedini, *The Life of Benjamin Banneker*, 2nd ed., 117.

201 **Ellicott then used these computations to set his own timepiece:** Louis Keene, "Benjamin Banneker: The Black Tobacco Farmer Who the Presidents Couldn't Ignore," White House Historical Association, https://www .whitehousehistory.org/benjamin-banneker?%20#footnote-14Keene,%20 footnote-13.

201 **On February 14, Andrew Ellicott made his first report to Thomas Jefferson:** Bedini, *The Life of Benjamin Banneker*, 2nd ed., 329.

201 **Ellicott and his crew worked seven days a week:** Bedini, *The Life of Benjamin Banneker*, 2nd ed., 125.

202 **the meridians and placement of the future landmarks of Washington, D.C.:** Tyson, *Banneker, the Afric-American Astronomer*, 11–12.

202 **Benjamin was paid $2 a day for this work:** Keene, "Benjamin Banneker: The Black Tobacco Farmer Who the Presidents Couldn't Ignore."

202 **the presence of the surveyors was announced:** *Georgetown Weekly Ledger*, March 12, 1791, reprinted in "Benjamin Banneker," PBS: *Africans in America*, https://www.pbs.org/wgbh/aia/part2/2p84.html.

202 **The designers of the capital rejected the overall grid pattern:** Eddie Glawe, "Feature: Benjamin Banneker," *Xyht Magazine*, February 13, 2014, Professional Surveyor Archives, https://www.xyht.com/professional-surveyor -archives/feature-benjamin-banneker/.

202 **Pennsylvania Avenue . . . was oriented to the movement across the sky of the star of Sirius:** Elaine Paulionis Phelen, "How Did Freemasonry Influence the Design of Washington, D.C.?," Masonic Philosophical Society, November 29, 2019, https://blog.philosophicalsociety.org/2019/11/29/freemasonry -design-washington-dc/.

205 **the great white slabs of stone that would be used to build the Presidential Palace:** The White House was referred to as the Presidential Palace at this time. Enslaved men were also used to quarry the stone for the palace and build its frame. Bob Arnebeck, *Slave Labor in the Capital: Building Washington's Iconic Federal Landmarks* (Charleston, SC: History Press, 2014), 65.

206 **there is no record of there ever being a debate:** Arnebeck, *Slave Labor in the Capital*, 42.

206 **Edmund Plowden hired out Gerard, Tony, Jack, Moses, Lin, and Arnold Plowden. E. J. Millarde sent his men Tom and Joe Millarde . . . :** The time sheet for the laborers for the White House, where these men are listed, is available in the National Archives of Washington, D.C. Arnebeck, *Slave Labor in the Capital*, 21–23.

206 **their "masters" were paid roughly twenty-one pounds a year for their work:** Arnebeck, *Slave Labor in the Capital*, 29.

206 **"What humanity! What a country of liberty. If at least they shared the earnings!":** Arnebeck, *Slave Labor in the Capital*, 11–13.

207 **"Banneker's deportment throughout the whole of this engagement":** Tyson, *Banneker, the Afric-American Astronomer*, 36.

207 **The commissioners held a celebration in April 1791:** Bedini, *The Life of Benjamin Banneker*, 2nd ed., 128.

CHAPTER 26: INSURRECTION

208 **"My roots are planted deeply in Georgia soil":** Raphael Warnock, "May My Story Be an Inspiration," Victory Speech for the Georgia Senate, January 6, 2021, https://www.youtube.com/watch?v=2wPPWJIsOvs.

208 **to plan a city in response to the astrological houses:** Elaine Paulionis Phelen, "How Did Freemasonry Influence the Design of Washington, D.C.?," Masonic Philosophical Society, November 29, 2019, https://blog .philosophicalsociety.org/2019/11/29/freemasonry-design-washington-dc/.

209 **We put on CNN and saw the footage of a vigilante mob:** "January 6 Insurrection at the US Capitol," CNN Politics, https://www.cnn.com/specials /politics/january-6-insurrection.

CHAPTER 27: THE CORRESPONDENCE

213 **the *Georgetown Weekly Ledger* and had announced his work:** Silvio A. Bedini, *The Life of Benjamin Banneker: The First African-American Man of Science*, 2nd ed., rev. and expanded (Baltimore: Maryland Historical Society, 1999), 141.

213 **Goddard, publisher of the *Maryland Journal* . . . had first proposed the U.S. Postal System to Congress:** Bedini, *The Life of Benjamin Banneker*, 2nd ed., 151.

214 **He offered Banneker a sum of three pounds for the publication:** Letter from Benjamin Banneker to Elias Ellicott, quoted in Bedini, *The Life of Benjamin Banneker*, 2nd ed., 171.

214 **James Pemberton, the president of the Pennsylvania Society for Promoting the Abolition of Slavery and the Relief of Free Negroes Unlawfully Held in Bondage:** Silvio A. Bedini, *The Life of Benjamin Banneker: The First African-American Man of Science* (Rancho Cordova, CA: Landmark Enterprises, 1972), 172–73.

214 **"Every instance of Genius amongst the Negroes is worthy of attention":** Bedini, *The Life of Benjamin Banneker*, 148.

214 **Senator James McHenry:** Bedini, *The Life of Benjamin Banneker*, 2nd ed., 169.

215 **"The whole commerce between master and slave":** Thomas Jefferson, *Notes on the State of Virginia* (New York: Penguin Group, 1999), 148.

216 **"never yet could I find that a black had uttered a thought above the level of plain narration":** Jefferson, *Notes on the State of Virginia*, 149–50.

216 **He knew that he himself was the scientist and thinker:** Britt Rusert, *Fugitive Science: Empiricism and Freedom in Early African American Culture* (New York: New York University Press, 2017), 38.

217   **Jefferson knew Benjamin to be someone talented and competent:** Bedini, *The Life of Benjamin Banneker*, 2nd ed., 166.

217   **"I suppose it is a truth too well attested to you":** Benjamin Banneker, "To Thomas Jefferson from Benjamin Banneker, 19 August 1791," Founders Online, National Archives, Boston Massachusetts Historical Society Special Collection, https://founders.archives.gov/documents/Jefferson/01-22-02 -0049.

218   **"view it in my own handwriting":** "Letter from Banneker to Jefferson," Benjamin Banneker's Astronomical Journal, Special Collections, H. Furlong Baldwin Library, Maryland Center for History and Culture, Baltimore, https: //www.mdhistory.org/resources/benjamin-banneker-astronomical-journal/.

218   **[Jefferson's] usual answer to abolitionist critique:** Ibram X. Kendi, *Stamped from the Beginning: The Definitive History of Racist Ideas in America* (New York: Nation Books, 2016), 122.

219   **"Sir, your most obedient and humble servant, Thomas Jefferson":** "Letter, Thomas Jefferson to Benjamin Banneker, 30 August 1791," Library of Congress, https://www.loc.gov/item/mcc.028/.

219   **"I have seen very elegant solutions of Geometrical problems by him":** "Jefferson in a letter to the Marquis de Condorcet," in Bedini, *The Life of Benjamin Banneker*, 159.

220   **Had the manuscript been presented to the Académie:** Bedini, *The Life of Benjamin Banneker*, 2nd ed., 168.

221   **[Sally] seemed "good natur'd" and "very fond of Polly":** A letter by Abigail Adams, in Annette Gordon-Reed, *The Hemingses of Monticello: An American Family* (New York: W. W. Norton, 2008), 194.

222   **[Sally] negotiated on behalf of their future offspring:** Gordon-Reed, *The Hemingses of Monticello*, 326–27.

222   **Jefferson's political opponents began accusing him of fathering these children as early as 1802:** Jefferson's onetime friend, then opponent, James Callender exposed Jefferson's secret on September 1, 1802, in the *Richmond Register*, writing, "By this wench Sally, our president has had several children." Kendi, *Stamped from the Beginning*, 129.

222   **the groundskeeper, who described Harriet as "very beautiful" and "nearly white," gave her money from Jefferson to join her brother Beverly in Washington, D.C.:** Gordon-Reed, *The Hemingses of Monticello*, 657.

223   **"I have a long letter from Banneker which shews him to have had a mind of very common stature indeed":** "Thomas Jefferson to Joel Barlow, 8 October 1809," Founders Online, National Archives, annotations by Princeton University Press, https://founders.archives.gov/documents/Jefferson/03-01 -02-0461.

CHAPTER 28: THE RIFT

227   **some of the main features in the oral histories were supported on paper:** There are many ways to glean information from the archives by reading between the lines. For instance, another relative of ours, named Colby Tate,

was brought before the Virginia Provincial Courts twice, to be tried for creating freedom papers for other fugitives from slavery. He was not found guilty of the crime, however, because he feigned illiteracy. He enters the historical record as a criminal, a forger of freedom papers, but by reading this record "against the grain" we can see that he was, in fact, literate and working for the cause of liberation. From an oral history by Robert Lett, December 2, 2021.

227 **Archives . . . masquerade as objective spaces, but they are far from it:** Tiya Miles writes, "While at times imposing and formal enough to seem all-encompassing in their brick, glass, and steel structures, archives only include records that survived accident, were viewed as important in their time or in some subsequent period, and were deemed worthy of preservation . . . even in their most organized form, archived records are mere scraps of accounts of previous happenings, 'rags of realities' that we painstakingly stitch together." Tiya Miles, *All That She Carried: The Journey of Ashley's Sack, a Black Family Keepsake* (New York: Random House, 2021), 27–28.

227 **the archives prime us to read the history of people of color through the lens of criminality:** For brilliant writing about the archive and criminality, see the work of Saidiya Hartman. Saidiya Hartman, *Wayward Lives, Beautiful Experiments: Intimate Histories of Riotous Black Girls, Troublesome Women, and Queer Radicals* (New York: W. W. Norton, 2019).

232 **"the tangled genealogies of slavery":** Harriet Jacobs, *Incidents in the Life of a Slave Girl* (Garden City, NY: Dover Publications, 2001), 68.

233 **the offspring of "masters" and slaves "invariably suffer greater hardships":** Frederick Douglass goes on to say, "The master is frequently compelled to sell this class of his slaves, out of deference to the feelings of his white wife; and, cruel as the deed may strike any one to be, for a man to sell his own children to human-fleshmongers, it is often the dictate of humanity for him to do so; for, unless he does this, he must not only whip them himself, but must stand by and see one son tie up his brother, of but a few shades darker complexion than himself, and ply the gory lash to his naked back." Frederick Douglass, *Narrative of the Life of Frederick Douglass, an American Slave, Written by Himself* (New York: Signet Classics, 1997), 4.

233 **53 percent of [white women] voted for Donald Trump in 2016:** Katie Rogers, "White Women Helped Elect Donald Trump," *New York Times*, November 9, 2016, https://www.nytimes.com/2016/12/01/us/politics/white-women-helped-elect-donald-trump.html; Lyz Lenz, "White Women Vote Republican. Get Used to It, Democrats," *Washington Post*, November 27, 2020, https://www.washingtonpost.com/opinions/2020/11/27/white-women-vote-republican-get-used-it-democrats/.

234 **By willing her enslaved people to the Society of Friends:** Silvio A. Bedini, *The Life of Benjamin Banneker: The First African-American Man of Science,* 2nd ed., rev. and expanded (Baltimore: Maryland Historical Society, 1999), 317.

236 **She wrote to Martha nervously about the findings:** Rachel Mason to Martha E. Tyson, December 5, 1847, in Bedini, *The Life of Benjamin Banneker*, 2nd ed., 317.

236 **if he could not be proven to be "of strictly African parentage":** Statement signed by Martha Tyson, undated, privately owned. Bedini, *The Life of Benjamin Banneker*, 2nd ed., 293.

237 **"I sent for a niece of Banneker, named Harriet Henderson":** Diary entry by Martha Ellicott Tyson, December 1851, in Bedini, *The Life of Benjamin Banneker*, 2nd ed., 294.

237 **they praised the "modesty" of the lady:** Bedini, *The Life of Benjamin Banneker*, 2nd ed., 84.

238 **"My father was a white man":** Douglass, *Life of Frederick Douglass*, 3–4.

239 **Banneker's biography . . . remained largely unknown by the reading public:** Bedini, *The Life of Benjamin Banneker*, 2nd ed., 299.

CHAPTER 29: PUBLICATION

241 **informing readers of the author's race:** Banneker's Almanac of 1792, Special Collections, H. Furlong Baldwin Library, Maryland Center of History and Culture, Baltimore.

242 **Benjamin's 1792 almanac had been presented in the House of Commons:** Silvio A. Bedini, *The Life of Benjamin Banneker: The First African-American Man of Science*, 2nd ed., rev. and expanded (Baltimore: Maryland Historical Society, 1999), 190.

242 **an essay proposing "A Plan of a Peace Office for the United States":** Benjamin Rush, "A Plan for the Peace Office for the United States," included in *Banneker's Almanac for the Year 1793*, Special Collections, H. Furlong Library, Maryland Center for History and Culture, Baltimore.

242 **The Pennsylvania Society for the Relief of Free Negroes . . . made plans:** Bedini, *The Life of Benjamin Banneker*, 2nd ed., 191.

243 **Banneker's next almanac of 1795 reached its widest-ever distribution:** Julma B. Crawford, "The Writings of Benjamin Banneker: Their Effect upon Concepts Regarding the Negro in America, 1750–1800" (master's thesis, Loyola University of Chicago, 1947), 44.

245 **"I recollect to have seen his Almanacs in my father's house, and believe they were the only ones used in the neighborhood at the time":** Martha Ellicott Tyson's interview with Charles Dorsey. Martha Ellicott Tyson, *Banneker, the Afric-American Astronomer* (Philadelphia: Friends' Book Association, 1884), 53–54.

245 **"I believe I should live fifteen years, and consider my land worth 180 pounds":** Letter by Benjamin Banneker is quoted by Martha Ellicott Tyson, but has never been seen by the Banneker-Lett family. It may have been part of the private Ellicott family collection. Tyson, *Banneker, the Afric-American Astronomer*, 33.

245 **"increase his knowledge on subjects":** Tyson, *Banneker, the Afric-American Astronomer*, 33.

245   **the parcels would be too small to be of service to anybody:** Tyson, *Banneker, the Afric-American Astronomer*, 33.

245   **"Sometimes he would be found watching the habits of his bees":** Tyson, *Banneker, the Afric-American Astronomer*, 34.

CHAPTER 30: RECKONING

255   **"The Maryland Archives has a copy of that transaction between Greenbury Morton and Benjamin":** "Benjamin Banneker Homestead, Site," https://mht.maryland.gov/secure/Medusa/PDF/BaltimoreCounty/BA-1141 .pdf.

CHAPTER 31: THE FINAL YEARS

256   **"when he was shut up in his house immersed in calculations, they would return and strip his trees":** Martha Ellicott Tyson, *Banneker, the Afric-American Astronomer* (Philadelphia: Friends' Book Association, 1884), 64.

257   **"If evil communications corrupt good manners":** Tyson, *Banneker, the Afric-American Astronomer*, 64.

257   **"Standing at my door, I heard the discharge of a gun":** August 27, 1797, entry in his journal, Special Collections, H. Furlong Baldwin Library, Maryland Center for History and Culture, Baltimore.

CHAPTER 32: LEGACIES

259   **"Maybe if those had been preserved, he would be more known to history":** Tiya Miles writes, "Compared to other groups with a stability afforded by earnings, wealth, or racial privilege, Black families' possessions were more likely to wind up in dump pits and rag bins, as elder members moved on or were pushed out during the height of Jim Crow segregation and racially motivated violence." Tiya Miles, *All That She Carried: The Journey of Ashley's Sack, a Black Family Keepsake* (New York: Random House, 2021), 267.

CHAPTER 33: BURNING

265   **continued to operate and strike the hours through more than half a century:** Martha Tyson wrote that Banneker's clock kept time throughout his life. Silvio A. Bedini, *The Life of Benjamin Banneker: The First African-American Man of Science*, 2nd ed., rev. and expanded (Baltimore: Maryland Historical Society, 1999), 45.

CHAPTER 34: FRAGMENTS

268   **archaeological dig . . . at the sites of Benjamin's cabin:** Banneker Homestead Archaeological Dig, Archaeological Collections of Maryland, Maryland Archaeological Conservation Lab, St. Leonard.

274   **"They lived in a world that would count people of color as objects":** Tiya Miles, *All That She Carried: The Journey of Ashley's Sack, a Black Family Keepsake* (New York: Random House, 2021), 165.

CHAPTER 35: THE ARCHIVE

279 **"set free and discharge all my negroes":** Edie and I visited the archives on September 16, 2021, and were able to see, touch, and photograph this original will. "1752 Will of Molly Welsh," Maryland Archives, Annapolis.

280 **British women . . . who had children with African men and then married British men:** T. H. Breen and Stephen Innes, *"Myne Owne Ground": Race and Freedom on Virginia's Eastern Shore, 1640–1676* (New York: Oxford University Press, 2005), 86–87.

281 **Harriet Jacobs spends considerable time and effort:** Jacobs's memoir, is filled with these instances of her trying to get a friend or family member to buy her children as a way of keeping them safe. Harriet Jacobs, *Incidents in the Life of a Slave Girl* (Garden City, NY: Dover Publications, 2001), 88–92.

283 **"it is still quite possible that she was Benjamin Banneker's grandmother":** Paul Heinegg, "Banneker Family," *Free African Americans of Maryland and Delaware from the Colonial Period to 1810*, digital archive, http://freeafricanamericans.com/maryland.htm.

285 **"Like the deadseeming cold rocks, I have memories within":** Zora Neale Hurston, quoted by Toni Morrison in "The Site of Memory," in William Zinsser, ed., *Inventing the Truth: The Art and Craft of Memoir*, 2nd ed. (Boston: Houghton Mifflin, 1995), 83–102, https://blogs.umass.edu/brusert/files/2013/03/Morrison_Site-of-Memory.pdf.

CHAPTER 36: ON BANNEKER LAND

288 **"Historians who don't believe that anything is true unless it can be separated out":** James David Audlin writes, "People who hold the modern literal understanding of reality become observing minds separated from reality, unable to bridge the gap into reality, which is forever out there beyond their perceptions. Conversely, the traditional person does not feel divorced from reality, but closely interrelated with it." James David Audlin (Distant Eagle), *Circle of Life: Traditional Teachings of Native American Elders* (Santa Fe: Clear Light Publishing, 2006), 71.

288 **I let the land instruct me:** My way of relating to land is largely informed by my childhood in nature with my parents, and by the teachings of Native American elders. It involves an attunement to the land, and cultivating an expanded awareness that can open to deep memory and guidance. It is a way of coming into relationship.

293 **the whole matrix of time coming to rest in the present moment:** James David Audlin writes that the traditional indigenous view of selfhood is that "our own selves are a sacred gift handed down by our ancestors. . . . We grow out of the soil nourished by our ancestors. We bend down and become the seed of our children's children. We all must carry ourselves as a sacred trust given to us by the Grandfathers and Grandmothers, for the people, past, present, and future." Audlin (Distant Eagle), *Circle of Life*, 83.

CHAPTER 37: THE END

296 **On October 28, 1806, an obituary ran in the *Federal Gazette*:** Silvio A. Bedini, *The Life of Benjamin Banneker: The First African-American Man of Science*, 2nd ed., rev. and expanded (Baltimore: Maryland Historical Society, 1999), 271.

ABOUT THE AUTHOR

RACHEL JAMISON WEBSTER is a professor of creative writing at Northwestern University and the author of four books of poetry and cross-genre writing. She has also taught writing workshops through the National Urban League, Chicago Public Schools, and Gallery 37, celebrating diverse voices and literatures. Rachel's essays, poems, and stories have been published in outlets including *Poetry*, *Tin House*, and the *Yale Review*. *Benjamin Banneker and Us* is her first nonfiction book. She lives in Evanston, Illinois, with her husband and daughter.